Environmental Choice,
Human Behavior,
and Residential Satisfaction

Environmental Choice, Human Behavior, and Residential Satisfaction

WILLIAM MICHELSON

University of Toronto

NEW YORK

OXFORD UNIVERSITY PRESS

1977

Copyright © 1977 by Oxford University Press, Inc.
Library of Congress Catalogue Card Number: 76–42617

Printed in the United States of America

ERRATA

Page 288, Table 8.6, line 1 of caption: First parenthesis should read
(Wives, Phase III)

Page 207: Replace map in Figure 6.8 with the map given below.

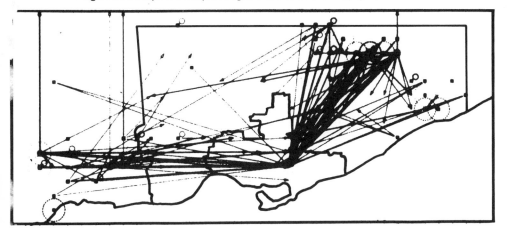

Page 208: Replace map in Figure 6.9 with the map given below.

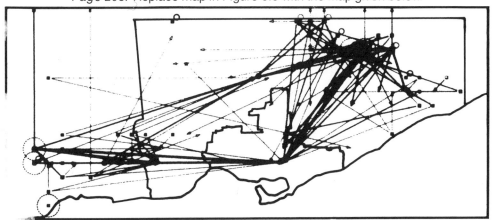

ENVIRONMENTAL CHOICE, HUMAN BEHAVIOR, AND
RESIDENTIAL SATISFACTION
by
William Michelson

ACKNOWLEDGMENTS

Before turning to the substance of this book, I find it both imperative for myself and perhaps worthwhile for the reader that I indicate the scope of support, collaboration, and cooperation that I received during the progress of the project described.

The primary sponsor for the research conducted was Canada's Central Mortgage and Housing Corporation (CMHC). It took considerable trust for CMHC to continue the substantial funding required during the several years that were necessary before any tangible result could appear. In this regard I am particularly indebted to Andrew Hazeland, under whose leadership the project was initiated, and to Samuel Gitterman, Robert Adamson, W. W. Struthers, Brian Randall, and John Auld at various other times. Two research grants from the Canada Council were also of critical importance to this study.

The research took place at the Centre for Urban and Community Studies, University of Toronto. This facility has been a most fruitful place in which to work, and the efforts of Directors J. Stefan Dupré, Richard Soberman, and L. S. Bourne are deeply appreciated.

The Ministry of State for Urban Affairs, Government of Canada, became the headquarters of members of the project staff for one year, when I served as an advisor there, and it provided strong computer support during that time. I thank M. Harvey Lithwick and Kar Liang for their help in that area. Advice of considerable value on administrative and legal questions was given us by Sydney Dymond, Q.C., of the Office of Research Administration, University of Toronto. I am grateful also to colleagues Hy Day, Jan Loubser, John Hitchcock, James Simmons, and John Ogilvie for substantive advice.

None of these results could have been possible without the hard work and ideas of a small army of research associates, assistants, and students. Since the contribution of each is in some way unique, let me merely name them, with the hope that each realizes my appreciation for the nature and degree of assistance provided: Brody Anderson, Cathy Barth, David Belgue, John Brants, Thomas Brecher, Jon Caulfield, Chris Cotterell, Carol Cox, Barry Crump, Les Cseh, Ellan Derow, Marcia Effrat, John Farley, Connie Guldemond, Linda Hagarty, Itamar Halevy, Joanne Hershoran, Brian Holly, Lee Joliffe, Leslie Kennedy, Jack Klebanoff, Janet Lytle, Kathy McDonnell, Ellen Michelson, Liviana Mostacci, Paul Reed, Ellis Roberts, Don Rogers, Anna-Rose Spina, Colin Stafford, June Steele, John Stewart, Beverly Thompson, Sandy Thompson, and Oscar Vallarino.

Interviewing for the first three phases of the study was conducted by the York University Survey Research Centre. This organization also coded the interview materials from Phases I and II of the study. RECON Limited of Toronto coded Phase III of the study. Lee Joliffe and Ellen Michelson administered the field activities of Phase IV, and Barry Crump coded these materials.

My thanks are due to these and also to the many members of the housing industry whose cooperation made this study possible. These companies are as follows: Alcan, BBC Management, Cadillac Property Management, Del Zotto Property Management, Limited, Edrich Construction, Greenwin Construction, Goldlist Construction, Marvo Development, Murray Menkes, Meridian Property Management, New Style Construction, Rice Development, Shipp Corporation, Limited, Alcan Design Homes, Apollo Real Estate, Arthur Blakely, Limited, Boston Homes, W. H. Bosley & Company, Limited, A. B. Cairns, Canada Permanent Trust Company, Cholkan Real Estate, Claus Clausius Realtor, W. H. Clipperton Real Estate, Costain Estates, Limited, Ralph L. Davidson Real Estate, Elidio DeCaires, Limited, William Dicker Real Estate, Richard Dowley Realtor, L. J. Fleck, Gibson-Willoughby, Gillen Associates, Hunter Telford Real Estate, Limited, Johnston & Daniel, Limited, H. Keith, Limited, E. Lawrence Real Estate, A. E. LePage, Uno Mankin Real Estate, Martin & Meredith Company, Limited, Matthews-Allen Company Limited, McArthur and Son Realtor, McLintock Homes, Mell Real Estate, Monarch Chartwell Construction, Limited, Ralph Nardi Real Estate, Emilio Platzer Real Estate, Ken Psillas Real Estate, Limited, Rideau Trust Company, Royal Trust Company, A. E. Scott, Clifford Smith Real Estate, L. S. Snelgrove, Robert Taylor, Limited, Treasure

Homes, United Trust, Mann and Martel Real Estate, Young and Biggin Real Estate.

The Housing and Urban Development Association of Canada gave generous moral support to this project. I am particularly grateful to Lloyd Gunby, William McCance, and Brian Lawrence for their advice and help. Donald Kirkup, then of the Real Estate Board of Metropolitan Toronto, also assisted greatly in providing necessary records and information. Liivi Currier and Heinz Loth created the drawings, graphs, and some maps found throughout the text. The Driver Licensing Division of the Ministry of Transportation and Communications, Province of Ontario, Mr. Richard Mackie, Head, provided considerable assistance in tracing families over time. Mrs. June Upshaw went out of her way to speed the tracing process.

Finally, I must express thanks to the families who gave as much time as they did to this particular study. In this regard I have two hopes: (1) that they may find the result worthwhile, and (2) that communication of the results has sufficient policy consequence to have justified their time.

The foregoing to the contrary notwithstanding, I have organized and written these materials entirely myself, and hence I stand responsible for all shortcomings.

William Michelson

Lund, Sweden
August 31, 1975

I am grateful to James J. Anderson, Mary Ellen Evans, and David Laufer at Oxford University Press for positive, professional cooperation in the progress and production of this book; and to Mary Pace, who typed the Index.

W. M.

Toronto, Ontario
February 22, 1977

CONTENTS

Chapter Six
Situated Behavior 182

Chapter Ten

Some Applications and Implications 354

ILLUSTRATIONS

TABLES

Environmental Choice,
Human Behavior,
and Residential Satisfaction

PREFACE

This book is about housing.

Most adults have lived long enough to have observed at least two different kinds of concern about housing. One is quantitative—too few housing units for those needing them. The other kind is qualitative—the units available are unsuitable for those needing them.

Quantitative problems come and go cyclically, dependent on the economy and on the extent of population changes.

Qualitative problems seem always with us. But their nature changes from decade to decade. Older forms of housing seem unsuitable for current demands. Yet, whatever is new and widespread brings with it public expressions of apprehension and concern. People suspect that new forms of residential environment do not fulfill their purposes while simultaneously conferring undesired side effects. Suburbs and high-rise apartments, for example, have successively been recipients of kudos and brickbats, depending on the point of view of the observer.

It is clear that housing is not purely a 'numbers game' but involves also the matching of people to appropriate housing. This question of matching led me to undertake the study described in this book. In the mid-1960s, although we still had not sorted out satisfactorily what the human consequences of the previous decade's suburbanization might have been, the public uproar about high-rise apartments was in its initial stages. One of the major characteristics of the high-rise was its potential to compensate for, through concentration, the profligate waste of land resulting from 'suburban sprawl.' In the debate about the various alternatives, governments were being pushed in all directions by those for and against the various alternatives in housing and location: for concentrated high-rise housing; for low-density detached housing; for orientation of the city as a more dense, public transit-oriented entity; for low-density cities oriented around the consumer as king and with carriage, as well as against all these things. The debate carried considerable invective about all these phenomena, some of which contained emotionally charged speculations about how people live in these various contexts.

Governments can affect the kinds of housing which get built, both directly and indirectly. Various levels of government can affect them directly through stringent land use and building controls. Typically, however, more indirect measures tend to support very heavily one qualitative trend or another in housing, depending on what strings are or are not attached to such activities as granting of mortgage supports. For example, federal lending policies, which placed a high priority on the security of loans, underlie much of the suburbanization following World War II. The high-rise would not be a reality without the indirect support of a variety of government programs. Even what the private market does with the money it raises is dependent on such factors as land value. Land value is a direct function of the extent to which the government permits the realization of capital gains, as well as its position on whether land is a resource or a commodity.

What bothered me at the outset of a research project which I shall describe subsequently was my feeling that few if any of the programs which created various forms of housing and development incorporated a sufficient understanding of their social implications for the persons who would eventually come to populate the housing created. Little sophisticated attention seemed given to the matching of occupant and residence.

Specifically, there was extremely little hard information available about the implications of living in high-rise apartments or in suburbia, both expanding rapidly under existing programs and conditions. I therefore sought to assess some of the social implications of several basic alternatives in residential environment which governments can and do stimulate or retard. Presumably, such an inquiry would also turn up how to improve any of the alternatives.

I assumed at the outset that people were rational in their actions, when their economic circumstances permitted, with the result that they matched themselves to housing on the basis of their own assessment of what kind of people they were and what they wanted to do with their lives. Such matching did not mean that all people were rational or could foresee all aspects of their new housing, but rather that many people choose housing for pragmatic reasons related to their ability to take advantage of particular opportunities inherent in the housing type and location. Those who did not 'self-select' themselves on that basis were thought more susceptible to problems after arrival, necessitating more vigorous adaptation or subsequent mobility. I assumed that there would be some 'congruence' between people and the kind of environment in which they chose to live. Hence, the central underlying questions which I thought should be answered were as follows:

1. To what extent does a particular residential environment tend to attract a particular type of resident? Do people envisage, when selecting a new home, how they will lead their lives after moving?

2. To what extent does a particular way of life become pronounced in a particular physical setting? Do aspects of the environment influence *what people do, with whom they do it, and where they do it* or, all else being equal, do they merely repeat the round of life which they formerly pursued in the physically different environment?

3. If a 'typical' way of life emerges in a particular setting, what happens to the new resident who fails to adopt it? Does he tend to move? Do social problems or illnesses develop? Or, on the other hand, are typical patterns only a statistical phenomenon, unrelated to successful adjustment to the residential environment?

4. What effect does the passage of time have on people's adjustment to their environment? Does it take longer for people to adjust to some settings than to others? What problems typically emerge in specific settings during particular time periods after settlement, and could they be remedied if anticipated?

In other words, my initial perspective was to consider the new home and location to which people would move as a *target* toward which they were aiming for reasons having to do with their behavior and aspirations. The target itself incorporated a specific range of opportunities and limitations, but the people would be assumed to find these acceptable and even desirable. Those persons moving to the same target who had not perceived it accurately would either adapt (so as to be consistent with the environmental opportunities and limitations), endure strain of an unspecified nature, or else move elsewhere after perceiving the incongruence of the match.

This was, essentially, a *static* view of the matching of homes and people. It assumed that people rationally choose, when able, residences which fit a single set of their ideas. It assumed that people would not move to less than the ideal at any time if the ideal were open to them. It assumed that satisfaction was related to fulfillment of the ideal; anything considerably different from the ideal would present problems.

As the project progressed, however, the results increasingly pointed to the necessity of wider, more dynamic perspectives.

The data pointed to the necessity of understanding the relationship of families and their housing with an intended pattern of repeated movement until and beyond the time when fulfillment of the ideal becomes possible. Evaluation of people's match with their housing had to be done not always in terms of what the family *really* wanted, but rather in many cases in terms of what they wanted for a finite period of time before doing something entirely different.

In short, moves to new housing could not be taken on their own but rather as part of a dynamic family-mobility cycle fueled by more than unforeseen discontent.

Moreover, the evaluation of housing and its social implications proved to be possible only through the understanding of the *relation* of aspirations to market availability. If people's life plans, for example, are predicated upon the pursuit of a sequence which eventually ends in an ivy-covered cottage, and they become aware that such homes are no longer available, this latter fact will have an overbearing effect on their life in and evaluation of their current home.

In short, the research pointed to the importance of the qualitative aspects of supply and to the factors which affect supply as major considerations in understanding the implications of currently existing housing units.

In other words, what people *do* may be a function of their situation. But what they do at any one time in a given situation may not necessarily reflect what people hope to do in another situation. Finally, what they think *about* what they do now is a function of the extent that objective factors may allow them to do that which they really want to do in the future.

These larger perspectives suggest that assessments of why people choose particular types of housing and location at any single point in time are not sufficient to explain the implications of housing, even when people are acting under relatively unconstrained circumstances. Investigating what people do within specific environmental contexts is not enough to explain whether such environments might usefully be duplicated in the future. Even evaluation requires a more comprehensive viewpoint, as 'mere' satisfaction does not indicate 'on what grounds' or 'for how long.'

The chapters of this book address themselves to the several questions shown crucial to an understanding of the match between people and housing—why people move, what they expect, what they subsequently experience, and what they think of it. Although policy implications become most readily apparent only with the material presented in the second half of Chapter 8, the basis for understanding my argument and conclusions is found piece by piece in the preceding chapters, which must be viewed conjointly.

Environmental choice, human behavior, and residential satisfaction are easily three different subjects, and previous writers have usually considered them as such. Many geographers, for example, have considered intra-urban mobility without investigating either behavior or satisfaction with the qualitative aspects of housing. Behaviorists, on the other hand, have not always found it necessary to consider motives or the satisfaction-producing aspects intrinsic to the context. Similarly, architectural practitioners have long been concerned with 'user needs' without being interested in questions of mobility. Since, however, I feel that it is essential to include all three concerns in any attempt to assess the implications of given types of housing and location, I shall trace in Chapter 1 the interrelationship of these three emphases in the creation of a viable framework for the understanding of housing, its uses and consequences.

Then, given the framework established, I shall turn in Chapter 2 to the kinds of motives, expectations, and priorities which we would expect to find concerning the particular kinds of housing and location pursued in our study: downtown high-rise apartments, suburban high-rise apartments, downtown single-family houses, and suburban single-family houses.

I describe our study—its methods, the people studied, the information gathered, and the modes of analysis followed—in Chapter 3.

The first three chapters, then, lay a foundation for the provision of 'answers' in the chapter to follow.

The first kind of answer, found in Chapter 4, is to the rather pragmatic question of how persons moving to different combinations of housing types and locations looked for and then found, after different lengths of searching, their new homes. It is illuminating in this regard to compare the extent that various people sought alternatives to what they chose. I demonstrate in this initial presentation of results the logic of analysis of data in the more complex chapters which follow Chapter 4.

In Chapter 5, I delve into the questions of why people moved, what they expected out of their new types of housing and location, and in what ways persons moving to different categories of housing and location differed from each other before consummating the move.

I present a picture of life among the same group of movers, once in their destination environments, in Chapter 6. The point of this chapter is to assess the extent that different social groups, performing largely differing types of behavior, did in fact emerge under the spatial opportunities and constraints characterizing their diverse new environments, as one school of environmental studies would have us expect.

Since Chapter 5 is devoted to preexisting differences and Chapter 6, to post-move differences, a crucial distinction must be made as to whether the regularities observed in the new settings are due to what the residents themselves bring to the settings or to the settings themselves. I therefore present in Chapter 7 the results of an analysis designed to indicate the basis (or bases) for behavior observed in particular residential settings.

None of the kinds of answers presented in Chapters 4 to 7 deal explicitly with what people think about these home environments. In Chapter 8, then, I go into considerable detail about not only what people think about their homes, neighborhoods, and locations, but also the basis for the evaluations that emerge. It is this discussion which points to the extreme importance of supply factors in the housing market.

I proceed to a longer-range view in Chapter 9, putting the expectations and evaluations discussed in the previous chapters to the test of information covering a longer period of time. I examine the extent and nature of subsequent mobility on the part of the persons we studied, as well as the validity of the assumptions they had held. These longer-range data also enable us to assess the generalizations gained from short-range intensive examination of residential mobility in light of the subsequent behavior of the same people.

The book concludes with a distillation of the relevant sections of the preceding material with respect to housing policy. While attention is given both to microscopic and macroscopic aspects regarding the creation of new housing and the preservation of old housing, the force of the preceding arguments puts a considerable stress on macroscopic approaches, even with the aim of improving satisfaction with more microscopic elements in the housing situation.

In constructing a publication such as this, there is invariably a tension between succinct communication and complete scientific documentation. A short list of conclusions and recommendations might be more direct, but it would suffer from lack of context and factual support. On the other hand, this project is based on more than a million pieces of data that found their way onto paper and ultimately filled the bookshelves lining the walls of three whole rooms. Even a single copy of the field protocols on which the data were collected totals several hundred pages. Thus, full documentation would be an unwieldy nightmare.

As a consequence, I shall endeavor to communicate the results as directly as I can without losing sight of the factual support for my assertions. On the other hand, I shall attempt also to document my assertions as fully as possible, within the constraint of decent communication. In short, while this effort may contain neither the extent of the factual data required by the purist nor the brevity and directness esteemed by the decision maker, the material to follow is selected and written to attempt a satisfactory balance between the two. Those with questions beyond the scope of that which is presented are welcome to contact me directly.

The empirical material for this book was gathered in the Toronto area. I do not pretend that Toronto is typical of all large cities nor that the problems of any two cities are identical. Nonetheless, phenomena such as those dealt with in this book are very seldom one hundred percent present *or absent* in any city. They reflect a scientific literature based on studies conducted in many countries, including most prominently the United States, Canada, Australia, England, and Sweden. I have personally observed these same phenomena as active components in housing dilemmas in many cities around the world, even when additional forces such as racial questions or crime may have a more immediate impact on how and where the more affluent sectors of the population live in other cities. Thus, while I do not assert the universal relevance of each kind of phenomenon I shall discuss, I regard the several of them as potentially potent in cities at an advanced stage of development when not countermanded by other forces.

Despite my explicit attempt to gather as many facts by as many methods as necessary to answer some of the foregoing questions with more than rhetoric and emotion, there is still no way to avoid whatever biases my own guidance and interpretation of the data introduce. I must acknowledge this at the outset.

Nevertheless, it is you, the reader, who not only determines whether the theory, documentation, and interpretation are found balanced and fair, but also who takes whatever subsequent actions are justified. With these prefatory remarks as guidance and background, I turn the book over to you.

Chapter One

A Merger
of Perspectives

A professor once explained the match between a home and its occupant. 'A giraffe can't live in a home that was built for a flounder!'[1]

In some ways, the suitability of housing for its residents may indeed be obvious. Unfortunately, however, in an increasingly complex urban world, the diversity of ways to design new homes and neighborhoods, combined with the considerable heterogeneity in the nature of the people who need to live in them, makes the degree of success in matching people and residential environments far less clear. The implications of new forms of housing and community for their residents are too seldom known with confidence either in advance or afterward.

Hence, when suburban, detached houses became widespread, popular attention was focused on the presumed negative consequences of 'suburbia.' When young people began to congregate in newly created downtown cliffs, the public wondered what this meant. When older homes of unique character (whether brownstones, townhouses, or haunted houses) started to be taken over by relatively affluent families, many asked what these people hoped to achieve. When families with children started to live in great numbers in high-rise apartments, additional queries were raised about personal and societal consequences.

People continue to question the consequences of new towns, new neighborhoods, new housing types, and new efforts to redevelop or rehabilitate old areas.

Many claims have been made about what new forms of housing and community should or do accomplish: 'Well planned neighborhoods restore grassroots democracy.' 'Suburban houses isolate housewives.' 'High-rise apartments emasculate men.'

Yet, no systematic or productive means of evaluating the social implications of different forms of housing and location in the city have been developed to the same extent as evaluation techniques in engineering, economics, or other sciences. In economics, for example, cost-benefit analysis is widely used, since money is a respected criterion for the success or failure of endeavors. But the recent emphasis on the creation of general social (or urban) indicators shows growing public awareness of the need to account for the qualitative aspects of public policies and practices. In short, despite a high level of curiosity and speculation about the implications of the many new kinds of home environment in which people live, the evaluation of housing has not become a standard practice supported by rigorous methods and reliable evidence.[2]

This book, the outcome of a research project, explores deeply certain social implications of two current and much discussed dimensions in the development of housing. These dimensions are particularly pronounced in the area of the study, Toronto, but they are found, dependent on local conditions, with varying degrees of relevance in many other cities of reasonable size. These dimensions are height (with high-rise apartments and detached single-family houses as the poles) and centrality (with distant suburban locations appearing in contrast to center city locations). Therefore, the downtown house and high-rise and the suburban single-family house and apartment will be closely examined.

The detached home in the central city has long been subject to destruction and replacement by so-called 'higher' land uses—commercial buildings or multiple-family dwellings. Yet, a current trend in many cities is for families to restore such older homes and fight against the tide of changes in land use. What do these families seek? What do they find? What social basis is there for preservation of downtown homes?

The downtown high-rise often replaces the downtown home. The former is often characterized as a cold setting promoting only anonymous relationships between fellow residents. It is handy to the downtown, giving greater numbers of persons reasonably easy access to centrally located facilities. Is the downtown high rise a functional substitute for the downtown house?

The suburban high-rise apartment generally contains many families. Many question, however, the desirability of raising children in high buildings. Others question the effects of suburban locations on various members of the family. Unfortunately, these questions have rarely been applied to those in high-rise buildings in suburbia.

The suburban single-family house was the *bête noir* of the 1950s and early 1960s. Many writers expressed concern over the effects of isolation as a consequence of land-use segregation. Others pointed to the effects on human contact thought to accompany low densities. Still others pointed to the effects of population homogeneity which characterize the typical suburban neighborhood.[3]

It is impossible to assess the implications of these or other types of environment without having some idea in advance about what to observe. I shall reserve a more complete discussion of the specific factors thought relevant to these particular types of home environment until Chapter 2. First, it is necessary to ask the more basic question as to what kinds of phenomena to pursue.

I would argue that a combination of conventional perspectives is required. This assertion in turn is based on a critical assumption: that *behavior is both motivated and reactive.*

When it comes to housing, most North Americans are not like mice put in a maze. We exercise some choice as to where we live. There are certainly conditions such as family finances and market supply which enlarge or restrict the number of choices open to us—from very many to none at all. Even when we have no choice at all, though, we generally enter the housing setting with some expectations of what life will be like in the new setting. These expectations may be realistic in some cases; in others, they may be highly unrealistic. Yet, our minds are not empty on arrival.

What we expect and what we experience are not necessarily identical, though. Most people will find some surprises in their new home environments.

My assumption at present is merely that one must reject the absolute and mutually exclusive dogmatisms of both perfect consumer choice and complete environmental determinism in assessing the social implications of particular forms of housing. Aspects of both emphases should be explored.

PERSPECTIVES ON HOUSING

Mobility and Choice

To learn what people bring to their new housing requires an understanding of why they choose their housing. Much research over the years has been devoted to residential mobility by sociologists and geographers who studied people's motives, their status, and the spatial structure of cities. These scientists have been more concerned with making generalizations about observed regularities than in designing the physical environment. Although the work of planners and architects might have been facilitated by knowledge of the motives and expectations of families that move, design practitioners have not actively pursued the study of residential mobility.

People choose housing for many reasons. One is obvious: newly arrived or newly formed families require housing. Yet, there is considerably more turnover than could remotely be accounted for by new families. People change residence for a number of reasons, not all of which are fully recognized.[4] Furthermore, the different kinds of reasons for moving tend to change through time, which scientific writings on mobility through the years reflect.

An early perspective, for example, treated housing and hence intraurban mobility as status conferring. Social scientists observed that people used housing as an instrument in 'keeping up with the Joneses.' Many early indices of social status used evaluations of family-dwelling units (cf. Warner and Lunt, 1941; Warner et al., 1957). Use of these indices was consistent with the underlying assumptions of urban ecology, that land values which accompanied urban growth would sort people out into economically homogeneous living areas; it was assumed that people would want to live in housing and neighborhoods commensurate with their incomes or even slightly beyond them, as a way of conferring something which the presence of affluence alone could not realize. A miser with $110,000 stashed under his mattress would have far less status than a person with the same amount displayed under his roof.

Geographers traditionally pursued a similarly simple theme they called 'place utility.' Since geographers customarily emphasize spatial relations, including the distribution of people in space, it is not surprising that this approach to housing choice focused upon the access that people had to have certain necessities in life. Proximity to a person's place of employment was a major consideration when this line of thought was introduced, as travel time varied greatly depending on the direction one had to travel during an era when most people were forced to use public transportation to get to work. Even in postwar years, researchers have shown this locational determinant of housing choice to be an important aspect of intra-urban mobility for segments of the population with limited resources (Goldstein and Mayer, 1964).[5]

In recent years, many geographers have noted a lessening relevance to housing choice of access to workplace, since in some cities automotive transportation more nearly equalizes commuting times. Nonetheless, geographers still employ the term 'place utility,' broadening this concept to include a wider range of urban attributes and amenities such as preference toward one or another 'side' of town (e.g., Simmons, 1968) or proximity to certain kinds of people or pastimes (Clarke and Cadwallader, 1973). If place utility continues to be broadened to include most interpersonal and behavioral aspects related to housing and location, there is a risk that the term will become too abstract for meaningful use.

In a landmark study, *Why Families Move* (1955), Rossi drew attention to family characteristics and how they relate to the home. He provided statistical documentation of the influence of the stage of the family's life cycle and of the internal space and storage capacities of dwellings as factors precipitating moves. Thus, families moved when they 'outgrew' their dwellings in an era of family formation, population growth, and large-scale private construction of family housing. Rossi hence introduced conceptions of demographic need to go along with status enhancement and locational efficiency. He did not attempt to differentiate the ways in which different forms of housing would satisfy the need, but then the choices were not so varied as they are today.

Rossi discussed also the social composition of neighborhoods as well as considerations of tenure in housing (whereby renters might be motivated to move so as to assume ownership status) as factors precipitating moves.

Social scientists generally analyze mobility in terms of two, often different factors: *push* (why people move away from their housing and/or location) and *pull* (why they select the particular new housing and/or location, instead of alternatives). Rossi's work strongly emphasizes both push factors and the degree that pull factors correspond with push factors, but not the extent and range of additional pull factors beyond those that correspond with push factors. In this respect, many specific design aspects of residential environment of interest to architects and planners are not considered.

Just after Rossi's work, a number of statistical studies began to indicate the importance of broader facets of people's lives in housing choice. The new studies showed that the educational component of status was frequently more relevant than strictly economic components in determining who would live with what neighbors in what neighborhood. It was not just purchasing power that led people to certain residences, but broader considerations covering both who their neighbors would be and what they might do there, both with the neighbors and more generally (Duncan and Duncan, 1957; Feldman and Tilly, 1960; Tilly, 1961; Wheeler, 1968).

In another approach, Bell (1958, 1968) sought to refute the perspective of status enhancement arguing instead that people moved to be with greater numbers of persons who were *already like themselves*. To Bell, the move from center city to suburb, for example, was not one to increase status, but rather to escape from increasing numbers of neighbors of a dissimilar social character and to gain a larger percentage of peers as neighbors.

Beyond this, however, Bell brought behavioral considerations firmly into the spotlight. He asserted that people would move to areas which provided the most appropriate opportunities to satisfy life styles they already emphasized but were not able to carry out as easily in less favorable surroundings. He suggested that people evaluate themselves in terms of what they most want to do with their lives and then, when able, select neighborhoods most able to satisfy them. Bell called this process *self-selection*.

Suburbs, for example, were thought to be most appropriate for the satisfaction of *familism*, while center city areas were thought more appropriate for such life styles as *careerism*, and *consumerism*. Bell did not specify the

place that housing type occupied in his schema; broad locational considerations appeared more salient to him. Since most suburban housing was
single family in the 1950s, the issue of housing type, although highly relevant now, may have been moot when Bell wrote about self-selection. More
recently, Gans (1967), among others, found self-selection a highly important explanation of suburban behavior.

Wolpert (1966) explored the psychological aspects of the decision to
move. Discussing the match between a family and its residential environment directly, he made clear that families might sustain mismatches between themselves and their housing under some conditions, without the
felt necessity for moving, while, at other times, they would endeavor to
move.

In this regard, he made the conceptual distinction between *stress* and
strain as encountered by people in their housing. While both stress and
strain are feelings experienced by family members as a consequence of
dysfunctional aspects of their home environments, stress is something that
people will tolerate over time because they receive something positive in
return which is more important to them than the negative consequences
of the mismatched elements of the situation. Traditionally, for example,
people have spoken of the 'trade-off' between distance and cost: some people are willing to undergo the stress of longer traveling times in return for
the lower cost of peripheral locations in metropolitan areas. If, on the
other hand, a condition is thought impossible to bear over the long run,
regardless of any benefits, the resulting feeling is strain, according to Wolpert. Strain, he feels, is an important precipitant of intraurban mobility.
The fruitfulness of this formulation is that it does not equate simple dis-
utility with mobility, nor does it equate moving with only certain periods
of life. Identification of dysfunctional situations without a priori overre-
action is the first step to understanding the incidence and distribution of
mobility.

Brown and Moore (1970) created a model of the dynamics of the residential adjustment and mobility pattern for a family, indicating that
strains and their resolutions might usefully be thought of as *recurrent*.
These authors indicate that the resolution of one set of strains does not
preclude changes occurring subsequently in the life and context of the
family, including, for example, changes in the environment and in family
structure, which may create stress and strain once again. Brown and

Moore show that the strain may be resolved not only by moving, but also by changing the nature of the existing residential environment (for example, adding a room) or by changing the needs precipitating the strain (for example, older children finding their own accommodation).

Brown and Moore's formulation of moving as cyclical is surely fruitful. It is clear, for example, that moves from grossly substandard housing to safe, clean, and new public housing relieve one area of strain in the life of a family. Nonetheless, sometime after the move, if not earlier, it may become evident that there is more to a residential environment than the one set of strains typically satisfied by that form of housing. That public housing tenants are not perennially happy and grateful is an obvious concomitant of Brown and Moore's model.

As models of mobility have become more sophisticated, both a wider range of reasons behind residential choice and more detailed specification of the dynamics of the move have been introduced. Yet, concentration has continued to focus on (1) *the move* and/or on (2) *the impact of individual moves for the spatial structure of the city.*

Nonetheless, cyclical explanatory patterns (i.e., those which explain recurrent incidence of mobility) may not be dynamic with regard to individual families. One can picture the cycle in Brown and Moore's model as resembling a vertical coil: families basically going around and around in response to specific but changing needs, which are accommodated in a relatively superficial fashion without really 'going anywhere.' The model does not imply any form of standard progression which families, if able, might follow. We may regard the coil form of cycle as a stationary, ad hoc type, in comparison to a more progressive cycle which responds to common changes that people undergo in their lives or to their strivings toward common cultural goals. The latter form of cycle might best be characterized by turning a vertical coil on its side and viewing both cyclical change, as represented in the Brown and Moore model, as well as dynamic progression toward an explicit set of goals. Figure 1.1 indicates one rendering of these two conceptions.

The Brown and Moore model makes it possible to understand both the normality of stress and strain and the ways in which resolutions may be reached. It does not suggest the source of or conditions for the criteria which precipitate stress and strain, nor give any indication that certain of these criteria appear in serial fashion. Turning their model into a pro-

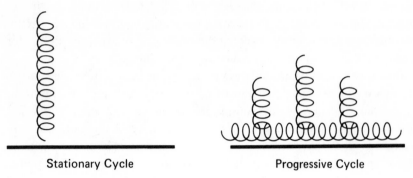

Stationary Cycle   Progressive Cycle

FIGURE 1.1.
THE CYCLICAL NATURE OF RESIDENTIAL MOBILITY: two conceptions.

gressive cycle makes it possible to deal with such matters of origin and order.

The progressive cycle implies that if certain changes in housing criteria come from expected changes in family need or from cultural goals, their occurrence does not necessarily come as a surprise in the lives of the people encountering them. People can move to a different form or location of housing or to a different location without the necessity of stress or strain in the old setting. The criteria behind choice of the current home may be seen as fully satisfied, and the criteria suggesting the need for a move may not create any current discomfort—merely the signal that a move would be necessary in order to satisfy progressively relevant criteria. While the search process for new housing would surely resemble that which occurs under the influence of strain in the existing setting, except perhaps for a lesser amount of pressure, moving under these circumstances becomes a matter of action, not reaction followed by action. The implications of this rethinking of the dynamics of moving will become apparent in the discussion at the end of this chapter.

User Needs in Housing

Architects generally employ a very different perspective on social aspects of housing, focusing on 'user needs.' This approach has concentrated largely on the physical attributes of housing that people want or need for the housing to be optimal. These physical elements are usually taken at face value as a basic core of necessities for most if not all people. In some cases, the particular needs of parts of the population, such as the blind or handicapped, are seen independent of the common needs of the whole population.

Architects have frequently expressed the wish that social scientists provide a standard checklist of user needs in housing so that their products could be found more suitable (cf. Broady, 1968; Gutman, 1972; Zeisel, 1975; Lasswell, 1974). Most materials coming from sociologists and geographers studying residential mobility have not been sufficient for the purpose, lacking specificity about the physical nature of environments serving as the context for mobility. Recent efforts to study the basic elements of home environment, so as to improve its functionality (e.g., Dalén & Holm, 1965), have still not resulted in satisfactory checklists.

Some have sought a universal basis for accommodating user needs in housing. Architects have often taken Maslow's (1943) theory of the hierarchy of needs as the foundation for such attempts. Maslow suggests that a series of human needs comes progressively into play as lower-order needs are satisfied. For example, safety from the elements, from animals, and from other people is a very basic need, one that must be satisfied for self-preservation. Yet, once the need for safety is satisfied, other needs, such as for self-esteem and self-actualization, require fulfillment. These higher needs must be considered when designing human housing. Rainwater (1966), for example, applied this theory fruitfully to explain the criteria which residents of a notoriously bad public housing project used as the basis for judging their environment, in contradistinction to criteria commonly employed by middle-class people—or, theoretically, by the same public housing tenants in a different residential situation.

The difficulty, however, with general theories of human need is that the physical specification of solutions is likely to take extremely diverse forms both in different cultures and classes within the same culture. It also does not attend to the specific needs of subgroups with various physical limitations, such as the young, the elderly, and the infirm.

In contrast, other design researchers have looked for those elements of the environment which appear to work most efficiently within specific institutions such as mental hospitals, airports, obstetrical wards, schools, offices, and kitchens. Standards, drawn up by professional organizations and government bodies and available for adoption by designers, generally have been codifications of pragmatic solutions which appeared fruitful.

However useful these standards are, they do not solve many of the problems which are part of the design process. We may know, for example, how to build an efficient kitchen, but we may not know whether we should build a kitchen at all in a potentially new unit of housing (or to install communal facilities instead). We may know how to design wards for schizophrenics, but we know less about what aspects of the ordinary home might produce schizophrenia. In short, the study of specific functional situations is a good beginning toward the study of user needs, but one addressing only limited questions at any one time.

Researchers have looked for user needs in many ways. Some researchers have studied people's *experience* with aspects of their environment. Evaluational studies are becoming far more common, as designers hope to capitalize on knowledge of personal experiences with what already has been built so that they might incorporate into new buildings and neighborhoods ideas inspired by this knowledge (cf. Michelson, 1968). These researchers have studied real-life reactions to environmental elements with such various methods as participant observation, photography, interviews, pencil and paper tests, and the like (cf. Michelson, 1975a).

When dealing with optimal elements of the environment, though, one cannot assume that people have already been exposed to them. People are not always able to give evidence on optimality from experience. Hence, researchers have devoted considerable effort as well to studies of public opinion. Many of these studies have been able both to ascertain public opinion about given elements, newly designed or existing, and to compare the importance of elements to each other. In this regard, researchers have used graphic and photographic materials (Peterson, 1967; Michelson, 1966), semiprojective techniques such as the semantic differential (Bechtel, 1975), and, of equal importance, the trade-off game, which attempts to simulate reality by forcing people to make choices as they might in real life (Wilson, 1962; Robinson et al., 1975).

The perspective of user needs suffers one typical shortcoming, however. It does not indicate the absolute value to the people observed or surveyed of the particular environmental elements under scrutiny. Some elements of the environment may work; others may not. Some may be specified as more important than others. But those elements to which the studied people react may be quite different from those which forced them to move, which attracted them to a new residence, or which became most salient to them after they moved. Indeed, if people follow a progressive pattern of *changing* needs, they may alter the relative importance of the various physical elements in their home environments over time.

While elements of the environment connected to user needs are omnipresent, they are not by definition uniformly important.

We need to approach the social implications of housing from both of the preceding perspectives. We need to know how people actually use their residential environments at any point in time, as well as their own interpretation of what they do. Therefore, we have to sort out both *intention* and *functional use* in the lives of people in order to answer the questions of this book. Ironically, these two perspectives are seldom brought together, however vitally complementary they may be.

Environment and Behavior

To this point, I have dealt only with residential choice and environmental elements which might satisfy certain functional and personal needs in housing. At this point, we might ask what 'happens' (in the most general sense) for which the physical elements of the home environment are more or less useful.

Some part of the answer lies in symbolism. The literature on mobility indicates that housing has status connotations, and one might easily add certain aesthetic properties which may prove pleasing or displeasing. Nonetheless, most of what spells the success or failure of the residential environment for families is behavioral in character.

Behavior occurs not in an abstract medium but rather under a definite set of spatial constraints. While much behavior is explained by cultural, social, and psychological factors, our interest at present has to do with the adequacy of spatial conditions for a wide range of desired and essential behaviors.

The literature on user needs is normally restricted to kitchens, bathrooms, garbage disposals, play spaces, well-defined institutional facilities, and the like. This literature pays less attention to other aspects of everyday behavior which are not tied as closely to the very basic fixtures in new buildings.

The literature on mobility, on the other hand, while bringing in broader life-style considerations as expectations in moving, largely fails to deal with how specific forms of behavior fit with specific spatial components of the new residential setting. Yet, design may have a bearing on whether expectations related to various life styles are fulfilled.

Therefore, to assess the implications of any particular residential environment, one must deal not only with moves and environmental elements but also with (1) whether expected behavior actually takes place, and (2) whether unexpected behavior, representing adaptation to the constraints of a particular residential environment, is deemed desirable by the residents.

A third necessary perspective, then, is one which is variously called environment and behavior, man-environment relations, ecological psychology, and other roughly similar names. This point of view is coming under increasing scrutiny by those who feel that a dynamic link must be made between sheer social intention on the one hand and design functionalism and/or determinism on the other.

Observers following the perspective of environment and behavior seek an explanation of behavior, when appropriate, with respect to its physical context. Usually, but not exclusively, the physical context is the *built* residential environment. Starting with some classic, original statements of this perspective (Hall, 1966; Sommer, 1969; Barker, 1968), many newer works have appeared of a more synthesizing character (Michelson, 1970b; Perin, 1970; Ittelson et al., 1974; Bell et al., 1973).

I tried previously to detail the place of behavior and other social considerations in the environmental context with the use of a concept called *congruence* (Michelson, 1970b). Congruence means taking certain salient aspects of the built environment, such as are present in the design of rooms, buildings, neighborhoods, and cities, as variables to be viewed in conjunction with other variables. Previously, space had been conceived by social scientists as effectively neutral in its bearing upon that which took place within it. Space was largely a *medium*, rather than a variable. Although some persons had taken quite the opposite stand, claiming spatial attributes determine behavior within the built environment, this perspective was surely not common, particularly among sociologists. I opted, simply, to put such spatial arrangements *into the same formula* as a wide range of social, cultural, and psychological variables, to assess their inter-relationships without a priori assumptions of freedom or determinism. I conceived of space as largely permissive, allowing people to do within it what they wish (all else equal), but as setting limits making very difficult or even impossible the performance of certain (possibly few) activities under certain circumstances.

Where the desired activity could, in fact, be accommodated by the given design, a state of congruence was deemed present. Where this was precluded by the design, a state of incongruence was declared. The thrust was that the latter state would lead to negative consequences of varying degrees of severity.

I made a distinction between mental congruence and experiential con-gruence. The former represented relations between people's behavior and environment in terms of whether they *thought* that the one would be con-sistent with the other—a vital factor in the acceptance or rejection of prof-fered solutions to environmental issues. Experiential congruence, on the other hand, would exist whenever the 'people side' and the 'environment side' were compatible, once the people had actual, realistic contact with the environment in question. Both types of congruence were felt essential to understanding the fruitfulness (or lack thereof) of built environments.

I encouraged the creation of an encyclopedic inventory of spatial designs and their congruence with a wide variety of human characteristics and behaviors, as a basis for the creation of future, more 'fitting' environments.

This formulation of congruence, despite the expressed meaning, may be easily misconstrued. The problem arising parallels a long-term tendency within the design professions to treat people *unidimensionally*, rather than *multidimensionally*. There was a day, for example, when clients or sub-jects of design were considered in very much oversimplified, stereotypic terms, along the line of only one of the many characteristics they pos-sessed. It was easy to identify groups of clients according to their main, shared characteristic, but this ignored many other characteristics that peo-ple as individuals always had as well.

For example, public housing authorities typically treated people in terms of their economic capacity. It was assumed that public housing was created for people who could not compete on the private housing market and who required new, safe, and decent housing made expressly for them.

Such recently constructed housing provided adequate shelter, but their designers did not consider that clients had varying family stages, ages, social problems, and interests. Poor families with illnesses were mixed in the same buildings with poor families with social problems. Teetotalers had alcoholics as neighbors, and single-parent families were provided the same kind of accommodations as families with both parents present. High-rise buildings were frequently considered equally appropriate for toddlers as for young adults or even old people. Hence, it is not surprising that many families found public housing undesirable, as it was planned only for their economic status and not for their everyday activities, and as it tended to reflect far more than the one dimension of their existence. More recent attempts have been made to plan public housing in terms of what various people do or need to do during the course of the day.

To jump to a different social class, let us look at the suburbs which were so prominently built in North America in the 1950s and 1960s. They were largely planned according to the considerations of raising young children. Planners conceived of separate houses on individual lots well removed from nonresidential activity as ideal for the care and socialization of toddlers. Nonetheless, when these young children grew into teenagers, they found such low densities and green spaces very undesirable, and required some form of transportation, usually unavailable, to participate in activities more suited to their ages. At the same time, the mothers of these toddlers were usually isolated from any form of commercial or recreational activity that might have made their days more interesting and efficient. Frequently, the fathers also were faced with longer commutes to work. The suburb is surely an example of unidimensionality—a fact only recently recognized.

Another example of unidimensionality is the planning of residential environments based on the kinds of interaction and activity which occur primarily during warm, pleasant weather. Yet, this is largely absent in most temperate or northern climates the greater part of the year.

While one may *analyze* environment and behavior according to the concept of congruence in such a disaggregated way, it is certainly dangerous to *plan* in that way. The question is how to bring all relevant aspects of people back together for the formal process of design, something for which there is some, but not much, precedent. It appears that the way to bring people back to an integrated whole for the purpose of planning is not to view people in terms of the 'labels' that social scientists customarily use to describe them, such as stage in the life cycle, social class, and so on. We do not know, for example, whether a person will emphasize what would be expected from social class, from ethnic memberships, from age-group relationships, or any other relevant label, when it comes to behavior within a specific setting. It is quite likely that two people with the same set of labels may regularly act very differently because of the individual priorities they put on the phenomena behind these labels. It is not the labels themselves which interact with environment. It is the behavior coming from one, some, or a blend of many labels which is actually what the environment must accommodate. We should design for regular behavior patterns.

There is no question that customary social scientific labels help *account* for such behavior patterns—in a post hoc, analytic way. Nonetheless, these labels are two steps removed from design, while the behavior patterns are only one step away. These labels are valid for the purposes of *explanation* and, although in a somewhat more risky venture, *prediction*. But for the purpose of *designing* more appropriate environments, the activity pattern-built environment equation is the most exact and relevant one.

In retrospect, I would have focused a previous book (Michelson, 1970b) more carefully around the concept of life style, indicating in what ways life style can be accounted for or explained by some of the more prominent nominal characteristics. But I would not have devoted just one chapter to life style and given the other variables independent treatment. Life style should be considered a higher-level concept than the others. It is a *synoptic* variable based on the concerns of the others, but more suitable for detailed design consideration.

All people do not share the same life style. Although people are in some ways totally idiosyncratic, one can still consider, for practical purposes, that the number of life styles to be taken into account varies somewhere *between* a very few (surely not one) and infinity. The design process must therefore assume diverse clienteles.

The input to congruence, then, is the relation between differential behavior patterns and the various aspects of physical environment—not nominal factors or labels. Environments, within the context of congruence, are *opportunity fields*, which, depending on their design, provide the opportunity for a certain (usually wide) range of behaviors to occur, although some behaviors are made difficult and others are precluded.

Assuming at any point in time fixed technology and resources, environments vary in the opportunities that they convey through land-use planning and housing design. Small children, for example, without a way to reach a park, however tremendous, and without other opportunities for play close to home, should be expected to congregate on steps and streets. Children whose building contains a play area will be less underfoot (although, as before, the presence of tot lots does not *determine* their use). Similarly, high-rise units with places designed for human contact are more likely to promote contact (as yards and gardens do for residents of single homes). In the halls, elevators, and lobbies constituting most public space in today's buildings, an excuse is needed for a person to remain in place, available for contact.

In short, since environment spells opportunity for some aspects of behavior and lack of opportunity for others, we should ask several questions about any neighborhood setting:

1. Does it preclude desired contacts or activities?
2. Does it provide realistic opportunity for the pursuit of desired contacts or activities?
3. Does it provide realistic opportunity to avoid undesired contacts or activities?
4. Does it preclude undesired contacts or activities?

Single-family homes may be weighed against high-rise apartments in terms of the opportunities they provide for family activities. Morever, aspects of the neighborhood and general location, for many everyday activities, must be taken into consideration in weighing the suitability of housing. The design researcher can probably quantify how well alternative environments satisfy carefully defined requirements, since opportunity is only valid in terms of specific degrees of access time, trouble, and expense. Sharpening the factors in the congruence equation in this way makes it easier to understand the *dynamics* of the relations discussed and studied, something not particularly true with the original formulation.

Following upon this emphasis on activity patterns an obvious question must surely be, But what about all sorts of other factors which seem to explain why people act the way they do in given spatial situations? What about, for example, the many factors discussed by environmental *psychologists?*

Recent developments make increasingly clear not only that a variety of perspectives on man-environment relations are legitimate, but also that these perspectives are complementary and perhaps subject to priority, according to the question asked. The context of man-environment relations is considerably broader than the considerations of any one perspective.

Several years ago (1971a), I wrote an article in the form of a fable as a way of relating these perspectives. It was based on the old saying, "You can lead a horse to water but you can't make him drink."

The fable centered upon the creation of a new, improved horse trough by a design team. Those on the team made many errors before producing a workable masterpiece, each error representing a new and complementary perspective. For example, first, they had to rule out social, physiological, and psychological reasons, about why horses would not drink from the newly designed troughs. They had to verify that the horses were thirsty, not preferring instead to play 'Cowboys and Indians.' They had to ensure that the vessel they were building was larger than a demitasse cup and had clear managerial procedures for the five horses involved, lest the field of opportunity was insufficient to meet the requirements called for by congruence. They had to ensure that the water was unchlorinated to satisfy the demands of those who knew about horse perception. They had to screen the drinking vessels for privacy, for the normative school of thought indicated that horses do not drink in public. They had to add swinging doors and a bar, while removing a bell tower and crosses, to provide a symbolically appropriate behavior setting for what they wished to do. But even this was not enough for the horses to drink, if their schedule or preference called for another type of behavior, like racing. Nonetheless, once all these 'hurdles' were overcome, despite the incredible simplicity of the design problem, there were no obstacles and the horses eventually drank.

When you put all these perspectives together, you discover that they form a relatively ordered set of filters between environment and the behavior assumed to occur within it. For example, when you start with a proposed new environment, the very first test it would have to pass is whether it provides a realistic opportunity for the eventual behavior to occur. If this is not the case, there is no sense in considering its perceptual, normative, or symbolic qualities. Nonetheless, once the opportunity has been provided, this does not ensure the occurrence of the behavior, and these other requirements must be satisfied one by one. The cultural elements, consisting of normative (cf. Hall, 1966; Sommer, 1969) and symbolic aspects (cf. Barker, 1968), actually seem closer to the occurrence of the behavior than the perceptual (cf. Downs and Stea, 1973; Lynch, 1960), as the perceptual must be operational before the two cultural types of evaluation can be made. If, on the other hand, the primary aim is to explain behavior rather than to judge the appropriateness of a design, then the perceptual, symbolic, and normative factors explain more completely why the particular behavior, and not some other, occurred in that environmental context.[6]

In any case, the perspective of environment and behavior draws on many forms of explanation but nonetheless focuses on the incidence of specific forms of behavior with respect to the characteristics of their physical setting, providing answers relevant to both social scientists and designers.

AN INTEGRATED PARADIGM

Figure 1.2 shows what the three complementary perspectives detailed above—mobility and choice, user needs, and environment and behavior—imply for the problem with which this volume deals. This paradigm resembles that of Brown and Moore (1970), in that it concentrates on the process of adjustment to, and life in, a single residence, although it does not deal with the selection of that residence.

The figure indicates first, at the top, that families are likely to have aspirations with respect to their housing. Such aspirations may or may not be connected with expectations concerning behavior in the physical setting, but in any case they precede life in that setting. Such aspirations may also go well beyond the immediate residence to which people are moving. People's aspirations may go several steps beyond the immediate move, with this move undertaken for vastly different reasons. Hence, another line and arrow from aspirations may well bypass the present physical setting and lead to future action once people have the ability to achieve these aspirations.

Also at the top of the paradigm are primary physical demands, such as the need for a certain number of bedrooms, which families may make on their housing and which may or may not be related to specific behavioral expectations.

In any case, initial aspirations or demands placed on the physical setting are then put to the test after exposure to the setting. Behavior may then occur as foreseen. This would of course be expected in cases that follow the theory of self-selection. On the other hand, it is possible, particularly from a perspective of environmental determinism, that unforeseen behaviors might occur as a consequence of the new physical setting. In either case, the onset of the results and behavior may be mediated by such persistent factors as perception and culture.

Moreover, behavior in the new setting may also occur without any

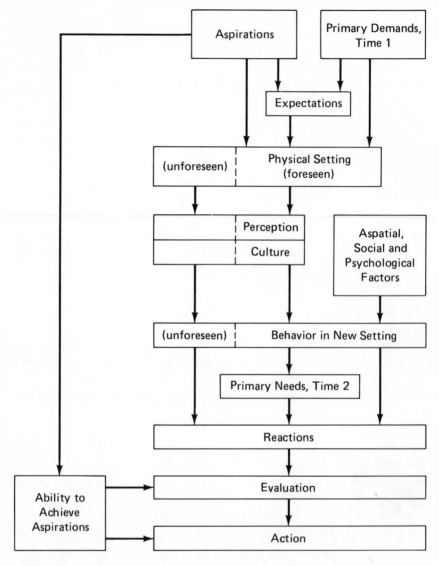

FIGURE 1.2.
THE SOCIAL IMPLICATIONS OF HOUSING: a paradigm.

stimulation by environmental factors. Social or psychological pressures, not to speak of popular culture and current fashion, may lead to behavior changes which merely coincide with residence in a new environment. Evaluation of 'situated behavior' surely requires sensitive examination about whether observed behavior is related to the factors behind housing choice, to the objective conditions of the setting, or to spurious correlation.

As Brown and Moore point out, it is possible that the primary demands which people place on their environment change with time. Such change may cause a reaction leading to a negative evaluation on the part of the residents and, possibly, action leading to a change of residence. However, reactions related to either the same or changed demands need not, of course, be negative. They can well be positive. There is also no necessity for needs to change, with reactions to the environment and eventual evaluation reflecting either the occurrence or nonoccurrence of what was expected and foreseen or the consequences of that which was unforeseen. While we customarily consider the effects of the unforeseen as negative, there is no reason why this is so.

In the above two cases—that of the foreseen and unforeseen behavioral consequences of the physical setting—a *balance* of reactions to different implications is a likely consequence, with the evaluation of the housing type based on the differential priorities assigned to the various components and reactions.

Nonetheless, it is imperative to stress that a third way through the model may make the previous two less relevant. Action may be based not on reactions or evaluation of the current home, but rather on the ability to achieve aspirations.

Another possibility is that once the ability to achieve longer range aspirations is realized, it will lead to a more negative evaluation of the present environment, regardless of the ability of that environment to satisfy the behavioral expectations originally placed on it. Festinger's theory of cognitive dissonance (1957) would surely suggest that, since people find it difficult to hold mutually exclusive opinions in their heads for long, they will tend to downgrade their existing residence in favor of what they now can achieve.

The ability to achieve aspirations may also play a part in the evaluation of the current home if that ability is *blocked* by objective circumstances. Blocked mobility may, on the one hand, lead to overglorification of the status quo in the absence of something better. It may, on the other hand, make the deficiencies of the existing home more glaring, since the family is not able to simply move on to the next home without 'looking back' upon the more negative aspects of the existing home.

The logic inherent in this paradigm (which includes the possibility of a long-term set of aspirations, suggesting movement with and without stress) implies a relatively simply progression through several broad stages, which are not necessarily equal in duration, in a *family-mobility cycle*.[7]

We might fruitfully conceive family mobility as comprising three general stages: (1) baseline, (2) incremental change, and (3) approximation of the ideal. Let us examine these one by one.

1. *Baseline stage*. That the baseline stage is the initial one is true by definition, but its placement also has implications about its character and the elements of environmental choice that might be thought relevant within it. It is the first stage either of the formation of a family or in a family's arrival within a given metropolitan area. It would be impossible for the couple to benefit from the experience either of their married life together, in the one case, or of their life in the particular metropolitan area, in the other case, as guides in the selection of this stage of housing. Hence, one could conceive that the effective factors in residential choice at this stage in the family's mobility cycle are those which are largely non-experiential criteria: economics, contacts, and obvious place utility (such as the trip to work). There is much in the literature, for example, to indicate the importance of easy purchase and resale of homes among persons entering a metropolitan area for the first time, as well as the importance of preexisting social contacts in the selection of initial accommodation (cf. Whyte, 1956; Tilly and Brown, 1967). Access to the workplace may be a major locational determinant of persons moving to a city from out of town. That nonexperiential factors may play a larger part at this stage does not rule out other factors in any absolute sense; obviously there is always a mixture of motives at every stage, and experiential factors may be thought to play a larger role at other stages.

2. *Stage of incremental change*. At any time most people have a sense of their ideal. Ideals are frequently culturally derived and shared. Yet, most ideals in housing are out of the range of short-run attainment for most people. More typical is the goal that makes 'striving for a lifetime' a frequently heard cliché.

For some years, no North American housing study has failed to show that the ideal among all subgroups of the population, no matter how defined, is the self-contained single-family house, frequently in low density areas (e.g., Lansing, 1966; Hinshaw and Allott, 1973). Yet, large segments of the population do not live in such residences. This separation of the ideal from the actual, however, does not retard intermediate mobility. There is no reason why people cannot and do not adhere to their aspirations (which the cynic might be tempted to call illusions) while making changes which incrementally satisfy pragmatic problems and interests which have arisen. Thus, Stage 2 can be seen to include a number of successive strains and resolutions from the baseline stage, continuing either indefinitely or until Stage 3 is reached. Indeed, successive iterations of Stage 2 can be, but do not have to be, steps in the direction of Stage 3. What Stage 2 suggests is that people may make a considerable number of moves over short or long periods of time with serious and pragmatic intentions but without the necessity that these moves bear directly on those things these people deem most important in housing.

3. *Approximation of the ideal.* While Stage 3 may never be attained for some families, its possibility is extremely important. The chance of achieving some approximation of one's ideal permits relative satisfaction with the various iterations of Stage 2, even though the latter may not be satisfactory in an absolute sense. Since ideals are seldom characterized in ironclad detail, approximations of them generally suffice for those without previous direct contact with their ideal.

If the ideal reflects by definition those elements of habitation which people consider most important, these will be emphasized in attaining the ideal, at the possible expense of some of the less important (but nonetheless real) factors which underlie housing choice at other stages in the family-mobility cycle. This would imply that some factors contributing to housing choice at Stages 1 and 2 will be *compromised* if necessary in order to achieve an approximation of the ideal in Stage 3. For example, travel time, which can be a major factor in Stages 1 and 2, may be traded off for privacy when a family obtains a self-contained house in Stage 3.

The juxtaposition of Stages 2 and 3 is highly important for several reasons.

First, this juxtaposition may help to explain why people may operate on different rationales at different points in time.

Second, it may also help to explain the apparent contradiction between lack of attainment of a strongly held ideal and concurrent short term satisfaction.

Third, it can help explain the basis for extreme and uncharacteristic frustration and unhappiness among those segments of the population which despair of ever attaining their ideal. Indeed, these segments—which would include many residents of public housing, whose physical or occupational disabilities suggest that public housing, while conferring some benefits, is the end of the road regarding mobility—may find it impossible even to consider further iterations in the Stage 2 cycle. Under these circumstances, one can expect (and one certainly finds) any initial satisfaction replaced by strain incapable of either the Stage 2 incremental amelioration or the Stage 3 approximation of the ideal, which are available to the rest of the population. A Swedish study demonstrates this point with considerable clarity (Egerö, 1967).

Within this paradigm of family mobility, pragmatic questions should be of more relevance at one stage in a family's moving cycle than at others. This does not mean, however, that these pragmatic questions are all of a kind. *Many* of the traditional explanatory factors are relevant to Stage 2 environmental choice. Furthermore, different types of reasons can support qualitatively different environmental choices within any stage. Thus, one may easily make a life cycle-related improvement in housing space without any bearing on status conferral. One may improve one's status while actually decreasing living space. One may seek out others like oneself without affecting either of the two previous factors.

All these quite logical and complementary phenomena have one thing in common, though. They refer to a person either taking his present situation and continuing it under more favorable conditions or of a person seeking an absolute gain either for its own sake or as response to a demographic event. One finds much less reference in the literature on mobility to the possibility that some people may discover areas of life in which they are relatively disadvantaged compared to their peers, where an action is intended to turn this perceived deficit into one of equality. This situation is generally known by the term *relative deprivation*. The action taken to overcome relative deprivation I shall call *deficit compensation*.

Under deficit compensation, some people might move in Stage 2 for reasons other than to achieve ultimate aspirations or to get something that other people do not have, let alone in reaction to life-cycle changes.

They might move, although without strain, if they are deprived relative to other people, where the disadvantage can be more easily remedied through a change of address. In essence, some people may move *not* to be the first on their block to have something or because it is painful not to have it, but rather because everybody else on their block already has it and because they can get it most easily by moving to a block in which it is a fixture.

My point is not that deficit compensation is the only process by which people make environmental choices in Stage 2, but rather that it is one which is not generally recognized but which may be relevant for some types of moves.

The argument, then, in this chapter is that to understand the implications of housing, one must consider: (1) moving as a repetitive process, (2) the direction of progression in this process as it is represented by the family's mobility cycle, and (3) the factors which come to play a part in consumer evaluation of the housing within the given iteration of this cycle. One must include such factors as (1) the minds of movers during mobility and choice processes, (2) those physical elements of the residential environment which are salient to the given family, as well as (3) the behavioral and other social patterns reflected in both of them.

Paradigms such as this do not by themselves answer questions. They are only more or less useful in guiding the search for answers. As a start, however, this paradigm suggests the need to search for *other than universal criteria* regarding the implications of any given housing type or location for any given segment of the population at any one time. It suggests that housing does not have to be perfect in order to satisfy the demands made of it. It suggests that satisfaction with housing does not necessarily denote that ultimate wants are being satisfied at the moment. It suggests that expressed satisfaction with the residential environment may coincide with the perception of severe faults by residents. Finally, it suggests, that, while the motivation for some moves may reflect psychological strains, such a condition is not a prerequisite for moving. All these suggestions, which are independent of such reasons for mobility as job transfer and macroscopic economic change, help make apparent why the current rate of residential mobility is so very high, so much so that statistics about mobility (e.g., 'one in five families moves every year') are often touted as representing the 'unbelievable but true.'

That most of these suggestions are also unconventional may indicate that the paradigm described, however obvious in appearance at first glance, may extend beyond what has been included in previous formulations.

Nonetheless, the perspectives necessary for a general understanding of the match between people and residential environment are at a very different level of specificity than the content relevant to the implications of particular housing types and locations. In Chapter 2, then, we turn to the discussion of what implications we should expect concerning the contrast of high-rise to single-family housing and of distant suburban location to central-city location.

NOTES

[1] Adapted from a cartoon by the late Danish humorist Storm Pedersen.

[2] See, e.g., the discussion by Onebokun (1974).

[3] There is considerable documentation, however, about the heterogeneity of suburban neighborhoods vis-à-vis each other (cf. Kramer, 1972; Clark, 1966).

[4] For an inventory of common determinants of intraurban mobility, see Sabagh et al. (1969).

[5] Ironically, Goldstein and Mayer are sociologists!

[6] A more detailed statement of this paradigm may be found in Michelson (1974).

[7] While the current discussion could justifiably focus on a person's succession of habitats from cradle to grave, I shall limit my focus to the conjugal family from marriage to approximately retirement age, as this is the group contributing to the bulk of intracity moves. Not coincidentally, it is also the group which directly or indirectly comprises the majority of the population; and it is a group whose welfare is a major concern in times of housing shortages, since the welfare of children is usually taken seriously.

Chapter Two

The Substance of Inquiry

This chapter focuses more closely on the expected social implications of high rise and single family housing, as well as on suburban and central city location. While the previous chapter identified the intellectual origins of such content, the present chapter will detail what people appear to seek in these various contexts, the environmental elements which seem salient, and the behavioral patterns presumed to emerge. We shall observe these both as reflected in writings and in the eyes of some of the developers of the kinds of housing studied.

I do not intend to single out just a single theme, a single hypothesis, or, as it were, any ax to grind. Instead, my wish is to make explicit a variety of existing hypotheses about these environments, while, in the study to be described in succeeding chapters, remaining open to serendipitous observations.

Nonetheless, I shall place one blinder on the ensuing discussion—an emphasis on the family during childbearing years. While this category of family is not the exclusive consumer of housing in the particular contexts involved, it is the one which the study to be described was geared to cover. Such a preoccupation, however, is not intended to denegrate other sectors of the housing market (e.g., the single or the elderly).

Before turning to the content per se, I must deal with some final questions of orientation, which follow from the discussion in Chapter 1. It is, after all, one thing to *note* a full range of orientations on the implications of housing, but quite another, to *treat* the intellectual contradictions inherent among the various perspectives. How shall we view the *relative importance* of motivated, conscious action by people, in contrast to 'environmental determinism'?

This is a question with a long and distinguished history.

Actions over the years by governments, which, on the one hand, attempted to replace slums with public housing and which, on the other hand, helped to create suburban housing, all contained clear assumptions about the beneficial functions of the physical units and external spaces created.

Governments assumed that social welfare was served by the creation of certain forms of housing and the elimination of others, rather than by the distribution of money directly to families, to command whatever they wanted in the market place. Some governments, for example in Sweden, have backed the creation of high-rise communities to provide families with strong supportive recreational and commercial services. In Sweden, too, some people thought that high-rise communities would provide the opportunity for political participation close to home, something hypothesized in North America to occur in well-planned, suburban-style neighborhoods (Perry, 1966).

In recent years there has been a backlash against physical determinism. Even when considering the plight of the poor, who largely lack a range of choice when forced into new housing, studies have emphasized that it is what people bring to their new housing that serves as the basis for understanding what happens there. Nathan Glazer, for example, declared in 1965 in *The New York Times Magazine*: 'We must root out of our thinking . . . the assumption that the physical form of our communities has social consequences . . . the truth is that social surroundings are more important in determining what happens to people than are physical surroundings' (pp. 57 and 59).

Present-day rejection of physical determinism normally takes a milder form, indicating a few, selected aspects of life as related closely to environmental elements, while citing antecedent social conditions for most behavior observed in given settings. Wilner et al. (1962) found some, but relatively few, expected improvements in health in a rehousing program studied. Schorr (1963), in a wide review of 'slum' conditions in the United States, and Daun (1974), in a more recent review of problematic conditions in a prototypic Stockholm housing project,[1] have both taken this approach.

In Chapter 1, I eliminated the possibility of either complete human rationality or complete environmental determinism, steering a middle ground using the guidance derived from each perspective. What this suggests at this point is that the salience of the one extreme or the other is not an 'across the board' phenomenon, but is dependent on the specific nature of the phenomenon or physical elements concerned. In many instances, one should expect a coincidence between human intentions and environmental opportunities, as environments are selected for their ability to transform wishes into reality. In this case, the perceptive person's environmental choice may be the imperceptive person's environmental determinism.

In any case, it is an *empirical* question about the extent and areas of application of each of the perspectives. Let us, therefore, examine what is suggested by the different perspectives concerning our selected types of housing and location without prejudgment about the primacy of the conflicting but necessary perspectives, as they affect housing and location.

THE VIEW FROM THE LITERATURE

This section introduces many of the implications commonly cited of the several combinations of housing type and location under study. These implications may come from one or more of the several perspectives discussed above, and this will be made explicit where relevant. We shall look at the opposing forms of housing, the contrast in location, and then the combinations of housing type and location (for those 'interaction effects' which may be thought unique to specific combinations of the two).

High-Rise Apartments

Two factors are almost always confused in any discussion of high-rise apartments: (1) the properties inherent in the high-rise building and (2) properties that only *appear* connected to them insofar as these buildings are constructed in a particular way.[2] A good number of the social implications of high-rise apartments are, in fact, implications of these buildings *as they are conventionally constructed*. It takes no great stretch of the imagination to contemplate buildings with total soundproofing, with cavernous living space, with service and recreation facilities near every suite, and so on. We may not expect such buildings under current economic conditions or under current methods of finance, but the limitations of the status quo are not necessarily inherent limitations to high-rise buildings per se.

On the other hand, some limitations which people relate to high-rise buildings may be thought inherent to the fact that they are tall, house many families under the same roof, and require elevator service to reach a reasonable proportion of the housing units.

One example of the latter type of implication is high residential density, which, according to one of its many definitions, means many persons per building. This term would apply invariably to high-rise apartments.

Let us therefore look first at the expectations contained in previous writings about the effects of living in high density settings, observing in the process the extent to which the specific nature of these concerns really applies to high-rise buildings.

The effects of density.[3] The most general of several approaches to density might best be called 'clinical.' Psychologists and psychiatrists have formed judgments as a consequence of their contact with individual patients about the effects of high density on human functioning (Plant, 1957; Cappon, 1972). They have generally drawn on environmental factors to account for breakdowns in either personal or family functioning, although one observer (Loring, 1956) emphasizes that high densities only 'aggravate or accelerate, not cause or motivate, any tendency to disorganization in a personality or group' (p. 167).

For some years, concerned observers had the same conclusions as clinicians. Journalists 'muckraked' against slum conditions and helped bring about public-housing projects which, although containing many families in a single area, nonetheless attempted to provide sufficient space for families within their own apartments (Steffens, 1931). Persons concerned with town planning and zoning contributed standards based on the assumption that too many people created poor conditions (Howard, 1898; American Public Health Association, 1946). Sociological thinkers such as Simmel (1957) and Wirth (1938) dealt in ideal-typical fashion with the presumed effects of high densities on individuals and social structures. Only in recent years have a few persons suggested some limited positive functions performed by high density (e.g., Jacobs, 1961).

Other persons used available statistics in order to assess the effects of living in high-density settings. Statistics are available on housing conditions, and various measures of density can be computed from them. Other statistics are available dealing with incidences of disease, crime, delinquency, and other pathologies. Coming as they do, however, from different bureaucracies involved with the same municipality and from organizations pledged to maintain the personal privacy of citizens, these statistics have always been stated in terms of *rates* for a geographic area, rather than in terms of the personal and environmental characteristics of individuals. The relationships then expressed between density and pathology are the consequences of analyses based on the statistical association of *aggregate* data. That is, they state whether a geographic area like a census tract—which can be generally characterized by one set of phenomena, such as high density—can also be characterized by one or more other sets of phenomena, including the various pathologies. These analyses do not say directly whether individuals are likely to encounter the inferred consequences of these differences in density, an inference which at times may be fallacious [referred to as the "ecological fallacy" (Robinson, 1950)].

Although these studies capitalize on availability of official statistics and, thus, present readers with problems of inference, they nonetheless deal with rich material providing the basis for considerable speculation. Schmitt (1966), for example, explored density in Honolulu, attaching considerable significance to the effect of crowded neighborhoods (in contrast to crowded dwellings) on signs of pathology. He also compared aggregate statistics on Hong Kong with aggregate statistics on American cities (1963). Since the population in very densely settled Hong Kong exhibited fewer signs of most pathologies than did more sparsely settled urban Americans, Schmitt entered the crucial modifying proviso that the effects of density can be strongly mediated by local culture, evolving in adaptation to and in support of changing, local density conditions. In other words, the same dense setting may be more or less conducive to pathology depending on the presence or absence of a suitably adaptive culture.

Galle et al. (1974) examined statistics available for Chicago, concluding that crowding inside the home, in contrast to crowded blocks, was an undeniable factor in the incidence of pathology. In elaborating this effect, which survived many statistical controls for social causation, Galle and his associates promulgated propositions concerning what they called "interpersonal press" *within* housing units.

At a higher level of generalization, Booth and Welch (1973) used aggregate data to explore the relationship of national density and aggression, with positive findings.

While most researchers would probably concede the desirability of using data on individuals rather than on areas as the basic unit of analysis, studies based on individuals are highly costly. High costs come from the necessity to seek out large samples of people in appropriate physical settings and then to obtain complex information on a wide variety of potential variables from them. Few such studies of density have been conducted, and these have been of limited scope.

Mitchell (1971), however, provided information about the effects of overcrowding in Hong Kong. His results documented the problems accompanying overcrowding within dwelling units, particularly dwelling units removed from ground level, but indicated as well that cohabitants of a dwelling unit could mitigate negative effects through skillful management of time and space. It was only when residents did not find themselves able to stagger their appearances at home, performing many daily functions outside the dwelling unit, that problems seemed severe.

Another study (Michelson, 1968a) traced the relation of home physical environment to the performance of a group of school children, holding relevant social factors constant. This study demonstrated within the limited population upon which it focused that high-site densities were strongly related to student performance within all strata of social ranking, while conditions of internal crowding were often successfully mitigated by the separation of activities within dwelling units of even modest size.

Despite the complementarity of these findings, these examples indicate the extremely narrow scope characteristic of studies to date on individuals, in contrast to the enormity of the problem arousing public concern.

Much public concern can be attributed to a series of studies taking still a different approach. A variety of studies, both in natural habitats and in highly controlled, experimental settings, have indicated that higher than 'normal' densities bring out effects ranging from 'antisocial' behavior to death among animals such as mice, deer, and woodchucks (Calhoun, 1963; Klopfer, 1969). These studies have commonly found that the increasing 'interpersonal' contact between animals living under conditions of higher density accompanies, at least coincidentally in time, a loss in the weight and functioning capacity of adrenal glands, which in turn are important to animals' defense mechanisms. Extreme caution must be exercised in translating the results of such studies to the explanation of human behavior, since people have additional capacities for adaptation, including a spoken and communicated culture. Nonetheless, studies such as these have unquestionably triggered off hypotheses concerning analogous phenomena within human populations. The consequences of overcrowding found among animals (given the label 'behavioral sink') have been applied directly to life in urban ghettoes.

The last of the different approaches to density consists of *experimental* studies on humans, normally conducted by psychologists and social psychologists. In these cases (e.g., Freedman, et al., 1971; Stokols, et al., 1973) conditions of differential density are purposefully created, and persons are brought in for the performance of a specific and finite set of tasks or behaviors, during which their reactions to the environmental conditions are measured. This approach affords considerable control over the situation of density under investigation. It allows factors in the process to be isolated and hence viewed more carefully. But, it also creates a situation where the main measure of density is a highly transitory and peripheral one in the lives of the persons surveyed, as compared to conditions of normal residential density.

Not surprisingly, results from the first several experiments in this relatively new approach have been ad hoc in character, although consistent sex differences in reaction to crowding have emerged. Women handle high densities better than men. The importance of separating transitory from quasi-permanent situations of density was underlined in an earlier analysis by Biderman (1963), which indicated that persons optimistic about their situation more readily survived situations of extreme density than did those pessimistic about the possibility of leaving behind such conditions.

Researchers have also used quasi-experimental settings in observing people like sailors on shipboard in highly dense settings which, while not permanent, were nonetheless natural (Roos, 1970). Such studies have shown both that crowded conditions create pressures on people, and that people are capable of taking adaptive measures to cope, even though such measures may not necessarily be desirable in the absolute to those involved.

From these various approaches, one expects a variety of potential ills from high density settings. These ills include threats to physical health, heightened aggression, family breakdown, inadequate child care, and personal disorder. While this literature cautions, in some instances, about the mediating effect of culture and about the necessary but insufficient nature of causal effect, a sober set of hypotheses is nonetheless presented to researchers wishing to refine their knowledge of these relationships. Besides these hypotheses, however, the previous literature leaves some major *issues* unsettled. These issues concern the nature of the independent variable, the dependent variables, and the dynamic processes which link the two together. Let us examine these problems briefly one by one.

The independent variable in this case is residential density. As the above discussion indicates, a number of different measures of density have been used, with varying and inconsistent results. Many people have assumed that crowding within the dwelling unit (normally expressed in terms of persons per room) is a natural and potent measure of density. Although the Galle et al. (1974) study suggests that this may be the case, several other studies cited have suggested that such internal crowding is less of a factor in accounting for pathological responses than are other conceptions of density (Schmitt, 1966; Michelson, 1968a), since people sharing the same immediate space may be more capable than larger groups of taking adaptive measures to compensate for their unfavorable situation.

A popular alternative to conceiving density in terms of internal crowding is conceiving it as the number of persons or families sharing a local area, such as an acre, a block, or a neighborhood. Although this conception has been supported by some studies, researchers have been more reluctant to specify *why* it should be expected to have this effect.

Still another definition concerns the number of families who share the same building. This definition combines some of the above concerns about competition for scarce resources with some of those about inability to escape from certain numbers of other persons, either in public areas or through the transmission of voices and other disturbances. This definition has not been used as frequently as the previous two.

Furthermore, some researchers have turned away from the measurement of objective density as it exists in physical space and turned instead to the social situations in which people *feel* the purported effects of their surroundings (e.g., Stokols, 1972).[4] These researchers argue that a dense spatial situation can not affect people until perceived or experienced. Nonetheless, the objective spatial parameters are in many instances both a context and a partial stimulus for what is perceived and experienced; these parameters are hence not to be discarded a priori.

As the nature of the independent variable has been so mixed, and as the approaches taken to research have been so different, it is perhaps understandable that such a wide variety of effects has been documented. To some extent, this is a function of the third problem, lack of adequate consideration of a dynamic process linking causes to effects. If this process is lacking, there is no reason to expect any specific set of outcomes to occur, permitting the scope of attention to range over a wide variety of possible effects. If you do not expect to find fish in a particular place, you spread your net more widely. Without exaggerating unduly, it may be fair to state that such processes as have been advanced have been frequently ad hoc and post hoc in character, following upon the results of analyses performed.

Some highly plausible schemes have emerged, however. One which links density to death and disorder through interactional and then physiological processes comes from the animal studies. Galle et al. (1974) conceptualized interpersonal press in crowded housing. Efran and Cheyne (1974) showed through experiments in public places that density necessarily involves invasions of personal space, resulting in stress. Zlutnick and Altman (1972) pointed out that one aspect of the high-density neighborhood is scarcity of environmental resources.

It is clear that this literature contains many frightening insinuations but few firm conclusions. In addition, very little of that part of the literature on density dealing with residential settings *necessarily* includes the high-rise situation. For example, there is no necessary relationship between internal crowding and residence in a high rise. There is also no necessary relationship between high-site density and residence in a high rise. There are at least two reasons for this: (1) a high-rise building may be surrounded by considerable space, yet stocked with ample facilities per capita, to avoid competition for scarce resources and (2) high densities in low-rise forms of housing are not only characteristic of many of the older sections of cities studied but are being consciously created today as alternatives to the high rise. Moreover, the one definition of density which is more or less coincident with the high-rise building, families per building, has not proven fruitful in previous studies. Hence, although we may investigate high-rise living with attention to the implications of high density, we should not automatically expect of the high-rise any particular set of outcomes in this connection.

Let us turn to what we might expect of the currently conventional high-rise building.

Social implications of the conventional high-rise building. The social implications of the conventional high-rise apartment *for families* lie strongly in the areas of user needs and situated behavior, insofar as the high rise is not a form of home families typically choose in response to deeply held motives. Most writers impute negative implications for family living for this form of dwelling. As one author put it:

Practically no one disputes that this form of home is unsatisfactory for the family with small children. It is a strain on the mother and an over-restricted environment, physical and social, for the child. [Jephcott, 1971, p. 130.]

Perhaps for this reason one cannot point to a wide variety of positive expectations motivating family choice of the high rise. While many persons find that ease of maintenance (i.e., somebody else does it for you) is a motivating feature for many older people to high-rise apartments as well as for some younger people without families, this motivation has never been found to apply to most families, who appear to prefer to be able to modify their home environment according to the changing needs of their families.

High-rise apartments have traditionally been rental accommodation, although condominium and cooperative arrangements are now taking hold. While rental status is extremely functional for families who are highly mobile or unable to amass the capital for owned accommodation, most people nonetheless find ownership preferable.

In many places, high-rise apartments are primarily in central locations, and people move to them in order to gain centrality. This, however, is not a direct function of the housing type.

Many think that condominium ownership in high-rise buildings confers an attraction which the high rise formerly lacked—investment potential and partial protection against arbitrary increases in the cost of accommodation. Some think that this is enough to turn the high rise from a negative to a positive form of housing. In the words of one enthusiastic developer:

We are finding that 96% of the people living in condominiums, whatever its form, are just nuts about it. They just love it. . . . Don't let anyone kid you—this is the life style of the future, it's preferred, it's the choice. [Capilano College Conference Center, 1974, p. 25.]

On the other hand, there is evidence that while ownership is preferred, a large percentage of those buying condominiums do not thereby come to accept them as optimal. They treat the condominium as interim accommodation, until they can move to a detached house (Norcross, 1973; Homenuck, 1973).

Its effects on behavior, however, cause high-rise accommodation to receive its worst image. Some observers cite the considerable social distance among the co-tenants in high-rise apartments, leading to a situation of

"I'm lonesome!"

FIGURE 2.1.
Drawing by W. Steig; © 1966 The New Yorker Magazine, Inc.

anonymity for the individual family (e.g., Rosenberg, 1968). This is normally explained with reference to the lack of areas in a typical building where people can naturally interact without having to excuse themselves to others for remaining in a particular place. Even people desiring social contact do not normally want to appear 'forward' or strange in areas of a building where the norms do not support socially acceptable forms of loitering. Other writers suggest that thin walls do not support extended, personal contact with neighbors who can hear what is said 'the night before' (e.g., Jephcott, 1971). In some cases, however, people move to high-rise precisely in order to divorce themselves from the pressure for social contact felt by some people in other forms of housing.

Many feel that high-rise buildings limit self-expression. When people cannot substantially alter their residential units or generally control the actions and policies of the managements of their buildings, self-expression is felt to be jeopardized.

The spatial characteristics of high-rise apartments limit the variety of discretionary activities possible within the home, in the eyes of many, as pursuits which are noisy or which require large numbers of other persons or private outdoor space are difficult. Hence, apartment dwellers are said to go out more frequently for entertainment, spending less time at home (Homenuck, 1973). As mentioned with respect to Hong Kong, Mitchell (1971) feels the reorientation of the daily timetable to include more 'outside' activity is a major form of adaptation to the high-rise residential setting.

When people remain at home, these limitations on activity may affect the roles of family members. Several authors, for example, suggest that the typically active, swashbuckling male-familial role is "emasculated" into that of "star boarder" (Wallace, 1952). Watching television and drinking beer substitute, according to this view, for more active or productive activities (Kumove, 1966).

Nonetheless, it is with respect to children that previous writers have asserted the most negative behavioral implications of high-rise. That children can do within their own dwelling units *few* of the typically noisy childhood pursuits without disturbing neighbors (Wallace, 1952) is a standard complaint. There is some debate as to whether the worst part of the problem is in the noise that children make under these circumstances or in the perceived necessity of parents that they must consciously inhibit children's noisy activities to prevent precipitating trouble (Raven, 1967).

When children go out, there is generally little if any place for them to do anything socially acceptable until they have gone down many stories to the ground, at which point the children are normally out of communication with their own dwelling unit. When children go downstairs unaccompanied, parents lose normal supervision and control. This problem of control creates pressure for the parents to accompany the children beyond the dwelling unit much more frequently than from the detached house with the private yard. One observer, for example, discovered that children in high-rise apartments are held back within the family circle for a longer period of time than are children in low-rise situations, but then once 'set free,' are relatively more free (Kumove, 1966).

In one study, researchers found few differences between school children living in the high-rise and single-family houses, but noted a lower level of motor ability among children living in high-rise apartments (Crawford and Virgin, 1971).

Then there are children's biological needs. It is not uncommon for children to urinate in lobbies and elevators if it takes as long as 20 minutes to get from the playground to the dwelling unit without intermediate opportunities for relief (Moore, 1969).

Such a physical gap between the component parts of the daily world of the apartment dweller leads to other sorts of problems. Teenagers, unable to do very much at home and typically without extensive recreational facilities tapping their energies in their environs, sometimes deface property as a means of working off steam. Whatever the actual cause of this behavior, it then becomes part of a vicious cycle, inasmuch as defaced buildings appear to lower morale and the sense of belonging. Such behavior is felt possible because corridors, stairways, elevators, and other spaces are situated throughout high-rise buildings, frequently out of range of normal surveillance.

One author (Newman, 1972) argues strongly that long hallways and entrances used by great numbers of persons make it difficult for residents to identify loiterers, who, shielded from view, may commit criminal acts. While building defacement may occur for relatively innocent reasons, conscious criminal activity (such as mugging, common assault, or rape) is seen as a growing problem which, while not necessarily caused by the spatial parameters of the conventional building, may nonetheless be well accommodated by them. Newman did not stress unsupervised underground parking facilities as another location providing opportunity for criminal activity, but he might well have.

Clearly, specific *design* aspects of buildings are involved in the presence and absence of the positive and negative behaviors just cited. Additional design aspects are also noteworthy. It has been shown essential to build windows and balconies to avoid deadly falls, particularly by children. Insofar as living space is generally considered a universal aspect of any form of home, economic pressures which limit the number of apartments with generous spatial dimensions or with many bedrooms are problematic for families. Tenants generally consider underground parking, regardless of the crime problem, undesirable (Homenuck, 1973). And while they appreciate good building maintenance, tenants with uncooperative management find this a sensitive issue in most buildings. These particular concerns contrast rather sharply with those associated with houses.

Single-Family Homes

Strangely, less has been said about single-family, detached houses *as types of housing* than about high-rise apartments. The many things claimed as relevant to houses refer in fact to the *suburban* detached house, a combination of dimensions—not housing alone.

In some respects, the house is considered the opposite side of the coin from the high-rise. Since most people own the homes in which they live, they consider this as an advantage of the *type* of housing, however spurious the actual connection. Ownership status also confers sovereignty, of a sort, over what occurs within the dwelling and on the ground outside, something typically lacking in the high-rise. Although this housing type excludes by definition shared walls and ceilings, audio and visual privacy are not guaranteed, something that critics of the high-rise often forget. Nonetheless, the 'privacy of a self-sufficient home,' whatever its factual basis, is a frequently given reason for choosing to live in the detached house.

Typically, however, the detached house provides considerably more space within the dwelling than does the apartment. Private control of outside space is lacking in the high-rise except through the provision of allotment gardens. Both these elements of the physical environment are related positively in people's minds to raising children (cf. Rossi, 1955), and many observers have pointed out that numerous postwar moves to the suburbs, particularly by less affluent people, were predicated upon the desire for a detached house (cf. Clark, 1966).

That one can go directly from dwelling unit to garden without long flights of stairs or elevators makes the outside space more immediate in the lives of family members.[5] One study, for example, indicated that the greater the functional distance which separated young mothers from outside space, the more they felt cooped up, reflected by preoccupation with their own physical ailments and problems (Fanning, 1967). Another study suggests that gardens may provide a more natural setting in which people get to know their neighbors (Michelson, 1970a; see also Wallace,

"Someday, son, all this will be yours . . . !"

FIGURE 2.2.
© King Features Syndicate, Inc., 1965

1952). Not surprisingly, gardening is an activity widely found among homeowners (Riesman, 1958; Michelson, 1967). Homeowners (and not *just* suburban homeowners) also have been found more active in church and civic activities (Homenuck, 1973).

In contrast to the high-rise, the house is supposed to provide adequate opportunity for handyman activities.

Downtown

Bell has suggested in his theory of self-selection that downtown locations, as compared to suburbia, were most appropriate for people placing a high value on what he called 'consumerism' and 'careerism,' and that those placing a strong emphasis on their work would find it most congenial to live close to their place of work (Bell, 1958, 1968). That commuting time, rather than mere emphasis on work, is involved in the selection of downtown locations was challenged by Gans (1967), whose data on suburbanites fails to show aggregate gains in commuting time for those moving from downtown to suburban locations.

Access to good restaurants, museums, live theaters, and concert halls—some of the components of Bell's consumerism life style—appears to be much greater among those living in downtown locations, since such facilities are typically clustered near the center of large cities. There is some evidence that they are a considerable magnet for persons moving to the center, as well as being frequently used by these persons after arrival (e.g., Abu-Lughod, 1960; Ross, 1965; Zelan, 1968; Michelson, 1967).

Persons moving toward city centers are generally attracted by the *convenience* of that environment, while those who are decentralizing are attracted by *aesthetic* components of the residential environment, according to another report (Ross, 1961).

But what part, if any, does housing type play in these aspects of location? Families choosing detached downtown houses gain the advantages of central location without sacrificing the normally preferred housing type, while those moving to downtown apartments indeed make such a 'sacrifice.' Are downtown apartment dwellers as committed to their situation as those in downtown houses?

Suburbs

Although Bell (1958, 1968) specified that life styles emphasizing 'familism' are most easily accommodated in suburbia (which strongly attracts families), it was unclear whether residents in suburban high-rise apartments are included. Similarly, Riesman (1958) spoke of an aura of low-keyed pleasure in suburban areas. Could he have meant suburban apartments as well as suburban houses? Unfortunately, Riesman and Bell provided no answers in their works.

More clearly associated with suburban location are such opposite sides of the downtown coin as longer commutes (in dispute), less emphasis on high culture (Zelan, 1968; Riesman, 1958), and more emphasis on aesthetics than on convenience (Ross, 1961). Despite the dispute about whether suburban commuting times are really longer, there is considerable evidence suggesting that suburbanites tend to compromise (or at least give lower priority to) accessibility, in favor of social and aesthetic qualities of their local neighborhood (Butler et al., 1968; Newman, 1974). This is particularly true when people have moved to the suburbs in order to escape what they consider deteriorating social conditions in their previous neighborhoods.

One researcher found that those who had been long-term residents of their previous neighborhoods were more likely to have moved in reaction to social or physical changes perceived as occurring in these former neighborhoods over time; they appreciated the social and physical qualities of their new neighborhoods. In contrast, those living less long in their previous homes were more likely to have moved on utilitarian grounds (Newman, 1974).

That suburbanites may sacrifice accessibility and that residents of short duration may have different criteria than those of longer duration in the choice of new housing is fully consistent with the dynamics of the family mobility cycle in Figure 1.2.

Homogeneity of social class within particular suburban neighborhoods is an apparent attraction to many. Beshers, for example, argued that the strong emphasis on social homogeneity in suburban neighborhoods is based on considerations of appropriate marriage partners for children (1962). Nonetheless, class homogeneity is frequently justified on the basis of more objective terms, the financial stability of real estate investments.

A recent study set in Halifax, Nova Scotia, contained an unusual but helpful analysis, wherein the behavior and attitudes of those living in the suburbs were contrasted not with center-city dwellers but rather with those in equally peripheral areas which contained local sources of employment (i.e., satellites). In this comparison, the researchers found, in addition to the expectedly longer work trips, a greater pursuit of active leisure, religion, and conversation, as well as a greater attitudinal emphasis on family life, on the part of suburbanites. These attitudes about family life, however, were not reflected in what these people *actually did* during the course of the average day (Harvey and Procos, 1974).

Downtown High-Rise Apartments

In some cases, the intersection of housing type and location produces a set of expectations or activities which goes beyond that expected on the basis of housing type and location alone. The so-called *interaction effect* is more than merely the sum of its parts.

Evidence from a study in Chicago suggests that young, single people come to downtown high-rise apartments with different expectations than do married couples. The downtown apartment, with its short-term rental structure, its largely efficient interior space, and its proximity to places of work and recreation, seems ideal for young persons able to pay the rents involved. Since large numbers of such persons share the premises, opportunities for friendship and social life are increased well beyond what is predictable on the basis of housing type or location alone. Indeed, the tenor of social life makes many married couples, particularly older ones, less happy with otherwise suitable accommodation (Wekerle and Hall, 1972).

One way to avoid this form of conflict is to clearly separate singles apartments from those intended for persons desiring more sedate existences. There seems to be a growing recognition of this problem. The result is a segregation of units by *life style*.

Downtown Single-Family Homes, Suburban High-Rise Apartments

Perhaps because downtown single-family homes and suburban high-rise apartments are, respectively, no longer typical of many large cities (Toronto, the site of the present study, definitely excluded) and recent trends, previous writers have not given them the serious treatment they deserve.

Suburban Single-Family Homes

The suburban house was a major postwar phenomenon, and it has since received extensive treatment, much of which lacks specificity and explanatory power.

One researcher summed up the variety of effects believed by previous writers to be a function of suburban residence. These were: (1) active participation in local organizations, (2) beyond this, much church going, (3) stylish consumption, including house decoration, (4) political conservatism, and (5) belief in continuing upward mobility (Berger, 1960). This researcher then showed these effects to be spurious, rooted more in the social composition of residents of just some suburbs.

Clark (1966), for example, indicates clearly in his work extreme differences in both *social opportunities*, which differ according to the kind of suburb, and *expectations*, which differ according to the social class composition of those in a given suburb. He suggests, moreover, an alternative to the conventional two explanations of suburban behavior (self-selection and environmental determinism). He considers suburban living a 'frontier' situation. Newness, rather than particular people or spaces, accounts for some of the typical suburban behavior observed. This third alternative, reflecting neither motivation nor *architectural* determinism, is worthy of further investigation—something pursued in the present study through the observation of families in both new and existing suburban homes and areas.

Many have asserted intense neighboring as both an expectation which residents have of suburban life and a behavior documented there (Whyte, 1956; Fava, 1956; Tomeh, 1969). Although the housing type is frequently credited for this behavior, neighborhood characteristics may also be an influence, as making acquaintances may be easier in homogeneous local neighborhoods.

Bell's (1958, 1968) familism theme appears most applicable to the suburban *house*. British studies, for example, show a change in emphasis from activities focused on the extended family to those based on the nuclear family after families moved from dense downtown locations to lower density suburban houses (Young and Willmott, 1957; Willmott and Young, 1960).

Nonetheless, devices intended to aid family living, such as private (often fenced) yards, few if any nonresidential land uses, and the absence of heavy traffic on residential streets, remove those who stay at home (either by choice or from lack of transportation) from commercial and recreational facilities, not to speak of contact with a broader cross section of the population than that found at home in the suburbs. Although many think such isolation good for young children, it raises problems in the lives of women and older children (cf. Gordon, Gordon and Gunther, 1961).

While some of the better examples of current suburban home building provide neighborhood facilities within easy access of individual residences, this is not something typical of suburbs of the postwar era, and such community facilities as have been built are more common in upper middle class suburbs. Most families moving to suburbia do so primarily for the home itself, secondarily for class homogeneity, and very little for facilities seen as costly and unimportant for daily life (Clark, 1966; Gans, 1967).

There is an additional literature on the role of *planning* in new communities (Lansing, Marans, and Zehner, 1970; Werthman et al., 1965), but the findings are intended to differentiate among different methods of development and different physical designs for suburban communities, rather than to shed light on implications of suburban home owning per se.

In all, a wide variety of 'hypotheses' about the social implications of high-rise apartments, single-family homes, downtown locations, and suburban locations comes from the scientific literature and public domain.

THE DEVELOPERS' VIEW

The above views are those of and about users of these home environments, as found in more or less scientific literature. In connection with the research to be examined in this volume, it seemed relevant to inquire how many and which of these implications were considered by persons in the development industry in the decision making and design processes concerning the housing studied. Meetings were arranged with about fifteen of the developers whose housing was occupied by families in our study, and we had wide-ranging discussions about the basis for their design decisions.

There appeared to be *relatively little* accounting for most of the above implications.

Decisions about what type of housing might be built on a site were a function of the setting and the cost of land, in light of how much a client might be expected to pay for housing built there. Since most families were thought incapable of paying what the going rate would be for ample space in new downtown buildings, downtown lots were filled with high-rise apartments with suites of meagre dimensions and few bedrooms. Suburban lots were utilized according to estimates about who could pay how much for houses of what size and quality, with high-rise apartments filling land either too costly for single houses or surplus for the needs of the affluent home buyer.

Design accommodated the amenities which families were felt to demand as well as those elements felt to enhance the sales possibilities of the final product. The developers stressed that they felt their duty was not to lead public taste, but rather to respond to it. As examples of such response, apartment developers emphasized larger kitchens and more ample cupboard space at that time. Since many apartment developers believed that apartment living was becoming a more permanent institution for families, greater amounts of storage space and additional places for indoor entertainment were created.

More specifically, those building downtown apartments stressed that the *image* of their buildings was more important to their design decisions than the actual utility of the buildings. Many of them built extensive social and recreational facilities within their buildings, including swimming pools, saunas, and the like, but they largely believed that these facilities were more important for selling the building than for the amount of use they were to receive afterward.

Those building houses felt that interior design was critical for sales, with sufficient recreation facilities (for example, in the form of playrooms) particularly important for popularity. They also stressed that they thought people wanted new suburban homes removed from commercial facilities, as the latter were thought to lower property value.

Although most developers stressed that satisfied customers were crucial for their continued business, they nonetheless evinced in their actions little concern for the everyday behavior of people who would live in the housing. If anything, 'image,' whether with respect to class or style, was felt the most vital element during the process of design.

SUMMARY OF CONTENT AREAS

A review of the various implications for family living thought relevant to these types of housing and location indicates a wide variety of phenomena deserving of pursuit. This includes at least the following:

1. financial aspects
2. life-cycle considerations, focusing particularly on childraising
3. neighbor characteristics
4. commuting
5. interpersonal relations
6. organizational activity
7. commercial activity
8. recreational activity
9. housekeeping activity.

Let us now turn to Chapter 3 for a description of the means for studying such diverse phenomena. We shall also pursue the accuracy of and the dynamics behind such implications of housing type and location in selected environmental contexts.

NOTES

[1] See also, e.g., Rosow (1961), Lee (1972), and Lipman (1969).

[2] Still another problem comes when people equate high-rise apartments with living in *any kind* of a multiple-family dwelling. I do not intend such an equation in this discussion. Although I have omitted consideration of the vast middle ground between high-rise apartments and single-family homes, this is done for the purpose of contrasting the potential extremes (despite the admitted internal heterogeneity among varieties of houses and high-rise apartments), rather than for equating them.

[3] Two recent and helpful syntheses consistent with the present discussion are found in Fischer et al. (1974) and Loo (1974). The present discussion is drawn from Michelson and Garland (1974).

[4] In a new, unpublished paper, "The Experience of Crowding in Primary and Secondary Environments," Stokols has started to explore in detail the differences between and among densities in different types of settings.

[5] Although the same degree of access is available in townhousing, it fails to serve the same purpose since, in all but the most superior townhousing units, the outside spaces are not arranged in such a way that feelings of private control plus space for activity are efficiently conveyed by the physical design.

Chapter Three

A Longitudinal Study

RATIONALE AND METHODOLOGY

The results of a study with the intellectual perspectives and substance described in the previous two chapters are not fully intelligible without an understanding of the methods used. In this regard, we must understand both how information was gathered and the logic by which answers were provided for particular kinds of questions. While it is necessary to specify whether, for example, a given research project used interviews or observation, it is necessary also to explain why the choice of either, as applied to a particular time frame and spatial setting, would produce data relevant to the potential resolution of the questions posed.

Let us, therefore, commence discussion of our study with an examination of the requirements put on methodology by the particular perspectives and substance.

REQUIREMENTS OF THE
RESEARCH DESIGN

Some important requirements of a study with the intellectual and substantive content sketched are as follows: research should be able to (1) differentiate between housing type and location, (2) assess the process of self-selection potentially operative, (3) involve people who have options about where they move, (4) involve a range of experience, (5) cover a period of time long enough to differentiate short-run from long-run considerations, and (6) examine a wide range of variables. Let us examine these requirements one by one.

Differentiation of Housing Type and Location

In order to explore the place of both housing type and location, the design of a study should be such that they vary independent of each other. Furthermore, these dimensions should be clearly differentiated. Yet, most previous studies on one or the other have not made clear how much of their findings were a function of housing type and how much of location.

There have been many studies of people moving from one environment to another (cf. Young and Willmott, 1957; Berger, 1960; Fried, 1973). Normally both housing type and location change in the move studied, so that before-and-after differences cannot be attributed to one factor or the other.

Several studies control carefully for location when assessing the effects of housing changes (Morris and Mogey, 1965; Wilner, et al., 1962). While these studies naturally fail to further our interest in location, their more unfortunate (but certainly understandable) difference from this study is that they were asking far different questions; their interests had to do more with management practices or housing quality than with the different effects of housing type on behavior.

Self-Selection Process

As discussed earlier, a full understanding of the type of relation linking man and environment requires knowledge of whether behavior in the new environment reflects preexisting emphases, traits, or behavior, or whether, on the other hand, this behavior is situation-specific, reflecting primarily post hoc experiences.

To answer this question, studies have to go back far enough in the moving process to measure preexisting, 'baseline' behaviors and expectations. Gans did this in his study of Levittown (1967) (which did not differentiate housing type and location), but many other studies positing particular behavior as functions of one or another aspect of environment are not able to demonstrate to what their findings might be attributed.

Involvement of People with Options

If housing choices are to represent meaningful decisions, representative of the wide range of criteria having to do with environmental selection, the people studied should have some range of options available to them. Otherwise, their criteria and choices reflect only the current constraints, not what the same people might do on other occasions with fewer or different constraints present.

Unfortunately, most of the before-and-after studies involve poor people, studied out of concern for their situation as potential victims or beneficiaries of housing policies. Either victim or beneficiary, the subjects of study had little say over whether or where they were to move. Thus, their reactions were not particularly related to any form of self-selection. This simplifies such studies. But it does not provide a model for studies which must link the questions of self-selection and subsequent behavior in 'majority' populations. Even Gans's subjects had severe financial constraints on their environmental choices.

Involvement with a Range of Experience

Some of the most suggestive studies have been microscopic in focus. Fanning's (1967) statistics about illness among housewives living above the ground floor, compared to those having direct access to gardens, is highly thought-provoking. But one wonders about a host of possibly intervening variables which cannot be explored in small samples taken from a single British armed forces base in Germany.

Similarly, the classic works on neighboring have been conducted in 'hot house' atmospheres—university campuses or single new suburbs, for example (Festinger et al., 1950; Kuper, 1953).

Although explanation is never complete or total, large numbers of subjects, found in a sufficiently great array of housing types or locations, enable the researcher to randomize out idiosyncratic findings or to control for suspected influences. Several studies on the meaning of planning among residents of planned and unplanned communities have shown strong results because the findings were based on a variety of settings (Werthman et al., 1965; Lansing et al., 1970). The same may be said of a survey on the meaning of condominium housing (Condominium Research Associates, 1970).

Longitudinal Perspective

The controversy over the purported effects of suburbs on people suggests the necessity to include time as a consideration. Many early studies of suburbs focused on life during the first year or two in the new environment, making the assumption that what researchers found was a final picture. As indicated in Chapter 2, Clark (1966) challenges this assumption, asserting that suburbs are different only because they are new. With time, according to Clark, life there will be no different from life elsewhere.

Without a longitudinal perspective, it is impossible to separate short-term from long-term effects. It is also impossible to measure the length of the 'term' in different environmental settings, assuming that it does vary.

Yet rare is the housing study that extends beyond a very few years (about two), although one study successfully restudied a Swedish housing project ten years after settlement and previous study (Krantz, 1968). In Britain, one investigator attempted to provide a longitudinal perspective by studying life in a second, supposedly comparable town which underwent the changes under investigation twenty years before (Willmott, 1962). However suggestive the results, a great deal of leeway must be given such conclusions.

Rare, if existent, is the panel study on housing covering a long range of time while also assessing the temporal pattern of change in between.

Examination of a Wide Range of Variables

As the previous two chapters suggest, the range of factors relevant to this problem area is wide, drawn from several intellectual perspectives. Hence, studies of the implications of housing type and location should optimally include a suitably wide range of factors. This has been the exception rather than the rule in previous studies, as the phenomena researchers typically investigate in environmental contexts are generally focused around one or another specific topic of social or psychological interest to the researcher, which by coincidence has environmental parameters (e.g., neighboring). As another research team recently wrote about housing studies:

The range of variables is limited, making it difficult or impossible to determine the relative importance of the variables actually studied with respect to overall satisfaction with the living environment. [Anderson et al., 1974, p. 1.]

DESIGN OF THE CURRENT STUDY

The preceding discussion indicates the major considerations which underlay the design of the present study. It would be presumptuous to claim that all problems were solved. This section indicates, however, decisions with reference to these considerations.

Differentiation of Housing Type and Location

Metropolitan Toronto and the suburban areas beyond include an unusually wide variety of housing choices within each of many locations. Large numbers of single-family homes mingle with the high-rise apartments normally found in the fringes of the central business district and within reasonable access to subway stops. Similarly, large numbers of persons in far-flung suburban locations live in high-rise apartments, side by side with residents of the expected single-family houses and row houses.

Thus, in Toronto, housing type and location are not synonymous with one another. Granted, if one wants a newly built single-family home, the search today is almost exclusively in the suburbs; but type and quality of structures are not tied exclusively to location.

We decided, for clarity in our research design, to emphasize extremes. We restricted our attention to single-family homes and high-rise apartments. Regardless of whether characteristic and expected differences appeared as a result of this comparison, the study of intermediate housing types would not have been expected to add anything in answer to the kinds of questions posed. We restricted our attention also to central and far suburban locations, skipping an intermediate zone.

Accordingly, we sought to study people residing in the four combinations of housing type and location represented by the above dichotomies: high-rise downtown, single house downtown, high-rise suburban, and single house suburban. The units were to be in more than one project in each case. Furthermore, these units were to be as comparable as possible; what this means in operational terms will be discussed shortly.

Self-Selection Process

In order to shed light on this process, it was necessary to find people who were about to move to the above combinations of environments *before* they had made their move. Indeed, to measure self-selection, it was desirable to talk with people about their current behavior patterns and about their expectations while they still lived in the pre-move environment and before intervening events added conditions which had to be rationalized.

In short, we wanted a *baseline* fund of information at the time of decision making. To do this, we arranged for a wide variety of agents with knowledge of environmental decisions of the sort in which we were interested—i.e., real estate agents, builders, high-rise rental agents, etc.—to tell us when appropriate families signed agreements to buy or leases to rent. We then contacted these families as soon as possible before they moved.

The relation of prior expectations and behavior to subsequent activity and adaptation would be assessed by continuing to contact these people after their move.

Involvement of People with Options

In order that housing choice would more nearly represent choice rather than acceptance of a needed commodity, we decided to study people somewhat more affluent than the average, who might, on financial terms alone, have been able to choose any one of the four combinations of environmental elements.

Since the subjects of study are relatively affluent, they, therefore, have more resources to use *in adapting to* their new situation. Because of this, any clear reactions which we can document as tied to the *spatial constraints* of their new environments will almost certainly hold for poor people. Certainly poor people have additional constraints as well on their life chances, but this does not obviate problems which might originate from housing type and location.

Given the emerging pattern, of a systematically varying environment and economically homogeneous people, we opted to keep the sample of people homogeneous in still another way by concentrating on a single large demographic group—married couples in the childbearing years with children (under 18) and, for some contrast, couples in the same age brackets but without children. Newlyweds in their first home were *not* sampled. We also avoided *areas* of the city with pronounced ethnic characteristics to eliminate an additional source of nonenvironmental variation in the data collected. Within the buildings and areas studied, however, a variety of ethnic backgrounds was included.

Involvement with a Range of Experience

To avoid the pitfalls of data based on particular, perhaps idiosyncratic, cases, we attempted a 100 percent sample of turnover in appropriate units in appropriate locations for as long as it took to get a suitably large sample. This meant that we contacted people moving to a large number of different buildings and neighborhoods, albeit within the greater Toronto area.

We set a total target sample of 800 families, divided equally among the categories, to have enough families for sufficient control in analysis. This figure also included consideration of an estimated 40 percent loss in the sample between the time we first contacted respondents and the end of the study period, a rate not nearly approached by the actual rate of about 20 percent.

Longitudinal Perspective

The long-range perspective, as well as an assessment of interim change processes, was accommodated by contacting families and receiving information not only before the move (Phase I), but also at fixed periods afterward: two months after (Phase II), one year after Phase II (Phase III), and four years after Phase II (Phase IV). Phase II was to assess *immediate* effects and adaptations. Phase III, to be done in the same season of the year (cf. Michelson, 1971b), was to assess regularized but still short-term changes, while Phase IV, still in the same season, was to discover eventual patterns, since any likely effects have emerged, the literature suggests, by the end of five years.

If people moved again before the end of the total study period, we would consider this valuable data. If the move was in the greater Toronto area, we would definitely retain them in the study. If the move took them elsewhere, usually for occupational reasons, we would note this but not continue to interview them. In Phase IV, however, we attempted to 're-trieve' all cases, to assess the actual pattern of residence of those in the original sample.

Examination of a Wide Range of Variables

Through several techniques, we attempted to obtain information about all the areas of content detailed at the end of Chapter 2. Wherever possible, we attempted to establish fact, rather than opinion, about behavior and environmental use. In some cases, however, it was important to seek out opinions concerning housing choice, expectations, values, and, with increasing necessity in succeeding phases, evaluation. Although we sought both fact and opinion, we attempted as far as possible to differentiate the two, although recognizing that neither is necessarily what it is purported to be.

These are, however, only general comments about study design. More specific details about techniques and procedures of data gathering and analysis need to be examined.

RESEARCH TECHNIQUES AND DETAILS

We shall turn now to a more detailed discussion of (1) sampling, (2) field techniques and instruments, and (3) aspects of analysis.

Sampling

Early in the planning of the study, we established fruitful liaison with such integral components of the housing industry as the National Home Builders Association (now Housing and Urban Development Association of Canada), the Metro Toronto Housebuilders Association, the Toronto Real Estate Board, and the Ontario Branch Office of the Central Mortgage and Housing Corporation (CMHC). These organizations were able to provide information, which, supplemented by searches in newspaper real estate advertising, and some personal observation, helped form an inventory of appropriate new and used dwelling units for study in the greater Toronto area.

In 1969, at the commencement of field activities, we found houses appropriate if they were fully detached and had a selling price of $35,000 or over, but in no case as much as $100,000. Appropriate apartments were located in modern high-rise buildings at least five stories in height and with elevators; the minimum rental acceptable was about $200 for two-bedroom apartments, although this varied somewhat by location. These figures were set to represent the upper-middle portion of the housing market at that time.

Family economic circumstances vary widely; CMHC went so far as to suggest that there was no relationship between the ability to place a down payment on a house and the earning capacity of the householder, due to extrafamilial sources of aid and assistance, or, on the other side of the coin, to inability to save. Therefore, our matching was on approximately

1   2

3   4

FIGURE 3.1.
THE FOUR CATEGORIES OF HOUSING TYPE AND LOCATION STUDIED IN TO-
RONTO: prototype scenes. (1) Downtown high-rise apartments; (2) Downtown single-family homes; (3) Suburban high-rise apartments; and (4) Suburban single-family homes. (*Photos by the author*)

equal monthly payment levels of $200 and upward (but not including
'top of the line' residences).

We defined location partly according to access to the center and partly
according to distance. Operationally, downtown location meant within a
ten minute walk of a subway station within city limits,[1] or on a bus or
trolley line leading directly to the central business district without transfer, or directly within walking distance of the central business district.
We defined suburban location as minimum travel time to the center.

Hence areas with fast highway transportation to the center had to be more distant than areas with less ready access. The suburban area included the major commuting areas vis-à-vis downtown Toronto: to Oakville in the west, Ajax in the east, and Thornhill in the north. Areas in between the downtown area and the suburban area were not eligible. An approximation of the sampling zones is shown in Figure 3.2. We left completely open where the respondents were living before the move.

Once we had an inventory of apparently eligible homes and areas, we made contact with the corporations concerned, with the assistance of trade and governmental officials. We attempted to establish a regular reporting system between our office at the University of Toronto and their rental agents and/or executives. This system provided a weekly report of eligible[2] respondents who had just rented or bought appropriate units. If the same high-rise developers had comparable buildings in which they were rerenting available units, we accepted respondents from these buildings as well.

To make an inventory of persons moving to new homes, we made similar arrangements with home builders.

Resale homes represented another set of circumstances. Due to the structure of the city, all downtown homes studied were resales. However, we wanted suburban resales as well to assess differences between newly settled and established suburban areas. The most comprehensive information on house sales is the record of deed transfers, compiled by municipal governments and published by commercial survey firms. However, since a 'closing' normally occurs only when the new owner is about to move in, this was too late for our purposes, as we required a reasonable picture of baseline behavior, rationales, and expectations.

The next best information network was the real estate profession, which had a list, published daily, of homes on the multiple listings service which had just been sold, with price and location as well as size and structure. We received this list regularly and contacted the realtors who had sold the homes for more details. All homes, however, are not multiple-listed (although the percentage of multiple-listed homes in Toronto is high). This was a particular problem with the range of downtown homes in which we were interested. We therefore sought out the real estate firms that dealt most actively with these homes and locations, and we established regular reporting systems with the firms.

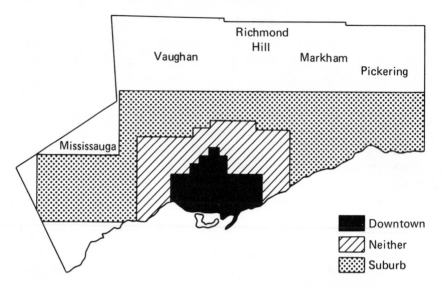

FIGURE 3.2.
STUDY ZONES IN GREATER TORONTO. (*Map by Lee Jolliffe*)

We had desired a subsample of rented houses, but there proved to be no available source of rental homes (which in any case are not numerous in Toronto) as comprehensive as the sources just described. We, therefore, eliminated this subsample.

In general, cooperation was enthusiastic and generous, particularly after it was made clear that the reporting systems would rely on *our* initiative. Only two high-rise developers refused cooperation. Not a single house builder or real estate firm refused.

These persons, however, had to come to grips with an important aspect of their professional ethics—disclosure of clients' names. They cooperated on an extraordinary basis, premised on a number of criteria: (1) the purpose of the study in aiding both the respondents and the industry, (2) sponsorship by CMHC and endorsement by housing and professional organizations, and (3) our promise to maintain the anonymity of respondents.

Our respondents, then, were a 100 percent sample of persons *naturally* moving through relevant sectors of the housing market, who met certain criteria of family structure and age. Nonetheless, while we did not sample among the respondents on our lists, our procedures were not watertight. Some transfer of relevant housing units occurred outside our information network. Since our project staff had no particular authority over the persons in rental or sales offices with whom we dealt (who were frequently low in their own organization's hierarchy and for whom their superiors' promises to us were an imposition), our inventory is not as complete as it could be.[3] In some cases, relevant respondents could not be used because they moved within the approximate week that we needed for an interview to be arranged—often unknown by the central management of their apartment buildings; we suspect on this basis a bias toward exclusion of families moving from outside Toronto or Canada, although many such families were nonetheless included. Many potential respondents turned out, when contacted by us, to be ineligible; knowledge of family characteristics by rental or sales agents was often incomplete, through no fault of their own.

That this procedure followed the lines of a natural experiment, finding appropriate categories of people enacting a real-life situation, meant that sampling and interviewing had to follow the pace of the situation studied. We could not enjoy the luxury of identifying and contacting respondents within a finite period of time known in advance. We were dependent on the vicissitudes of the housing market.

The housing market at the time of the study proved as unkind to us as it was to the housing industry. A boom was just finishing as we began our inventory in June 1969. From that point until after we concluded our initial fieldwork, sales and rentals were slow. This meant holding open our sampling processes until Christmas of the following year. Not only were new buildings standing scarcely rented, but families were renewing leases rather than switching buildings.

There was also a structural obstacle to filling all the cells of our sample design quickly. Only a small percentage of downtown apartments were rented to married couples in the childbearing years who were not newlyweds, whether or not they had children. Very few were rented to families with children.

In many buildings the bedroom count of the apartment units was too low to encourage family occupancy. In most, children were allowed only if newly born or over fourteen years of age. In any case, for reasons ex-

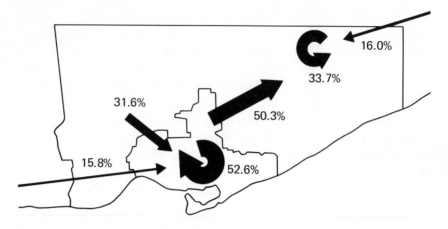

FIGURE 3.3.
ORIGIN OF MOVERS TO STUDY ZONES.

plored in the study, not many families with children *sought* downtown apartments, even when these were available to them.

Sampling, therefore, extended over a lengthy period due to both market and demographic reasons.

Of the 989 eligible families approached, 77 percent consented to participate in the study, an acceptable figure. Families who could not be located or who refused to participate were 20 percent of the total, while families whose particular circumstances (e.g., a language not spoken by any of the interviewing staff) made contact impossible constituted the remaining 3 percent. The final sample, therefore, consisted of 761 families.

The then current homes and locations of these families, when from Toronto, were widely and evenly distributed. About one in six families came from other places. Figure 3.3 shows that more than half (52.6%) of those moving to downtown locations already lived in this zone. Another 31.6 percent were becoming more central as a consequence of their moves, while 15.8 percent were arriving from out of town.

On the other hand, suburban locations represented a decentralizing change to a greater percentage of movers. Just about half (50.3%) came from less peripheral locations to join the third who were relocating within suburbia. Sixteen percent came from out of town, comparable to the downtown figures—something *not* expected by previous writers who stressed that families making intercity transfers gravitate to suburbs (e.g., Whyte, 1956).

The move represented a change in type of housing to about 40 percent of both house and apartment movers, while about 60 percent of each were not making such a change.

The homes to which they were moving were distributed fairly randomly all throughout the eligible zones. No emphasis was given one or another *side* of the city.

Families continuing to participate in Phases II, III, and IV numbered 686 (90.1%), 593 (77.9%), and 617 (81.1%), respectively. The increase in response from Phase III to Phase IV is antiintuitive. It reflects partly our desire in Phase IV to gather final information on families who moved from Toronto after Phase II, who had not been contacted in Phase III, and partly more thorough efforts to achieve completed research protocols.

The completed Phase I sample was distributed as follows according to the housing types and locations which served as sampling criteria:

high-rise downtown	109 families (14.3%)
single house downtown	94 families (12.4%)
high-rise suburban	286 families (37.6%)
single house suburban	272 families (35.8%)
(a) new—209	
(b) resale—63	

The skew of cases to suburban zones is a function of the supply and flow of housing during the period of sampling. We cut off sampling in suburban areas in the latter stages, while continuing in downtown categories until we had close to 100 in each cell.

Throughout subsequent phases of the study, somewhat more apartment dwellers dropped out, reflecting their undoubtedly greater rates of mobility. However, their percentage of nonresponse was not disproportionately high. In Phase IV, for example, the lowest response, 71 percent, was from those who had moved to downtown apartments, compared to an overall response rate only 10 percent higher. Those moving to single homes, regardless of location, responded at a rate approaching 90 percent while 77 percent of families who had moved to suburban apartments were still in contact at the end of the study. There are no differences of note between respondents who dropped out and those who did not, other than such minor differences as place of residence.

The reader must keep in mind that the sample does not include either young singles or families in or approaching retirement. Although these groups are frequently posited as prime occupants of high-rise apartments, the purpose of this study was not to canvass all occupants of high-rise but rather to assess the attractions and effects of the high-rise for families.

As the distribution of housing units would suggest, the percentage of families with children is lower in downtown apartments than in any other category. Nonetheless, each category of housing and location contains families with and without children. Within categories of housing type and location, the age distribution of the families' *youngest* children is relatively similar, although slightly more of the 'babies' in downtown high-rise apartments are thirteen or over than in the other categories. The youngest children in families interviewed were usually under thirteen but there was almost an even division between those with preschoolers and those with school-aged children.

There are no dramatic differences between categories of ages of *all* children in the family, although children moving to the suburban high-rise are a bit younger than the others. Distribution of children among the various age categories is quite liberal.

The sampling criteria succeeded in producing respondents with greater than average economic positions. The median family income at the time of moving was about $13,000. About 40 percent earned over $15,000 (but only 16 percent earned over $20,000), while about 12 percent earned less than $9,000. Income figures for husbands show that *some* relatively costly housing is being occupied by men earning nonroyal incomes; 42 percent of households interviewed had more than one wage earner.

Income figures are borne out with reference to occupation. About 60 percent of the men in the sample fall into the categories of either 'executive and manager' or 'professional and technical,' with the remainder almost evenly split between white-collar and skilled blue-collar positions. About half the working wives are in the professional and technical group, while the others are mainly in the clerical category.

There is considerable spread in the education level of respondents, something the earlier work showing nonequivalence of income and education clearly anticipates. More than 20 percent of husbands and wives did not complete high school, while, on the other hand, almost 50 percent of the husbands received postsecondary education, most of them *completing* university degrees, with many receiving postgraduate training. Many wives, although not receiving as much training as their husbands, are, nonetheless, relatively well educated.

In sum, although external constraints prevented the original sampling plan from being realized exactly, a workable sample meeting the intended social criteria was drawn.

Research Instruments and Procedures

We thought interviewing desirable to obtain most of the content sought for a number of reasons:

1. the amount of the data necessary
2. the complexity of requesting different information from different members of the family.
3. the need for the highest possible response rate
4. the necessity for personal contact to retain families in our panel from one phase of the study to the others.

We, therefore, used the interview technique as the main source of data for the study.

Nonetheless, we realized that often some very subjective or dynamic types of data—not easily recognized or communicated—are necessary to complement what one learns from survey data, to interpret the latter, or to confirm them. Thus, two doctoral students conducted participant-observation studies, living for an extended period of time in relevant settings.

They gathered material on our subject for which the interview is an inappropriate technique. In this, our two observers followed the basic theoretical orientations of Erving Goffman (1959, 1963, 1971) and Edward Hall (1966). Goffman's work has been concerned with the unspoken rules of everyday behavior, many of which are manifested in spatial preferences which bring about privacy, contact, and so on. Hall has written and lectured widely about the concept he calls *proxemics*, the cultural component of spatial behavior; his work deals with how people arrange themselves physically so that their interaction follows the rules of their culture.

Several specific questions in our study were pursued in depth through personal experience coupled with systematic observation methods:

1. How do people use or adapt to the space allocated to them in a high-rise building? That is, what do people feel they can do inside their apartments? Where within them do they perform these activities?

2. How do people allocate and use public and semipublic space in high-rise buildings? Large amounts of space in corridors, balconies, lobbies, laundry areas, recreation areas, and 'green' are not formally assigned to individual tenants. Yet, people initiate informal rules on who will use them, in what pursuits, and under what circumstances.

3. Hall asserts that space is used according to the stage in the life cycle. To what extent is this true *within* high-rise?

4. What is the impact of *formalized* authority and maintenance on residential attitudes and behavior? (Cf. Reed, 1972.)

Results of the observational work are used as a basis for both interpreting and going beyond the more literal survey data. The bulk of the data was nevertheless collected by survey techniques. Individual interview schedules were prepared in each of Phases I, II, and III for wife, husband, and child.

Within each family, the basic interview was to be with the wife. Supplementary though lengthy interviews were to be held with husband and one child, if there was one aged ten to seventeen at the outset. In those families with more than one eligible child, a random number system preselected the child to be interviewed.

We generally asked only the wife factual questions about the family and its moves, but information about financial and labor force matters was obtained from the husband whenever possible.[4] If the husband did not cooperate, we would ask the wife for the factual family information normally on her husband's protocol.[5]

A number of questions were placed on more than one of the interview schedules. These were the questions likely to draw differing responses: on subjective topics, like rationales, expectations and evaluations, and on individual routines such as interaction, memberships, activities, and interests. The children's protocols required special wording.

We had clear indications in the years following Phase III (one year and two months following the move) that a very high proportion of families was moving to still another home. This, of course, was highly relevant, not only with respect to the housing and location selected at the outset of the study but also to mobility more generally.

These subsequent moves, nonetheless, distorted the categorical basis for comparison of the various kinds of movers. In essence, we would lose the 'control' in the study design after Phase III for those who moved again. Since there was also evidence that behavior patterns measured during Phase III had begun to stabilize, we decided to make our long-range contact with the families (four years and two months after the move) focus on a more succinct set of questions about mobility and residential satisfaction, which would still be relevant to all families who were originally part of this panel study. This decision did not exclude the use of questions worded to permit exact comparison of cases over all phases of the study.

Given our emphasis in Phase IV, however, on broad coverage of the original sample *regardless* of current location, posing many specific questions to validate conclusions drawn from earlier phases of the study, we used a mail questionnaire in this final phase. When we did not receive answers from respondents, particularly during long periods of uncertainty about the postal service, we elicited with considerable success the required information over the telephone.

Several additional comments on interview content should be made.

Many questions having to do with choice and/or evaluation are first open-ended, then followed by a closed-ended checklist. We anticipated that priority aspects of subjective areas would form the primary basis for answers to the open-ended questions. On the other hand, we wanted to assess the relevance of a wide variety of factors, not all of them likely to be mentioned spontaneously by respondents; hence, we included closed-ended checklists. The latter type of question is particularly suited to between-phase comparison.

In Phases II and III, we wanted to learn how respondents *thought* they had changed or adapted, while comparing *more standardized* records on their behavior with similar records from previous phases. Although there is never a basis for claiming absolute validity for either open- or closed-ended information, we felt it advantageous to have a basis for cross-checking. In fact, divergence between the two, when it occurs, is a social fact of some importance.

This complementarity applies particularly to a component of the interview schedule called the *time budget*. Questions comprising the time budget require that a respondent itemize what he or she did during a given period of time (in our case, the day before—always a weekday— plus the previous Sunday), including, in chronological order, what was done, with whom, and where. A wide range of recent studies indicates not only the validity of such an approach, once certain basic procedures are followed, but also the fruitfulness of its application to questions of design and planning. The time budget produces a picture of what people do which contains both interpersonal and spatial dimensions and which is in continuous, quantitative form. Results can be both analyzed statistically and mapped graphically.[6]

Although the time budget ties together the various types of activity a person undertakes during the day, not to speak of the intersection of activities of various members of the family (cf. Carlstein et al., 1968; Hägerstrand, 1972), *detailed* consideration of important activities still requires individual sets of questions on each of them, as many are unlikely to occur within the period sampled by the time budget.

The time budget and the specific sets of questions on such areas as organizational membership, neighboring, and pastimes are highly complementary, although each performs a unique function—the former integrative and the latter definitive. While they are not expected to produce materials of the same degree of depth, they can be used as cross-checks upon each other.

Some discussion of field procedures is necessary to understand the timing of Phase I interviews, as well as the retention of families in such a longitudinal study.

When we received a 'name' and relevant new address as part of the inventory of movers, we immediately forwarded them to York University Survey Research Centre,[7] the interviewing subcontractor, together with the moving date, if known. York then mailed each of two letters that had been prepared to these people. One letter was on University of Toronto letterhead, explaining the study and requesting an interview. The study was introduced as one on moving, one in which the persons contacted were indispensable and irreplaceable. The other letter was on York letterhead, detailing and legitimating the interview procedures to be followed, while showing also the cooperation of both major universities in the area on the study.

An interviewer then visited the pre-move address, first assessing the eligibility of the family and then attempting to interview the wife, if the family was eligible. After having completed the wife's interview, preferably during the day, the interviewer attempted to arrange separate and private interviews with the husband and, if relevant, a child. Six attempts were made at different hours and days to find respondents before abandoning an address.

Interviewers were all mature women, trained in interviewing and briefed for the project by both our study staff and the York staff.

The interviews were lengthy. Wives generally took about 90 minutes on their interview schedules, while husbands took about 75 minutes and children 45 minutes. Those being interviewed felt that the sessions were hard work but not unpleasant. The reinterview rate indicates no great negative effect, and interviewers report a good deal of commitment on the part of respondents to the study, something clearly indicated by the high response to the mail questionnaire.

One problem appeared to come from interviewers who felt that they were imposing too much of a burden on the interviewees, particularly with the time budgets. It took some experience with these instruments to convince the interviewers that the time budgets could be done as compulsively as necessary without anyone the worse for wear.

During Phase I, we thanked but did not pay respondents. Their general affluence made wage payment inappropriate. However, when we approached respondents for a second series of interviews about two months after they had moved, we presented them with a 'housewarming' gift (a box of assorted jams and jellies under the label of a prominent department store),[8] before the interviewer brought up more mundane intentions. We also thanked respondents by telephone between Phases II and III, at which time we assured them that the information tendered was being put to good use.

Ideally, each interviewer should have contacted the same families during every phase. To reduce costs, however, the interviewing subcontractor assigned interviewers on a geographic basis. Only when respondents moved only a minimal distance did the same interviewer follow a family from Phase I to Phase II. Interviewers generally stayed with the same families in both Phases II and III, however.

We also telephoned respondents about half way between Phases III and IV. At that time, we not only thanked them, but we asked about their immediate intentions to move. A check of this kind not only maintained respondent loyalty, where it existed, but it helped to locate and keep track of mobile respondents.

In Phase III, interviewers asked about the existence of a person who would always know where to find the respondent family. This also proved critical in tracing respondents over the three-year gap between Phases III and IV. Even that, however, was not enough to trace many families who had moved during this period. The survey researchers' normal friend, the utility company, was willing to cooperate in providing information about address changes, but this data was of little use when dealing with apartment dwellers, who, for the most part, were not billed directly for their utilities. The single most useful source of information[9] on repeat mobility was the Motor Vehicle License File of the Province of Ontario, access to which made it possible to trace many families otherwise unreachable.

The high success rate of the mail questionnaire is due to several factors, one of which was the sense of commitment built up among respondent families. In addition, however, two follow-up letters, at two-week intervals, were succeeded as necessary by contact with the persons suggested by the respondents, by resort to the various official sources of address changes, and to follow-up by telephone. Once we were able to find respondents and institute personal contact, there were very few refusals (approximately 2%).[10]

Answers received by telephone were slightly sketchier than those placed, perhaps with more time for thought, on paper. Nonetheless, there is no evidence they are different in kind. One possible difficulty with the telephone contact is that the answers are thereby given by just a single member of the household, rather than allowing for discussion and possible consensus among family members.

Aspects of Analysis

Coding of interviews was conducted under the substantive supervision of study staff but under the roof of the coding subcontractors. Production techniques were followed, coding similar questions at the same time and dividing coders into specialties, so that not every coder had to master every complex detail. Checking procedures were followed.

Most codes followed standard coding practices and require no explication. There are three exceptions: (1) activity codes, (2) geo-codes, and (3) the master code.

There is a danger that a coding scheme with too few categories of activity will be insensitive, although statistically elegant, while one with too many categories will be too difficult both to code and to analyze subsequently. For purposes of relative completeness and balance, as well as comparability, we adapted the 99-category code used in the Multi-National Time Budget Study (Szalai et al., 1972; *American Behavioral Scientist*, 1966). While we made only very modest modifications in husbands' and wives' time-budget codes (such as the addition of a category for packing to move), we took liberties in wording, within the general structure of the set of codes, when setting up a code for children's activities.

Some questions dealt with items having geographic reference. We wanted, for example, to relate the location of people's friends, jobs, stores, etc., with reference to their old and new homes. Geographic reference points facilitate examining distance, clustering, and direction—although their relevance is mainly for the trends examined in *later* phases of the study. To create geographic reference points, we divided the greater Toronto area into a square-mile grid, designed so that main roads fell within grid squares rather than as boundaries. Any location within a square mile grid was treated as in its center, and distances of a mile or more were calculated accordingly as the sum of the north-south and east-west sides of the triangle. We meant this to reflect the most likely distance traveled given the grid road system of Toronto, rather than distance 'as the crow flies.' Distances of less than a mile were coded according to more specific, descriptive criteria (e.g., next door, same block), while locations outside the greater Toronto area were coded by miles, according to standard mileage charts. Many, but not all, questions containing locations were geo-coded.

The final item of coding worth special mention is probably the most important. A number of open-ended questions dealt with aspects of choice of environment, compromises, and expectations. The questions drew answers which were not identical, but which had a great deal of overlap, due to the wide range of answers given any single question. The answers included considerations of interior and exterior features of the homes, social and locational features of neighborhoods, demographic and behavioral aspects of the family and its daily routine, and economics, to speak in general terms. We could have coded each question according to an idiosyncratic, finite list of categories, but each list would have been long; furthermore, interquestion comparability would have been confusing. In addition, we saw some substantive merit in the creation of a complete inventory of the relevant environmental considerations with which our study commenced and which appeared in its progress.

We therefore created a *master code*. With it, we could use the same set of values to deal with all relevant open-ended questions, enabling direct comparison of answers to the different questions. The code also included all the answers to *closed*-ended questions on the same subjects.[11]

Despite its length, the master code is insufficient. Knowing of people's concern about size of rooms, for example, does not tell us whether the rooms are 'too big' or 'too small.' Discussion of bus stops does not indicate whether the problem of or benefit from them (depending on the question) comes from their being 'far' or 'close.' Such evaluations of size, quality, or distance, require a complementary set of codes, which we named the *orientation code*. Thus we coded each answer to an open-ended question with one or more five-digit codes, the first two digits of which are the orientation code and the last three of which are the master code.

In practice, we referred in analysis mostly to the master code, as we knew the orientation from our acquaintance with the interview materials. However, in those cases in which the orientations were not self-evident, we tabulated the orientation code with the master code, and the meaning became clear. Although use of these codes requires knowledge of a complex set of categories and potentially long computer printouts, our experience justified continued use of this code. Indeed interphase trends (and potential interstudy comparisons) become more fruitful with use of the master code.

Several general comments are in order about analysis, apart from the details accompanying particular analyses.

This is clearly a longitudinal study using great amounts of data. Several problems of incompleteness arise. First, there is the problem that all those families who participated in Phase I of the study did not necessarily participate at later phases, as was mentioned concerning the sample and response rates. The question arises of whether only information gained from persons who participated in all phases should be used, or whether the fullest information about any time period should be consulted, regardless of the fact that the sample in some phases is more inclusive than in others?

Our analyses to some extent follow both potential approaches. When trend analyses of changes in opinion and behavior occurring among individual families are calculated, they clearly rely only on those answering at all relevant points in time. When cross-sectional analyses are made about the state of affairs during any one phase of the study, all persons present during that phase are drawn upon, even if they might have dropped out of the study later; this presents the fullest possible picture of the context under analysis. As mentioned earlier, the dropout bias appears extremely slight, and in practice the results based on the 'full' sample in any phase differ insignificantly from those based on the 'trend' sample.

Another variation of this problem is that not all participants answered all questions satisfactorily. Since there must be some degree of 'give' in a matrix with so many items by so many persons, we did not drop respondents with the occasional 'missing information.' As a consequence, the tables for all questions do not necessarily add up to the total sample size appropriate to the table. We note, however, the number of persons with missing information, where relevant.

For these reasons, there is a variety of valid totals for the various tables presented in succeeding chapters. While the reader might prefer to worry about only a single total of persons or answers, sensitivity to the demands of the current data set make this impossible.

The nature of the sample raises another question. Technically, the sample is not one of a population. It attempts to approximate a population chosen for the purpose of comparative analysis rather than to represent persons in a particular area like Metropolitan Toronto, Ontario, or Canada. Although the 'sample' presents, for comparative assessment, some critical, systematic differences in population and residence characteristics, the nature of the sampling process makes invalid the question of whether such differences as are found between the various categories of home environment investigated are large enough or small enough to represent differences between *all* people fitting these categories in some larger agglomeration. Direct projection of any larger population is clearly out of order.

Hence, normal statistical tests of significance are inapplicable to the present data set and, therefore, not used. What we learn and think about the results must meet standard canons of logic and consistency, as well as the substantive demands placed by previous work.

We have turned for this purpose to relatively simple and straightforward analysis. On any question, do the differences between contrasting groups appear large or small? Moreover, are they consistent with answers to other questions and do they add up to larger patterns? Much of the data, time budgets excluded, is qualitative in character. We have tried wherever possible to retain in categorical form the closest possible approximation of the spirit and meaning of the data.

We have resisted current trends within social science to reduce all categorical differences to numbers on a scale, even if this might result in more statistically elegant analyses. How one assigns numerical values to categories of qualitative variables is often arbitrary. When these variables are then used to measure the degree of correlation or variance explained, the amount of variance shown by these newly created variables in relation to other variables reflects largely their mode of operationalization, not their inherent characteristics or meaning. This may constitute an *answer*—a consequence of statistical manipulation—but not one representing fully or accurately what the researcher really wishes to measure (cf. Felson, 1974).

We, therefore, prefer less elegant but substantively more sensitive measures.

In two cases, however, we resorted to precisely the technique just decried. Certain of our variables were turned into quantitative variables through the use of so-called 'dummy variables' and then entered into factor analyses. It is critical to stress, however, that this was the last stage of analysis, rather than the first. We ran the factor analyses only after having tabled all the variables included within them in nominal categories, representing their original structure, and after having established their interrelations and meaning. The factor analyses were created *not* to discover findings and patterns but rather to *confirm* whether we could demonstrate such patterns in a more parsimonious form than the original plethora of contingency tables.

Our customary form of analysis, due to many aspects of this particular study, consists of inspection of a number of tables involving the relationship of two, three, and sometimes more variables but without the assistance of statistical tests of significance. Although statistics are intended to clarify whether numbers make sense and say something, they are not the only mode of doing so; in the present case their use would violate the logic which serves to justify them.

———————

Having now discussed the intellectual, substantive, and methodological underpinnings of the current study, I shall turn to what the study says. The first set of answers, serving as the subject of Chapter 4, concerns how people find their housing. This chapter is also an introduction to the logic of inquiry subsequently pursued.

NOTES

[1] N.B. The City of Toronto is a compact city with political boundaries covering only a small percentage of the area in Metropolitan Toronto.

[2] To the best of their knowledge.

[3] Our success in some organizations increased when we started to pay our informants $1.00 per name.

[4] Sample interview schedules are in the data bank of York University Survey Research Centre.

[5] There were 527 completed interviews and 218 partial protocols from the husbands in Phase I. Husband cooperation improved in later phases. Of 202 eligible children, 82 percent completed their interviews in Phase I, 166 in all.

[6] For intensive discussion of the time budget as a research tool and as applied to the substantive context, see Szalai et al., 1972; Michelson, 1975b, and 1975c; and Michelson and Reed, 1975.

[7] Hence referred to as York.

[8] Individuals pretested indicated a strong preference for this type of gift.

[9] Particularly since the telephone company does not maintain change-of-address records for more than six months.

[10] For various techniques of follow-up, see Ekland (1966). We found it impossible to rely on the Canadian post office for either prompt delivery or for useful return of mail sent to respondents who had moved. Slight misspellings of street names led to letters and questionnaires being thrown out rather than returned. Letters sent to people who had *not* moved were returned to us by the post office. Follow-up was difficult when mail took several weeks to cover several miles and when erratic service led to follow-up letters being received before original questionnaires. It was a matter of chance whether letters sent to persons who had moved were returned to us, the sender, as they should have been. All these experiences occurred during periods when postal

employees were *not* on strike. There were other difficulties when they were. In contrast, the efficiency and courtesy of Bell Canada, the telephone company, was remarkable. Our inquiries received immediate and definitive answers in every case, regardless of the time of day or night.

[11] For details of the code, see Michelson, Belgue, and Stewart (1972).

Chapter Four

The Search
for Housing

Before we turn in the following chapters to the social implications of the various housing types and locations studied, it might prove useful to introduce the logic of analysis by applying it to a relatively simple topic which is yet of considerable interest to those concerned with residential mobility, both from the academic and from the practical side—*how people find their new housing*. Here we are not concerned with why they move, what they expect, or what they find, but only with the mechanics of locating a new place to live.

Previous studies on the search for housing have dealt with questions such as length of search, direction of search, the fund of urban knowledge and personal contacts which guide the search, number of units of housing inspected, and the types of agents or materials which proved most useful during the search. (See, for example, Barrett, 1973; Adams, 1969; Rossi, 1955; Brown and Moore, 1970; Moore, 1972; Simmons, 1968, 1974; Gad et al., 1973.)

These studies have typically sought generalizations concerning the dimensions of the residential search just mentioned. Studies progressively examine new metropolitan contexts, to confirm or refute previous generalizations and, it is hoped, to uncover additional areas where generalizations can be made.

The logic of the present study, however, differs from the previous ones which take mobility as a relatively general, although dynamic process. The paradigm sketched in Chapter 1 suggests some ways in which such generalizations can be made even more dynamic through the elimination of certain assumptions about inevitable similarities in trends of movement. Chapter 2 illustrates as well some of the considerable differences in orientation with which people approach qualitatively different types of housing and location.

In this chapter, we shall initiate the logic of inquiry which asks whether various patterns are explicable in terms of choice of housing type, location, or combinations of the two. Studies of the residential search typically concentrate just on homes for purchase. They provide little *differentiation* regarding the residential search for the housing type and location of destination (other than whether the location selected is on the basis of one or another characteristic of the mover).

Here, we shall ask whether the choice of housing, location, or both is associated with differences in each of the following aspects of the house-hunting process:

1. length of the thought process which preceded active search for new housing
2. length of the active search
3. number of dwelling units inspected
4. type and location of homes inspected but rejected, and
5. sources of information employed during the search for housing

In each case, we must ask whether environmental choice is related to the aspect of the search process, but also whether this relation involves persons changing from one type of housing to another and/or from one type of location to another, any more than it involves those remaining within the same housing type and location. In other words, are whatever generalizations uncovered related to the characteristics of the destination or only of *change to* that type of destination?

Length of Thought Process

People spend longer, on the average in *deciding* to look for new housing than they do in actually inspecting and choosing it. The median length of thought before starting an active search in our whole sample is over two months, while the search itself is typically less than one month. While those who took longer to decide to look for housing also tended to take somewhat longer in the active search process, the lengths of the two processes are not highly related.

The critical question under investigation here, however, is whether the length of these processes differs according to the type of housing or location chosen. The first way to assess this kind of question is to view the factor thought related to housing and location choice, in this case length of thought process, with each of the categories of housing and location. Reference to these same factors, aggregated according to the type of *change* in housing and/or the type of change in location, may then be necessary, to understand whether the relation observed is one which reflects the specific kind of housing or location chosen or the nature of change undertaken.

For example, the first section of Table 4.1 shows the relation between combinations of housing type and location and the amount of time families took to decide to look for new housing. It shows that although families buying single-family houses in the downtown zone took slightly longer

Table 4.1
Time Taken for Decision to Move, by Mobility

| | Time Taken for Decision to Move | | |
| | Two months or less (%) | More than two months (%) | (N) |
Type of Mobility			
Destination Environment			
Apartment downtown	45.8	51.5	(105)
House downtown	39.1	60.9	(92)
Apartment in suburbs	44.1	55.9	(279)
House in suburbs	44.6	55.4	(258)
Total Respondents			(734)
Missing Information			(27)
Change in Housing Type			
House to house	48.0	52.0	(198)
House to apartment	50.7	49.3	(67)
Low-rise to house	33.7	66.3	(83)
Low-rise to apartment	43.8	56.2	(89)
Apartment to house	37.1	62.9	(62)
Apartment to apartment	44.9	55.1	(214)
Total Respondents			(713)
Missing Information			(48)
Change in Location			
Downtown to downtown	38.4	61.6	(104)
Other Toronto to downtown	49.2	50.8	(63)
Other city to downtown	53.3	46.7	(30)
Suburbs to suburbs	48.1	51.9	(177)
Other Toronto to suburbs	41.5	58.5	(270)
Other city to suburbs	54.0	46.0	(89)
Total Respondents			(733)
Missing Information			(28)

to decide to move, the overall differences between those moving to homes and those moving to apartments are relatively minor. Furthermore, virtually no difference is indicated between those moving to downtown as opposed to those moving to suburban locations.

Nonetheless, one might ask whether those *changing* housing types or locations took longer to make such a decision to move, something perhaps hidden since these persons are only part of the total sample. For changes in housing type and location, respectively, one must refer to the second and third parts of Table 4.1.

With respect to housing type, this material shows that families making the change from apartments (high or low rise) to single-family detached houses do in fact take somewhat longer to decide to move than those moving from one detached house to another. While only 52 percent of those moving from one home to another take over two months to decide to move, 66.3 percent of those moving from a low-rise apartment to a house and 62.9 percent of those moving from a high-rise to a house take over two months to decide to move. On the other hand, there appear to be no consistent differences of this kind among those moving to apartments. A small but consistent difference throughout this second part of the table is that those moving to apartments from any given type of housing take less time in deciding to move than those moving to houses.

With respect to changes in location, the data indicate that those remaining within their respective locational zones take longer to decide to move than those whose move represents a significant change in location. This no doubt reflects that job changes are commonly a factor in locational change, especially among those making intercity moves; in such cases, decisions about residential mobility follow job change decisions without much delay.

The length of time necessary to initiate the mobility process is in no way related, however, to the mechanics of the subsequent search process. There are no differences on this basis in how many dwelling units were inspected or what sources of information were consulted.

Length of Active Search Process

The same logic of analysis as in the last section, when applied to Table 4.2, leads to clear differences separating those moving to new houses from

Table 4.2
Search Period, by Mobility

Type of Mobility	Length of Search Period		
	One month or less (%)	Over one month (%)	(N)
Destination Environment			
Apartment downtown	75.9	24.1	(108)
House downtown	47.8	52.2	(92)
Apartment suburbs	67.6	32.4	(284)
House suburbs	45.5	54.5	(266)
Total Respondents			(750)
Missing Information			(11)
Change in Housing Type			
House to house	53.4	46.6	(202)
House to apartment	73.1	26.9	(67)
Low-rise to house	31.0	69.0	(87)
Low-rise to apartment	68.5	31.5	(89)
Apartment to house	40.3	59.7	(62)
Apartment to apartment	69.8	30.2	(222)
Total Respondents			(729)
Missing Information			(32)
Change in Location			
Downtown to downtown	58.6	41.4	(104)
Other Toronto to downtown	62.5	37.5	(64)
Other city to downtown	78.1	21.9	(32)
Suburbs to suburbs	58.0	42.0	(181)
Other Toronto to suburbs	50.2	49.8	(279)
Other city to suburbs	75.2	24.8	(89)
Total Respondents			(749)
Missing Information			(12)

those moving to apartments in the length of the active search process. Hence, there is a need to concentrate on the upper two sections of Table 4.2, although not ignoring the third.

The first part of the table shows that those moving to houses take considerably longer to look for their new housing than those choosing apartments. Over 50 percent of those who move to houses took over one month to search for their new homes, while about 30 percent of those moving to apartments took that long.

The next part of the table indicates that although this difference is present regardless of the amount of change in housing represented by the choice of new home, those moving to detached houses from some other kind of housing took longer in their search. There was no such differentiation among the different types of movers to apartments. The family buying its first home may well be more hesitant and less certain when in the search process, while the established homeowner may be more certain in 'snapping up' just the home desired when it appears on the market.

Reference to the section of the table on location change indicates only the not surprising finding that those moving to Toronto from other cities typically spend much less time in the search process than those already resident in the local area. The alternative may be a park bench!

Number of Dwelling Units Inspected

As one might expect from the length of the active search process, there is a tremendous difference among those who chose apartments and those who chose houses in the number of units they inspected before the choice was finalized. Home buyers looked at very many places during the search process. Table 4.3 indicates that about three-quarters of the home buyers looked at seven or more housing units, compared to only about one-third of those who eventually chose apartments. The slight differences indicating greater shopping on the part of suburbanites, regardless of housing type, are not large enough to demand further investigation or elaboration.

One may use Table 4.3 also to assess whether the shorter length of the search process among those moving from one detached home to another means that they looked at fewer homes or whether they felt able to act on knowledge of their desires when appropriate homes were recognized. The latter explanation appears more plausible, since the differences in *number* of homes inspected according to housing change among home buyers are extremely minor. The speedier resolution of the search among those moving from one home to another may well reflect that they had more definite criteria as to what they wanted, even though they inspected a variety of potential new homes.

The section of the table on location change, as expected from the preceding discussion, does not indicate many differences. The one most worthy of citation, however, is most ironic. Those moving to suburban areas from out of town, shown in Table 4.2 as taking a disproportionately

Table 4.3
Housing Units Inspected, by Mobility

| Type of Mobility | Housing Units Inspected | | |
	Six or fewer (%)	Seven or more (%)	(N)
Destination Environment			
Apartment downtown	68.5	31.5	(108)
House downtown	27.8	72.2	(90)
Apartment suburbs	66.1	33.9	(277)
House suburbs	23.2	76.8	(250)
Total Respondents			(725)
Missing Information			(36)
Change in Housing Type			
House to house	25.8	74.2	(190)
House to apartment	65.1	34.9	(66)
Low-rise to house	25.3	74.7	(83)
Low-rise to apartment	65.2	34.8	(89)
Apartment to house	19.7	80.3	(61)
Apartment to apartment	68.6	31.4	(216)
Total Respondents			(705)
Missing Information			(56)
Change in Location			
Downtown to downtown	49.1	50.9	(104)
Other Toronto to downtown	51.6	48.4	(62)
Other city to downtown	50.0	50.0	(32)
Suburbs to suburbs	43.1	56.9	(174)
Other Toronto to suburbs	51.0	49.0	(263)
Other city to suburbs	36.0	64.0	(89)
Total Respondents			(724)
Missing Information			(37)

short time to search for their housing, nonetheless inspect a disproportionately large number of housing units before coming to a decision. While short, the search process is clearly frenetic, presumably organized by personal acquaintances or employers in advance of arrival in town (cf. Tilly and Brown, 1967).

Alternative Types of Housing and Location Inspected

Table 4.4 shows that people choosing single-family homes confine their search largely to such homes, few of them inspecting low- or high-rise

Table 4.4
Housing Type(s) Inspected, by Mobility

Type of Mobility	Alternative Housing Type(s) Inspected			
	Single house (%)	Low-rise (duplex, row, other) (%)	High-rise apartment (%)	(N)*
Destination Environment				
Apartment downtown	13.9	34.3	+	(108)
House downtown	+	10.9	4.3	(92)
Apartment suburbs	25.4	34.2	+	(284)
House suburbs	+	3.8	1.1	(266)
Total Respondents				(750)
Missing Information				(11)
Change in Housing Type				
House to house	+	2.0	1.0	(202)
House to apartment	22.4	22.4	+	(67)
Low-rise to house	+	4.6	2.3	(87)
Low-rise to apartment	22.5	32.6	+	(89)
Apartment to house	+	17.7	4.9	(62)
Apartment to apartment	22.1	37.4	+	(222)
Total Respondents				(729)
Missing Information				(32)

* More than one answer permitted; cells with + are 100% by definition.

apartments in their search for new housing. Although the search which ends in the purchase of a home seems generally restricted to houses, this is particularly the case among families who already have been living in single, detached homes. There is no evidence of their having seriously considered the alternatives.

In contrast, those eventually choosing high-rise apartments typically inspect not only high-rises, but detached houses and low-rise apartments as well. What this means about orientations to housing, the family mobility cycle, and evaluation of housing is treated in depth in Chapter 8.

The same sort of bias is uncovered when locational change is considered. Families choosing downtown locations are much more likely to consider the suburbs than suburban movers are to consider the downtown. These orientations are indicated in Table 4.5.

In any case, both Tables 4.4 and 4.5 give evidence of a degree of asym-

Table 4.5
Location(s) Inspected, by Mobility

| Type of Mobility | (Location(s) Inspected | | (N)* |
	Downtown and non-suburban (%)	Suburbs, rural, and other (%)	
Destination Environment			
Apartment downtown	+	23.1	(108)
House downtown	+	26.1	(92)
Apartment suburbs	3.2	+	(284)
House suburbs	3.0	+	(266)
Total Respondents			(750)
Missing Information			(11)
Change in Location			
Downtown to downtown	+	22.1	(104)
Other Toronto to downtown	+	20.3	(64)
Other city to downtown	+	40.6	(32)
Suburbs to suburbs	2.2	+	(181)
Other Toronto to suburbs	4.3	+	(279)
Other city to suburbs	1.1	+	(89)
Total Respondents			(749)
Missing Information			(12)

* More than one answer permitted; cells with + are 100% by definition.

metry in housing choice which is not related at face value to such factors in the lives of families making the moves as some writers would have expected—such as typical workplace, direction of daily travel, areas of the city best known—as these factors would have suggested a centralizing rather than decentralizing bias.

One might ask whether asymmetries in the search for housing type reflect different, previous experience with various forms of housing. Those developing high-rise apartments, for example, believe that the acceptance of this form of housing is a matter of public education. Once people experience high-rise living, it is said, they will accept it. It is ignorance which promotes the type of hostility shown by opinion polling at present, high-rise developers claim.

Such a claim is not supported by the data in this study. Table 4.6, for example, concentrates on just those husbands and wives moving from houses or low-rise situations, to see whether previous experience in having lived in a high-rise apartment is more likely to predispose a move to the

Table 4.6
Experience in High-Rise, by Change in Housing Type

Change in Housing Type	Percentage Having Lived in High-Rise*			
	Wives	(N)	Husbands	(N)
House to house	32.7	(205)	31.1	(148)
House to apartment	28.4	(67)	28.6	(49)
Low-rise to house	33.3	(81)	41.2	(51)
Low-rise to apartment	31.6	(79)	31.8	(66)

* Those living in high-rise in Phase I excluded.

high-rise. There are actually very few differences among the categories of housing change according to prior residential experience. Nonetheless, without exception a greater percentage of those moving to *houses* have had experience in a high-rise than among those moving to high-rise apartments. Although the size of this difference must not be exaggerated, the contrary of the customary idea is suggested. Experience with high-rise living predisposes a family to move to a house, not to an apartment.

In fact, those with prior experience in a high-rise were not more predisposed even to *inspect* a high-rise during the period of active search for new housing.

It is clearly legitimate to ask in this context *why* people selected what they did rather than an alternative, but this is best answered within its full context in the next chapter. Here, though, we may pursue some idea of the trade-offs emerging from the selection process. They are available in capsule form as answers to a question about how life would be different if respondents had chosen opposite housing types and locations. These answers indicate the tendency for housewives who have chosen homes to feel that apartment living would have given them too little inside space and no garden and that it would have been harmful to their children's upbringing as well as to their own personal happiness. Women moving to apartments thought of the extra housework possible in single homes, with less ability to participate in active pastimes than possible in the high-rise complex. Their husbands did not disagree but put less attention on inside items and more on finance; many husbands moving to apartments felt they could not afford houses at this time. This is particularly true among those moving from homes, mainly rental homes, to apartments.

Those choosing to live downtown felt the suburbs would have lacked easy access to goods, services, workplaces, and recreational facilities, while those moving to suburban locations felt that downtown areas largely lacked private open space and suitable neighborhood social characteristics. Husbands and wives are remarkably similar in these perceptions, which are considerably more crystallized than those concerning differences in housing type.

Sources of Information

We asked respondents where they received the information that led them to their final choice of housing. We also used a checklist to assess all the sources of information they consulted during the search process. Answers to both questions show heavy reliance on several sources of information: newspapers, real estate agents, and 'driving around' [a phenomenon Clark (1966) referred to in his work on Toronto suburbs]. Information from friends and relatives did not appear to be either widespread or important. The reputations of developers and builders (despite advertising) turned out to be the least important of the elements involved in the search. As one might expect, however, sources of information consulted proved differentially effective according to the housing type and location people chose.

As Table 4.7 indicates, newspapers are consulted much more frequently by people moving to apartment houses than by those moving to single-family homes. Furthermore, although the differences are not so great, people retaining the same type of housing consult newspapers less than those changing housing type.

While people searching for apartments may thus *look* at newspaper advertising more than those searching for houses, the former are even more likely to find their new housing this way. As reported in Table 4.8, newspapers are much more effective as sources of productive information about apartments than they are as sources about houses. This may, however, reflect the practice of going directly from a newspaper advertisement to a rental agent, when looking for an apartment, while the search for a home may go from a newspaper to a real estate agent, and only indirectly to the vendor of a particular house, leaving the real estate agent as the effective party.[1] Just as with respect to their role as an initial source of information,

Table 4.7
All Sources Consulted, by Mobility
(*Percentage*)

Type of Mobility	All Sources Consulted*						
	Newspapers	Friends	Real estate agents	Relatives	Driving around	Builder's reputation	(N)
Destination Environment							
Apartment downtown	69.4	27.8	21.3	4.6	51.9	5.6	(108)
House downtown	69.6	33.7	94.6	9.8	54.3	1.1	(92)
Apartment suburbs	71.1	22.9	12.7	9.5	55.6	5.3	(284)
House suburbs	57.9	27.4	61.7	14.7	77.1	12.4	(266)
Total Respondents							(750)
Missing Information							(11)
Change in Housing Type							
House to house	53.5	28.7	67.8	11.9	70.3	12.9	(202)
House to apartment	67.2	20.9	9.0	9.0	58.2	1.5	(67)
Low-rise to house	64.4	25.3	67.8	9.2	67.8	4.6	(87)
Low-rise to apartment	79.8	24.7	19.1	8.9	49.4	6.7	(89)
Apartment to house	79.0	33.9	79.0	24.2	80.6	6.5	(62)
Apartment to apartment	68.5	25.2	14.4	6.8	55.4	6.3	(222)
Total Respondents							(729)
Missing Information							(32)
Change in Location							
Downtown to downtown	63.5	28.8	54.8	8.7	49.0	2.9	(104)
Other Toronto to downtown	75.0	29.7	54.7	4.7	57.8	3.1	(64)
Other city to downtown	78.1	37.5	56.3	6.3	59.4	6.3	(32)
Suburbs to suburbs	56.4	19.9	35.4	9.9	70.2	6.1	(181)
Other Toronto to suburbs	67.7	26.5	33.3	12.5	62.7	10.0	(279)
Other city to suburbs	73.0	31.4	48.3	14.6	67.4	10.1	(89)
Total Respondents							(749)
Missing Information							(12)

* More than one answer permitted.

Table 4.8
Most Effective Sources Consulted, by Mobility
(Percentage)

Type of Mobility	Most Effective Sources Consulted*						(N)
	Newspapers	Friends	Real estate agents	Relatives	Driving around	Builder's reputation	
Destination Environment							
Apartment downtown†	38.9	10.2	16.7	0.9	24.1	4.6	(108)
House downtown	20.7	8.7	79.3	5.4	14.1	1.1	(92)
Apartment suburbs	44.0	15.1	10.2	5.9	32.4	4.9	(284)
House suburbs	18.7	11.2	39.4	4.5	44.7	12.0	(266)
Total Respondents							(750)
Missing Information							(11)
Change in Housing Type							
House to house	14.4	12.4	48.0	4.5	39.1	12.9	(202)
House to apartment	46.3	11.9	6.0	4.5	37.3	1.5	(67)
Low-rise to house	24.1	5.7	49.4	4.6	34.5	3.4	(87)
Low-rise to apartment	52.8	12.3	13.5	5.6	24.7	5.6	(89)
Apartment to house	29.0	9.7	53.2	4.8	33.9	6.5	(62)
Apartment to apartment	38.2	14.9	12.6	3.6	30.6	5.9	(222)
Total Respondents							(729)
Missing Information							(32)
Change in Location							
Downtown to downtown	25.0	8.7	49.0	3.8	18.3	1.9	(104)
Other Toronto to downtown	34.4	9.4	42.2	1.6	18.8	3.1	(64)
Other city to downtown	40.6	12.5	40.6	3.1	28.1	6.3	(32)
Suburbs to suburbs	23.2	9.4	22.7	4.4	45.3	6.1	(181)
Other Toronto to suburbs	35.1	16.5	22.9	5.4	34.8	9.3	(279)
Other city to suburbs	39.3	11.2	32.6	6.7	34.8	10.1	(89)
Total Respondents							(749)
Missing Information							(12)

* More than one answer permitted.
† Miscellaneous sources not quoted in this table, keeping this category under the expected minimum of 100%.

newspapers are more helpful for families *changing* from one form of housing type or location to another than they are to those not changing.

Real estate agents are consulted mainly about houses, and their effectiveness is considerably greater than their rate of consultation indicates. Our respondents used real estate agents more for downtown moves than for suburban moves, and the effectiveness of real estate agents seems greatest with downtown housing, even including downtown apartments.

'Driving around,' on the other hand, is more a suburban method for finding a home. Its effectiveness seems to be mainly limited to the suburbs, as the data in Tables 4.7 and 4.8 show it to be a very ineffective way of looking for downtown housing.

This chapter, therefore, has illustrated with more 'guidance' than is possible in the succeeding chapters (which are more complex) the logic of the analysis used to assess the extent to which behavior may vary, not only by housing type and location but also by changes in each. In the case of the succeeding chapters, we shall add to this basic logic of inquiry the question of whether the differences observed in the phenomena may not also, or indeed primarily, be due to social factors or to combinations of social and environmental factors.

However, the evidence of the current chapter supports the merit of pursuing differences according to housing choice, location choice, and to changes of the two. At present, one or another of the environmental variables is related to the length of time spent deciding to move, the length of active search, the number and type of alternatives considered, and the sources of information sought and found effective within this search. The mechanics of mobility are surely not identical among dissimilar groups of movers.

NOTE

[1] It is relatively common, moreover, for the newspaper advertisements about one home to precipitate a visit to a realtor, who then sells the purchaser a different home. In such cases the realtor is the effective source of information, despite the prior role of the newspaper.

Chapter Five

Environmental Choice

One major perspective for understanding the implications of residential environment is that of what people bring to the new setting. Why do people move? Why do they choose a particular home or location? And what do they expect upon arrival? People may want what they do not have at present. They may think that the new environment will satisfy their requirements. On the other hand, the characteristics and activities of movers may *already* reflect the nature of the environment to which they move.

In the first situation, people match themselves with their new settings to gain something they do not have or cannot do in their present setting. In the second instance, they are finding a more compatible setting to do what they already do. While both are instances of self-selection, the former represents the process of deficit compensation as well. Both would indicate that families moving have mental congruence about their new homes. Whether these families subsequently find experiential congruence is the subject of Chapter 6.

At present, we must ask which reasons for mobility are found in the current sample subgroups? To what extent do the different destination environments reflect unique motives and expectations? To what extent, within a sample already stratified by certain broad ranges of the life cycle and degree of affluence, are there strong differences in *preexisting* characteristics and behavior?

The previous chapter showed considerable differences among the categories of residential environment regarding search behavior. The present chapter applies and expands upon the logic of Chapter 4 with more complex subject matter. As a consequence, it is not feasible to reproduce the full data set underlying every point. Nonetheless, the discussion to follow is based upon reference to the same form of empirical support, only with more succinct reference to it.

FACTORS IN THE MOVE

Let us start by examining the factors which families claim underlie their moves. Such an examination shows many things.

First, most of the kinds of factors customarily explaining intentions to move from one home to another, summarized at the end of Chapter 3, are given support by the families studied here.

Second, different factors play different roles among people moving to the various combinations of housing types and locations.

Third, while husbands and wives generally tend to exhibit the same emphases regarding their residential situation, some factors are given heavier emphasis by one sex than by the other.

Fourth, families attempt to 'solve' many problems in housing without needing to change the type of housing or location, although such a change is directly involved in attempts to solve some difficulties.

Fifth, certain 'benefits' thought attached to specific forms of housing and location are mainly appreciated by those who do *not* have them in their current housing, while others seem universally appreciated regardless of the home environment at the point of origin.

Sixth, one must differentiate between prime reasons for moving and benefits which people expect to get after having made their choice.

Finally, we should pay special attention to what people want of condominium apartments, as compared to rental units.

Let us look at some of these phenomena, with specific reference to (1) why people move away from their former housing, (2) why people choose their new housing, and (3) what compromises they make in return for these benefits.

'Push' Factors

We asked people directly why they were leaving their former homes. Up to four answers, completely open-ended in character, were coded with the master code. We placed no priority on the order of the answers given.

Since the master code is so specific, it is unreasonable to expect any one or several of the coded reasons for moving to accumulate a very high percentage of the answers given. In fact, as the items are most meaningful at their most specific level, without aggregating to higher order categories, the answers are well distributed among the possible codes. Nonetheless, it is clear that some items were chosen far more frequently than others. The average probability of choice for any single item is 2.8 percent; yet some items were chosen by a very much higher percentage of husbands and wives.

The most prominent reasons given by wives for leaving their former homes are as follows (in descending order): amount of space (19.7%); job change (13.0%); management of previous home (10.9%); noise, dirt, and similar intrusions from the outside (10.9%); dislike of the type of housing occupied (10.4%); dislike of the tenure of housing (10.4%); the type of people in the neighborhood or area (8.5%); number of bedrooms (8%); difficulty of access to place of work (7.9%); and eviction from the previous residence (6%).

Husbands showed roughly similar rationales: space within the dwelling (19.3%), dislike of form of tenure (11.3%), job change (10.7%), management practices (8.6%), difficulty of access to job (8.6%), dislike of type of dwelling (8.4%), external noise and dirt (5.4%), and lack of indoor recreational facilities in the area (5%).

Such a complete disaggregation of mobility rationales may hide more general agreement on the critical role for mobility of particular aspects of the environment. In Table 5.1, the distribution of all rationales given to aggregations of specific codes (i.e., higher-order categories) making up the master code indicates that no one level of environment or social consideration was paramount among the whole sample. Approximately equal reference was made to unit interiors, the immediate exterior setting of the former dwelling, the type and tenure of the unit itself, the social aspects of the neighborhood, and changes anticipated in such areas as family and

Table 5.1
Reasons for Move Away from Current Home, by Sex

Reasons*	Sex	
	Wives (%)	Husbands (%)
Unit interior size and layout	17.7	15.8
Unit interior features	3.2	3.0
Exterior setting	15.9	15.7
Dwelling unit	18.7	20.2
Neighborhood	13.9	13.1
Access	6.5	8.3
Family composition	14.2	13.5
Interaction with people	1.4	0.5
Leisure activities	0.5	0.9
Fiscal considerations	7.0	8.7
Other	1.1	0.2
Total Reasons	1703	955

* Up to but not necessarily four reasons per person.

job (between 13 and 20% each of all reasons given). Only such broader considerations as access to certain locations, interaction, leisure, and fiscal considerations ranked considerably lower as reasons for leaving a home, as would be expected from earlier writings. This distribution of mobility criteria is remarkably similar for husbands and wives.

Nonetheless, why people want to move is not unrelated to where they intend to go. Those moving to the various combinations of housing type and location studied do not have the same reasons for moving. Rather, once broken down according to housing type, location, and combinations thereof, the specific rationales are emphasized by certain subgroups much more than the aggregate statistics suggest.

Furthermore, some reasons for moving away which do not appear strongly emphasized in the aggregate turned out to be important for one or another of the subcategories.

Finally, those in the different subcategories cite a smaller number of the rationales for moving which appeared important in the aggregate approximately equally, an 'across the board' demonstration of importance.

Let us look at some of these effects according to destination environment.

The wives moving to single-family homes are more likely than those moving to apartments to cite as factors precipitating the move: (1) too little space (23% among those moving to homes versus 16% among those moving to apartments), (2) the kind of dwelling (17% to 4%), and (3) the kind of tenure (15% to 4%, with the latter percentage made up entirely by those moving to *condominium* apartments). In contrast, those moving to high-rise apartments are more likely to state as reasons for moving from their previous home than those moving to houses the following: (1) problems with the management (19% to 2%), and (2) increases in rent (7% to 1%).

Locational choice does not reflect particular problems at the place of origin.

With combinations of housing type and location, the move to the downtown high rise appears associated with three reasons for moving: (1) intrusion of noise and dirt from outside the current home (21.1%, as compared to an overall average for wives of 10.9%), (2) distance from place of work (12.8% versus 7.9%), and (3) number of bedrooms (12.8% versus 8%).

Several items given emphasis in the aggregate are held regardless of the destination environment. These include dislike of previous neighbors and job change.

Although husband-wife disagreement is generally minimal, the relation of push factors to destination environment among husbands differs in some significant ways from the case of the wives. Only the husbands moving to *suburban* houses, for example, stress the space inadequacies and the type of their previous housing, not those moving to downtown houses. Husbands moving to apartments stress noise and dirt less than their wives, almost to the point of equality with those moving to houses. Emphases on bedrooms and on access to work are not found among the husbands.

The husbands exhibit several small but suggestive emphases of their own. Only those moving to suburban high-rise apartments decry the lack of recreation facilities on their previous premises. They are also more likely to complain that their previous housing was a poor value for the money, potentially reflecting the same factor.

Do these reasons for moving away reflect primarily the particular characteristics of the unit being vacated or the generic characteristics of housing type or location? These data show occurrences of both phenomena. Those dissatisfied with the type and tenure of their housing, for example, almost exclusively move from one or another form of multiple dwelling to a single-family house. For example, 46 percent of the husbands and wives moving from high-rise apartments to houses indicate a dislike for the former type of housing, as compared to virtually none of those moving from one home to another.

In contrast, those dissatisfied with their existing home because of external noise and dirt, problems with management, and sharp increases in rent are almost exclusively living in a high-rise and moving to yet another high-rise. The nature of the problem does not necessarily dictate a move out of a high-rise. Men who complain about a lack of recreation facilities in the current home are moving from apartment to apartment, presumably in the quest of better on-site facilities.

Unexpectedly, moving to houses to get more interior living space is put forward more by those living in houses than by those living in apartments as a primary reason for leaving the current dwelling. Among the men, for example, 34.8 percent of those moving from one detached house to another say they are leaving for reasons of space, as compared to 17.9 percent of those moving from a low-rise multiple dwelling to a house and to only 9.8 percent of those moving from a high-rise to a house.

Greater space is undeniably involved in the move from a multiple dwelling to a house, but greater space may not be as precipitating a factor in the move as it is among those already owning houses. This suggests that people feel some inadequacies more strongly than others; type and tenure of housing, for example, may outrank living space as the predisposing factor in mobility *until* the former two have been satisfied.

Such priorities among criteria may help explain why recently built housing in the Toronto area of relatively modest dimensions, under government programs to facilitate home ownership, have received tremendous consumer support, despite industry suggestions that the public really wants big houses with all improvements. The preference for ownership of a detached dwelling among those paying rent in multiple dwellings is so great as to override concurrent desires for the maximum possible living space, where both cannot be achieved simultaneously.

As might be expected, those moving closer to the center of the city find greatest fault before moving with their access to work. Among the wives, those moving to downtown apartments were most likely to stress problems of access to work; a third of those moving from the suburbs to downtown complained in this manner, compared to 15.4 percent of those moving in-wards from in-between areas and only 4.7 percent of those already within the downtown zone. It is even less surprising that out-of-town movers are doing so with reference to job changes.

Although we sought to discover the primary reasons why people would consider leaving their current housing through the use of open-ended questions, we also wanted to assess whether certain *characteristic* problems in housing were associated, either across the board or in differential fashion, with the types of mobility studied. Therefore, we presented each respondent with a list of factors commonly associated with residential mobility. Respondents were to point out as many as they found in any way related to their move.

As expected, many more factors are cited in answer to a question inventorying rationales than to one asking for primary reasons. Since overall emphases indicated by these data are no more than a function of the items presented to the respondents, let us turn immediately to the comparison of those moving to different housing types and locations.

Those moving to houses, husbands and wives alike, are more likely to be trying to solve inadequacies in: number of bathrooms (by about 2 to 1), outside space (2 to 1), form of tenure (but for the condominium apartments subsample, 100% to 0%), household space for additions to the family (about 2 to 1).

Among those moving to high-rise apartments, husbands and wives agree about pre-move inadequacies in: kitchen or laundry facilities (2 to 1); interior maintenance (2 to 1), privacy (2 to 1), exterior appearance of their home (3 to 2), building management (3 to 1), characteristics of neighbors (more difference for the men than for the women), and access to recreation (5 to 2). In addition, wives moving to high-rise apartments are dissatisfied with preexisting distances to work.

As to primary reasons for moving, few of the rationales in the inventory are related to the location chosen. One finding is surely expected: those moving downtown are twice as likely to have complained about the distance to downtown. In addition, men moving downtown are twice as likely to have complained about mass transportation in the premove environment,

One interaction effect is worthy of attention. Almost half of both husbands and wives cite as a reason for moving that they could simply afford a better home than their old one—a matter of *status*. Although only a third of those moving to the other forms of housing and location note the relevance of this factor, much more than half of those moving to suburban homes cited it—a phenomenon consistent with observations in the literature.

Problems accompanying a change from apartment to house include outside space, privacy, tenure, and additions to the family. On the other hand, problems predisposing moves into a high rise are those already encountered in another high-rise building. In other words, some forms of problems in a high-rise are unsolvable within the confines of the high-rise building, while others merely militate toward a change of building. No problems associated with the single-family home, however, lead the families in this study to seek refuge in the high-rise.

As with the primary reasons for moving, moves to single-family homes reflect problems met in other such homes which can be satisfied without changing housing type. These problems include, for example, inadequate numbers of bathrooms (something particularly noted by the men) and dissatisfaction with local schools.

It is worthy of note that dissatisfaction with housing status relative to purchasing power is stated *least* frequently by those moving from houses to apartments, who, as additional data will indicate, feel a marked status loss in the move.

Changes in location reflect exactly the characteristic dissatisfactions expected. Those whose moves represent centralization are much more likely than others to stress existing dissatisfactions with public transportation, access to workplace, and distance to downtown. For example, 63.6 percent of the husbands moving downtown from the suburbs cite inadequacies in public transportation, compared to 21.6 percent moving there from intermediate areas and to only 5.7 among those remaining within the downtown zone. Comparable figures with respect to complaints about distance to work are 72.7 percent, 29.7 percent, and 14.3 percent. Similar figures reflect the views of their wives.

In short, while many push factors are indicative of particular types of move undertaken in response, solutions differ in terms of whether *changes* in housing type or location are necessary. Furthermore, there are considerable differences between problems which may precipitate moves and those which just happen to be solved in the process of moving. While there is considerable agreement among husbands and wives about their mutual situation, this reaches its highest level with the latter form of problem.[1]

In any case, this analysis of reasons underlying moves indicates the relevance of continuing to include a wide variety of factors in assessing the implications of specific forms of housing and location. The data do not suggest the uniform relevance of a selected few reasons for moving but rather the differential importance of many according to the environmental context involved. Such a pattern is exhibited even more strongly with the reasons why families choose their new housing.

'Pull' Factors

We assessed the factors that pulled people to the several types of housing and locations, also with both open-ended and closed-ended questions, to gather both primary rationales and a full inventory of motives.

Although our methodology was the same in eliciting primary pull factors as it was for push factors, with an identical probability according to chance for any single master code item to be mentioned (2.8%), people gave many more reasons for choosing their new homes than for leaving their former homes.

Despite an expected correspondence between push factors and some pull factors, some criteria attracting people to a new setting are largely unrelated to problems encountered in the previous residence. This is consistent with the paradigm sketched in Chapter 1, and it differs from the implications of the earlier strain models of mobility. Furthermore, some of the consequences expected from the move are mentioned most frequently by persons moving into a housing type for the first time, for whom the environmental element cited is novel. Thus, environmental choice may involve a number of positive expectations apart from the resolution of problems.

As with pull factors, there is a high degree of agreement between wives and husbands, both on the items chosen and the relative emphasis accorded them. Space within the home, for example, was given as an attraction by 21.6 percent of the wives and 20 percent of the husbands. Other factors agreed upon are layout (20.1% and 15.6%), access to workplace

(15.4% and 19.7%), on-site recreation facilities (15.0% and 18.6%), the new home as an investment (11.2% and 11.4%), the modernity of the new home (11.4% apiece), public transit (11.3% and 7.2%), number of bedrooms (10.5% and 7.4%), access to shopping (9.3% and 5.5%), building management (8.1% and 6.8%), and fixtures and appliances within the home (7.5% and 5.5%).

In some cases these differences between husbands and wives are more extreme. Social characteristics of the neighborhood represent the choice factor mentioned most frequently by the men (21.1%), while only 12.2 percent of their wives cite them—an important item among wives but surely less prominent than among their husbands. In addition, husbands stress neighborhood aesthetics (7.8%) and safety (6.6%), compared to only an insignificant percentage of their wives.

In contrast, wives are more likely than their husbands to mention elements of a more microscopic scale. The type of housing (7%), the looks of the residential building (6.6%), the size of the lot (6%), the facilities in the local area for children (5.8%), the lack of external noise or dirt (5.7%), and the presence of family rooms (5.4%) are comments not matched by similar responses from the male head of the household. An astonishing 15.4 percent of the wives state that a particular side of town in which they will locate (for example, "the west end") is important in their choice, compared to only 2.8 percent among their husbands.

Table 5.2 shows a wide and inclusive distribution of rationales for residential choice according to aggregated master code categories, as was the case with push factors. Nonetheless, Table 5.2 differs from Table 5.1 in some respects. Interior aspects of the dwelling unit and the social characteristics of the neighborhood are more important in attracting people to a new home than in propelling them away. In contrast, changes of job and family size, while important precipitants of mobility, do not particularly aid in the specification of where families will go. In addition, access to various land uses and facilities, often mentioned as relevant to mobility but yet given low priority in many opinion polls, appears far more relevant as a pull factor than as a push factor; indeed access is as important as most other leading factors among the persons in this particular study, although the observation of our whole sample in aggregate may be misleading since this sample does not represent a normal universe.

The factors which appear in aggregate as important in residential choice,

Table 5.2
Reasons for Choice of New Residence, by Sex

	Sex	
Reasons*	Wives (%)	Husbands (%)
Unit interior size and layout	25.0	21.2
Unit interior features	4.8	4.6
Exterior setting	17.6	16.3
Dwelling unit	9.8	10.7
Neighborhood	18.3	20.2
Access	17.0	17.9
Family composition	1.4	1.1
Interaction with people	0.3	0.2
Leisure activities	0.4	0.5
Fiscal considerations	5.3	7.2
Other	0.1	0.1
Total Reasons	2481	1538

* Up to but not necessarily four reasons per person.

are, nonetheless, almost entirely specific to particular choices of housing type, location, and combinations thereof.

Ironically, no particular feature of houses attracts people uniquely. Rather, impressions of the social characteristics of the neighborhoods in which their houses are found differentiates those moving to houses from those moving to apartments. Both husbands and wives choosing houses are more likely to cite neighborhood characteristics as a pull factor than those selecting apartments. A somewhat greater percentage of men choosing single-family homes (about 23% versus 17%) cite greater amounts of space than do those moving to apartments. But this is not matched by the pattern of response given by their wives; among the latter, for example, 24.8 percent of those moving to downtown apartments say they are doing so for the living space (against a sample average of 21.6%), while men moving to that same setting are about 5 points *below* the sample average of 20.1 percent in citing that same factor—surely a difference in orientation (one to which we shall return).

Those moving to high-rise apartments—both husbands and wives— place uniquely strong emphasis on the presence of on-site recreation facilities (about 25% of the wives and over 30% of the husbands, as compared to virtually none of those moving to houses). They choose their homes for their modernity (about 20%) about five times as frequently as do house movers. Proximity to work place is about 50 percent more important among persons moving to apartments than among those moving to houses.

The choice of a downtown location reflects a strong desire for public transportation, particularly on the part of families moving to downtown apartments. Wives moving to downtown houses cite public transit twice as frequently as do their husbands, although the percentage cited for both is above the aggregate average.

Certain aesthetic and possibly utilitarian factors are unique to the downtown house. Sixteen percent of wives moving to downtown houses (compared to an aggregate average of 6.6%) cite the aesthetics of their new home as a reason for choosing it, while 15 percent of their husbands cite the aesthetics of the neighborhood in which the home is located (compared to a sample average of 7.8%). Practically the only people in the sample stressing as a virtue that their housing units are old are women moving to downtown houses. One out of every nine mention this as a factor. These women are also much more likely to stress a preference for living in the downtown area as a reason for choice; more than one in four do so, almost twice as many as stress this factor when choosing downtown apartments.

The suburban apartment, as a unique combination of housing type and location, appears to have purely utilitarian attractions. Both husbands and wives cite as a reason for the choice the proximity of shopping facilities, a land use more frequently mixed with high-density housing in Toronto's suburban areas than with single-family homes. In addition, about one of seven wives mentioned the presence of facilities for children as attractions of the suburban apartments. Many suburban apartment complexes in the Toronto area have incorporated indoor-outdoor recreation facilities and actively welcome children.

Those moving to suburban houses, in contrast, cite reasons which pertain to their individually held home and grounds as reasons for choice. More than four times as many husbands and wives moving there cite layout as a feature of attraction than do so with respect to any other combination of housing and location. About one in eight mentions the availability of an extra room or two for recreation, such as a family room, a feature barely mentioned at all about any other setting. The outside lot is another positive feature for this subgroup, a feature found not at all in the apartments and far less as an attraction among those moving to downtown homes. Finally, more than one in five, particularly among the men, stress the choice of the single house as an investment. While most of those moving to suburban condominiums do so as well, they are but a small number within the suburban apartment category.

Many attractions to one or another form of new housing reflect the *change* in housing type or location undertaken by the respondent family. For example, those moving to houses from multiple dwellings are far more likely than those merely moving from one house to another to mention each of the following elements: layout, private grounds (especially those moving from a low-rise, which usually provides some access to outside space, but normally neither very much space nor private control over it), the social characteristics of the neighborhood (husbands only), and the investment aspects (especially those moving from high rises).

Among those moving *to* high-rise apartments, the families who are moving from houses are most likely to cite proximity to shopping and children's facilities, as such proximity is not typical of suburban detached houses. Regardless of the status losses families making such a move often encounter, they are at the same time filling a deficit with this utilitarian aspect of the environment.

In some cases, improvements within the same housing type, such as in internal space among homeowners and in management practices among apartment dwellers, serve as attractions. In other cases, people moving to apartments anticipate such benefits as on-site recreational facilities, regardless of where they live before moving.

Regarding locational change, those moving to downtown houses are more likely to see downtown as a desirable section of town in which to live if they already live in or near it, or if they are moving to Toronto from other cities, than if they are moving downtown from the suburbs.

Among all those moving downtown, it is predominantly those who are moving from the suburbs who stress job location and public transportation as important factors. These factors clearly represent the solution to a problem more than an abstract preference for a section of town.

One special case needs particular comment. The description in Chapter 1 of the family-mobility cycle placed recent arrivals from other cities into Stage 1, since those people were felt to choose housing on limited, nonexperiential criteria. One of the major choice factors was said to be job location. Among the men arriving from out of town within the present sample far and away the most frequent reason for choice of their new residential setting is job location, whether they move downtown or to the suburbs. A strong second among the downtown movers is the quality of public transportation. These men cite many of the other factors far less frequently than do intracity movers. This trend is less pronounced among their wives, although these same emphases are found.

Thus, the primary reasons for environmental choice reflect both the kind of change undertaken by individual families and the particular opportunities of the destination setting.

In contrast, the *total range* of benefits, as measured by closed-ended items, which families expect from housing is wide. Indeed, what may be a strong primary factor in the choice of, say, an apartment but not a house, may be a function more widely satisfied by houses, but not sought as a *primary* reason for buying them. Why people do things is equivalent to more than just the explicit opportunities afforded by any environmental setting.

The benefits anticipated more by those moving to new houses than by those moving to new apartments are: inside space, layout, number of bedrooms, number of bathrooms, the lot, the aesthetics of the housing unit and neighborhood, the ability to accommodate an increase in family size, and the investment.

Those moving to apartments are more likely to stress: kitchens and laundry equipment, privacy (at least relative to their previous dwelling), and access to recreational facilities.

About one-third of the families, husbands and wives alike, moving to apartments and to *new* single-family homes cite the quality of the building management and the developer, respectively.

Those moving to the downtown area cite public transportation, access to work, and access to downtown itself about twice as frequently as those moving to suburban locations. All except those moving to suburban single-family homes recognize access to shopping facilities as a benefit, probably with some degree of accuracy.

In contrast, there is no item uniquely shared by *both* suburban housing groups. Suburbia clearly means different things according to the context of housing in which a family is located.

A family's ability to make alterations in its home is seen as an attraction only among those moving to downtown houses. Ironically, it is only the wife who sees this as an attraction.

As might be expected from the corresponding push factor, only those moving to single-family suburban homes are likely to stress their ability to afford a better house as a reason for purchasing the new one.

The degree of change involved in the move influences what benefits people anticipate. For example, 78 percent of those moving from a high-rise apartment to a house anticipate greater internal space as a benefit, as compared to only 70 percent of those moving from house to house, the reverse of our finding on internal space as a primary motive for housing choice.

Other benefits of the house seen most clearly by those in multiple dwellings include: layout, number of bedrooms, outside space, aesthetics of the house, ownership, social character of the neighborhood, neighborhood aesthetics, accommodation for additional family members, investment aspects, and status in relation to purchasing power.

Those moving from a house to an apartment are uniquely low in citing most expected benefits, while the rationale behind such a move may be indicated by the one instance where this subgroup is uniquely high: lower housing costs.

People moving from one house to another do not anticipate any single benefit more than do those moving from apartments to houses. Perhaps the former families are either more realistic about what the home will permit or perhaps more blasé about benefits they have realized already from the purchase of their first home.

In contrast, families moving to high-rise are generally more likely to anticipate specific improvements if moving from another high-rise, rather than from either a lower-rise multiple dwelling or from a house. The former are more likely to foresee improvements in such areas as building management and privacy, as these are characteristic problems with high-rise which the respondents hope might be solved through a more judicious selection of buildings.

Families anticipate several benefits regardless of the change in housing involved. For example, those moving to houses appreciate the number of bathrooms there, regardless of the type of dwelling from which their move originated. Similarly, those moving to high-rise apartments look forward to excellent proximity to on-site recreational facilities (about 55% across the board). Nevertheless, such findings of relatively undifferentiated appreciation of anticipated benefits are more the exception than the rule. Those changing housing type have the most frequent and various expectations.

The data linking locational change to anticipated benefits parallel those with primary reasons for locational choice. The very highest citation, for example, of public transit, proximity to work, and proximity to downtown is made by those moving to the downtown area from out of town. In the case of public transit and proximity to downtown, this is nearly matched by those moving downtown from the suburbs, although those in or near the downtown already clearly appreciate these factors as well.

Men moving downtown from the suburbs and families from out of town cite proximity to work most frequently. About 50 percent of wives moving to downtown locations cite job location as a criterion regardless of where their move originated.

In short, different environments have different attractions, although to a large extent these are dependent on the housing types and/or locations from which families are moving. While these attractions are surely part of objective spatial structure, what they *mean* to the people moving to them is in part conditioned by the orientation of the particular mover. This, again, is consistent with the paradigm in Chapter 1.

One should note again the high degree of consistency between the answers of husbands and wives. Such agreement, does not, of course, imply that husbands and wives within the same family will give the same reasons. Any attempt to assess intrafamilial agreement using the questions just cited is fraught with difficulty, since there is always some degree of indeterminancy as to whether spouses acting independently will actually select items on which they in fact agree. There is no chance for them to compare their respective meanings and interpretations of items in an interview schedule before selecting them. An analysis we conducted of whether items were chosen by both spouses or by just one is inconclusive, as it shows that the percentage of occurrences in which both spouses agree is largely a function of whether specific factors are those frequently chosen. We found a high of 41 percent agreement on the size and layout of the dwelling unit and a low of 11.6 percent agreement on specific features found in the dwelling unit, with the more macroscopic considerations in between these two figures. We cannot, however, construe such statistical disagreement as necessarily equivalent to actual disagreement between spouses.

Compromises

In addition to problems with the original residence and benefits from the new one, residential mobility may reflect compromise. As our paradigm indicates, people do not necessarily intend to achieve all they want in housing through any single move. They may be aware of drawbacks in the new environments they choose.

Nevertheless, people are either less aware of, more reluctant to discuss, or anticipate fewer compromises than regarding push and pull factors. Very few factors are chosen by a high percentage of the sample, and even in these cases the figures almost always reflect drawbacks associated with a more specific type of housing or location.

With respect to open-ended statements of compromise, those moving to a high-rise are more likely to stress amount of living space (particularly husbands moving to a downtown high-rise, more than a quarter of whom suggest a drawback), the housing type itself (except for the wives in a downtown high-rise), and the aggregate costs of housing (again, a somewhat greater stress on the part of the husband).

The compromise about living space is one which exists regardless of whether the families are moving to high-rise from homes or other apartments. The drawback about the type of housing is particularly strong among those husbands moving to high-rise from something else. The problem of cost is one which is most acute, by a wide margin, among those moving from one high-rise to another.

Those moving to houses more often mention a lack of sufficient numbers of bedrooms (husbands only) and of an insufficiently large lot. These complaints are not related to the type of change in housing attempted by the family.

Certain drawbacks are uniquely associated with particular *combinations* of housing type and location. The downtown house, husbands and wives strongly agree, represents a compromise on its kitchen and laundry facilities, shared driveways, and parking. In houses generally, these problems are more related to the characteristics of the destination environment than they are to the nature of change involved in the move.

Just as many of the suburban home buyers found the purchase of their new home an attraction in terms of its investment qualities, a minority of approximately 15 percent find it a compromise on the same criterion. This, too, is regardless of where the families were moving from.

Several compromises were mentioned relatively frequently with respect to location. Husbands share concerns about children's safety on nearby streets, train tracks, and the like, and these concerns are not specific to housing type or location.

Less shared concerns include the following: nearby construction among those moving to new suburban houses, poor public transportation on the part of suburbanites generally, distance to work on the part of husbands moving to suburban apartments, and distance to the downtown area on the part of husbands moving to suburban houses. In addition, 10 percent of the husbands moving to downtown high-rise apartments feel that they will be too close to the downtown area, in contrast to less than 1 percent of their wives.

One might note that these findings on compromises add to several others in suggesting that the downtown high-rise may be one context which reflects greater than average husband-wife disagreement. Additional material in this chapter will shed further light on this question.

The only one of these compromises reflecting particular locational *changes* rather than across the board recognition of a problem, lies in commuting to work among the husbands whose move involves decentralization (i.e., to the suburbs from areas closer to downtown).

A closed-ended checklist of problems foreseen in the new environment confirms many of the same compromises, but provides the opportunity for respondents to add some others as well. Among the additions worth noting are two. Women moving to suburban houses are about twice as likely as the average to mention that they think they will be too far from shopping. Men moving to high-rise apartments refer to one of the factors strongly mentioned in the literature. More than one in seven foresees a lack of place for constructive activity in his new home, especially if moving to a high-rise from other forms of housing.

Although we did not assume children to be potential decision-makers in the family, it may, nonetheless, be fruitful to indicate some of the draw-

saw. Due to small subsample sizes, this discussion will be
omparison of children moving to high-rise apartments and
n the suburbs. Children moving to apartments are more
ned with amount of living space (16.7% versus 4.3%) and
1 inability to keep pets (12.5% versus 0%). In contrast,
: moving to houses saw as drawbacks the number of bedrooms in the dwelling unit (26.1% versus 12.5%) and the size of the
grounds around their home (17.4% versus 4.2%).

The Condominium High-Rise

In Chapter 2, I gave the condominium high-rise apartment special attention. As a building, it contains many of the attributes of the conventional high-rise typically scorned in answers to opinion polls, while
it possesses also the esteemed attribute of ownership. In the present
sample, there is a subsample of thirty-six families who moved to condominium high-rise apartments within the suburban zone. While this is a
very small subsample, it is large enough to compare with those renting
similar apartments to assess any blatant differences in orientation separating the two.

Those choosing condominiums almost entirely concentrated their primary reasons for choice on financial factors; about half mentioned the investment involved, and just under one-third mentioned their preference
for ownership. These two categories of answer alone account for 27 percent of all the reasons given for choice of their new housing. In contrast,
some factors typically mentioned by the suburban apartment renters, such
as recreation facilities for themselves and their children, building modernity, management, and proximity to work, were barely mentioned at all
by the condominium buyers.

On the closed-ended list of choice factors, renters cited every item more
frequently as relevant to their choice *except*: good price (50% to 0), preference for ownership (44% to 0), number of bedrooms (80.6% to
45.2%), and number of bathrooms (44.4% to 32%).

One therefore suspects a different orientation in the selection of condominium housing in comparison to rental housing. That one of every
five condominium families stated that they were making a compromise

about the type of housing, in comparison to only about one in twelve of the families moving to rental apartments, supports this suspicion.

What explains the differences between condominium buyers and renters? Within these two subsamples, the condominium owners appear somewhat better educated; 67 percent of them are in managerial or professional and technical positions, as compared to 45 percent of the renters. Nonetheless, both groups have virtually the same family income levels. It is not clear that such differences in rationale as reflect the purely financial aspects of the condominium are merely reflections of this degree of educational background. Condominium buyers have slightly smaller families, but it is similarly difficult to make a logical connection between this and the findings reported.

The motives and expectations of movers are surely important. But, as the paradigm in Chapter 1 suggests, these are not the only phenomena necessary to understand the implications of housing.

Therefore, I shall turn to a more detailed analysis of the baseline characteristics and behaviors of the families moving to these housing types and locations. Many points in the preceding discussion are thereby amplified.

SPECIFIC MOBILITY FACTORS

In this section, I shall focus on the implications for housing choice of (1) financial aspects, (2) life-cycle considerations, (3) neighbor characteristics, (4) commuting, (5) interpersonal relations, (6) organizational activity, (7) commercial activity, (8) recreational activity, and (9) housekeeping activity. These are, of course, the factors isolated in the literature review in Chapter 2.

Financial Aspects

Researchers once believed that financial considerations were a determining factor in the choice of housing. We saw in the preceding section that fiscal considerations were present but not prominent among rationales for housing choice outside the ranks of condominium buyers. We saw in Chapter 3 that, despite the sampling procedures, there were income differences among husbands studied. We must ask, therefore, whether patterns of income are related to differential environmental choices in a highly deterministic way.

The first problem in exploring this question is how to measure income—husband's income or family income? The implications of this distinction are major.

Table 5.3 shows the particular combinations of housing and location people have chosen, together with husband's income. Such a table conveys the direct impression that housing choice is almost purely a function of the husband's income. For example, 48.4 percent and 47.4 percent of the husbands moving to downtown and suburban high-rise apartments earn under $9,000 a year, compared to only 14.7 percent and about 12 percent of their counterparts moving to houses.

This is relatively consistent with the rule of thumb indicating that one

Table 5.3
Husband's and Family Income, by Destination Environment
(Percentage)

Destination Environment	Income										(N)	
	Under $9,000		$9,000–$11,999		$12,000–$14,999		$15,000–$20,000		Over $20,00			
	Husband's	Family	Husband's	Family	Husband's	Family	Husband's	Family	Husband's	Family	Husband's	Family
Apartment downtown	48.1	12.9	24.7	13.9	13.4	30.7	7.2	25.7	6.2	16.8	(97)	(101)
House downtown	14.7	5.6	19.3	11.1	19.3	21.1	18.2	22.2	28.4	40.0	(88)	(90)
Apartment suburbs	47.4	20.0	36.0	28.7	12.1	29.5	3.3	18.2	1.1	3.6	(272)	(275)
House suburbs	10.4	4.4	18.7	9.3	31.3	26.4	23.1	35.2	16.5	24.7	(182)	(182)
Resale house suburbs	18.4	13.3	21.7	15.0	23.3	20.0	21.7	30.0	15.0	21.7	(60)	(60)
Total											(699)	(708)
Missing Information											(62)	(53)

can afford to buy a home worth three times annual income. Since the minimum priced house studied was $35,000, this put the majority of house purchasers above the rule of thumb income minimum of about $12,000, while the majority of apartment movers fell below.

Nonetheless, a very different picture is shown when family income is considered. Table 5.3 shows also that family income is markedly lower *only* among the *suburban* apartment movers. While the family incomes of those moving to downtown apartments are marginally lower than those of the house buying groups, the difference is much less than when only husbands' incomes were considered. Those families moving to downtown apartments are relatively affluent; indeed, fewer of them earned under $12,000 than among those buying resale houses in the suburbs. The big difference is in the wife's income.

Wives moving to downtown high-rise apartments are *much* more likely to work, and the addition of their income to that of their husbands creates a family income quite comparable with that of the homeowners. Within the downtown high-rise sample, 78 percent of wives work, compared to 46.9 percent in suburban apartments and just under 30 percent in single-family houses, regardless of location.

At the time of Phase I in the study, regulations governing the allocation of mortgages considered the husband's income almost exclusively. Hence, the current income of the husband may be more relevant to housing choice than family income, however different the two figures. The income differences associated in cross-sectional analysis with housing choice may reflect, moreover, not absolute cleavages in the population but rather differences in length of time spent in careers. The ages of those moving to apartments are considerably lower than among those moving to houses. Seventy-five percent of the wives, for example, moving to downtown high rises are under thirty, as are 55 percent of the wives moving to suburban apartments. While this makes the suburban high-rise movers an older group, more than 70 percent of the house moving groups are *over* thirty. This, with the usual adjustment for the husband's age, would indicate a far greater likelihood that the income of the husband in the downtown high rise represents an earlier phase in a career pattern, with expectations of improvement.

Husband's current income, then, had a considerable limiting effect on choice of housing type under restrictive lending regulations since revised.

Nonetheless, it did not determine entirely what people chose, for income does not appear closely related to *locational* choice.

That husbands' income may set limitations on housing types chosen, in combination with stage in career and mortgage regulations, does not mean that income was a major factor in the inducement to move and to choose a particular dwelling. Income may help explain what *some* people do *not* choose, but it does not go far in explaining what people actually select.

An analysis of the open- and closed-ended rationales for choosing the several types of housing and location indicates only slight, random differences in the mention of fiscal considerations. The same is true when monetary factors are examined in relation to the husband's income level. The limiting but not determining function of income is underscored further by answers to the question of why people rejected other homes they had inspected during the search for housing. Fiscal factors were cited as 42.8 percent of all reasons by those with husbands earning under $9,000, 31.9 percent by those $9,000-$14,999, and 32.8 percent by those $15,000 and over. The expected differences are there, but they are not major.

Students of city structure in recent decades have pointed out the indeterminancy of income in this regard and suggested other aspects of socioeconomic status as more sensitive determinants of residential choice. They have turned to the husband's occupation (cf. Duncan and Duncan, 1957; Wheeler, 1968) and education (Feldman and Tilly, 1960; Tilly, 1961), as these factors are thought to reflect not just purchasing power but more of an underlying consensus on priority among potential consumer expenditures.

Education is highly related to choice of *location* in this study, but not to housing type. University graduates constitute more than half of those moving *downtown*, in comparison to a third of those moving to suburban houses and to less than a seventh of those moving to suburban apartments.

Data on occupation in Table 5.4 support the findings on education. Those moving downtown are predominantly professionals and technical workers and only secondarily managers. Those moving to the suburbs are predominantly managers, with a wide variety of other occupations as well.

In this study, the effects of income, on the one hand, and of education and occupation, on the other, appear to be relatively independent of the choice of environmental setting. Education may underlie life style better than income. Moreover, cultural and specialized institutions are generally

Table 5.4
Husband's Occupation, by Destination Environment
(*Percentage*)

Destination Environment	Husband's Occupation						(N)
	Manager	Professional, Technical	Clerical	Sales	Craftsmen	Other	
Apartment downtown	18.0	51.0	13.0	6.0	9.0	3.0	(100)
House downtown	29.3	46.7	5.4	5.4	7.6	5.4	(92)
Apartment suburbs	21.1	24.4	8.4	10.5	23.3	12.4	(275)
House suburbs	36.8	34.8	2.0	13.9	7.5	5.0	(201)
Resale house suburbs	46.0	25.4	1.6	7.9	12.7	6.3	(63)
Total Respondents							(731)
No Answer							(30)

in or near the centers of large, old cities, and hence access to professional jobs may demand a degree of centralization. But while income differentials have been mapped according to centrality in an inverse relationship in North America (Burgess, 1925) and in a direct relationship in Latin America (Caplow, 1949), there is no previous documentation of a direct relationship between *educational* and *occupational* levels and centrality.

Rossi (1955) indicated that home *ownership*, another financial consideration, is a prime motive for moving. What influence does the desire for ownership, or the desire to rent, have in the various decisions on housing choice reported by our respondents?

First, there is a strong relationship between present tenure and prospective tenure. Those who own their current dwelling are almost exclusively buying *another* home. Among those currently renting, a clear majority will be renting again; this, however, may be a function of the sample.

It is more fruitful to assess the origins of those moving to the specific destination categories. Of all the suburban homes studied, most of them newly built, about 60 percent will be occupied by persons already owning homes. Only about 40 percent are being bought by people moving into home ownership.

The picture is different downtown, however. Fifty-seven percent of the homes are being bought by persons currently renting, virtually the opposite of the suburban pattern.

Those in the study moving from homes to apartments differ from those moving from house to house with regard to their initial form of tenure. Half of those leaving a single home for a high rise had been *renting* the former dwelling. In contrast, 87 percent of those moving from one house to another were owners.

We have seen so far then that homes in the suburbs are primarily taken by people already owning their homes and that renters turn to ownership more than owners do the reverse. We have not as yet assessed whether these differential choices represent more general feelings about tenure. Is there still a large group among the renters who prefer renting, or do the aggregate trends accurately reflect an underlying preference in the sample for ownership?

The desire for ownership is extremely high regardless of what tenure people have before their current move. Among those renting, about 81 percent of both husbands and wives prefer ownership, while about 95 percent of owners prefer this.

This position on ownership prevails within all categories of move, although as might be expected, a larger *minority* favoring renting is found among those moving to apartments (regardless of where they currently live). In no category of change in housing type, however, do fewer than 63 percent prefer ownership.

Some spokesmen for the housing industry argue that there are generational differences in desire for ownership. Younger people, they say, wish the more flexible rental arrangements. Table 5.5 gives no such indication. Younger age groups express the same level of desire for ownership as do older groups.

Table 5.5
Desired Tenure of Wife, by Age of Wife

Age of Wife	Desired Tenure		(N)
	Own (%)	Rent (%)	
15–24 years	86.1	13.9	(115)
25–29 years	85.4	14.6	(226)
30–34 years	87.3	12.7	(157)
35–39 years	88.7	11.3	(97)
Over 40 years	88.4	11.6	(147)
Total Respondents			(742)
No Answer			(19)

Hence, desire for ownership in the sample is pervasive; but while ownership serves to influence *some* family moves, *most* moves require other means of explanation. The desire for home ownership is not always satisfied by a given move. That home ownership is generally acknowledged to be one of the cultural goals for which families aim, this goal is seen as a motive for future moves, while interim moves are made for other, shorter range reasons. In Chapter 9 we shall see evidence on what these families do over a longer time period.

Stage in the Life Cycle

Past studies show (cf. Rossi, 1955; Mann, 1973) stage in the life cycle as a major factor in residential mobility. Given the extreme stratification in the present sample, the addition of children to a family is the aspect of the life cycle most fruitfully explored here. Data cited earlier in this chapter indicate that respondents employed considerations of family and space both for moving and for the choice of residence. Let us examine these considerations in greater depth.

When sampling we experienced difficulty in finding families with children moving to appropriate downtown high-rise apartments, as well as childless families moving to suburban houses. Unavailability and restrictive management policies may have hindered the former type of family in finding certain types of housing.

Hence, the sample shows two-person households as mostly but not exclusively destined for apartments (slightly more of them downtown than in suburbia), three-person households for suburban apartments, four-person households for suburban apartments and houses, and five-person and larger households for suburban houses. Within our study, single houses and suburban location are both positively and additively related to family size.

Nonetheless, given the nature of the sample, this type of finding is tautologous, as it only reflects where people are rather than what they do *in response to* family pressures. A more dynamic approach is necessary. What are the consequences of *need for* space on mobility and, more specifically, on the choice of particular environments?

Although the data are not completely linear, they show that aspects of interior space within the home are cited by larger families as reasons both for 'push' and 'pull' far more than among smaller ones. Among families with six or more children, for example, more than a third of the push factors cited had to do with space and rooms, compared to about a sixth of those in families with two, three, or four members. The same kind of differences, although less extensive, apply to factors pulling them to new housing.

The same pressures on space are shown with respect to additions to the family. Spatial considerations are more important as push factors in those cases in which children represent *recent* additions to families. Hence, families whose youngest children are below teenage years are more likely (about 20% to 7%) to cite space as a *push* factor than those whose youngest are teenaged. Younger childless couples[2] weigh spatial factors much more heavily than older childless families.

Still another question to ask is, however, if these factors are related to a *change* of housing type consistent with the overall pattern. For example, if large families are found predominantly in houses after the move, are houses uniquely able to provide more space, or is this space gained regardless of the type chosen? In the latter case, family-oriented needs would motivate the move but not the choice of housing *type*.

The majority of all family-size categories (between 54% and 63%) stayed in the same type of housing. The remainder were nearly evenly divided in the direction of their moves. The percentage of families moving to single-family homes from some other housing type varied from 19 percent among three-person households to 23 percent among four-person households, an extremely modest range.

Without question, respondents in the different family-size categories started from different kinds of housing: those without children, more from high rises, and the larger families, more from houses. Nonetheless, most respondents increase their space without making the move which people consider 'obvious' with respect to matching family size with housing type: from apartment to house. One may recall that those most frequently moving to increase their household space are those moving from one house to another.

Reference to the recency of arrival of the youngest child produces the same conclusions.

In contrast, however, family considerations are very much related to change of location. Families without children are overrepresented in the downtown category (as a function of the sample). Many of these childless families, though, are *moving to* the center from outlying areas. Larger families are not, on balance, already in the suburban areas that we defined; they are *moving to* these suburban areas from more central locations and from out of town. Only the families of six and more are not for the most part moving *to* the suburbs, but this is because they are there already. Table 5.6 shows these results.

Movement to suburban areas is tied as well to the *recency* of the latest addition to the family. Those with infant children are more highly overrepresented (60.5% of them) in the move to the suburbs than are others. Those without children are overrepresented in moves to downtown from elsewhere, as was suggested above (26.5% of them).

Therefore, it is clear that there is some relation between family composition and movement to the suburbs. Is it, however, a function of voluntary choice having to do with the presence or absence of children in a family? This is answered affirmatively in response to a question on how respondents think their lives would be different if they were to live in the same housing type as that selected, but in the opposite location. Those with children, regardless of the number or age of them, were far more likely to stress differences in the character of their neighborhood, particularly as a place for children, if they were to be in the opposite location

Table 5.6
Location Change, by Number in Household
(*Percentage*)

	Location Change				
Number in Household	Downtown to downtown	Centralizing and outside Toronto to downtown	Suburbs to suburbs	Decentralizing and outside Toronto to suburbs	(N)
Two	27.9	26.0	10.6	35.6	(208)
Three	11.5	7.7	17.3	63.5	(156)
Four	7.4	5.2	28.7	58.7	(230)
Five	6.9	11.9	36.6	44.6	(101)
Six or more	10.8	9.2	46.2	33.8	(65)
Total Respondents					(760)
Missing Information					(1)

(i.e., downtown for most). On the other hand, those without children, reflecting their downtown location on balance, were much more likely to stress the loss of access to various facilities, of which the job is a prominent one, if they were located elsewhere.

Suburban locational choice then greatly reflects family considerations. Furthermore, for those without children, a downtown location is not just a matter of taking what others do not want; it is also a positive choice, on grounds of access.

That the choice of downtown location among the childless is positive is supported by the many women moving to downtown apartments who work (78% as cited earlier). In general, the childless wives in our sample were more likely to work than those with children; 80 percent of those without children have paid employment, compared to a clear minority among those with children, *regardless of the ages of these children*. Working wives answer the question of what differences in life would occur in the opposite location stressing considerations of access considerably more frequently than their nonworking counterparts.

These several pieces of evidence indicate that selection of suburban locations on the part of women with children is based primarily on considerations related to the children. Choice of downtown by the childless is related to the fact that most of these women work, as they are equally capable, in financial terms, of selecting suburban locations. Hence, choice of *downtown* locations, particularly among apartment dwellers, is closely related to a combination of family and work status among the wives. This may help indicate why the wives are so much more positive about the spatial aspects of these residences than are their husbands. The possible connection between this move and considerations of travel time and distance will be sketched in a subsequent section.

Thus, regarding family structure, interior space demands are common, particularly with larger families and families increasing in size. Although satisfaction of these demands does not commonly involve a change of housing type, when this does occur, it is in the direction anticipated. However, locational choice is very much related to family structure, with suburban locations reflecting considerations for children about the neighborhood and downtown locations, primarily for apartment dwellers, reflecting that most childless wives work.

This set of findings is consistent with Bell's notions (1958, 1968) of suburban familism and downtown careerism, although careerism in the present study reflects the *wife's* actions (not the husband's) and is not necessarily permanent, reflecting a relatively young average age of the wife.

Neighbor Characteristics

The central question approached in this section is whether a desire for upward social mobility strongly influences environmental choice or whether, in contrast, movement merely results in a 'coming together' of status equals. In general, data support the latter hypothesis. Nonetheless, there are distinctly different orientations toward the social characteristics of the residential environment depending on whether the move involves single-family housing or the high-rise. There is also a considerable difference in how people regard the *status* characteristics of their neighbors in comparison to their *personal* traits.

Previous work has indicated that the wife is more dependent than the husband on contacts in the immediate residential area (cf. Gutman, 1961). Hence, we should expect, and do find, that wives are more sensitive than their husbands to the potential characteristics of their new neighbors, something conditioned through perceptions of existing neighbors. This occurs despite the unexpectedly high citation of neighbor characteristics by husbands as *rationales* for moving to single-family homes, discussed in the first part of this chapter.

Let us look at some of the support for these conclusions. We asked respondents to compare themselves with, first, their present neighbors and, then, their anticipated postmove neighbors—using educational and economic criteria. Only a minority of both husbands and wives thought that 'most' of their *current* neighbors were the same as themselves on any of these criteria. More said that they were similar to 'some' or 'few' or 'none,' and many did not know their neighbors well enough to answer the question. Of those answering 'some,' 'few,' or 'none,' most claimed that the neighbors were *lower* than themselves both educationally and economically. Fewer people claimed an educational similarity than an economic one, confirming the notion of greater differentiation by education.

In contrast, but as expected, the new neighbors were seen by 65 percent of the wives and by about 63 percent of the husbands to be the same as themselves educationally, but a minority (30% and 25%) imagined that their neighbors would be superior to themselves.[3]

The relation between perceived similarity and the decision-making process can be observed regarding the different reasons people cited about push and pull. One can compare the percentages of those citing any item of a general category in the master code about residential choice who felt that most of their neighbors were or would be similar to themselves. If lack of similarity were an effective factor, then the percentage of persons citing the neighborhood rationale for moving, who felt similar to most of their neighbors, would be lower than the same percentage calculated for those citing other rationales.

Table 5.7 shows that this is indeed the case. However, the pattern of proof follows the lines of difference in neighborhood salience according to sex, as mentioned earlier with respect to the detailed categories. *Wives'* perceptions of neighbors' characteristics are related to the move away, while *husbands'* are related to the choice of new housing. A positive interpretation is that husbands took cues for action from the feelings of their wives.

These data indicate that: (1) people not only leave what they see as heterogeneous settings for more socially homogeneous settings, but that (2) heterogeneity and homogeneity are operative in the choice process, and that (3) women treat social composition more as a push factor while men see it more as a pull factor in moving.

But is this general trend toward homogeneity related to any particular *change* in housing type and/or location?

It is useful, first, to look at persons unable to speak about the socioeconomic characteristics of their neighbors. Those moving to high-rise apartments are considerably less likely both to know the characteristics of their current neighbors and to anticipate the characteristics of their future neighbors. It matters little whether people live in high, medium, or low housing before their move. Knowing or not knowing the socioeconomic characteristics of neighbors is much more a function of type of future residence; people knowing less of their neighbors 'self-select' themselves for high-rise. This much is consistent with the popular mythology that high-rise residents are people cut off from their neighbors.

Among those able to assess their neighbors, both husbands and wives moving to high-rise apartments feel more *similar on socioeconomic criteria*

Table 5.7
Push and Pull Factors, by Similarity to Neighbors

Reasons	Similarity to Pre-move Neighbors (% of those giving each reason as a push factor who felt similar to most neighbors)				Anticipated Similarity to Future Neighbors (% of those giving each reason as a pull factor who expect similarity with new neighbors)			
	In Education		In Economic Level		In Education		In Economic Level	
	Wives	Husbands	Wives	Husbands	Wives	Husbands	Wives	Husbands
Space of unit interior	29.0	29.7	33.2	33.8	31.4	39.5	40.1	39.6
Unit interior—other	22.8	23.3	39.7	33.3	38.9	30.2	39.7	38.6
Immediate exterior setting	22.8	19.1	34.9	23.7	36.5	37.3	37.4	35.7
Type of dwelling unit	22.6	20.6	34.5	23.8	33.5	39.5	31.7	36.8
Social aspects of neighborhood	20.7	15.4	30.0	33.6	35.6	42.0	35.3	40.2
Access	20.1	21.8	33.6	33.3	32.1	43.8	39.1	40.1
Fiscal considerations	33.6	20.7	44.0	34.5	37.9	37.8	28.6	37.9
(N)	(438)	(224)	(609)	(295)	(557)	(429)	(555)	(474)

to their present and future neighbors than do people moving to single houses. Again, it matters little in what building people currently live; self-selection is critical.

House-movers who do not feel equal to their present neighbors are more likely to feel *superior*. House-movers, again when not feeling similar, are more likely to feel *inferior* to those they are joining. Although perceived similarity with future neighbors is the major overall trend, 'moving up in the world' (at least on the basis of who one's neighbors will be) is concentrated more heavily among those moving to houses, even from other houses.

We could trace no variation in perceived socioeconomic characteristics of neighbors to location.

These findings on socioeconomic homogeneity might surprise believers in high-rise heterogeneity. These findings are quite consistent, however, with financial constraints on housing choice. Nonetheless, perceptions of heterogeneity do not rest purely on socioeconomic criteria. There are many other differences among people to create impressions of heterogeneity.

We asked each respondent which of twenty-seven personal characteristics he or she thought applicable to premove neighbors, to anticipated new neighbors, and to himself or herself.

We can observe, first, whether people's *knowledge* of the nonsocioeconomic characteristics of their neighbors varies by housing type and/or location. The number of traits wives mention about both their pre-move neighbors and their anticipated new neighbors varies most strongly by prospective housing type. People moving to houses know more about their neighbors than do those moving to apartments. About a third of those moving to apartments mention as applicable three or fewer traits, compared to less than a fifth of those moving to houses. These differences between destination categories persist regardless of housing type at point of origin. Those moving to houses mention many more traits. This result is consistent with wives' knowledge of the *socioeconomic* characteristics of their neighbors. Husbands do not, however, follow suit. Their professed knowledge of neighbors does not vary by type of residence.

Location is not related to knowledge of characteristics of neighbors, the popular suburban literature to the contrary notwithstanding.

A second way to view these traits is with the number of traits which people claim to have *in common* with pre-move and future neighbors. On this criterion as well as with the previous one, wives moving to houses have higher scores on both old and new neighbors than those moving to high rises, regardless of original housing type. The house-movers feel more *personal* similarity with neighbors than do apartment movers, despite perceived *socioeconomic* differences with the same groups of neighbors. Again, men do not follow the simple pattern of their wives; and location is not a factor in this context.

These two ways of observing nonsocioeconomic characteristics of neighbors involved simple counts, looking at the traits independent of their individual meanings. A third insight comes from seeing how citation of specific traits varies by housing type and location.

Since wives moving to houses know more of the characteristics of their current and future neighbors than those moving to apartments, what we must note now is twofold: (1) *clear* differences when the neighbors of those living in houses are mentioned most frequently as having any specific trait, and (2) *any* differences when traits attributed to the neighbors of apartment residents are most frequent.

For wives, there is some agreement that those living in houses currently have neighbors who are higher than the neighbors of apartment dwellers on: (1) pride in property appearance (75% to 22%), (2) neatness (53% to 35%), (3) living for the family (49% to 28%), (4) efficiency (23% to 9%), and (5) handiness (35% to 12%). High-rise residents see their current neighbors more frequently as: (1) withdrawn (24% to 15%) and (2) sloppy (25% to 6%).

Husbands know less about their current neighbors. Nonetheless, there is clear agreement as to the current neighbors of house dwellers being much higher in: (1) friendliness (75% to 46%), (2) pride in property appearance (72% to 20%), (3) readiness to help (60% to 27%), (4) neatness (48% to 28%), (5) living for the family (49% to 20%), (6) child-orientation (47% to 22%) and (7) handiness (42% to 10%). The neighbors of high-rise dwellers are relatively high on: (1) modernity (32% to 17%), (2) outgoingness (14% to 12%), (3) liveliness (18% to 17%), (4) being 'with it' (13% to 6%), (5) withdrawal (39% to 19%), (6) sloppiness (22% to 6%), and (7) laziness (14% to 4%). Indeed, while husbands seem to know less about their neighbors, they make a clearer differentiation of them by housing type. Although some of the descriptions are negative, they are given as much by those retaining the very housing type containing such neighbors as by those changing their housing type.

When turning their attention instead to the traits of future neighbors, female respondents report expectations consistent with their previous observations, although suggesting fewer of the negative characteristics. Virtually the same predominant characteristics of 'house-neighbors' emerged as before. The only difference was the replacement of efficiency by child-orientation (30% to 17%). A somewhat more flattering picture of future neighbors of apartment dwellers emerged; they are seen as higher regarding: (1) modernity (39% to 29%), (2) liveliness (23% to 17%), and (3) living for the present (12% to 6%).

Men moving to houses add only the expectation of efficiency (by 20% to 10%) in their new neighbors. Among apartment movers, men do not agree with their wives that neighbors are more likely to be modern and lively. Instead, they use the adjective 'withdrawn' (9% to 5%), a more negative perspective.

There was no variation in these characteristics attributable to downtown versus suburban locations, something of a surprise.

Although the present evidence has little to say about careerism or consumerism except that traits such as 'expensive tastes,' 'cultural,' 'with it,' and 'wrapped up in work' did *not* vary by housing type or location, some evidence is available about families. Only people moving to houses stressed 'living for the family' and 'child-oriented' as descriptions of new neighbors. Mention of these traits does not vary by location.

Nonetheless, this finding contrasts with the one which shows that large families are mostly moving outward, partially because of the characteristics of the new neighborhoods. This may indicate a gap between personal actions and stereotypes of what others are doing in response to similar problems. Families compromising in the short run by moving out to suburban apartments rather than suburban homes, may not have been aware of how many others were doing the same. The designation of high-rise neighbors as withdrawn supports the earlier data that people know less about their neighbors when in high-rise apartments.

While we explored the *degree* of trait similarity which the different categories of wives saw about themselves and their current and future neighbors, four charts were drawn. The vertical axis of each depicts the percentage of mention of each of the personal traits on the horizontal axis. The lines on the charts represent the categories of person to whom the traits refer—self, current neighbor, and future neighbor.

The major messages of Figures 5.1 through 5.4 can be stated succinctly:

1. Women moving from one single-family house to another are relatively similar to their current neighbors, and they do not expect their new neighbors to be very different.

2. Women moving from single-family houses to high-rise apartments express great similarity between self and *pre-move* neighbors and anticipate a great difference between self and future neighbors. These women identify with their current neighbors and sense a change will occur after they move to a high-rise. This category of mover does not self-select environment on the basis of a personal match between self and neighbors.

3. Women moving from high-rise to house indicate great similarity between self and *future* neighbors, and a large difference between self and current neighbors. These women assign positive traits to themselves and to their future neighbors and negative traits only to their present neighbors.

4. A pattern which is similar to but weaker than the previous one describes those moving from one high-rise apartment to another. It is interesting to note the optimism thus expressed, as it supports earlier evidence that many respondents expected considerable improvements from moving from one high-rise apartment to another.

Whether any or all these perceptions and anticipations are realistic is another question, addressed in the next chapter. In any case, it appears clear from the above that: (1) those in high-rise feel personally dissimilar to their current neighbors and seek to change their situation through a move, and (2) those in houses feel similar to their neighbors and either retain or lose this by the nature of their move. Therefore, results concerning the social characteristics of neighbors strongly suggest the following:

1. Social characteristics of people's neighborhoods are a factor regardless of the type of move among our respondents.

2. Many respondents see themselves as socioeconomically superior to

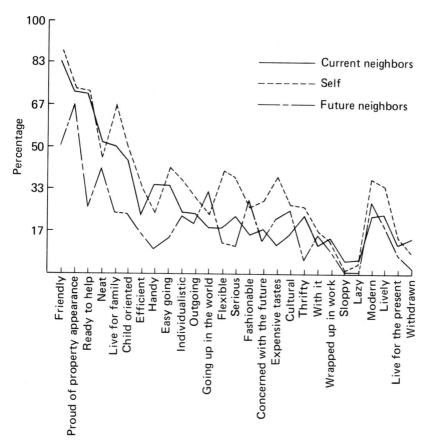

FIGURE 5.1.

HOUSING CHANGE (WIFE): House to House. Personal traits attributed by women changing residence to their current neighbors, their future neighbors, and themselves, among those moving from one house to another.

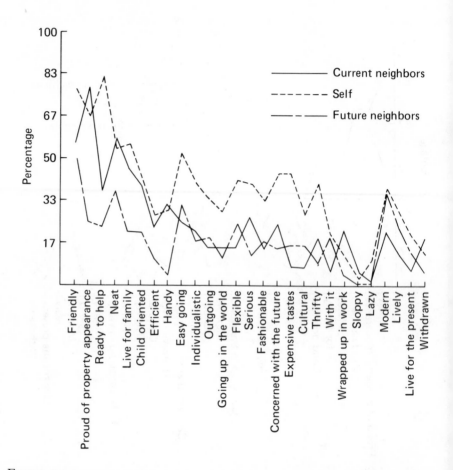

FIGURE 5.2.

HOUSING CHANGE (WIFE): House to High-rise Apartment. Personal traits attributed by women changing residence to their current neighbors, their future neighbors, and themselves, among those moving from a house to an apartment.

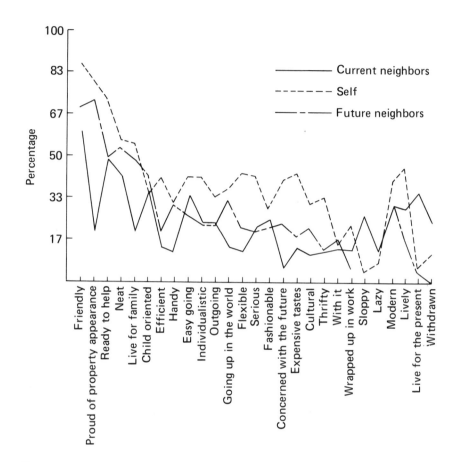

HOUSING CHANGE (WIFE): High-rise Apartment to House. Personal traits attributed by women changing residence to their current neighbors, their future neighbors, and themselves, among those moving from an apartment to a house.

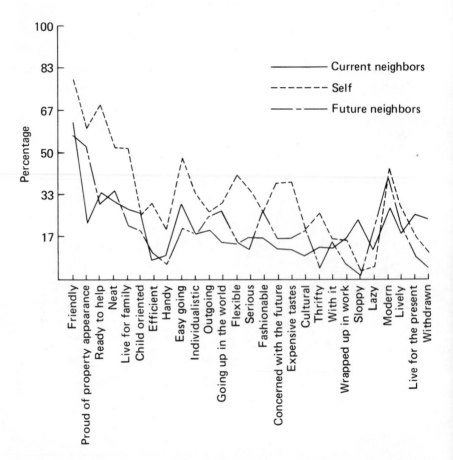

FIGURE 5.4.
HOUSING CHANGE (WIFE): High-rise Apartment to High-rise Apartment.
Personal traits attributed by women changing residence to their current neighbors, their future neighbors, and themselves, among those moving from one
apartment to another.

their present neighbors and similar to their anticipated new neighbors.

3. These similarities and differences with neighbors influence the decision-making process. They are not incidental.

4. Concerning point 2, apartment movers see themselves on more of an equal basis with neighbors, while those moving to houses feel they experience more upward social mobility.

5. Those moving to high-rise apartments are far less knowledgeable of either the socioeconomic or the personal characteristics of their neighbors.

6. Respondents attribute different personal traits to house dwellers and high-rise dwellers, the former more positive than the latter, as reported both from experience and from anticipation.

7. Residents of high-rise apartments report more personal dissimilarities regarding their neighbors, and they expect somewhat more similarity after the move. In contrast, those moving from houses to high-rise apartments expect less similarity thereafter, but they obviously make the move on other grounds.

8. We did not find self-selection in terms of neighbors' social characteristics to vary by location.

Interpersonal Relations

The previous section showed evidence among apartment dwellers of perceived socioeconomic similarities, which is asserted as a requisite for intensive neighboring by some writers (Keller, 1968; Michelson, 1970b). But findings also support the nature and extent of dissimilarity described there for an expectation of isolation among apartment dwellers, a common observation. To what extent, then, are the actual interpersonal relations of those moving to apartments different beforehand from those moving to homes? Are there different expectations of subsequent interpersonal relations? What accounts for such observed differences?

The patterns of interpersonal contact among persons in the study vary little by residential setting—certainly not in the direction anticipated. We can resolve the contradiction between what people perceive to be the nature of their social milieu and the social life they actually lead by paying attention to where people make friends.

We asked respondents to give information about the three people they feel closest to (socially) inside and outside their neighborhoods.[4]

This provides measures of frequency of contact with specified people with whom respondents feel close. It must be clear, however, that this procedure does not provide measures of other possibly relevant phenomena including: (1) total amount of contact encountered by the individual and (2) the structure of a person's network of contacts. Nonetheless, since network studies indicate that the first three persons mentioned in naming lists of intimates are usually those seen frequently (Shulman, 1972; Wellman et al., 1971), the present procedures enable one form of assessment of whether people are isolated before their move.

The data do not support any notion of high-rise residents as withdrawn individuals. In this regard, men have a different pattern of contact than do their wives, although neither is relatively isolated.

Wives' differences in interaction with local friends vary by future *location*. Future suburban wives see their local friends slightly more frequently than do those downtown. Women moving to the downtown area see about 55 percent of their friends at least once a week, compared to about 65 percent among those moving to the suburbs. Although the differences are not great, they suggest self-selection, inasmuch as no such variation reflects the respondents' current residential setting.

With regard to Clark's (1966) explanation of life in new suburbs cited earlier, people moving to a new suburban home do not socialize more with their neighbors before their move than do people moving to resales. If there is to be a difference between these groups, it occurs after the move, as Clark suggests.

There is no variation whatever by either housing type or location regarding wives' frequency of interaction with contacts living *outside* their neighborhood.

Husbands vary only slightly according to future housing type, not location, in frequency of seeing their friends. This variation applies both to intra- and extra-neighborhood contacts. High-rise movers see somewhat *more* of their friends than do those moving to single-family houses, although this difference is not very large.

A great majority of people in both housing categories make regular telephone contact with these same persons, but the slim and inconsistent differences in amounts of telephone contact by housing categories do not alter the general lack of a pattern concerning frequency of interpersonal contact.

Although the results are hardly dramatic, it is abundantly clear that people in high-rise apartments are not isolated from their close contacts.

Reference to the time budgets enables us to see similar phenomena beyond the bounds of a finite list of close friends. The weekday time-usage figures, for example, show that the average number of minutes people spent with others not residing within the household is not related to their current or future home environments.

One should note, however, that women moving from one high-rise to another spend nearly twice as much time (280 minutes) in the company of others than do those in any other category. This is directly attributable to a greater likelihood of working, as an average of 170 of these minutes is with work colleagues. The downtown apartment movers nonetheless devote the same average time as the others to visiting relatives (a half hour) and only 19 minutes less time with friends and neighbors (about 55 minutes and 36 minutes, respectively), with the latter differences *not* attributable to work status.

The Sunday pattern is simply one of slight differences, but shows that those already in apartments spend the most time with outside contacts (about 166 minutes versus 135 among those in houses).

The same findings hold for husbands both on weekdays and Sundays.

Attendance at parties and receptions is still another indication of interpersonal relations. The data on husbands and wives, weekdays and Sundays, fail to uncover large or consistent differences with either current or future home environment.

Different housing types, then, do not on the basis of the present evidence appear to attract persons with variant frequencies and amounts of interpersonal contact. Another dimension of social life is *where* people meet. Inasmuch as different housing types have been thought to contain different opportunities for home entertainment, it is not inconceivable that families with different *loci* for their social life do not choose the same home environments. There is, however, virtually no variation of any kind regarding entertaining at home.

What clearly does differentiate interpersonal contact along the lines of the environmental contexts under scrutiny is the *origin* of the contacts people have. While social life may not vary according to amount or place, it does vary according to *where people make their friends*—with implications which reflect the residential settings.

Wives, for example, living in single homes and low-rise multiple dwellings before the move met well over 50 percent of their local friends casually inside the neighborhood, compared to only 28 percent among residents of high-rise. Nonetheless, house and low-rise occupants who are moving to houses are more likely to have met their friends this way than those moving to high-rise.

Those *living now* in high-rise met well over 50 percent of their associates either by birth (i.e., relatives) or through communities of interest (such as school, mutual friends, work). Those *moving to* high rise are more likely to have met friends at work, particularly those going to downtown apartments (21.5%).

Women moving to suburbs, even from nonsuburban areas, are more likely to have met their friends in the neighborhood, rather than in a miscellany of other places, including at work. Husbands demonstrate the same patterns.

In stark contrast, there are no noteworthy differences about where *extra-neighborhood* friends were made according to either housing type or location, current or future, for either husbands or wives.

That people in and/or moving to suburbs and houses met local contacts in the neighborhood itself, while the high-rise and downtown residents met them on a nonlocal basis, is further substantiated by answers to another question asking with what type of person a respondent has his or her most frequent contact. We noted whether respondents made reference to a relative, a nonrelated neighbor, or a (nonrelated, nonproximate) friend, representing three logically different patterns of first acquaintanceship.

Both future housing and future location are related, additively, to the type of person chosen. As Table 5.8 indicates, those moving to houses and to suburbs are each more likely to have neighbors as most frequent contacts than those downtown and in apartments. Those moving to both house and suburb are doubly more likely. Choice of 'neighbors' in this regard is generally instead of 'friends,' while the selection of 'relatives' remains practically constant across categories of home environment.

We also asked about people's most personal contact (apart from spouse). Few choose neighbors for this role. While husbands split almost evenly between relatives and friends regardless of environment, wives heading to

Table 5.8
Relationship of Most Frequent Contact Reported by Husbands/Wives,
by Destination Environment
(*Percentage*)

| | Relationship | | | | | | | |
| Destination Environment | Family or Relative | | Neighbor | | Friend | | (N) | |
	Wives	Husbands	Wives	Husbands	Wives	Husbands	Wives	Husbands
Apartment downtown	28.9	27.4	11.5	8.8	59.6	63.8	(104)	(80)
House downtown	31.9	29.3	26.1	12.1	42.0	58.6	(88)	(58)
Apartment in suburbs	34.2	30.1	26.9	17.9	38.9	52.0	(275)	(196)
House in suburbs	39.8	31.8	31.5	26.7	28.7	41.5	(251)	(176)
Total							(718)	(510)
Missing Information							(43)	(17)

downtown locations are much closer to friends in this context than are suburbanites, the great majority of whom cite their relatives.

Residents of single-family houses and suburbs are both likely to have neighbors as their most frequent, though not most intimate, contacts, have met them in the neighborhood, and see them casually around the neighborhood. This is in contrast to downtown and high-rise residents, whose contacts come more from a community of interests, often involving the job and with less of a basis in locality.

We have not yet explored several potential explanations. The most obvious is the stage in the life cycle. Mothers and fathers are more likely to have casual access to neighbors through their children than childless spouses. Mothers of young children are less likely to take outside employment, thus lacking one alternative source of contact. People met through children are extremely likely to be neighbors. That husbands' friendship patterns were found to follow those of their wives suggests a greater influence of life-cycle stage than work status in making friends. Fathers, after all, have access to neighbors through children *without* a corresponding debit in the area of work contacts.

We, therefore, analyzed the data on social interaction according to whether a family had children. The results supported our expectations. Indeed, life-cycle stage is unquestionably a more effective explanation behind variation in interaction[5] than housing type or location.

That this is the case, however, in no way eliminates particular interaction patterns with which people are selectively choosing different home environments, even if the explanation lies in a third variable. If people choose environment on the basis of family and work status (which are in practice closely linked) and if a particular interaction pattern accompanies a given family-work status, then we must expect certain types of interaction (or at least sources of it) to vary from one environmental setting to another.

Environment may not cause the behavior. Neither may people necessarily choose the environment because of an existing interaction pattern. However, choice of environment with reference to another factor, family-work status, brings about the kind of environment-interaction match described in this section. It is not an accident, although it is causally spurious. And it ends up assisting in the creation of myths about reasons for the kinds of interaction present or absent in places like high-rise apartments and suburbs, such as that apartments 'create' anonymity and suburbs, gregariousness.

These 'myths' are found in the expectations of the movers. Consistent with their expressions of personal compatibility with their prospective new neighbors, 49 percent of the women moving from high-rise to single homes expect more contact with their new neighbors than with their current neighbors. Although some people moving to apartments (and from one to another) also expect increased contact (or no less than the same amount), the apartment to house group expects far and away the biggest increase—the rest *well under* 49 percent.

Similarly, women going to suburban houses said they expected to entertain friends more when we asked how their lives and use of time might change after moving.

We shall examine how well they realized all these expectations in the next chapter.

Organizational Participation

Participation in organizations is still another aspect of personal contact, but at a more formal level. The message of previous research is that people moving to suburbia are 'joiners.' Moreover research indicates that they do not suddenly catch a club 'infection' but were already joiners in their old neighborhoods, seeing an attraction in a new social atmosphere with a potentially rich collective life (Gans, 1967; Michelson, 1961). We assessed this theory with our data.

One can measure the intensity of organizational participation, ranging from nominal membership to great amounts of time and effort committed. However, our respondents proved to be very low in participation of any kind. Half the wives belonged to no formal organizations and another quarter belonged only to one. A quarter of the husbands belonged to none, and more than half to no more than one. The time budgets showed an average of less than a minute a day devoted to organizational activities. For this reason, we looked at participation only in terms of: (1) number, and (2) types of organizations.

There are great differences in membership according to future housing type. Over 80 percent of those choosing high-rise apartments are likely to hold membership in only one organization, or none, regardless of the type of current housing. Since we counted union and professional memberships, many of those working have an "automatic" membership, hence the link of none and one to form a category. In contrast, about a third of the wives and half of the husbands moving to houses belong to two or more, again without distortion by current residence.

Organizational membership does not vary by location.

There is some but not very strong evidence of the higher participation previous writers had led us to expect among those moving to newly built suburban homes, as compared to single-family houses in already settled suburban areas. Whether differences of 5 percent among the wives and 8 percent among the husbands show enough of a preexisting difference to settle the 'self-selection'—'newness of area' debate on participation in new suburban areas in favor of the former is questionable, particularly since participation is even higher among those moving to *downtown* houses (by another 6 percent)!

These findings on membership *do not*, however, reflect life-cycle stage, age, family income, or the wife's working status.

The types of secular associations in which people hold membership do not vary significantly by housing type or location. Church membership, on the other hand, provides some evidence of self-selection of housing. The Sunday time budgets show exactly twice the percentage of participation, 20 percent to 10 percent (and twice the average time devoted), among those moving to houses, as compared to those moving to apartments. Only those moving to houses from *high-rise* apartments do not follow this form of self-selection. The ultimate explanation in this case appears to be the presence of school-age children.

The relative lack of several kinds of public activity among those moving to high-rise may contribute to the general perception of apartment dwellers as withdrawn, regardless of the real cause.

Commuting

At one time, researchers saw commuting as a prime factor in residential selection. At this point, we must assess in more detail the part that commuting plays in the kinds of moving decisions dealt with here.

Women *moving to* high-rise apartments currently live disproportionately further from their jobs than do wives in all other categories. Over 40 percent live more than 6 miles from their work place, of whom almost 40 percent live more than 10 miles away. The other housing and location categories contain between 28 and 34 percent in the former regard. Women living in downtown apartments are also the fewest working within a mile of home. Husbands moving to downtown apartments join with those moving to downtown houses in living closer to their jobs than those in the suburban categories, although those moving to the downtown homes are clearly the closest before moving (68% already within 5 miles, compared with 46% for those moving to the downtown high rise).

Travel *time* may be a more crucial basis for understanding moving behavior, however. On the basis of direct questions about travel time, both husbands and wives moving to downtown high-rise apartments have the longest commutes of any pre-move group. Only about 30 percent of wives moving to downtown apartments have commutes of less than half an hour, compared to over 50 percent of those moving to suburbs. The husbands of the former are particularly high in work trips, over 45 minutes in length.

We clarify the meaning of pre-move disadvantage among those moving to downtown locations, particularly to apartments when examining *change* in location. As Table 5.9 indicates, wives moving from outlying locations to the downtown area are *considerably* farther from work before the move than any other group of women, while their husbands are not uniquely disadvantaged.

In terms of travel *time*, however, both husbands and wives making centralizing moves are high in travel time relative to the others, again the wife considerably more so. Table 5.10 shows these figures.

The time budget confirms the initial plight of the wife moving downtown from the suburbs, as her average commuting time is 15 minutes more daily than that of any other category whose move originates from the Toronto area. The time budget does not support the plight of her husband, although it does show that men who are centralizing start with higher commuting times than men remaining within the downtown zone—the basis for feelings of relative deprivation. Men moving to suburbia, in contrast, all start with still longer commutes.

The contradiction between travel time and distance among husbands is

Table 5.9
Pre-move Distance to Work, by Location Change
(Percentage)

| | Distance in Miles | | | | | | | | | |
| | Less than 1 | | 1–5 | | 6–10 | | 11+ | | (N) | |
Location Change	Wives	Husbands	Wives	Husbands	Wives	Husbands	Wives	Husbands	Wives	Husbands
Downtown to downtown	16.7	9.7	65.0	57.3	13.3	25.2	5.0	7.7	(60)	(103)
Outside Toronto to downtown or centralizing	6.5	6.2	28.3	37.0	41.3	28.4	23.9	28.3	(46)	(81)
Suburbs to suburbs	22.8	3.5	38.6	22.7	15.8	22.1	22.8	51.7	(57)	(172)
Outside Toronto to suburbs or decentralizing	14.2	5.9	56.0	35.1	20.6	31.0	9.3	28.0	(141)	(339)
Total									(304)	(695)
Missing Information									(—)	(76)

Table 5.10
Pre-move Duration of Work Trip, by Location Change
(*Percentage*)

Location Change	Duration in Minutes									
	1–14		15–29		30–44		45+		(N)	
	Wives	Husbands	Wives	Husbands	Wives	Husbands	Wives	Husbands	Wives	Husbands
Downtown to downtown	10.0	12.1	26.7	34.3	58.3	42.4	5.0	11.1	(60)	(99)
Outside Toronto to downtown *and* centralizers	7.0	8.4	16.3	28.9	39.5	26.5	37.2	36.1	(43)	(83)
Suburb to suburb	24.5	10.6	35.8	31.3	30.2	35.6	9.4	22.5	(53)	(160)
Outside Toronto to downtown *and* decentralizers	14.6	8.5	33.6	33.8	31.4	36.3	20.4	21.5	(137)	(317)
Total									(293)	(659)
Missing Information									(–)	(102)

resolved, as might be expected, with reference to *mode* of travel. Although a slim majority of the 'centralizers' drive their own cars to work, many more of them use mass transit than do those making decentralizing moves. Mass transit use then, turns short distances into longer commutes.

Furthermore, prospective residents of downtown use the same modes of travel as those already downtown, while prospective suburbanites drive cars as much as those already in suburbia. Husbands' mode of travel appears to play a part in locational decisions. Husbands seem to change location rather than preferred mode of travel where one mode makes traveling a certain route disadvantageous.

Wives' modes of travel do not resemble that of their husbands. Those remaining in downtown areas differ as expected from those remaining in suburbia (22% versus 82% driving to work), while the group of wives changing locations are in between these two extremes.

That husbands reflect more evidence of continuing a form of preference in mode of transport than do wives is supported by data illustrating intra-family priorities. When a family has but one car, the husband has first crack at it. The wife commonly drives herself to work only when a family has two cars. In one-car families, 73 percent of husbands drive to work, only 15 percent lower than in families with two cars.

At this point, then, we have seen that wives moving to downtown apartments are most distant from work before the move, both in miles and in time, while many of their husbands are more distant than they want to be in travel time, due largely to their choice of mode of transportation. We must ask, however, if this particular housing choice actually involves lowered travel times. Does not the suburban move, moreover, also take into consideration the reduction or maintenance of travel time?

While families cannot gauge travel time accurately until after the move, they can see distance relatively objectively in advance.

We studied that subsample of residents who maintained the same job from Phase I to Phase II, comparing distances from home to work, as they would change from before to after moving.

The only category of people showing a decrease in distance to work following the move is the group moving to downtown high-rise. The decrease is tiny, however; virtually as many increased as decreased. But within all other categories, the increases in distance to work were appreciable.

Consistent with expectations, those moving *from* outlying areas *to* the downtown area (whether to house or apartment) substantially decreased their distance to work. Sixty percent of the husbands decreased their distance, while only 25 percent increased, the rest remaining stable; fully 80 percent of the wives decreased their distance to work. In contrast, those remaining within the same general type of location experience a moderate net *increase* in distance, while those moving to the suburbs from elsewhere have a most substantial increase in travel distance (69% and 80%, for husbands and wives).

In sum, only those centralizing (usually to apartments), make moves with clearly shrinking effects on distance to work. This is consistent with the significantly greater percentage of working wives moving to downtown apartments, underlying the rationale for such a move. It appears an excellent example of the deficit compensation process. We shall examine what this means in terms of daily travel time after the move in the next chapter.

Commercial Activity

Data on people's frequency of use of certain facilities indicate a considerable selection of home environment related to life style. Tables based on housing and location *changes* show that those *moving* to an environment possessing spatial opportunities are already more frequent participants in congruent activities before the move.

With respect to restaurant meals, for example, we would expect movers to high rise (entertainment *outside* the dwelling unit) and to downtown (closer to large numbers of establishments) to be more frequent participants. Over 10 percent more of the families living in a low-rise accommodation but moving to high-rise apartments patronize restaurants at least several times a month than do those moving to houses. Regarding location change, the most frequent users are those moving in a centralizing direction, although the difference of 10 percent between high and low is not dramatic.

As expected, those moving downtown from elsewhere already patronize places of public entertainment most frequently. Almost 50 percent of the centralizers participate in public entertainment at least several times a month, while all other categories participate at a level of around 29 percent. There is no differentiation by housing type.

Shopping facilities in Toronto are quite decentralized. The central business district is only one of many areas in which to purchase goods. Perhaps as a consequence, there is *no* relationship between the location chosen and the preexisting frequency of shopping for clothes.

The time budgets potentially shed additional light on the use of city facilities. Time budgets are normally useful in making a more precise assessment of time spent on common everyday behavior, because people do not always have an accurate notion of the time they spend on routine activities. Direct estimates of time devoted to housework and commuting, for example, are notoriously unreliable. While the time budget does not escape problems concerned with accuracy of recall and the social acceptability of answers, it has the advantage of pinpointing activities to a very particular time frame, which, in context, is less loaded in its implications to the respondent. Although what an individual might do during the day(s) assessed may be unusual for him or her, the aggregation of usual and unusual activities within analytic categories provides a relatively accurate picture of daily life for that group of persons.

However, because infrequently performed activities are likely to be registered in the time budgets of very few in any sample, such activities as might be relevant to the present discussion as attendance at night clubs, movies, or live theater, are characterized by impossibly thin data in time-budget results. On the other hand, 'meals taken outside home'—an approximation of eating in restaurants—occurs regularly enough for observation.

There is some support, with qualifications, for the theory of self-selection regarding the patronage of restaurants. In the weekday time budgets of both husbands and wives, centralizers are most likely to eat out, although the husbands' figures reflect an emphasis among *all* who will live in the center (those already there included).

Wives moving to apartments eat out more than those moving to houses, a difference not found among their husbands. Furthermore, these differences are not reflected in the Sunday time budgets.

Given the large numbers of working wives among those moving to downtown apartments, together with the lack of differences among husbands and of a similar pattern on Sundays, female work status appears to underlie differences in time given to restaurant meals.

Examination of the data indicates that working wives eat out more than do nonworking wives, regardless of residence. Nonetheless, among the working wives alone, the very same differences by destination environment appear. That these differences do not appear among the nonworking wives reduces the self-selective effects to just the working wives—undoubtedly a function of the lesser likelihood of the latter having children to draw them back to the apartment for supper. Hence it is not surprising that size of family makes these differences even more pronounced, but only after the *second* child!

Pastimes

Participation in some pastimes varies by the chosen housing type. There is general agreement on two counts, however: (1) husbands and wives are likely to stress the same preexisting interests in conjunction with particular moves, and (2) all matching of activity to setting has to do with the environment *chosen*—not the current environment, again indicating self-selection on the basis of activity. The match-ups are as follows:

Movers to House	*Movers to Downtown*	*Movers to Suburbia*
Church	Reading	Gardening
Cards	Movies or plays	Watching sports (H)
Gardening		
Reading (W)		
Sewing or knitting (W)		
Sports participation (H)		

Wife only (W)   Husband only (H)

Respondents moving to high-rise apartments are not strong participants in any professed pre-move pastime activity.

These data indicate once again that many of the activities associated with a given housing type or setting are not spawned in that setting but represent a selective migration of particular persons to particular settings.

Activities which people propose to commence, apparently unable to carry out in their current setting, vary quite simply by setting chosen. Both husbands and wives moving to single houses expect to take up gardening, if they have not already. Both of them expect to participate in athletic pastimes, if moving to high-rise apartments. This latter expectation is consistent with the reasons cited for choice of environment early in this chapter.

It is interesting to see that men moving to apartments expect more active athletic pastimes, although they are lower than house movers in terms of their pre-move participation in this activity. This may indicate not that high-rise movers are *more* interested in athletics but that they are using an opportunity in environmental design to redress a deficiency which they had not previously overcome by other means (such as athletic club memberships)—i.e., the process of deficit compensation.

Some writers have suggested that home environments need not provide for certain recreational activities as long as people were to have alternative living arrangements for vacation periods. However, the current study data show no such connection of people's choice of housing type and location to their vacation patterns.

The time budget also sheds light on participation in some pastimes (churchgoing already having been mentioned with respect to formal organizations). Among those living in houses both before and after the move, 16 percent were found to garden on the day in question, as compared to 9 percent among those moving from houses to apartments. Ten percent of those in low-rise apartments but moving to a house reported gardening activity, as compared to only 2 percent in similar accommodations moving to high-rise. Gardening, however, reflects the wife's work status inversely, and does not hold on Sundays or for husbands. Nonetheless, whatever the reason, it is a pattern of activity which at least one member of the family *brings to* the new home, appearing not just as a function of demands placed by this residence.

People play cards too infrequently for the time budget to prove efficient as a source of evidence.

The time-budget data confirm reading, particularly of magazines and newspapers and on weekdays, as done more by those moving to houses than by those moving to apartments and by decentralizers. Nonetheless, this appears primarily a function of nonworking status, as working wives participate in this pastime only half as much as their nonworking counterparts.

Although sewing and knitting are also inversely related to work status, the main variation lies between the wives moving from one house to another (of whom 15% record this activity on the weekday, compared to only 5% among those moving from houses to apartments). This distinction is not found within any other current housing type, and it is not explicable with reference to family size.

The last recreational characteristic of those moving to houses is participation in sports. Whether men or women moving to high-rise apartments really have a deficit in this regard before their move is unfortunately not resolved by time-budget data. Apartment movers have neither a real deficit or advantage before their move.

Television watching is a frequent pastime on which the time budget provides useful information. Both husbands and wives moving to downtown single-family homes are uniquely low in television viewing (on weekdays and Sundays). They average only two-thirds the amount of viewing characteristic of the others, with those moving to apartments the heaviest TV watchers. That apartment movers are highest in television viewing indicates the possibility that Wallace's hypothesized 'star boarder' was someone who existed before the move to the high-rise, not necessarily just a product of it.

In any case, a look at pastime activity suggests that people practice some behaviors consistent with their new environments before they move, albeit sometimes as a function of still another factor such as family size. This does not, however, rule out the form of self-selection; people also move to selected settings to develop new pastime activities, such as participatory sports.

Housekeeping Activity

Somewhere between the worlds of paid employment and pure leisure lies the area of household activity. This includes such things as cleaning, making repairs, dishwashing, and laundering. In this regard, movement to a particular combination of housing type and location, the downtown high-rise, is more significantly related to existing behavioral differences than is either change in housing type or in location alone.

On weekdays, for example, wives moving to downtown apartments average 38 minutes on food preparation, compared to about twice that amount among those moving anywhere else. They spend 17 minutes on dishwashing, again half the usual amount. Their average of 27 minutes on indoor cleaning is only about 40 percent of the average among the others, while the 12 minutes they spend on laundering and ironing is only about a third to a quarter that of the others. The time they devote to home repairs, 18 minutes, is up to half of that in any other category.

One might ascribe these differences to the greater propensity of wives moving to downtown apartments to work. As the day has only 24 hours, a trade-off is usually considered necessary when one form of activity characteristically requires a large and regular input of time (cf. Staikov, 1970). Nonetheless, with the sole exception of daily household repairs, both working and nonworking wives, analyzed separately, show exactly the same patterns with respect to destination environment. And in the case of this one 'exception,' the nonworking wives nonetheless follow the pattern.

One response to such differentials in housework is to question how the group doing minimal housework gets by. An associated question to this is, 'What really *needs* to get done?'

The answer to the first question is to forego the assumption that the wife should necessarily do all the housework. On weekdays, for example, the husbands moving to downtown apartments are unique both in the percentage of time they put in on dishwashing, indoor cleaning, and home repairs. With respect to indoor cleaning, for example, not only does 8 percent participation on the given day interviewed far outpace the others, but among those who do participate, an average of 1½ hours was spent at it, in comparison to well under an hour within all the other categories.

Furthermore, on Sundays, the amount of time wives moving to downtown apartments spend on household work more nearly approaches that of the other categories regarding food preparation and indoor cleaning, while they spend somewhat more time than on weekdays on dishwashing and home repairs. Far more time is spent by those moving to downtown apartments than the others on laundering and ironing on Sundays, an average of 2½ hours put in by the former 'making up' for what was not done during the week.

Despite the Sunday work and husbands' contributions, the total work put in by families moving to downtown high-rises on these household activities still does not equal that within any of the other groups of movers.

The underlying differences separating the downtown apartment group could also be their typical lack of children. Generally, children make demands on the daily timetable, which women bear whether or not they work; children also create additional demands for housework. That both working and nonworking wives moving to downtown apartments are unlikely to have children, in comparison to the much higher frequency of offspring among both working and nonworking wives in the other categories, places relatively fewer demands for housework on the former.

Nonetheless, analyzing time devoted to the various types of housekeeping according to whether a family has children does not remove all the differentials reflecting housing type. Differences between those moving to downtown apartments and those in the other categories on indoor cleaning remain great even after control for children. Just over a third of the childless wives moving to downtown apartments report cleaning their homes on the weekday surveyed, compared to around half within each of the other categories; the differential is about the same but at a higher level of participation among the wives who have children (about 55% to just over 75%).

Although most wives do prepare food on the given day, the amount of time they devote to it largely follows this pattern among the categories of destination environment. Laundering follows this pattern as well, except in the case of the wives without children moving to downtown houses, who are exceptionally low on this activity. Only with dishwashing does the pattern disappear once controlled for whether or not the family has children.

There is no disputing that the presence or absence of children has a tremendous effect on time usage. The average housework figures double and triple when women with children are compared to the childless. The average time devoted to indoor cleaning, for example, among the childless is around a half an hour, compared to somewhat over an hour among those with children. The former average 10 to 15 minutes in laundering and ironing, compared to a half hour to 45 minutes for the latter. That this effect is so strong, however, does not negate the pattern reflecting self-selection in housing, which largely survives. Furthermore, women moving to houses, particularly suburban houses, expect that their daily routines in the future will contain increased amounts of housework.

In any case, at present we see families with two working spouses and no children, who already put in the least housework, moving to the most efficient destination environment, both in terms of access and space within the dwelling unit. Combined with the findings in the other sections, it provides renewed support for the theory of self-selection.

THE EMERGING PICTURE OF
ENVIRONMENTAL CHOICE

The data gathered before people moved illustrate that there were distinct, *qualitative* differences among the people moving to the four primary categories of housing and location: downtown apartments, downtown houses, suburban apartments, and suburban homes. The distinction is not merely that of one category wanting a little more than another or of some people representing a little more of certain characteristics than others; no continuum is involved. The differences are of kind rather than amount. What emerges logically from the welter of perspectives and factors according to types of housing, location, and combinations thereof?

Single-Family Homes

People buying homes are largely interested in increasing their amount of usable space and in either achieving or maintaining home ownership.

While, by and large, they are people who feel personally similar although economically superior to their former neighbors, they are friendly and active with neighbors, and they wish to move to a residence where *more* of the neighbors are like themselves. A noticeable minority of these people make the move in an effort to enhance their own status (i.e., they think their new neighbors will be superior to themselves).

Women moving to houses *already* spend more of their time on child care and housework than do those moving to apartments, and they expect to do more housework still in the new home; part of this difference, however, is due to the fact that fewer '*house*wives' hold jobs.

People moving to houses are generally more interested in gardening and other home- and family-centered activities. They are more active in organizations and churches.

People moving to houses, even downtown houses, generally have more automobiles than do people moving to high-rise apartments, and they use them to drive to work.

High-Rise Apartments

In contrast, people moving to apartments are primarily seeking homes with more space than they had previously. The desire for more space is not something satisfied only by single-family housing, and most respondents satisfied needs for more residential space as a consequence of their moves, whether they moved to houses or to apartments.

What those moving to apartments do not usually satisfy is the desire to own their unit, a desire held virtually as strongly by apartment renters as by home buyers.

Although families choosing high-rise apartments exhibit no unusual interests or prior participation in leisure pursuits or organizational activities, sporting facilities on the premises of most of the high-rise complexes studied are important attractions to these families.

While families moving to high-rise apartments are every bit as social as anyone else, seeing friends as frequently and entertaining them just as much in their own homes, these friends are nonetheless not chosen among visibly immediate neighbors but rather are made through nonlocal communities of interest: school, workplace, and mutual acquaintance. While these families see their new neighbors as socioeconomically similar, their personal view of them is less distinct, more negative, and as not similar to themselves.

This friendship pattern is related to the many more wives living in high-rise apartments who hold jobs than do those in single-family homes. Nonetheless, the particular patterns by which friends are made is typical of men moving to high-rise apartments as well. Underlying all these are differences in family composition; children lead to adult social contact, in the absence of which other paths to friendship are used. This phenomenon helps account for the antisocial image of high-rise apartments.

Downtown

With respect to the dimension of location, people choosing downtown locations are generally more highly educated, and are more likely to be professionals (husbands and wives). Even within relatively high levels of socioeconomic status, there is a clear division between professionals seeking downtown locations and managers seeking suburban locations. Associated with this major difference is a set of cultural influences. Families choosing downtown locations are much more interested than suburbanites in cultural and culinary pastimes congruent with those physically located in downtown Toronto.

Suburbs

Suburbanites are drawn from the ranks of those living in more central areas with growing families. Few people already resident in suburban areas choose to live downtown; downtown residences are normally filled from those already downtown, from adjacent intermediate areas, and from out of town.

Downtown Apartments

Within our general range of families within the childbearing years, those moving to downtown apartments are clearly younger. Although we excluded newlyweds from the sample, downtown high-rise families are much less likely to include children and much more likely to have both husband and wife at early stages of their respective careers. The husband's income is relatively low, although future prospects are good. The wife's income contributes to a healthy family income but her income did not count for mortgage purposes and hence toward the purchase of alternative accommodations, at the time of our initial survey.

The downtown apartment comprises the strongest example of different contact patterns found.

Location is very important in the choice of a downtown high-rise apartment by these relatively affluent families. They are least likely of all the groups to own automobiles and most likely to use public transportation. Since, in most cases, two members of the family are employed, decent access to the place of work is a special consideration.

Even before moving to downtown high-rise apartments, the wives spend a great deal of time *away* from their homes, but this is not primarily a function of their housing but of their employment and family status.

Downtown Homes

The husband moving to a downtown house is generally older and more advanced in his profession, and the wife does not work in three out of four cases. High family income is a function of the husband's earnings, therefore qualifying fully in mortgage computations.

Although the usual desires for internal space and for home ownership are satisfied by downtown houses, locational elements are of considerable importance. Travel to work is initially favorable for most. The families are typically drawn from elsewhere in the downtown area, somewhat more than half of them taking the leap from rental accommodation to home ownership.

Suburban Apartments

The apartments are generally larger, with more bedrooms than those in the downtown areas. As should be expected, many more families with children choose these units than choose downtown high-rise units. These families anticipate that these units will satisfy their needs for a greater amount of space.

Yet the choice of these units is generally made over such alteratives as older low-rise housing units in more central areas of the city on the rationale that suburban neighborhoods are more suitable for raising children. These families appreciate the prospect of on-site recreation facilities. A lower family income narrows the range of alternatives in family housing available to these people.

Suburban Homes

If the families moving to downtown homes put priority on locational requirements (having fulfilled basic housing requirements), those moving to single-family houses in the suburbs would seem to put a priority on

their homes and on the characteristics of their neighbors. The status en-
hancing quality of the suburban single-family home, as compared to its
purely spatial and tenure-oriented considerations, is brought out by the
fact that most persons buying these homes are already homeowners in
suburban or in intermediate locations. The new home is a larger dwelling
in a more socially acceptable neighborhood. Housewives expect more
housework, more entertaining, and less ease of access to shops and recreational facilities.

I assembled the above figurative 'clusters' of qualitatively different factors underlying and accompanying choice of the different types of environment through the inspection of numerous discrete relationships. Their
appearance as clusters is based on such criteria as consistency and logical
complementarity. A large and dispersed literature, as well as the paradigm
outlined in Chapter 1, guided this task. It was critical to retain the data as
close as possible to their original form, relying, then, on the presence of a
coherent substantive framework to unify the results. The import of most
of the findings will be developed in later chapters, especially Chapter 10.

I felt it tempting but dangerous to consider quantifying all variables at
the start, throwing them into one or another popular form of analysis and
then attempting to explain the results post facto.

Nonetheless, once the data are examined as closely as possible to their
original structure and with regard to their substantive meaning, it is highly
desirable to confirm that such patterns as do emerge in fact contain unify-
ing elements apart from the analyst's imagination. It is also desirable to
observe such clusters in more succinct form than the original analyses
provided.

Therefore, solely for the purpose of confirming the plausibility of the
general interpretation of the specific findings, we listed in quantitative
form all the variables described in the preceding discussion, many of them
broken down into their component values and expressed as one or zero,
when present or absent, and then used as input to a rotated factor analysis. We are not concerned with the exact amount of explanation of the
emergent factors, due to the amount of total variance created by the input
of so many variables as well as due to the liberties taken in the quantification of so many of these variables. The point was to see whether general
clusters emerged statistically which are consistent with the individual relationships and conclusions previously observed.

Ten factors of significant size emerged. Although they explain 32.04 percent of the variance, their most critical property is that they confirm the previous logically constructed clusters. Nine of the ten are centered around aspects of residential environment and mobility. Let us look briefly at the theme and leading characteristics of each of these factors.

Factor 1—Active Men (Variance explained 6.72%)
This is the only predominantly non-environmental factor, and it is based almost exclusively on variables intertwining a variety of leisure activities and degrees of knowledge of and contact with current and future neighbors. This pattern contrasts almost entirely with variables representing expression of no interest in the various pastimes inventoried.

Factor 2—Continual Renters (Variance explained 5.01%)
This factor contains families who rented previously and who are about to again. They are not knowledgeable of the personal characteristics of their neighbors but expect that their future neighbors will be economically similar. They met their current local friends through nonlocal communities of interest. The wife commonly works. The family does not have children. It is not interested in gardening or most other forms of recreation. The members of the family are outside the home an above-average amount, but while at home they watch television more than most.

Factor 3—Downtown Apartment: Working Wife
(Variance explained 3.76%)
This factor relates predominantly to information from the wife. Besides the defining characteristics, these families are characterized by the absence of children, the use of public transportation, and time spent away from home and with work colleagues. These people have met their friends nonlocally, but they anticipate seeing their new neighbors more than their old ones. This kind of family contrasts with those where the husband's income is high, who have children, and who spend more time at home and on housework, child care, and passive leisure.

Factor 4—Moving to Downtown House (Variance explained 3.13%)
The women whose answers contribute predominantly to this factor are in families with high income and education. The men are professionals. Although children are present, their presence is not a strong factor. These

people are interested in culture, not in playing cards or watching television. They contrast with those moving to suburban apartments, with no interests other than watching television. The latter group has a strong expectation of increased participation in sports.

Factor 5—Moving to Suburbs (Variance explained 2.94%)
The families in this factor are more likely to have more than one car, and they use their cars to get to work; they have children; and the wife, who already does considerable housework, expects still more. The husband is a manager, and the members of the family have little interest in cultural pursuits. In contrast, those moving downtown have fewer children, take public transportation to work, and are interested in plays but not gardening.

Factor 6—Suburban Home to Suburban Home
(Variance explained 2.47%)
These families feel they are moving to a more socially homogeneous neighborhood. They met their friends locally, and they belong to civic groups. Although moving to another house, they still expect problems regarding space. The wife is alone a good deal on weekdays, while the husband spends the weekend in the company of guests more than the average.

Factor 7—Move from Apartment to House
(Variance explained 2.15%)
The family has children. The wife spends an inordinate amount of time on housework and in child care. The family goes to church. They tend to watch television and devote much time to passive leisure. They are not particularly interested in participating in sports.

Factor 8—Move from Outside Toronto to Apartment
(Variance explained 2.08%)
These people are moving from outside Toronto to apartments, either downtown or in the suburbs. In either case, a major factor in the choice was the *location* of the building. They expect an increase in weekday sports participation. This is not a move made in response to the need for more living space.

Factor 9—Decentralizers (Variance explained 1.95%)
These families are moving from houses in the in-between area to suburban locations. They are very close to their former neighbors and expect to be so with their new neighbors. They are active in religious activities, in sports, and in civic groups. They are interested in gardening. The major reason their new home was chosen had to do with its neighborhood.

Factor 10—Change of Residential Environment
(Variance explained 1.77%)
This factor contrasts those changing housing and/or location with those who do not. Those changing expect more problems both in their housing and in their daily routines.

The factors that emerged in this analysis reiterate succinctly some of the major themes from this analysis of environmental choice. Those who move are making choices, of both housing type and location, which reflect different criteria for the choice of housing, different personal and family characteristics, and different expectations of what they will find. The qualitative differences among these types of move are confirmed by the blend of different factors in the manner observed.

These factors, like the outcome of the various discrete analyses, stress the environment *chosen*, together with the rationales and characteristics of those choosing, much more than these factors stress the current settings from which the families are being drawn.

The message of this chapter, then, is the importance of understanding fully the exact nature of what people bring with them to their new housing as a basis for understanding the subsequent implications of the new setting.

Nonetheless, as expressed in Chapter 1, it is too much to expect perfect rationality. The characteristics of the destination environment may precipitate effects which were not anticipated by all new residents, leading to more distinct or to different patterns of behavior and difficulties than were originally anticipated. The next chapter, therefore, examines the lives of these families in their new homes and locations.

NOTES

[1] Note, however, that such an agreement is easier to achieve operationally with the closed-ended form of question.

[2] Our techniques did not *in Phase I* explicitly elicit family increments planned or in progress among the younger families, except where volunteered.

[3] A large minority felt unable to answer the question and are not counted in this distribution. This inability has some meaning, to be explored shortly.

[4] The definition of neighborhood was left to the respondent.

[5] See Gans (1962b) on this point.

Chapter Six

Situated Behavior

My argument in the previous chapter is that families with any degree of choice do not view new home environments as 'black boxes' upon arrival. They choose different forms of environment to represent different needs and wants. In some instances, they have expectations they intend to fulfill within the spatial opportunities of their destination environments. In other instances, they have preestablished patterns of behavior which they anticipate the new environment will support. Indeed, our analysis of environmental choice indicates that those changing environments have *greater* expectations of what they may subsequently find and do, which, while possibly unrealistic, are certainly different from the theoretically opposite position, in which they lack expectations and are potentially vulnerable to whatever forces may be found within the new environment.

Nonetheless, to what extent are the rationales and expectations about life in the new homes and locations supported by subsequent experience? Do the differential patterns of behavior, activity, and social characteristics explored in the previous chapter emerge? In essence, to what extent are many of the assertions about life in different residential settings justified by the actual *experience* of the persons in this study?

In this chapter I shall explore in some detail what emerges within each of the environmental settings pursued. The main body of data utilized for this purpose is that gathered from wives, husbands, and children in Phase III, about one year and two months following the move. I shall point out where Phase III data diverge from the shorter run effects noted in Phase II, only two months after the move. This is the last phase in which intensive interview data were gathered, although I shall draw upon the final information on these respondents, gathered some three years later but in considerably more succinct form, for confirmation (see Chapter 9).

In the present chapter I emphasize the overt *patterns* characteristic of the various environmental settings. The extent that such patterns reflect preexisting expectations or behaviors, on the one hand, or the exigencies of the destination environment, on the other, will be the subject of the next chapter. Let us again look at the various substantive areas of interest one by one.

SPECIFIC FACTORS

Financial Aspects

No one would expect income to be radically transformed as a consequence of moving to a particular environment. And this did not happen in the present case. Not surprisingly, patterns of income are unchanged from the previous chapter.

Although the relative distribution of husbands' incomes is literally unchanged during the approximate year and a third separating Phase III from Phase I, save for an across-the-board increase in the income levels, the picture of working wives is less sharp than before. The percentage of working wives among those who by now had moved to high-rise apartments downtown shrank from 78 percent to 64 percent, while the percentage of working wives in single-family houses edged up to about 32 percent. Those who moved to suburban apartments maintained their approximate 50 percent participation in the labor force. Although not as dramatic as preexisting behavior may have suggested, the relation between home environment and working status for the wife is nonetheless high.

Stage in the Life Cycle

A higher percentage of families who had moved to the high-rise were caring for babies (21%) than among those who had moved to houses (17%). Even a sixth of the wives who had moved to *downtown* apartments now had babies—not unrelated to their drop-off in outside employment.

While the suburban apartment families do contain a somewhat higher percentage of infants than do downtown apartment families, the reverse is true among those who moved to houses, eliminating any generalization about location in this regard.

Although family starts are occurring without particular regard to the characteristics of the new environment, a maldistribution of older children remains. Those in the downtown apartments, who had been predominantly childless, do not within a year acquire older children, while well over half the families in all the other home environments, suburban apartments included, do have children above infancy.

That we found significant numbers of babies in the downtown apartments challenges the widespread assumption that families choosing high-rise living are thereby inhibited in childbearing. We should, perhaps, rephrase the question, and ask whether these families choose not to have children or whether, more probably, once the children start to arrive, the families choose not to remain in the high-rise housing, leading to a paucity of children there. The Phase IV data reported in Chapter 9 helps to clarify the answer to this question.

Critics have pointed out that the lower densities found in suburbs require that women drive children from place to place throughout the day. The 'mother as chauffeur' is a strong lament in some books on suburbs. Yet, our comparison of the time budgets of suburban and downtown wives, both living in houses and with approximately the same family responsibilities and lack of commitment to outside jobs, shows virtually the identical amount of time devoted to accompanying the child outside the home. Within both groups, 24 percent took their children somewhere at least once during the previous weekday, amounting to an average of 49 minutes each among those in the downtown houses and 48 minutes each among those in suburban houses.

There is a similar concern over the time that fathers spend with their children. The hypothesis that suburbanism is related to an emphasis on familism assumes that suburban fathers will spend more time with their children, despite whatever rigors may be involved in commuting. The time-budget data show this assumption to be unfounded, whether the reference is to weekdays or Sundays. About the same percentage of fathers spend the same amount of time both in the care of older children and in spending recreational time with them, whether they live in downtown houses or suburban houses.

Neighbor Characteristics

The social characteristics which our respondents brought to their new neighborhoods were detailed in the last chapter. The question now is whether, upon arrival, the respondents found the educational and economic similarities they expected. Furthermore, do they find the personal characteristics of neighbors consistent with their own?

A majority of husbands and wives in almost all the destination environments now see their neighbors as economically and educationally similar to themselves. Only among those in downtown houses do fewer than about 55 percent find themselves economically similar, and in this case it is 44 percent, accompanied by a greater percentage of 'don't know' answers. The same situation is true with regard to educational similarities, but the exceptional category comprises those in suburban apartments.

The basis of economic similarity differs somewhat from category to category. While a plurality in each of the settings calls their new neighbors 'middle-class,' 32 percent and 41 percent in downtown and suburban houses respectively see their neighbors as 'upper-middle class' while an additional 6 percent of those in downtown houses term them 'upper class.' This then leads to the designation of neighbors as middle class or higher by close to 90 percent of those moving to houses. In contrast, only about two-thirds of those moving to apartments say the same. The latter are more likely to see some neighbors as lower or working class. Husbands in suburban apartments are particularly likely to make this assessment, 26 percent of them doing so. In light of the respondents' own incomes, what they attribute to their neighbors is consistent with their expressions of similarity.

With respect to educational similarity, those downtown, finding their neighbors similar to themselves, indicate higher levels of education, consistent with the respondents' own educational backgrounds. This is also true among those living in single-family houses. Table 6.1 indicates that housing type and location are additive regarding education; neighbors are felt to have university degrees most frequently by those in downtown houses and least frequently among those living in suburban apartments, with the levels in downtown apartments and suburban houses somewhere in between. In contrast, an overwhelming majority of those in suburban

Table 6.1
Basis of Educational Similarity When Perceived, by Housing Type and Location
(*Percentage*)

| Housing Type and Location | Basis of Educational Similarity When Perceived | | | | | | (N) | |
| | Maximum high school or vocational school | | Maximum some university | | University degree or higher | | | |
	Wives	Husbands	Wives	Husbands	Wives	Husbands	Wives	Husbands
Apartment downtown	45.7	50	34.8	29.2	19.6	20.8	(46)	(48)
House downtown	21.2	19.4	28.8	25.0	50.0	55.6	(66)	(36)
Apartment suburbs	80.9	74.0	12.1	17.9	7.0	8.1	(157)	(123)
House suburbs	45.8	35.0	24.1	23.8	30.1	41.3	(166)	(143)
Total							(435)	(350)
Not Applicable or Missing Information							(158)	(99)

apartments believe that their neighbors are similar in possessing only high school or vocational training, with the downtown-house group least similar in this regard and the other two categories again in between.

When respondents see neighbors as having educational levels dissimilar to themselves, those downtown are more likely than not to feel superior, while those in suburbia, particularly in suburban houses, are more likely to feel inferior (an aspect of status climbing expected by some of them before they move).

It is interesting to note that respondents answered these questions more easily in Phase III than in Phase II, just following the move. Wives in suburban houses and husbands in suburban houses and apartments had particularly high 'don't know' rates at that point.

We also asked about interest similarity between respondents and their neighbors. There was little difference in this regard among the categories of residential environment; over 50 percent in every category said that some or most of their neighbors shared their interests. The *nature* of interests differentiates the settings, however. Only 5 percent of downtown apartment families mentioned 'family' as a shared interest, in contrast to about 30 percent among all the other categories of respondents. Only the downtown-house families stress an interest in civic activities, while only those in suburban houses stress working on their home. Men in the downtown houses are unique in their stress on work, while the wives in downtown apartments lead the other categories of wives in expressing a shared interest in work. Both husbands and wives who moved to apartments cite an interest in active leisure, while husbands and wives in the downtown apartments share a high interest in social life. Therefore, the basis of interaction among neighbors is quite different from setting to setting.

Respondents were aware of most of these interests already in Phase II. Moreover, the emphasis on social life by those in downtown apartments was very much more intense immediately following the move (mentioned by about 20% more at that time than in Phase III). Social life was also a strong, immediate postmove emphasis among the wives in downtown houses, but it was reduced in Phase III to only a relatively low level.

On what people know about the personal characteristics of their neighbors, the husbands' patterns diverge from those of their wives. Women who moved to houses typically assign more traits to their neighbors than do those who moved to apartments. About 85 percent of those in suburban houses and 72 percent in downtown houses cite at least six of the traits on our list as applicable to their neighbors, compared to only about 65 percent of those moving to apartments. In contrast, it is only the husbands in suburban houses who stand out as knowledgeable of neighbors; 77 percent of them choose 6 or more traits, as compared to just over 50 percent among all the other categories. While the wife's pattern of knowledge about neighbors was already established in Phase II, the husbands in suburban houses gained their more lucid impressions later in the first year of residence.

We found no differences in ability to identify traits of neighbors by people in new suburban areas as compared to older suburban areas.

Both housing type and location are related to the extent that respondents feel themselves personally similar to their neighbors. Residents of single-family houses and suburban locations perceive the greatest personal homogeneity. Thus, both husbands and wives in the suburban houses are highest in perceived personal homogeneity; over 50 percent of them feel similar to their neighbors on six or more of the traits. In contrast, only about 20 percent of those in the downtown apartments report the same degree of similarity, while those in downtown houses and suburban apartments are between the two extremes. The feeling of homogeneity among those in the suburban houses was again something that developed only *after* Phase II.

In any case, the respondents foresaw the relation of personal homogeneity to housing type while the literature stressed its relationship to location.

Nonetheless, we might explain such differences in perception with reference to the *number* of neighbors known by respondents. More apartment families, for example, know none of their neighbors at all (roughly a quarter of the respondents), while, on the other hand, those in houses (particularly the wives) know a greater number of families. While differences according to location are not noteworthy among those living in houses, the families in downtown apartments are much less likely to know their neighbors than those in suburban apartments, no doubt reflecting the lower incidence of mobile children among the former. Although apartment dwellers are more likely than those living in houses to be friendly with unmarried individuals within their neighborhoods, this does not sufficiently change the overall pattern of their knowing fewer of their neighbors.

Children do not follow the same pattern as their parents. Children living in suburban apartments are more likely to know large numbers of other children in the immediate neighborhood than do those living in suburban houses. Suburban apartments may well provide more opportunity to do so. Close to 40 percent of the children living in suburban apartments know twenty or more neighboring children, compared to slightly less than 20 percent of those in suburban houses.

What about the particular content of the traits which respondents say they share with neighbors? There is no overlap among the emphases shared by residents of downtown apartments and those shared by families living in downtown houses. The former characterize themselves as both lively and withdrawn, as well as fashionable. They are particularly unlikely, relative to the others, to see themselves as child-oriented, proud of property appearance, doing things as a family, or neat. In contrast, husbands in the downtown house characterize themselves and their neighbors as wrapped up in work, while their spouses agree that they and their neighbors are ready to help, serious, efficient, and cultured, though not necessarily modern.

Suburbanites more frequently view themselves and their neighbors as easy going. Beyond that, however, residents in suburban apartments simply do not assert the existence of unique types of personal similarity.

In contrast, both wives and husbands in suburban houses modestly observe similarities described as ready to help and efficient (like the downtown homeowners) but also friendly, flexible, proud of property appearance, doing things as a family, and neat. Only the wives see themselves as fashionable, while their husbands see themselves as lively, wrapped up in work, and handy.[1]

This assessment of the personal characteristics of self and neighbors shows considerable differentiation among the characteristics assigned to each of the combinations of housing type and location, with few spread broadly over either housing type or location without further specification. Those in suburban houses find great amounts of similarity with their neighbors on positive traits. Those in downtown houses find fewer, but very positive points of similarity. Those in downtown apartments are much more negative than many of the others, while those in suburban apartments have few unique sources of similarity.

To sum up this section, a reasonably cogent picture of socioeconomic similarity among neighbors emerges, which is related partly to housing type and partly to location. Although knowledge of neighbors varies by housing type and, in some cases, by the interaction of housing type and location, perceived personal homogeneity varies by housing type and location in combination. What emerges is a picture of relatively homogeneous groups of neighbors in terms of socioeconomic status, with considerable differences in the kind and amount of personal homogeneity serving to contrast homeowners to apartment dwellers. In most respects, this pattern is consistent with expectations, although the extent of differentiation is greater than expected.

Interpersonal Relations

We can view interpersonal relations in a number of ways. Let us turn first to an examination of the three people with whom the respondent feels closest, on the one hand within his or her neighborhood and on the other hand outside the neighborhood.

With respect to extra-neighborhood friends, there are very few differences by housing type or location. Differences, for example, in the frequency with which people see friends are tiny, although both husbands and wives living in downtown apartments see them the most frequently. Also, where they get together varies minimally, scarcely supporting assertions that apartment dwellers do not entertain at home. Slightly more than 70 percent of all such get-togethers involving wives occur at home, regardless of housing type or location, as do about two-thirds of those involving husbands.

Both husbands and wives label close to three-quarters of the persons named as 'friends,' rather than relatives, again with only minimal variation. Suburban women include about 10 percent more relatives among their close contacts than do downtown women, with a corresponding difference among their husbands of approximately 5 percent.

Both men and women living in downtown apartments are somewhat more likely to have met their friends at work, but otherwise there are no differences on how extra-neighborhood friends were met. Surprisingly few of those friends used to be neighbors, ranging from 6 percent among those in suburban houses up to 11 percent among those in downtown houses; this underlines the earlier finding that some people see neighbors frequently, but relatively few form very personal relationships with them (cf. Keller, 1968).

Turning to close contacts *within* the respondents' local neighborhoods, we see that the new differences in frequency of contact run 'in favor of' apartments, not, as expected, houses. Women in suburban apartments see 38.7 percent of their local friends several times a week or more, compared to 30 percent in the suburban-home category and to under 25 percent in both of the downtown categories. The same modest downtown-suburban difference is found with respect to husbands, with only a slight difference separating the types of people living in suburban housing.

Apartment dwellers visit with their local friends most at home, but this is clouded somewhat by husband/wife differences. For example, although the wives in suburban apartments see 64 percent of their local contacts at home, those in downtown apartments resemble those in both downtown and suburban homes at around 56 percent. Husbands, both downtown and suburban, who live in apartments see about 58 percent of their local friends at home, compared to slightly under 50 percent of the homeowners, with minimal locational effects. This house-apartment difference, however, appears to be part of a trade-off between seeing friends at home and seeing them casually around in the neighborhood; the latter occurs more frequently among homeowners, particularly suburban homeowners, amid more ample spatial opportunities for casual contact.

These small differences are logical and tied to spatial opportunity. But one thing they do not show is a structured *inability* of apartment dwellers to meet other people. The participant-observation conducted as part of this study brought out strong norms in the high-rise building against casual contact in the public spaces in and around the building, with a strict taboo preventing a tenant from leaving his or her door open to connect the outside world to the inside world of the dwelling unit. Nonetheless, when acquaintance has been made, the apartment unit itself apparently does not serve as a barrier to entertaining, despite assertions that its relatively smaller size may be restrictive.

As might be expected, the *paths* to local friendship differ strongly between those living in apartments and those living in houses. Suburban housewives made three quarters of their local contacts through their children or casually within their current neighborhood, compared to 52 percent by those in downtown houses and around 40 percent by those in the apartments. In contrast, those living in the apartments found their friends more frequently in so-called 'communities of interest,' school, work, and mutual friends. That *both* husbands and wives in downtown apartments are particularly high in this latter regard indicates the role that the absence of children plays in friendship formation.

The single person other than spouse seen most frequently is not normally a neighbor; only about 20 to 25 percent of the residents in the various settings name neighbors. Nonetheless, such citation is almost double in Phase III what it was in Phase II, showing an increase in contact with neighbors over time. Residents of newly built suburbs list neighbors more frequently than do those in existing suburbs, but the difference of only about 2 percent is hardly dramatic. Friends and relatives constitute the bulk of frequent contacts, again without differences by environment.

Even fewer cite neighbors as the most personal contact they have, although, ironically, those in downtown apartments claim this most frequently (but only 10% of the wives and 7% of the husbands). Otherwise, residents of downtown houses feel closest to nonrelatives, while all categories show the reverse.

The nondifferences are of most significance for this analysis of interaction with neighbors.

We also investigated the mutual-aid practices of our respondents. We were concerned with the extent that people drew upon neighbors in a variety of problematic situations. Very few in any residential category say they would turn to a neighbor for advice about taking a job; they clearly favor friends, relatives, and professionals for such advice. A minority feel that they *could* expect this from a neighbor: 30 percent of suburbanites compared to about 20 percent of those living downtown.

About 10 percent more of the wives in suburban homes (40% of them) than in any other form of housing say that they would turn to a neighbor to borrow a small amount of cash when the banks are closed. This does not, however, reflect potential ability to do so, as about 60 percent of those in every category except the downtown apartment feel they *could* turn to neighbors, with 60 percent in downtown high-rise feeling *unable* to do so. Among husbands, ability to borrow from neighbors is equated to home ownership (believed by 65% of the homeowners versus 45% of the apartment dwellers). Surprisingly, then, those living in high-rise apartments downtown are slightly more likely than the others to *actually* do so, perhaps a function of their actual financial condition.

With respect to just 'shooting the breeze' with neighbors, suburban residents lead the way. Consistent with their characterization of neighbors as easy going and familiar more than half the suburbanites turned to their neighbors for amiable chatter, compared to about 40 percent of those living downtown. Among the wives, housing type is also a differentiating factor, with those living in houses coming together with their neighbors more frequently. For the wives, then, conversation with neighbors is highest among those in suburban homes and least in the downtown apartment, with the other two settings in between. Suburban husbands and wives (upward of 70% of them) expect that they *can* turn to their neighbors for small talk, as compared to those downtown (closer to 45%).

About 90 percent of husbands and wives in suburban houses agree that they would call on neighbors to borrow a food staple or tool. About half or more in the other categories feel the same way, but no other category approaches the suburban house. While those in downtown houses are next most likely to feel this way, their strength of feeling resembles that of the apartment dwellers more than the extreme of those in the suburban houses. It is not surprising that a similar proportion and distribution feel they can expect this in turn from their neighbors.

We asked women with children who would take care of the children in the event of varying lengths of maternal illness. About 10 percent more suburbanites than downtown residents would call on neighbors during illness, except the most extreme length of illness, three months, in which case virtually no neighbors were considered. Within categories of location, differences in housing type were minimal.

Thus, the extent that people feel they can and do turn to neighbors varies according to the type of aid involved. Suburbanites rate higher when it comes to sociability and child care. Housing-type differences are also of relevance when something in the form of a tangible object, like money, food, or tools, is involved.

Many think mutual aid varies according to whether a suburb is old or new, due to the need for mutual assistance in 'frontier' territory. Investigation of four forms of mutual aid for the wives and three for the husbands (discounting advice about jobs) indicates that in only one case does the suspected form follow. A higher percentage of people in the new suburban houses turn to their neighbors than do those in resale suburban houses only in the case of the wives borrowing food. In every other case, those in the more settled neighborhoods turn to neighbors more frequently than do their counterparts in new homes.

The above differences are extremely minor. Nonetheless, such findings continue to disprove the theory that suburban life takes the form it does simply because it is new.

The time budget provides a complementary perspective on interpersonal relations. Instead of a focus on particular types of friends or activities, it takes the day as its focus, assessing intergroup differences with respect to what happens during that particular time period.

Thirty-seven percent of those living in houses, compared to about 29 percent of those living in apartments, had formal visits with other people on the weekday in question. This constitutes an average of about 40 minutes during the day for the former, as compared to about 30 minutes for the latter. The average time reflects, however, the different degree of participation, because the average time devoted *just by those who did participate* was approximately the same in all groups. Counterbalancing these home visits, is the preponderence of people in downtown high-rise settings who visited with others in eating or drinking establishments. Since suburban apartment residents are less than a third as likely to do this, this last group comes forward as the lowest in formal visiting with other persons.

Contact with friends and neighbors need not be formal. When we assessed the extent that daily activities with a minimum time of 15 minutes involved friends or neighbors, we discovered that there are virtually no differences in the percentage of contact with these people by the wives in the various settings. Between 40 and 49 percent in all residential settings see friends or neighbors during the given weekday. Nonetheless, the wives in suburban houses spend more time with these people, devoting about three hours a day to such company. This is about three quarters of an hour more than the others spend. Ironically, the very same subgroup, women in suburban houses, spends the most time alone as well.

The Sunday pattern helps to underscore the findings of the preceding chapter on the strong influence of work and family status on interpersonal relationships. As before, Sunday patterns dispel generalizations from the daily data. For example, wives do not vary by home environment in the number of formal visits at home on Sundays or the time they devote to them. Although wives in downtown apartments are still somewhat more likely to meet with other people in restaurants on Sundays, the actual difference of 12 percent to 8 percent is minimal. And, with respect to all activities spent with friends or neighbors, it is the downtown high-rise group which engages in these activities more on Sundays, although not to any great extent.

That housing type or location alone plays a major part in the incidence of interpersonal contact is further dispelled by the data on husbands. While husbands visit formally with other people very seldom during the weekday (only about 12% of them do so), with only insignificant variations by residential setting, they spend much more time with other persons over meals or drinks on commercial premises. Homeowners eat out with others almost twice as frequently as renters. Job seniority and affluence are more plausible explanations, though, than housing tenure!

The husbands' pattern differs once again on Sundays, when suburbanites, regardless of housing type, visit more frequently, and downtown residents meet others in restaurants more frequently. Like their wives, men in downtown apartments see friends and neighbors most on Sunday, but again without the existence of any particular relationship to housing type or location.[2]

A comparison of children living in suburban apartments and suburban houses indicates no differences in Phase III with regard to visiting or daily contact with friends and neighbors, although reference to Phase II data shows that the children in the apartments may have started visiting somewhat sooner. Sundays show no greater differences.

In sum, the general observation which must follow, not just from the time-budget information but from that on close contacts and mutual aid, is the absence of a general deficit of personal contact among those living in high-rise apartments. Such differences as occur in how people meet their friends, in mutual aid, and in the type and occurrence of daily and Sunday contact are explained not by a single factor, but by a series of factors including work status, family size, the relative affluence of homeowners, and the social image of the suburbs. There are no singularly advantaged or disadvantaged groups.

Organizational Activity

While the last chapter showed prospective homeowners as greater participants in formal organizations before the move, the literature suggests that suburbanites are likely to join new organizations in their destination environments.

Although close to 50 percent of the wives and husbands did join new organizations, there is no noticeable difference in this regard by housing type or location. Such differences as occurred have to do with the *type* of organization joined. Those purchasing houses typically join civic organizations, such as ratepayers' groups.[3] About one in five, both downtown and in the suburbs, joined civic organizations.

There are no significant differences by housing type regarding new memberships in social and recreational organizations (which account for about three-quarters of all new memberships). It is easy to understand why apartment dwellers join this kind of organization in great numbers; most large complexes have recreation clubs which organize the use of on-site facilities. That this may underlie the equality of *new* memberships among the apartment dwellers, in contrast to their deficit in total memberships, is indicated by another finding. About 65 percent of the organizations which wives in apartments joined lie within the same square mile radius as their homes, compared to only 30 percent among those wives living in houses. The same distinction holds for the husbands, only not as sharply.

Homeowners go to church far more than do apartment dwellers, *although a majority of the entire sample attends no church at all.* About half the house-dwellers attend church, however, compared to 30 percent of those in suburban apartments and 24 percent of those in downtown apartments. Homeowners also attend more *frequently*, about 30 percent of them attending at least several times a month.

The time-budget data on church attendance on Sunday support the conclusions drawn from the direct questions on church attendance.

The differences in participation in religious practice by children living in suburban houses and apartments shows that the breakdowns of housing type do not merely mask differences in life-cycle stage, as had been suggested by baseline data. Only about 10 percent of the latter went to church on the given Sunday, as compared to 33 percent of the former—both figures representing trends clearly in effect already in Phase II.

Church participation, however, should not necessarily be viewed as an aspect of participation in the organizational life of the *local* neighborhood. The majority of churchgoers travel at least outside their own immediate dwelling area, 87 percent of them driving to church. Some suburbanites travel particularly long distances to churches that previously commanded their loyalty in other parts of the city.

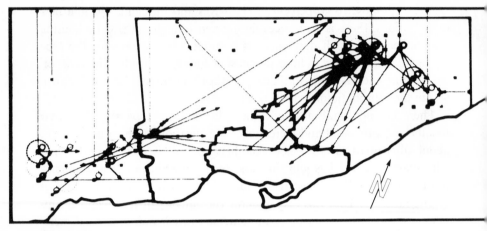

GOING TO CHURCH. Relation of home to place of worship, among suburbanites.

■ Home
/ Where they go,
  if more than 1 mile

○ Within a few blocks
⊙ Within same square mile

Figure 6.1, for example, indicates the central direction and distance
which many suburbanites travel when going to church. Lines on the map
connect the square-mile area in which families live with those where they
go to church. The larger circle denotes that a family worships farther
than a few blocks of home but within the same square-mile grid. An
asterisk denotes that a family goes to church within a few blocks of home.
(This map and others like it were computed on a Cal-Comp machine
adapted so that the information to be put on every map was emitted in
the form of light onto photographic film. Hence, the more people who
go to or from a particular place or who take the same path, the darker
will be the information on the map.)

Churchgoing is but one *extra*-neighborhood orientation for services and
recreation on the part of suburbanites. I shall describe others subsequently.

Commuting

It was clear in the last chapter that the move to downtown, particularly by those moving to downtown apartments, involved lessening uncharacteristically long distances to work on the part of the wives. While the husbands moving to downtown apartments were not all that disadvantaged in terms of distance,[4] that they and their wives used public transit more frequently than those in other settings had the practical result of longer travel times.

Following the move, the working wives in downtown apartments continued to take public transportation (almost 60% of them) or to walk (another 12%) more than the working wives in any other group. The wives in downtown houses, as well as the husbands living in both types of downtown housing, split about 50-50 between public and private forms of transportation to work. In contrast, close to 90 percent of the husbands and wives in suburban houses drove their own automobiles to work, while 65 percent of the wives in suburban apartments drove either in their own car or in a car pool, leaving slightly over 30 percent either on public transportation or on foot.

Among the wives the combination of different distances to cover by different means of transportation results in commuting times which are roughly similar. Both the mean and the range of travel times are approximately the same immediately following the move.

Among the husbands, those who moved to the downtown zones do not have uniquely short commutes. Somewhat over 50 percent of men in downtown apartments and houses alike say they commute less than thirty minutes each way, as do an equal percentage of those living in suburban apartments. Only about 35 percent of men in suburban houses have this short a commute; more than a quarter travel over 45 minutes each way.

In short, while the change of residence results in the elimination of greater than average discrepancies in travel time and, for the wives, distance, such a move did not create a situation of net overall advantage in travel time to those previously disadvantaged. Mode of transportation is a critical factor in this regard.

The information on travel to work reported within the context of the time budget contains typically higher commuting times than does information given in response to the direct questions, indicating a tendency to underestimate in answer to the latter type of question. Nonetheless, the time budgets do not indicate alternative patterns.

Accompanying such important aspects of the work trip as distance, mode of travel, and time, is directionality. Figures 6.2 through 6.5 show that those husbands and wives living downtown focus much more on one zone, namely *downtown*, with respect to their places of work, while those living in the suburbs are very much more diffused. Some of the latter work downtown, while others work in a variety of locations in and around the city. Husbands' workplaces are somewhat more scattered and distant than those of the wife.

Commercial Activity

Now that the families studied have moved to their new housing types and locations, we may analyze several dimensions of commercial activity. We may look at the frequency with which the respondents participate in each of the types of commercial activities studied. We can look also at the distance, mode of transport, directionality, and selectivity characteristic of these respondents' commercial activity.

First, let us look at frequency. There are no appreciable differences in the frequency that people in different residential settings shop for groceries and sundries, everyday necessities for which most people do shop often. On the other hand, there are some differences with respect to more specialized goods and services, reflecting both personal priorities and differences in daily routines.

Suburbanites appear to be more active than downtown residents, for example, in shopping for *clothing*. About 40 percent of the suburban women shop for clothing once a month or more, compared to about 25 percent of those living downtown.

In contrast, women in downtown apartments eat out more frequently than the others. Forty-four percent go to restaurants more than once a month compared to less than 30 percent of the women in any other category.[5]

Those living downtown attend public entertainment more frequently; about 10 percent more of them go out more than once a month than

FIGURE 6.2.
WORK TRIPS. Relation of home to workplace, among suburban wives.

■ Home   ⊙■ Within a few blocks

╱ Where they go,   ⦂⸽⸽⦂ Within same square mile
   if more than 1 mile

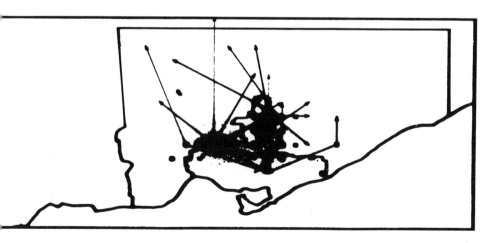

FIGURE 6.3.
WORK TRIPS. Relation of home to workplace, among downtown wives.

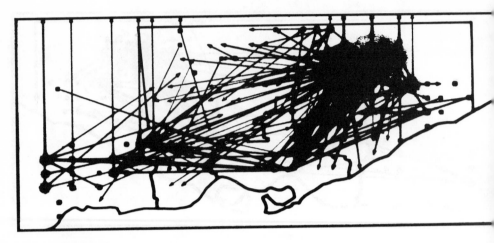

FIGURE 6.4.
WORK TRIPS. Relation of home to workplace, among suburban husbands.

■ Home   ⌐■ Within a few blocks

╱ Where they go,   (·⁚) Within same square mile
╱ if more than 1 mile

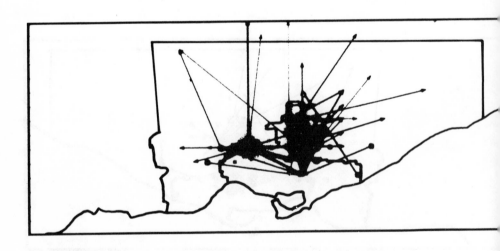

FIGURE 6.5.
WORK TRIPS. Relation of home to workplace, among downtown husbands.

among the suburbanites (25% to 14%). This leading figure of 25 percent, however, is considerably down from the percentage of frequent attendants registered in Phase II, right after the move; at that time more than 40 percent of the downtown apartment group and about 30 percent of those in downtown houses said that they went out to public entertainment more than once a month. This change downward is consistent with other instances in which those moving downtown, especially to apartments, participated in one or another of the major attractions of their new housing shortly after moving, with reductions in the level of activity thereafter.

Compared to these relatively mild differences in frequency, certain differences in *access* appear quite striking. Those living in suburban homes travel significantly farther on everyday commercial trips than families in all the other categories of residential environment. For example, about 50 percent of the residents of downtown apartments and houses, as well as suburban apartments, live within a mile of where they buy food. Only 20 percent of those in suburban houses live within a mile. More than a third of the latter live more than 3 miles from where they buy their groceries, compared to less than half that percentage among the others.

Seventy percent of the apartment dwellers find sundries within a mile, as do 50 percent of those living within downtown houses. Only 30 percent of those in suburban houses buy sundry items in the immediate neighborhood around their homes.

The same is true for clothes. Just under 5 percent of those in suburban homes manage to shop for clothes within 2 miles of home, although from 18 to 30 percent of the others do so. More than 50 percent of the former travel more than 7 miles to shop for clothes, anywhere from two to six times the percentage of families in the other categories traveling that far.

Are suburban homeowners farther from everything else or are they simply more selective as to where they go? We can observe selectivity indirectly by looking at whether the stores respondents patronized for these particular goods are the closest ones available. The suburban homeowners are no more selective than the suburban apartment dwellers about groceries and sundries, but they are slightly more so about clothes shopping. Of the various stores patronized by the suburban homeowners, 65.5 percent of the clothes stores were not the closest to home, as compared to 51.2 percent for those living in suburban apartments. Thus both groups demonstrate some selectivity, not merely one or the other.

FIGURE 6.6.
MIXED LAND USE IN SUBURBIA. Suburban apartment dwellers with everyday shopping goods mixed into their local neighborhoods are more likely to use local facilities and go places on foot than are residents of suburban homes whose neighborhood settings are more segregated this way. (*Photo by the author*)

Residents of suburban houses travel almost exclusively by automobile. They travel by car to 93 percent of the grocery stores cited, to 86 percent of the stores which sell sundries, and to 91 percent of their clothing stores. The use of the automobile in this respect is like chicken and egg. Where people's homes are remote from commercial land uses because of zoning practices, they may feel that the car is necessary; yet, once in the car, people have the freedom to travel further and to be more selective about the establishment patronized. This would suggest that attraction is more important than proximity, within certain bounds, in explaining many suburban commercial shopping patterns. The presence of so many attractive shopping centers throughout Toronto suburbs may attest to this.

The suburban apartment group provides an interesting example. Many projects have commercial facilities within them or nearby. Fewer families drive for everyday purchases than among those living in nearby but less well-integrated houses. For example, 38 percent walk to buy groceries (as do 41 percent of those in downtown apartments). Both reach about two-thirds of their destinations for sundries on foot. Those in suburban apartments walk to 20 percent of the places where they shop for clothes, compared to only 3 percent of their counterparts in suburban houses and 17 percent of those in downtown apartments. Although the majority of shopping trips for groceries and clothing among people in suburban apartments is still by car, these data nonetheless indicate that if stores exist within walking distance, people will convert the opportunity to deal locally into some degree of local shopping, with some resistance to temptations to travel further and further afield.

Those living in downtown apartments are equally as proximate to everyday shopping goods as people in suburban apartments. Those in downtown houses are generally not so close. Hence, while the latter may walk for something like sundries (37.4%), three quarters of them still drive for groceries.

Clothing shopping illustrates a difference in the downtown situation, as compared to suburbia. Residents of downtown take public transportation on about 30 percent of all trips to shop for clothing, reducing automobile travel without affecting patterns of walking to immediately proximate locations. When people *can* walk, they often *do*. Public transportation, when available in a well-developed form, is a direct substitute for automobile travel to some destinations, such as clothing stores and workplaces.

Families living in suburban houses also participate more in mail or telephone-order commerce. More than 75 percent of them order things from catalogues for home delivery, 10 percent more than do people in downtown houses and 20 to 25 percent more than those in suburban and downtown apartments, respectively.

Among those who order, the people in suburban houses do so more frequently—36 percent of them ordering more than once a month. In contrast, those living in downtown houses are more likely to know the personnel in the places where they shop.

If we turn our attention to places of recreation, we see that those in the suburbs travel further. While roughly three quarters of the restaurants and places of entertainment patronized by downtown residents are *within* five miles of home, approximately the same proportion is *more than* five miles away from those living in the suburbs.

There are only minimal differences in the mode of transportation used for these activities, since they are more likely to occur in the evening, when more personal forms of transportation are seen as desirable. Hence, despite proximity, the majority of downtown residents drive when they go out for meals or entertainment. About 75 percent of them drive to restaurants, with most of the remainder taking public transit or walking. With respect to entertainment, 61 percent of those in downtown apartments drive; 26 percent go there by public transit, while some walk. Eighty percent of those in downtown houses drive to places of entertainment, with the remainder divided equally between public transit and their own legs. Nearly *all* suburbanites drive when going out in the evening.

Figures 6.7 and 6.8, for restaurants, and 6.9 and 6.10, for public enter-

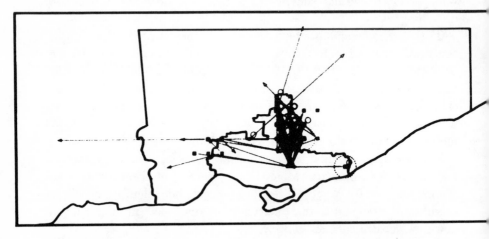

FIGURE 6.7.
RESTAURANT TRIPS. Relation of home to restaurants patronized, among families in downtown houses.

■ Home

/ Where they go, if more than 1 mile

Within a few blocks

Within same square mile

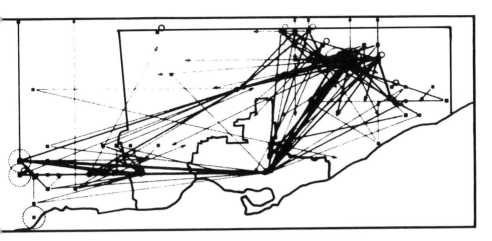

FIGURE 6.8.

RESTAURANT TRIPS. Relation of home to restaurants patronized, among families in suburban houses.

■ Home

/ Where they go,
  if more than 1 mile

Within a few blocks

Within same square mile

tainment, indicate the tremendous continuing attraction of the downtown for residents of both suburbia and downtown. These maps compare only residents of houses in the two locations, to keep family and wife's work status roughly equal. While the resident of downtown finds it an attraction, uses it, and bears whatever nuisance value may be attached to it, the downtown area is surely not his exclusive domain. He does not use the more modest suburban attractions reciprocally, though.

The time budget data cited on interpersonal relations are also relevant here. The habits of downtown residents in meeting friends in commercial eating and drinking spots support the data in the present section.

In sum, then, there are different explanations of shopping and entertainment patterns. Regardless of the explanation, however, those in suburban houses travel farther than the others. With shopping, length and mode of

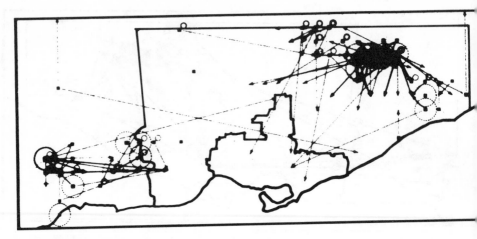

FIGURE 6.9.
AMUSEMENT TRIPS. Relation of home to places of public entertainment patronized, among families in suburban houses.

■ Home

/ Where they go,
  if more than 1 mile

Within a few blocks

Within same square mile

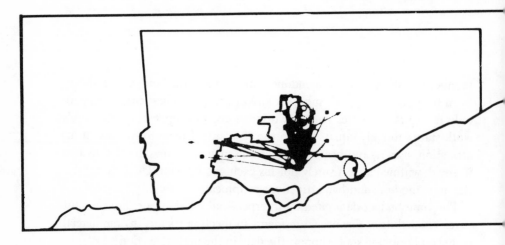

FIGURE 6.10.
AMUSEMENT TRIPS. Relation of home to places of public entertainment patronized, among families in downtown houses.

travel are a function of land use integration and the degree of availability of mass transit. With entertainment, the explanation lies in the distribution of the places to which people wish to go.

Pastimes

I have already touched upon those aspects of recreation that involve large-scale commercial facilities and membership in organizations. Let us now examine participation in a variety of recreational activities.

It would be surprising if those living in houses did *not* participate more actively in gardening than those in apartments. As expected, the overwhelming majority of both husbands and wives living in houses say that they participate in gardening. Furthermore, a high percentage of those who participate say that this pastime is of considerable importance to them. Attribution of importance to gardening by husbands is twice as frequent (71% versus 35%) in the suburbs as downtown.

It is also not surprising that those who move downtown go to theaters to a greater degree. Approximately 65 percent of those husbands and wives who moved to either housing type in the downtown area go out to theaters, as compared to only about 40 percent among those living in the suburbs. We must note once again that the downtown apartment dwellers started reaching their level of participation at the beginning of Phase II, while those in the downtown houses only resumed their previously high participation as the year went on.

Those who move to downtown houses are the *least* likely to watch television, as expected from their previous habits. Almost 40 percent of the wives and 27 percent of the husbands claim not to watch television in downtown houses, compared to only about 15 percent of husbands and wives in the other categories. Few, however, feel television watching is something important.

There are few differences concerning sports participation by home environment in Phase III. About 40 percent of the wives and husbands in all categories claim to participate. Nonetheless, our examination of Phase II data shows considerably greater differences in favor of high-rise residents. At that time, roughly 50 percent of them participated in sports activities, compared to about 35 percent of the wives and about 40 percent of the husbands living in houses. Hence, we have another instance of short-range differences dissipating over time.

There are several unexpected pastime differences to note. Suburbanites are much more likely to play cards than are people living downtown (who presumably are out on the town more). Well over 50 percent of suburbanites claim they participate in this activity, compared with only 35 to 40 percent of downtown residents.

Both husbands and wives in the downtown apartments are more likely to have photography as a pastime than those in any other category. Half the husbands and 32 percent of the wives say they pursue photography, as compared to an average of 35 percent and 22 percent, respectively, in the other categories. Photography is an engrossing hobby easily pursued in the downtown high-rise.

Finally, men living in apartments claim that they are interested in stereo more than do their counterparts living in houses. Almost three-quarters of the former claim such an interest, as compared to only 56 percent of the latter. While this is a refinement of the television watching, beer drinking stereotype, it may be part of the same syndrome suggested by the literature.

No patterns worth mentioning were found with respect to the following pastimes: church-affiliated activities, youth work, mechanical-electrical work, reading, sewing, observing sports, extension courses, playing musical instruments, and collections, as these pastimes are either so universal or so rarified that differences according to home setting are not meaningful.

Data from children complement those from their parents. A quarter of the children in the suburban high-rise, for example, cite photography as a hobby, compared to only 10 percent of those in suburban houses. More in the high-rise (67%) listen to stereo than in houses (58%). More in the apartment watch television and think it is important than in the house, although the differences are very minor (about 6%). Those in houses participate more in arts and crafts (27% to 15%) and in collections (33% to 20%), probably reflecting greater amounts of space at home.

On the other hand, 35 percent of those in the suburban high-rise belong to youth organizations, compared to 12 percent living in suburban houses. This is not the same pattern shown by their parents. But it reflects differing opportunities in their immediate milieu, a scale of environment of greater relative importance to children.[6]

One might argue that these various differences reflect to some extent, the older average age of children in the high-rise. Nonetheless, all the findings persist when broken down by age.

Time-budget data on recreational activities support very strongly the conclusions drawn from direct reports. With respect to participation in sports, for example, time-budget data indicate no differences according to housing type and location in either participation or amount of time devoted in Phase III; these data show a clear pattern, however, in Phase II. At that time, residents of a high-rise were about 75 percent more likely to participate in active sports on Sunday than were those in houses, with lesser differences in the same direction on weekdays.

Thirty-four percent of the wives and 40 percent of the husbands in downtown houses watched television on the weekday surveyed, as compared to about 60 percent of persons in the other housing types and locations. On Sundays, slightly more people watch television, but the difference between those in downtown houses and all the others remains the same. Incidentally, children in downtown houses appear to follow the same pattern of television viewing as their parents.

Women living in houses are much more likely to pursue other forms of passive leisure, such as reading magazines and newspapers and holding casual conversations on weekdays, as well as to spend more time while doing so, than their counterparts living in apartments. This distinction in time use continues even after working status is held constant. Nonetheless, these latter types of passive leisure do not vary by housing type on weekends or with respect to male participation.

One can view the relationship of spatial opportunity to participation by analyzing the location of sports activities. For example, 71 and 73 percent of women in downtown and suburban apartments, respectively, play their sports within the same square-mile grid in which they live (presumably taking advantage of opportunities on site), compared to only 40 and 26 percent of those in similarly located houses.

In this section I have shown the development of certain pastimes in environmental contexts that provide appropriate opportunity for them to occur. The greater *immediacy* of adoption of some of the expected pastimes among those who moved to downtown high-rise apartments, with subsequent lessening of emphasis later on, deserves special attention. So does the situation of those moving to houses, who took longer to commence even that which they expected. I shall return to this difference later in the book.

Housekeeping Activity

Household activity does not differ with respect to home environment in any uniform way. Different activities are relatively more and less frequent in the different types of housing and location.

All but those in the downtown high-rise category emphasize food prep-aration, for example. Over 90 percent of the wives in downtown houses and suburban apartments and homes prepare food sometime during the weekday, compared to 76 percent of those in downtown apartments. The former spend more time on it, from 71 to 87 minutes when they do it, while the average amount of time those in downtown apartments spend on food preparation is only 60 minutes.

Indoor cleaning follows the same pattern. Only 46 percent of the women in downtown apartments do this on the weekday of the time budget, compared to 66 percent of the women in downtown houses and suburban apartments and 74 percent of those in suburban houses. Simi-larly, even when they do some indoor cleaning, the women in downtown apartments spent an average of 58 minutes on that job, compared to over 80 minutes in each of the other categories.[7]

On the other hand, washing dishes is a household activity whose per-formance on the day in question differs according to *location*. The subur-banites are more likely, by about 20 percent, to have washed dishes than the downtown women (about 75% to about 55%). Nonetheless, when the job is done, it requires approximately an equal amount of time.

Still a different pattern is represented by laundering and ironing, which only about 25 percent of apartment dwellers do on the weekday in ques-tion, compared to close to 45 percent of the residents of houses. In this case, however, the percentage of participation bears no resemblance to the amount of time spent in the process, which follows no pattern whatever.

Time devoted to food preparation, indoor cleaning, dishwashing, laun-dering, and ironing on weekends does not vary to any noteworthy degree by housing type or location.

Whether the weekday variations are by housing type, location, or both of them, participation of those in downtown apartments is always lowest. One, therefore, suspects that again the wife's work status accounts for different uses of time.

When we control each figure on participation by working status, we see that, within any housing type, the working wives do the household activity less on the given day than do the nonworking wives. Given that there is a higher percentage of working wives in the downtown apartments, this would tend to depress the figures in that category.

Nonetheless, when the working wives and the nonworking wives are taken separately and their participation compared by category of environment, the very same pattern emerges. For both working and nonworking wives, those in downtown high-rise apartments are least likely to prepare food on the day in question or to do indoor cleaning. Those in apartments are less likely to do the laundry. Those downtown are less likely to wash dishes.

In short, the environmental context and the working status of the wife appear to have independent effects on the performance of these various household activities.

Furthermore, the presence of children continues to act independently of working status and home environment in its effect on housekeeping activity.

Although husbands are more likely to take on tasks such as food preparation and dishwashing if a wife works, the same general level of 'nonperformance' is maintained in the various home settings within the ranks of men whose wives do not work, and a similar but slightly more active nonpattern exists among the men whose wives do work. On Sundays, there is a distinct pattern with respect to cooking; only men in suburban homes do it. Our time budgets may have picked up backyard barbeques, although the codes are not that specific.

The literature makes one suspect that men in houses spend more time on repairs and construction than do men living in apartments. This is confirmed. The daily rates of 13 percent participation in houses as against about 5 percent in apartments are clearly in the expected direction, although hardly staggering. As might be assumed, the weekend pattern is stronger, showing about 29 percent of the men in the downtown houses (almost always older houses) and 19 percent of them in suburban houses engaging in such work on the given Sunday, as compared to only about

6 percent of the men in apartments. In Phase II, twice as many husbands in downtown houses had reported doing repair work as in Phase III, and they were also spending more time at it. This reflects not just the task of living in a house, but that of taking over an older house.

THE EMERGING PATTERN IN
THE NEW ENVIRONMENT

As in the previous chapter, the preceding discussion has focused on the different substantive areas where we thought the implications of housing type and location were to be found. To view the different implications of the dimensions of housing type and location under study, it is necessary to regroup the various findings accordingly.

Single-Family Homes

The percentage of wives living in single-family houses who work, although low, is increasing. These women have children of all ages. Their neighbors are largely middle and upper-middle class, as well as highly educated. Families living in houses feel they know personal characteristics of their neighbors better than do those living in apartments; the former feel very similar to their neighbors. They are acquainted with more of their neighbors, and they extend mutual aid in very tangible forms. They are church-goers, join civic groups, and social-recreational organizations, although the latter are not necessarily locally based. They tend to see their friends casually around the neighborhood more frequently. When they need everyday shopping goods, they almost certainly drive for them. They participate actively in gardening and in repair work, and they spend more time reading periodicals and holding conversations.

High-Rise Apartments

The families studied are likely to have young babies. The salaries of the husbands tend to be lower, as are the educational levels of the neighbors, who are designated as middle and working class. The apartment residents feel they share an interest with their neighbors in active leisure, and the children know many other children within the project. Apartment dwellers visit with their local friends more within their dwelling than out in the neighborhood, but they do not suffer a lack of contact with other people. They are likely to join local, on-site recreation organizations. They participate unusually actively in sports shortly after moving, but this decreases as time passes. They are more likely to walk for everyday shopping needs.

Downtown

Those living downtown are likely to share a very high level of education with their neighbors and also an interest in an active social life in the period right after their move. Yet there is no overlap in the traits which residents of downtown houses and apartments feel they share with their respective neighbors. They are close to downtown places of entertainment, such as the theater, and they attend more frequently. They tend to use public transit more frequently for trips to work and to shop for clothes. Although their jobs are focused on the downtown area, downtown residents do not have uniquely low commuting times, because of high mass transit use.

Suburbs

Suburbanites have a somewhat lower educational level than those living downtown, and those in both housing types agree on a characterization of themselves and their neighbors as easy going. Mutual aid is based on personal assistance rather than on assistance involving material objects. They shop for clothing more frequently. They are farther from places of entertainment, and they go less often.

Downtown Apartments

The women in downtown apartments are the most likely to hold paid employment. While they are not likely to have older children, many have new infants. They say they share interests with their neighbors in an active social life and in a stress on paid employment. They feel they share a lack of stress on family matters with their neighbors. Personally, however, they think they have mostly negative points in common with their neighbors. They met more of their friends at work, rather than in the neighborhood. The type of mutual aid most frequently practiced with neighbors is monetary, by the husband. They are great patrons of restaurants, perhaps as a consequence of performing the least amount of housework. They emphasize photography as a pastime.

Downtown Homes

The men living in downtown houses tend to have high incomes, and they feel that they share an interest with their neighbors because they emphasize work. Although they feel they share few traits with their neighbors, compared to those living in suburban houses, those that are mentioned are extremely positive and flattering. The men have the easiest access to their jobs. They watch less television than those in the other groups.

Suburban High-Rise Apartments

Those in suburban apartments demonstrate very few unique behaviors and specify no unique personal characteristics or points of similarity to neighbors. They are more likely, however, to have older children than their downtown counterparts, and these children are more likely than those in suburban houses to be interested in stereo, television, sports, youth organizations, and photography.

Suburban Homes

Families in suburban houses do the most housework, as expected, and they feel that they share an interest with their neighbors in their homes. The men, particularly, feel a great degree of personal similarity to their neighbors, and both husbands and wives feel that they share a great number of positive personal traits with those around them. People living in the suburban houses are uniquely wedded to their automobiles for work trips and for shopping, and they generally tend to travel further, with some suggestion that they are more selective about where they choose to shop. Their children participate more frequently than those in suburban apartments in arts and crafts activities and in various sorts of collections.

If the above interpretation of the trends emerging from various discrete relationships is correct, a number of specific social characteristics and behaviors are associated with people's housing type and location. In addition to phenomena sorted out according to these two dimensions, still others are uniquely associated with particular *combinations* of housing type and location (all but the suburban apartment).

The data drawn on for the present chapter resemble those of Chapter 5. They required considerable interpretation in the process of assessing the nature of life in the different residential settings. Therefore, we performed the same type of *confirming* rotated factor analysis on the variables shown relevant to the understanding of postmove behavior as on similar premove data.

However, while the data in the present chapter show what occurred in the different settings after the move, they do not indicate what people *thought* of their settings. These data do not show the *meaning* of these phenomena. Such considerations, evaluation and meaning, are also essential in understanding the implications of such phenomena as neighbor characteristics and social behavior in the residential context, and they are examined in Chapter 8.

Due to the essential place of these latter considerations with respect to the more descriptive and distributive content of the present chapter, the factor analysis which reflects these materials will be introduced only after the main thrust of Chapter 8. To factor analyze the present materials alone would be incomplete, and to introduce an abbreviated result of a later chapter's content would serve to rob the latter of its primary purpose.

What can be said at present, however, is that once again the variations in housing type, location, and combinations thereof are essential organizing elements in all but two of the twenty factors which meet standard requirements and which together account for over 46 percent of the variance. Every housing type, location, and combination appears in at least one factor, certainly consistent with what has emerged in the present chapter. Even the occurrence of factors describing suburban apartments appear, containing evaluative and comparative elements which put this housing type into greater perspective.

However, what this material does not say about the various forms of behavior and differentiation described, which appeared *predictively* in the last chapter and *descriptively* in the present one, is whether the phenomena observed reflect preexisting characteristics and intentions of the families or responses to the unique characteristics and properties of environments to which they moved.

Chapter 7, therefore, examines whether the patterns observed in Phase III were brought to the new setting, with or without intention, or came about only as a consequence of the move, without prior intention. Such a chapter puts into a position of confrontation two of the major perspectives drawn upon in Chapter 1, showing the impact of each on our portrait of man-environment relations.

NOTES

[1] No pronounced emphases were found related to lazy, with it, sloppy, live for the present, expensive tastes, thrifty, individualistic, concerned with the future, and going up in the world.

[2] In any case, it is worthy of attention that the Sunday emphasis among those in downtown high-rise apartments of meeting with friends and neighbors was even more pronounced in Phase II than what was observed in Phase III, indicating that the interpersonal relations of these people were established more quickly after the move than were those of families in the other settings.

[3] The Canadian usage of 'ratepayer' is equivalent to the American term 'taxpayer.'

[4] Researchers generally treat commuting time as something to be minimized or 'traded off.' Nonetheless, some people do like long commutes, for psychological and other reasons.

[5] These commercial patterns were solicited from only the wives, although to represent the whole family. But it seems likely that some information, such as for restaurants and shopping for clothing, deals only with female patterns.

[6] What constitutes physical exercise for children is defined very differently by children than it is for adults. Given this ambiguity, discussion of it is omitted, although the differences between categories are not great.

[7] The amount of time spent on housework decreased considerably from Phase II to Phase III, presumably after the chores of moving were completed.

Social Attraction vs. Physical Determinism

ACCOUNTING FOR
SITUATED BEHAVIOR

The juxtaposition of Chapters 5 and 6 poses a critical question. How are social and physical determinism, even of the modified kinds considered here, reconciled? Chapter 5 lends strong backing to the theory of self-selection, that people with already established behavior patterns wish to continue or develop them by selecting congruent housing types and locations. Chapter 6 proceeds to show an even more extensive and complex pattern of differential behavior after people have been exposed to their new home environments.

The two poles of social and physical determinism are not no mutually exclusive as might appear at face value. People's different expectations and preexisting behavior are not unrelated to the actual spatial characteristics of their new homes and locations. As was emphasized in Chapter 1, people's predispositions to select particular residential environments are based on reasonable but not perfect knowledge of the physical characteristics of what they choose. The physical environment which serves as stimulus and setting for subsequent behavior is not just a determinative physical body, but one which the persons moving to it have imbued with meaning. In fact, the polar influences of social and physical determinism which set the framework of this chapter are hardly justified in such unrefined terms.

The results cited in Chapter 6 suggest a trinity—a 'package,' so to speak, wherein persons, like the working wife and the childless, seek to establish certain patterns of behavior and activity (specific uses of time, utilization of downtown facilities, and so on), and choose a residential setting likely to permit this (for example, downtown apartments). Emergent behavior is often closely related to social factors, yet is partially dependent on congruence with the home environment. Hence, all three elements must be considered together in mutually explanatory form. The physical environment does not cause the behavior; yet, it is not irrelevant, any more than the nominal characteristics of the family *alone* cause behavior.

Despite, then, the necessity stressed here of bringing both the forces of intention and determinism together in assessing the implications of residential environment, the relative strength of each in any given situation is an empirical question. We do not know a priori which purported 'effects' appear only after the move and within the particular physical context. Although 'before' and 'after' are closely related, it is imperative to gauge the *accuracy* of expectations, as well as the *strength* of the influences emanating from the physical setting which families subsequently experience.[1]

Therefore, in this chapter, we shall look at the extent that expectations were realized. We shall also assess the extent to which what eventuated can be traced, on the one hand, to prior attributes and expectations or, on the other hand, to the physical aspects of the new housing type and/or location.

The logic of analysis in this context utilizes the longitudinal design of the study. We focus predominantly on families who participated in each of the first three phases of the study, comparing the amount and direction of change in their responses to questions of rationale, priority, and behavior from before their move to a year and two months after the move. I analyze as appropriate, the extent that what people expected materialized, as well as the extent to which such different patterns shown in the previous chapter associated with different residential settings had become more pronounced within the new settings, a reflection of the new environment.

A picture emerges strongly supporting the rationality of the expectations people had when planning their moves. Yet, despite the generally high accuracy of such expectations, the door was by no means closed to unexpected occurrences of both a positive and negative nature. Analysis of the emerging patterns following the move, furthermore, shows that situated behavior is a function both of self-selection and of environmental influences. Let us first explore the rationales and environmental elements which were in respondents' minds before they moved.

EXPECTATIONS AND REALITY

In interviews with husbands and wives throughout the first three phases of the study, we presented closed-ended inventories of elements comprising what at first were expectations and, then, realities concerning the new home environment. As was indicated in Chapter 5, these inventories covered initially what proved troublesome in respondents' previous housing and what seemed to be the apparent benefits and drawbacks in their prospective housing. Use of the same items following the move helps answer such questions as the following:

1. Were preexisting problems remedied?
2. Do satisfactory items in the new home extend beyond the solution of problems in the previous home?
3. Were expectations of potential benefits realized after the move?
4. Are benefits realized mostly anticipated or are they an unexpected discovery?
5. Were aspects imagined beforehand to be drawbacks shown to be negative by subsequent experience?
6. To what extent were the dysfunctional elements of the new home anticipated?

Each of these questions can be viewed two ways: *generally* (i.e., to what extent most expectations are realized or experiences anticipated) and *specifically* (according to the housing type and location involved).

In general terms, most of what people expected to solve problems and to achieve benefit came to pass. Table 7.1 lumps together three different kinds of expectations subject to realization.

The first row on this table links reasons for moving away from the previous home with aspects of the new home found satisfactory. This indicates roughly whether problems raised in the former dwelling were solved

Table 7.1
Expectations Realized, by Housing Type and Location
(*Percentage*)

Type of Expectation	Apartment downtown		House downtown		Apartment suburbs		House suburbs	
	Wife	Husband	Wife	Husband	Wife	Husband	Wife	Husband
Problems to be solved	69.3	63.2	65.8	62.8	68.7	62.0	65.0	60.7
Benefits anticipated	77.4	70.9	75.0	69.5	77.5	71.6	75.4	67.8
Drawbacks anticipated	57.6	56.2	48.5	57.9	55.5	66.8	57.6	60.0

in the new home. The numbers represented in the table refer to the percentage of people who cited one of the closed-ended elements in Phase I as a reason for moving and who also cite it in Phases II or III as being satisfactory in their new home. Almost two-thirds of problems were solved in the new home, although wives were just slightly more likely to have their expectations realized than their husbands. Differences according to housing type or location are so minimal as to ignore (although consistently indicating more solution of problems among those moving to apartments than to houses).

The next row in Table 7.1 deals with the link between benefits which people anticipated of their new homes and locations and in Phase I the elements judged in Phases II or III to be satisfactory. In this case, an even higher percentage of expectations was subsequently realized. The difference in fulfillment of expectations between husbands and wives grows, although the generally high level of both is noteworthy. There are again extremely slight differences in favor of the realization of expectations on the apartment dwellers.

In Chapter 5, we noted that women moving from multiple dwellings had the most extensive set of expectations about benefits that would accrue as a result of their move to detached houses, more so than people moving from one home to another. At that time, we questioned whether this reflected a more blasé attitude on the part of those already living in homes about benefits which had accrued to them or unrealistic expectations on the part of those moving to houses for the first time. Breaking the trend data down according to the type of change in housing that was undertaken indicates limited support for the latter hypothesis. Only about 73 percent of the expectations held by women moving from multiple dwellings to houses were realized, compared to 78 percent among those moving from one home to another. No such difference exists among the husbands.

The third row in Table 7.1 indicates the link between areas which people felt to be drawbacks in their new homes and elements deemed unsatisfactory after arrival. People report fewer compromises than problems solved or benefits fulfilled; but, nonetheless, more than 50 percent of the expected compromises turned out to be realized. Confirmation of anticipated drawbacks was highest among the suburban men and lowest among the wives in downtown houses, but again within a narrow range of variation.

Although there is no particular standard on which percentage of the expectations realized is high or low, I interpret these levels as being relatively high. It appears that most of what people expected in their new homes and locations in fact came to pass.

Nonetheless, these figures aggregate a number of dissimilar elements of residential environment. Do the different categories of housing type and location satisfy specific criteria concerning housing type and locations in differential fashion?

If we turn, first, to problems in the previous residence requiring solution, the data show that some types of problems are more easily solved than others within given residential contexts. Table 7.2 shows this phenomenon.

Downtown apartments, for example, are relatively low on solving most problems of internal space within the home; yet they are high, together with suburban apartments, on solving internal maintenance problems and, together with downtown houses, on solving the original problems of access to public transportation.

Downtown houses are less likely than suburban houses to provide a final solution to any of the internal problems of the home except the total amount of space inside. But they are far superior in solving problems of *outside* space, privacy, and access of most kinds.

Although suburban apartments strongly fulfill expectations about improved storage space and access to recreational facilities, both of them anticipated by many prospective residents, the suburban apartment is lower than the other categories in a number of respects.

The suburban house demonstrates a high degree of solution of problems on internal characteristics of the dwelling unit, in contrast to relatively low solution of previously existing problems of access to various goods and services.

Table 7.3 indicates differences according to housing type and location in the percentage of expected *benefits* which families realized in their new homes.

Those moving to apartments are most likely to report that their expectations were realized regarding proximity to recreation facilities, confirming the emphasis on these facilities previously reported. Apartment movers also realized their expectation of easier internal maintenance more than did those moving to houses. There is a particularly *low* degree of fulfillment among the small proportion of apartment movers who expected privacy.

Those moving to houses, both downtown and in the suburbs, are not linked to a uniquely high degree of realization of any single factor, although their levels are generally high on many of the internal aspects of the dwelling unit; but those in suburban apartments have also realized many of these same anticipated benefits.

Downtown-suburban differences are more common. For example, suburbanites, regardless of housing type, are more likely to realize their expectations regarding storage space, the presence of open space, and proximity to schools, while typically failing to realize to a greater extent than those downtown such elements as access to good public transportation, access to downtown, and access to work among the wives.

Some fulfillments or lacks thereof are unique to particular combinations of housing type and location. For example, those in downtown apartments did not get a sufficient number of bedrooms, although, as indicated in the previous chapter, family needs began to change, in many cases, after the move. These families least appreciate anticipated satisfaction with open space surrounding their buildings. The wives in high-rises do not like the aesthetics of their buildings as much as they thought they would; their husbands share the same lack of fulfillment on this point, but they are not out of line with husbands moving to other categories of residence. One

Table 7.2

Problems in Previous Residence Solved through Move, by Destination Housing Type and Location

Problems for Solution	Apartment Downtown				House Downtown				Apartment Suburbs				House Suburbs			
	Wife		Husband		Wife		Husband		Wife		Husband		Wife		Husband	
	(%)	(N)	(%)	(N)	(%)	(N)	(%)	(N)	(%)	(N)	(%)	(N)	(%)	(N)	(%)	(N)
Size of home, rooms	85.7	(21)	76.0	(25)	96.9	(32)	94.1	(17)	94.9	(59)	79.5	(39)	97.1	(68)	91.5	(59)
Layout of rooms	87.5	(16)	64.3	(14)	94.1	(17)	66.7	(9)	85.7	(49)	66.7	(30)	96.4	(56)	97.6	(41)
Number of bedrooms	71.4	(21)	56.3	(16)	90.6	(32)	75.0	(16)	89.3	(75)	78.4	(51)	94.6	(93)	90.9	(66)
Number of bathrooms	62.5	(8)	60.0	(5)	77.8	(18)	63.6	(11)	88.9	(36)	74.2	(31)	94.3	(70)	91.1	(56)
In-home equipment	90.0	(20)	82.4	(17)	62.5	(8)	30.0	(10)	87.5	(56)	75.0	(36)	80.6	(36)	85.7	(21)
Storage or closet space	65.0	(20)	42.1	(19)	66.7	(27)	64.7	(17)	90.1	(71)	73.8	(42)	90.0	(80)	84.7	(59)
Interior noise transmission	66.7	(21)	60.9	(23)	68.8	(16)	50.0	(8)	22.5	(40)	29.4	(34)	47.6	(21)	47.4	(19)
Repairs/Alterations	88.9	(18)	76.9	(13)	75.0	(12)	55.6	(9)	81.6	(76)	67.3	(52)	55.6	(45)	53.3	(30)
Size of lot or outside space	50.0	(10)	36.4	(11)	83.3	(30)	88.2	(17)	83.8	(37)	69.7	(33)	78.3	(60)	58.7	(46)
Exterior noise transmission	41.7	(24)	55.6	(18)	56.3	(16)	73.3	(15)	42.6	(54)	38.8	(49)	58.7	(46)	38.5	(39)
Design, Appearance of home	84.6	(13)	73.3	(15)	92.9	(14)	70.0	(10)	89.1	(46)	54.5	(33)	97.2	(36)	86.8	(38)
Parking facilities	100.0	(13)	75.0	(8)	73.3	(15)	66.7	(3)	75.6	(41)	65.6	(32)	86.8	(38)	78.8	(33)
Management or developer	62.5	(16)	50.0	(14)	0.0	(2)	0.0	(2)	59.6	(47)	57.9	(38)	57.1	(14)	33.3	(15)
Social character of neighborhood	53.8	(13)	66.7	(9)	63.6	(11)	33.3	(12)	47.6	(42)	38.2	(34)	70.3	(37)	29.0	(31)
Type of neighbors/co-tenants	50.0	(12)	41.7	(12)	58.3	(12)	50.0	(6)	48.9	(45)	41.4	(29)	54.3	(35)	39.3	(28)
Distance to country/green spaces	76.9	(13)	50.0	(6)	100.0	(4)	37.5	(8)	92.6	(27)	84.6	(13)	100.0	(19)	84.6	(13)
Quality of schools	100.0	(1)	50.0	(2)	88.2	(17)	75.0	(8)	88.9	(36)	81.3	(16)	82.8	(29)	91.7	(12)
Design, Appearance of neighborhood	68.8	(16)	76.9	(13)	91.7	(12)	81.8	(11)	89.8	(49)	77.5	(40)	97.2	(36)	72.7	(33)

Transportation facilities	100.0 (13)	100.0 (10)	80.0 (11)	90.9 (10)	90.9 (33)	54.5 (11)	72.2 (18)	50.0 (12)
Distance to job/work	100.0 (16)	91.7 (15)	90.9 (12)	81.1 (11)	81.1 (53)	82.8 (29)	51.5 (33)	69.2 (26)
Location of friends	83.3 (6)	71.4 (8)	83.3 (7)	91.7 (6)	91.7 (12)	76.9 (13)	83.3 (12)	76.9 (13)
Location of relatives	37.5 (8)	100.0 (5)	100.0 (4)	86.7 (1)	86.7 (15)	63.6 (11)	81.0 (21)	65.0 (20)
Distance to shopping	88.9 (9)	100.0 (6)	100.0 (4)	91.7 (4)	91.7 (36)	86.7 (15)	73.7 (19)	100.0 (5)
Distance to recreation facilities	100.0 (14)	100.0 (15)	50.0 (7)	94.1 (2)	94.1 (51)	92.1 (38)	68.0 (25)	66.7 (12)
Distance to downtown area	100.0 (17)	100.0 (10)	77.8 (12)	69.0 (9)	69.0 (29)	72.7 (11)	57.1 (14)	58.3 (12)
Location of schools	100.0 (1)	38.2 (2)	75.0 (17)	91.7 (8)	91.7 (36)	87.5 (16)	86.2 (29)	100.0 (12)
Housing costs	44.4 (9)	20.0 (7)	0.0 (5)	63.6 (1)	63.6 (22)	44.4 (9)	30.0 (10)	0.0 (0)

Table 7.3
Fulfillment of Benefits Expected, by Destination Housing Type and Location

Benefits Expected	Apartment Downtown Wife (%)	(N)	Apartment Downtown Husband (%)	(N)	House Downtown Wife (%)	(N)	House Downtown Husband (%)	(N)	Apartment Suburbs Wife (%)	(N)	Apartment Suburbs Husband (%)	(N)	House Suburbs Wife (%)	(N)	House Suburbs Husband (%)	(N)
Size of home, rooms	94.4	(36)	77.8	(27)	96.7	(60)	96.4	(28)	94.8	(115)	87.5	(72)	98.1	(154)	91.1	(112)
Layout of rooms	87.9	(33)	87.0	(23)	91.2	(57)	86.2	(29)	91.3	(127)	77.6	(76)	97.0	(167)	89.4	(123)
Number of bedrooms	68.0	(25)	54.5	(22)	93.2	(59)	82.4	(34)	88.0	(100)	85.3	(75)	97.3	(150)	89.4	(113)
Number of bathrooms	50.0	(8)	80.0	(5)	83.8	(37)	72.7	(22)	91.5	(71)	81.8	(44)	97.2	(141)	87.4	(103)
In-home equipment	82.4	(34)	70.8	(24)	65.0	(20)	40.0	(10)	84.0	(81)	77.2	(57)	86.5	(74)	89.8	(59)
Storage or closet space	66.7	(27)	57.7	(26)	75.6	(45)	55.6	(18)	89.0	(118)	75.6	(82)	90.9	(132)	83.9	(87)
Interior noise transmission	75.0	(8)	64.3	(14)	40.0	(5)	71.4	(7)	58.8	(17)	47.1	(17)	50.0	(8)	66.7	(15)
Repairs/Alterations	78.6	(14)	72.7	(11)	62.2	(37)	63.6	(11)	85.3	(34)	72.7	(22)	68.1	(47)	59.1	(22)
Size of lot or outside space	61.5	(13)	35.7	(14)	88.2	(51)	88.0	(25)	85.5	(62)	65.9	(41)	84.0	(94)	68.9	(61)
Exterior noise transmission	30.0	(10)	57.1	(14)	100.0	(5)	100.0	(2)	51.9	(27)	40.0	(25)	75.0	(20)	33.3	(18)
Design, Appearance of home	75.6	(41)	74.2	(31)	86.7	(60)	77.1	(35)	90.2	(102)	70.3	(74)	94.9	(176)	87.7	(122)
Parking facilities	100.0	(12)	77.8	(9)	60.0	(10)	100.0	(3)	88.9	(27)	71.4	(21)	86.4	(22)	89.5	(19)
Management or developer	75.0	(20)	58.3	(24)	0.0	(1)	0.0	(1)	56.7	(67)	71.4	(56)	70.6	(51)	44.2	(43)
Social character of neighborhood	60.0	(15)	72.7	(11)	62.5	(16)	30.0	(10)	56.1	(41)	39.4	(33)	72.5	(40)	38.9	(36)
Type of neighbors/co-tenants	54.5	(11)	40.0	(15)	68.0	(25)	46.2	(13)	52.0	(25)	30.4	(23)	80.6	(31)	33.3	(24)
Distance to country/green spaces	78.3	(23)	66.7	(15)	82.4	(17)	54.5	(11)	95.7	(69)	87.5	(40)	92.6	(54)	88.9	(45)
Quality of schools	71.4	(7)	66.7	(3)	86.0	(43)	75.0	(24)	91.6	(83)	84.3	(51)	85.7	(98)	80.6	(67)
Design, Appearance of neighborhood	85.3	(34)	86.2	(29)	91.1	(56)	76.3	(38)	91.2	(113)	80.7	(83)	96.1	(154)	79.8	(114)
Transportation facilities	100.0	(56)	97.5	(40)	100.0	(50)	91.2	(34)	90.6	(85)	71.1	(38)	80.4	(56)	68.8	(16)

Distance to job/work	89.7 (39)	83.3 (30)	82.6 (46)	93.3 (30)	78.2 (78)	85.5 (55)	62.7 (59)	80.6 (36)
Location of friends	71.4 (14)	80.0 (15)	85.2 (27)	76.5 (17)	85.4 (41)	75.0 (28)	86.2 (29)	70.0 (20)
Location of relatives	100.0 (6)	80.0 (10)	82.4 (17)	66.7 (6)	84.4 (32)	66.7 (18)	89.7 (29)	75.0 (16)
Distance to shopping	91.4 (35)	91.7 (24)	92.1 (38)	83.3 (24)	91.9 (111)	91.3 (69)	86.4 (59)	88.9 (36)
Distance to recreation facilities	90.9 (44)	87.8 (41)	89.7 (29)	62.5 (16)	93.0 (114)	92.2 (77)	84.8 (46)	72.4 (29)
Distance to downtown area	97.4 (38)	94.3 (35)	96.3 (54)	94.3 (35)	80.0 (45)	71.0 (31)	70.4 (27)	71.4 (14)
Location of schools	71.4 (7)	66.7 (3)	83.7 (43)	76.0 (25)	93.8 (81)	94.1 (51)	86.6 (97)	84.3 (70)
Housing costs	50.0 (6)	50.0 (4)	0.0 (3)	12.5 (16)	66.7 (21)	62.5 (8)	7.7 (13)	0.0 (5)

major difference between husbands and wives in the downtown high-rise is satisfaction with the amount of space within the unit. Almost 95 percent of the wives have realized their expectations in this regard, compared to only 78 percent of their husbands, who are far less fulfilled this way than those moving to any other form of housing. Although internal space is but a single criterion of housing choice, it continues a series of husband-wife differences within the downtown high-rise.

The downtown house uniquely fulfills husbands' expectations of proximity to their jobs, but it does not fulfill expectations of functional elements such as kitchens and laundry areas. The latter certainly reflect the age and relative condition of the different housing units.

The only noteworthy aspects of the suburban high-rise in this regard are that husbands notably lack fulfillment with the interior layout and privacy of their dwelling units.

Suburban houses, on the other hand, are unique in terms of both partners liking the looks of their home as expected and agreeing that they are more distant than expected from most goods and facilities. In addition, the wives realize an unusually high degree of their expectations about the social characteristics of other people living in their neighborhood.

Since compromises were volunteered far less readily than reasons for moving or benefits expected, the breakdown of compromises realized by housing type and specific substance is not particularly fruitful. Nonetheless, the data appear to confirm some of the more obvious areas of compromise, such as internal space among those who move to apartments and access to goods and services among those in suburbia.

Aspects of New Homes Anticipated

A complementary way of looking at the same phenomena is to ask what percentage of those elements in the new home which proved satisfactory or unsatisfactory had been anticipated. Table 7.4 reports information parallel to Table 7.1 from this perspective.

Changes in the mechanics of coding between the phases eliminate the possibility of 100 percent anticipation of elements contributing to the satisfaction and dissatisfaction noted in post-move phases, simply on oper-

Table 7.4
Elements of New Homes Anticipated, by Housing Type and Location
(*Percentage*)

How Anticipated	Elements Anticipated							
	Apartment downtown		House downtown		Apartment suburbs		House suburbs	
	Wife	Husband	Wife	Husband	Wife	Husband	Wife	Husband
Solution to problem	25.5	24.0	22.6	21.0	25.7	20.0	22.0	20.1
Benefits expected	42.7	39.6	51.1	40.9	42.5	33.0	44.1	36.4
Compromise made	19.5	20.9	22.6	31.2	17.0	19.4	21.6	24.0

ational grounds. The percentage of elements which were in fact anticipated is far below the operational possibility of approximately 75 percent,
however, indicating a considerable amount of serendipitous discovery by
residents in their new environments. For example, only about a quarter of
the things which people find good about their new homes and locations
are responses to problems reported in Phase I. In this regard, husband-wife
differences and housing-location differences are extremely minimal.

As might be expected, somewhat more of the elements of the new
homes found satisfactory had been expected to be so. In this case, however, the wives had anticipated a reasonably higher percentage than did
their husbands. The husband-wife difference eclipses the very slight difference in favor of the homeowners over apartment dwellers regarding
anticipation.

Although more than half of what people felt in Phase I to be drawbacks were confirmed after moving, these represent only a small proportion of the items judged in later phases to be unsatisfactory. In this respect, there are few differences by sex or residential context worth noting.

By and large, then, although peoples' expectations proved relatively accurate, they did not foresee all that they could have. In fact, the residential setting contained much for good and for ill that had not been
anticipated.

No generalizations are in order about the percentage of aspects foreseen
according to change of housing type or location. There is no consistent

Table 7.5
Satisfactory Aspects of New Housing Anticipated in Response to Pre-move Problems,
by Destination Housing Type and Location

Satisfactory Aspects of New Housing	Apartment Downtown				House Downtown				Apartment Suburbs				House Suburbs			
	Wife		Husband		Wife		Husband		Wife		Husband		Wife		Husband	
	(%)	(N)	(%)	(N)	(%)	(N)	(%)	(N)	(%)	(N)	(%)	(N)	(%)	(N)	(%)	(N)
Size of home, rooms	32.7	(55)	42.2	(45)	41.3	(75)	27.1	(59)	29.5	(190)	20.8	(149)	31.3	(211)	30.0	(180)
Layout of rooms	29.8	(47)	24.3	(37)	24.2	(66)	12.5	(48)	24.4	(172)	15.0	(133)	27.0	(200)	24.0	(167)
Number of bedrooms	46.9	(32)	40.9	(22)	42.0	(69)	27.9	(43)	43.2	(155)	30.1	(133)	45.1	(195)	37.3	(161)
Number of bathrooms	20.0	(25)	14.3	(21)	25.9	(54)	19.4	(36)	24.6	(130)	21.5	(107)	33.8	(195)	31.7	(161)
In-home equipment	33.3	(54)	33.3	(42)	11.1	(45)	12.5	(24)	31.4	(156)	22.1	(122)	16.6	(175)	13.4	(134)
Storage or closet space	29.5	(44)	24.2	(33)	33.3	(54)	29.7	(37)	40.5	(158)	25.2	(123)	38.9	(185)	35.2	(142)
Interior noise transmission	34.1	(41)	46.7	(30)	23.9	(46)	14.8	(27)	10.7	(84)	14.1	(71)	11.4	(88)	13.2	(68)
Repairs/Alterations	29.1	(55)	21.3	(47)	19.1	(47)	14.3	(35)	39.5	(157)	26.5	(132)	18.5	(135)	15.2	(105)
Size of lot or outside space	17.2	(29)	21.1	(19)	40.3	(62)	34.9	(43)	19.7	(157)	20.9	(110)	29.6	(159)	23.3	(116)
Exterior noise transmission	40.0	(25)	41.7	(24)	23.7	(38)	33.3	(33)	39.0	(59)	37.3	(51)	30.0	(90)	19.0	(79)
Design, Appearance of home	20.8	(53)	25.0	(44)	20.0	(65)	14.9	(47)	24.7	(166)	15.0	(120)	17.7	(198)	19.4	(170)
Parking facilities	23.6	(55)	12.5	(48)	23.9	(46)	6.3	(32)	18.5	(168)	14.9	(141)	20.9	(158)	19.7	(132)
Management or developer	21.7	(46)	17.5	(40)	0.0	(4)	0.0	(0)	28.3	(99)	25.6	(86)	9.1	(88)	9.3	(54)
Social character of neighborhood	26.9	(26)	23.1	(26)	14.0	(50)	17.4	(23)	22.7	(88)	20.3	(64)	22.6	(115)	14.3	(63)
Type of neighbors/co-tenants	17.1	(35)	17.9	(28)	14.0	(50)	13.6	(22)	24.2	(91)	18.8	(64)	16.2	(117)	17.5	(63)
Distance to country/ green spaces	25.0	(40)	9.1	(33)	9.5	(42)	13.0	(23)	14.0	(178)	7.8	(141)	10.3	(185)	7.2	(152)
Quality of schools	5.6	(18)	10.0	(10)	27.8	(54)	15.4	(39)	24.4	(131)	11.7	(111)	14.3	(168)	8.1	(135)
Design, Appearance of neighborhood	19.3	(57)	20.8	(48)	15.5	(71)	19.1	(47)	24.3	(181)	21.8	(142)	17.4	(201)	16.2	(148)

Transportation facilities	18.6 (70)	15.6 (64)	14.5 (76)	15.7 (51)	18.3 (164)	4.9 (122)	11.2 (116)	7.1 (85)
Distance to job/work	25.8 (62)	21.1 (57)	19.6 (56)	18.9 (53)	36.8 (117)	19.8 (121)	19.1 (89)	16.2 (111)
Location of friends	11.1 (45)	17.1 (35)	8.8 (57)	12.5 (40)	8.0 (138)	8.3 (121)	6.6 (152)	8.9 (112)
Location of relatives	9.4 (32)	9.7 (31)	10.0 (40)	3.1 (32)	12.3 (106)	8.1 (86)	14.9 (114)	12.3 (106)
Distance to shopping	13.1 (61)	10.5 (57)	5.8 (69)	9.5 (42)	17.7 (186)	8.0 (163)	8.6 (162)	3.6 (137)
Distance to recreation facilities	23.0 (61)	21.4 (56)	11.1 (63)	2.9 (35)	27.4 (175)	23.0 (152)	13.0 (131)	6.8 (117)
Distance to downtown area	25.0 (68)	14.3 (63)	15.8 (76)	11.7 (60)	16.5 (121)	7.4 (108)	7.7 (104)	6.7 (105)
Location of schools	4.5 (22)	13.3 (15)	26.8 (56)	15.8 (38)	22.8 (145)	11.3 (124)	14.3 (175)	8.1 (149)
Housing costs	25.0 (16)	22.2 (18)	4.3 (23)	0.0 (15)	18.7 (75)	5.8 (69)	5.5 (55)	0.0 (43)

pattern indicating that those keeping either the same housing type or location were able to anticipate more of what happened.

As Table 7.5 indicates, relatively few of the specific elements viewed as satisfactory in the new home are to any extent related to pre-move problems. Nonetheless, among those most likely are those aspects dealing with the interior of the dwelling unit. In this regard, those moving to downtown high-rise apartments are most likely to have anticipated the benefits they have achieved, underlining some characteristics of incremental change they are making in their housing.

Table 7.6 indicates a similar view about which benefits were fully anticipated, singling out internal aspects of the dwelling unit. In this regard, those moving to houses are most likely to have anticipated more of the specific elements of internal space within the dwelling. Nonetheless, that apartment movers are more likely and downtown house movers least likely to have anticipated their satisfactions about kitchen and laundry facilities is not surprising given the relative age of these homes.

One should note as well that those who move to suburban houses discover much more satisfaction with their access to goods and facilities than they had anticipated. This does not necessarily make such access good, but it is not as bad as many had anticipated.

One noteworthy element of the detailed distribution of *dis*satisfactions anticipated is the uniquely low percentage of difficulties encountered in suburban apartments which were anticipated. Insofar as these apartments appear to reflect a residual choice of environment more than was the case with the other three categories, it is not surprising that respondents there freely identify post-move difficulties not anticipated.

In sum, this analysis of expectation and realization indicates that a great number of expectations regarding problems to be solved, benefits anticipated, and compromises made was carried into the new home environment and in many cases, fulfilled. Nonetheless, many more factors turned out to be relevant to the new home than had been anticipated along any of these three lines. Some criteria on which people select and then evaluate their housing are more likely to have been anticipated than others, while many of these criteria are likely to be fulfilled in different fashions according to the housing type or location to which people move.

Let us now turn from specific criteria of housing to broader considerations.

Before they moved, about two-thirds of the families expected changes in their daily and Sunday patterns of life. There were no major differences in housing type and location in this regard. To what extent was adaptation necessary?

After their move, the families report having taken varying lengths of time to adapt.

A year and two months after the move, those who had moved to high-rise apartments, particularly those downtown, felt that they had adapted to whatever changes were necessary very much more quickly than did those who had moved to houses, particularly suburban houses. Table 7.7 indicates this critical difference in the *period* of adaptation. That over 60 percent of those moving to downtown apartments and 55 percent of those who had moved to suburban apartments, in contrast to only 39 percent of those in suburban houses, had felt at ease within the first month is strongly supported by the data already examined, which showed intensive use at first of recreation and public facilities among the former, as well as an immediately active social life.

On the other hand, many activities characteristic of the suburban home-owners occurred only with the passage of time. Almost 40 percent of the wives and 30 percent of the husbands living there took between four months and a year to feel at ease—a much longer period of time than in any other category. Both suburban location and single-family housing appear to be directly related, in additive fashion, to the length of time necessary for adjustment.

Thus, while most families throughout all categories of residential context anticipate changes in their daily lives, apartment housing in downtown locations appears most supportive of 'instant living,' while families cope with the types of changes occurring in single houses and suburban locations more slowly.

Respondents find it difficult to enunciate clearly the kind of changes in their daily routines which have occurred as a consequence of their moves. Nonetheless, people tell of some changes in answer to open-ended questions.

For example, the women who move to downtown high-rise are very much more likely (55% versus about 30%) to mention lowered commuting times. This does reflect a change, since 89 percent of those moving downtown from the suburbs and 60 percent of those from the in-between

Table 7.6
Satisfactory Aspects of New Housing Anticipated as Benefits, by Destination Housing Type and Location

Satisfactory Aspects of New Housing	Apartment Downtown				House Downtown				Apartment Suburbs				House Suburbs			
	Wife		Husband		Wife		Husband		Wife		Husband		Wife		Husband	
	(%)	(N)	(%)	(N)	(%)	(N)	(%)	(N)	(%)	(N)	(%)	(N)	(%)	(N)	(%)	(N)
Size of home, rooms	61.8	(55)	46.7	(45)	77.3	(75)	45.8	(59)	57.4	(190)	42.3	(149)	71.6	(211)	56.7	(180)
Layout of rooms	61.7	(47)	54.1	(37)	78.8	(66)	52.1	(48)	67.4	(172)	44.4	(133)	81.0	(200)	65.9	(167)
Number of bedrooms	53.1	(32)	54.5	(22)	79.7	(69)	65.1	(43)	56.8	(155)	48.1	(133)	74.9	(195)	62.7	(161)
Number of bathrooms	16.0	(25)	19.0	(21)	57.4	(54)	44.4	(36)	50.0	(130)	33.6	(107)	70.3	(195)	55.9	(161)
In-home equipment	51.9	(54)	40.5	(42)	28.9	(45)	16.7	(24)	43.6	(156)	36.1	(122)	36.6	(175)	39.6	(134)
Storage or closet space	40.9	(44)	45.5	(33)	63.0	(54)	27.0	(37)	66.5	(158)	50.4	(123)	64.9	(185)	51.4	(142)
Interior noise transmission	14.6	(41)	30.0	(30)	4.3	(46)	18.5	(27)	11.9	(84)	11.3	(71)	4.5	(88)	14.7	(68)
Repairs/Alterations	20.0	(55)	17.0	(47)	48.9	(47)	20.0	(35)	18.5	(157)	12.1	(132)	23.7	(135)	12.4	(105)
Size of lot or outside space	27.6	(29)	26.3	(19)	72.6	(62)	51.2	(43)	33.8	(157)	24.5	(110)	49.7	(159)	36.2	(116)
Exterior noise transmission	12.0	(25)	33.3	(24)	13.2	(38)	6.1	(33)	23.7	(59)	19.6	(51)	16.7	(90)	7.6	(79)
Design, Appearance of home	58.5	(53)	52.3	(44)	80.0	(65)	57.4	(47)	55.4	(166)	43.3	(120)	84.3	(198)	62.9	(170)
Parking facilities	21.8	(55)	14.6	(48)	13.0	(46)	9.4	(32)	14.3	(168)	10.6	(141)	12.0	(158)	12.9	(132)
Management or developer	32.6	(46)	35.0	(40)	0.0	(4)	0.0	(0)	38.4	(99)	46.5	(86)	40.9	(88)	35.2	(54)
Social character of neighborhood	34.6	(26)	30.8	(26)	20.0	(50)	13.0	(23)	26.1	(88)	20.3	(64)	25.2	(115)	22.2	(63)
Type of neighbors/co-tenants	17.1	(35)	21.4	(28)	34.0	(50)	27.3	(22)	14.3	(91)	10.9	(64)	21.4	(117)	12.7	(63)
Distance to country/green spaces	45.0	(40)	30.3	(33)	33.3	(42)	26.1	(33)	37.1	(178)	24.8	(141)	27.0	(185)	26.3	(152)
Quality of schools	27.8	(18)	20.0	(10)	68.5	(54)	46.2	(39)	58.0	(131)	38.7	(111)	50.0	(168)	40.0	(135)
Design, Appearance of neighborhood	50.9	(57)	52.1	(48)	71.8	(71)	61.7	(47)	56.9	(181)	47.2	(142)	73.6	(201)	61.5	(148)

Transportation facilities	80.0 (70)	60.9 (64)	65.8 (76)	60.8 (51)	47.0 (164)	22.1 (122)	38.8 (116)	12.9 (85)
Distance to job/work	56.5 (62)	43.9 (57)	67.9 (56)	52.8 (53)	52.1 (117)	38.8 (121)	41.6 (89)	26.1 (111)
Location of friends	22.2 (45)	34.3 (35)	40.4 (57)	32.5 (40)	25.4 (138)	17.4 (121)	16.4 (152)	12.5 (112)
Location of relatives	18.8 (32)	25.8 (31)	35.0 (40)	12.5 (32)	25.5 (106)	14.0 (86)	22.8 (114)	11.3 (106)
Distance to shopping	52.5 (61)	38.6 (57)	50.7 (69)	47.6 (42)	54.8 (186)	38.7 (163)	31.5 (162)	23.4 (137)
Distance to recreation facilities	65.6 (61)	64.3 (56)	41.3 (63)	28.6 (35)	60.6 (175)	46.7 (152)	29.8 (131)	17.9 (117)
Distance to downtown area	54.4 (68)	52.4 (63)	68.4 (76)	55.0 (60)	29.8 (121)	20.4 (108)	18.3 (104)	9.5 (105)
Location of schools	22.7 (22)	13.3 (15)	64.3 (56)	50.0 (38)	52.4 (145)	38.7 (124)	48.0 (175)	39.6 (149)
Housing costs	18.8 (16)	11.1 (18)	0.0 (23)	13.3 (15)	18.7 (75)	7.2 (69)	1.8 (55)	0.0 (43)

Table 7.7
Length of Post-move Adjustment Period, by Destination Housing Type and Location

	To 1 Week		2 Weeks–1 Month		2–3 Months		4 Months–1 Year		(N)	
	Wife	Husband	Wife	Husband	Wife	Husband	Wife	Husband	Wife	Husband
Apartment downtown	32.3	24.5	30.6	34.7	22.6	24.5	14.5	16.3	(62)	(49)
House downtown	31.0	25.6	16.9	25.6	23.9	20.9	28.2	27.9	(71)	(43)
Apartment suburbs	25.5	30.8	27.7	29.4	20.2	22.4	26.6	17.5	(188)	(143)
House suburbs	20.4	28.6	18.4	24.0	21.9	16.2	39.4	30.5	(201)	(154)
(N)									(522)	(389)
Missing Information or Not Applicable									(71)	(60)

zone mention lowered commuting times, compared to 32 percent of those moving from one part of the downtown zone to another. These women also are more likely to mention that their use of leisure time has changed (32.2% versus about 20% for the others), although this is not related to a change of environment; this more likely reflects the move to a superior building, as suggested in Chapter 5.

Almost 60 percent of suburban apartment dwellers report changes in where they shop, compared to under 50 percent among the others. This reflects the opportunity to shop virtually at home in their new complexes.

Both husbands and wives moving to suburban houses report considerably more contact with their neighbors than before. This does not reflect a change in housing type, nor a move to the suburbs. The data show it more likely a matter of self-selection, surely heralded by the personal similarities which people anticipated before they moved that they would have with their new neighbors.[2]

Fifty-seven percent of women moving to *new* suburban houses mention increased contact with neighbors, compared to only 48 percent of those moving to resale houses. Comparable figures among husbands are 51 percent and 47 percent, respectively. While the previous evidence presented on Clark's hypothesis was largely indeterminate, these data give some backing to his association of newness to increased neighboring in suburbia. This difference also reintroduces the possibility of a contextual influence on neighboring.

Let us now turn to a more detailed examination of the specific areas of substance, based less on open-ended questions and more on the pattern of changes in answers to factual questions at different phases of the longitudinal study. In the present chapter, we must examine the extent and direction of changes observed, asking whether behavior already exists before the move, occurs as desired within the spatial opportunities of the new setting, and/or appears in response to a change in housing type or location.

CHANGE WITHIN SPECIFIC FACTORS

Financial Aspects

People chose homes and locations within limitations of husband's and family income. Subsequent moves may be partly a function of the same phenomena. However, one would not expect a change in income as a function of residential change. When residential changes involve great changes in income, it is the job change which precipitates the residential change, not the reverse. In any case, we noted in Chapter 6 that across-the-board increases were realized within each of the various categories of housing type and location.

Stage in the Life Cycle

About 7 percent of the families who responded in Phase III had enlarged their families since moving. Mobility, of course, does not conceive children. The critical question at present is whether (1) people moved because they just gave birth to, expected, or wanted an additional child, or (2) when people moved, they felt able to accommodate a child, who would only then be conceived. Data already cited indicate that a greater percentage of families in downtown high-rise apartments had new babies after the move, while families in the other categories were more likely to have had them before moving.

Unfortunately, our data are inadequate to determine the answer to the question posed. We do not know, for example, how many of the wives in downtown apartments were pregnant at the time they moved nor when, during the first year and two months after the move, the new infants were born.

While it is true that the need for more space was a common reason for moving, size of family was related only to suburbanization, not to the housing types chosen. Nonetheless, expected increases in the family were shown as mildly related to the choice of a house rather than an apartment.

That moves to apartments were not primarily associated with expectations of new children is indicated also by the high percentage of working wives moving to downtown apartments, with very strong reference to decreasing the length of their commuting time. Yet, many of them then had children within the first year and two months. That many of the house movers had infants sooner and that many of the apartment movers had their infants later may indicate a motivating force of this kind for environmental choice among the former only. Furthermore, it is highly unlikely that the amount of space in downtown apartments made families think of having children. Indeed, it is more likely that conceiving these children made the families involved think of the move to still another residence. We can assess this particular chicken-and-egg question better with data in the next two chapters.

Time-budget data offer some indication, though, that family increases among those in downtown apartments were mostly a postmove phenomenon, in contrast to those moving to houses. From Phase I through Phase III, 17 percent of the wives in downtown apartments increase the time devoted to infant care, while only 3 percent decrease this kind of time use. In contrast, women in all the other categories show marked aggregate decreases in the amount of time they spend on baby care over this period of time, with those moving to houses showing the greatest decreases. There is only a marginal decrease of 4 percent among those who moved to suburban apartments.

There is a compensating increase in the care of older children among the house movers, reflecting that the infants they had before moving were now considered children. Those who moved to apartments (especially to downtown apartments where 92 percent do not contribute to the care of older children during the course of the day) do not give evidence of similar changes.

Some, but not strong, evidence that the babies born after moves to downtown apartments were not originally part of the rationales for moving is offered by the fact that while 17 percent of the wives there devoted more time to baby care by Phase III, only 8 percent had reported such increases as of Phase II, several months following the move. We cannot, however, account for the time of arrival of the additional children within the intervening period.

In Chapter 6, we answered negatively the question whether fathers in suburbia were spending more time with their growing children than those in downtown houses. We must ask now whether the suburban figures at least reflected increases in this form of fatherly behavior. Again, the answer is No. The fathers in suburban homes decreased the net amount of time they spent with the older children in their families, in contrast to a modest increase among those in downtown houses. With respect to recreation time spent with their children, the suburban fathers showed a net increase of 5.5 percent, but this pales in comparison with the net increase of 18.4 percent among those husbands in downtown houses. This confirms the finding of Harvey and Procos (1974), indicating more attitudinal than behavioral support for familism among suburbanites.

Neighbor Characteristics

The social composition of the neighborhood to which people move is something about which they have expectations, but this is not something which they personally bring with them or which they themselves 'perform' after arrival. Therefore, we shall assess whether the similarities in neighborhood composition reported in Phase III reflect an increase in the economic and educational similarity of the new neighbors. If so, is this increase encountered as a consequence of change in housing type or location?

In Chapter 6, we observed that there are differences in personal characteristics of neighbors by housing type and location after the move. Family members living in houses typically know a greater number of their neighbors, know more about them, and feel more similar to them than do those living in apartments. Those moving to suburbs also feel similar to their neighbors. To what extent do these perceptions relate to changes in housing type or location?

With respect to economic similarities, more than half of those who moved to each of the categories of housing type and location feel that more of their new neighbors than their former neighbors are similar to themselves. This is particularly the case in the suburban single houses, where 76 percent of the wives and 70 percent of the husbands feel this way. It is also markedly more the case among those moving to *new* suburban areas, compared to already settled suburban areas, with a difference of almost 20 percent among the wives and 30 percent among the husbands in this regard. Since many have said that perceived homogeneity is a prerequisite for neighborhood contact, this provides a second firm piece of evidence in favor of Clark's hypothesis on suburban neighboring.

Not many (only about 10%) of the families in any category feel that fewer of their new neighbors are economically similar to themselves than their old neighbors. The feeling of increasing economic homogeneity is not tied to particular *changes* in housing type: majority support for this belief is strong regardless of the type of change in housing.

Men who have changed to more central locations believe most strongly that more of their neighbors are economically similar to themselves; 75 percent of those moving downtown from the suburbs feel this way, compared to 67 percent of those moving from intermediate areas and only 54 percent of those already downtown.

Among their wives, it is those already in the suburbs who believe most in the occurrence of an increase in economic homogeneity (75%). Fewer among those moving from intermediate areas (66%) and from downtown (57%) have experienced such an increase.

Both husbands and wives in the various categories of residence feel that their new neighbors are more like themselves educationally than their old neighbors. About 50 percent in each category feel this way, with the 62 percent of those in suburban houses representing the greatest feeling of educational homogeneity among both spouses.

According to both husbands and wives, educational homogeneity improves the most when undergoing locational change, regardless of the direction. About 70 percent of the centralizers feel that more of their new neighbors resemble themselves educationally, compared to 45 percent of those who remained downtown. On the other hand, about 58 percent of those decentralizing felt this way, compared to about 50 percent of those remaining within the suburbs. This finding helps underline the importance of education in spatial differentiation.

Change in housing type is not related to observed changes in the educational similarity of neighbors.

With respect to *interest* similarities among neighbors, people again found a greater amount of similarity among the new neighbors than among the old. In this case, however, somewhat less than 50 percent (40% for the wives, and 45% for the husbands) claimed that more of their new neighbors were similar to themselves than their old neighbors, with the remainder divided virtually evenly among the 'same number,' 'fewer,' and 'don't know.' It is interesting to note that a higher percentage—about 60 percent—had observed a greater similarity among their new neighbors in Phase II, but this level decreased over time as people got to know their neighbors.

Again, change in housing type is not associated with this movement toward greater homogeneity. As with economic homogeneity, however, there were differences by change in location which took different forms depending on the observation of the husband or wife. Husbands who are decentralizing (about 60%) observe a greater similarity between their own interests and those of their neighbors than before, while only 37 percent of those remaining within the downtown zone see an increase in similarity. Among the wives, it is those who are decentralizing (about 45%) who see increasing similarity, compared to 33 percent among those remaining within the suburbs.

Why husbands and wives diverge in these impressions according to different changes in location is unclear. Nonetheless, the general pattern of increasing perceived homogeneity is undisturbed by these minor inconsistencies in degree of increase.

In Chapter 6, we saw that the number of other families which respondents know locally is strongly related to whether they live in a house or apartment. Our analysis of these data on housing change indicates that this finding is not a function of the type of changes undertaken. Among those husbands now living in apartments, for example, between 26 and 28 percent of them know none of their neighbors regardless of whether they came to the apartment from a house, a low-rise apartment, or another high-rise. On the other hand, among the husbands now living in houses, the range runs between 6 and 9 percent. Hence, this finding cited in Chapter 6 supports the theory of self-selection, since those moving to apartments were considerably less likely in Phase I to know various characteristics of their former neighbors.

We found the same house-apartment differences with respect to knowledge of neighbors' personal traits. Once again, this difference exists regardless of the kind of housing change undertaken. Since the Phase I evidence showed the same divergence clearly, there are grounds for suspecting that a selective process has brought people with particular histories of neighbor relations into congruent settings.

We found perceived similarity with new neighbors to vary both by housing type and by location. Once again, our analysis of change in home environment does not alter the previous findings. In the case of perceived similarities, however, the premove data had indicated that such perceptions varied according to the home environment where people then lived— not the prospective housing type or location. Therefore, the finding of perceived similarities which reflect the environment to which people are exposed both before and after the move, regardless of the change undertaken, forms an example of 'situated behavior' rather than self-selection.

In short, respondent observations on social characteristics of neighbors give evidence of both self-selection and the actual formation of economically and educationally more homogeneous groupings of households. Families who moved to suburban locations and single-family homes also found greater personal homogeneity among their new neighbors, which was independent of the kind of move they were making.

Interpersonal Relations

We saw in the preceding chapter that contact with close friends does not vary by housing type with respect to either the amount or the place of contact. Only the path which people follow in making friends varies by housing type (although not by location). Those living in houses are more likely to meet local friends around the neighborhood through their children, while those in apartments, originally less likely to have children, were more likely to have met friends through communities of interest.

These findings do not vary according to the kind of change in housing undertaken.

Nonetheless, these paths to friendship also characterized the same groups of people *before* they moved. The presence or absence of children, which normally underlies how people make friends within local areas, is a phenomenon that most people *brought with them* unchanged from their previous dwellings, giving an undeserved post-move appearance of determination to the housing type. This is an example of self-selection as the process behind behavior spuriously assigned to dwelling types.

We saw also in Chapter 6 that certain types of mutual aid vary according to housing type and location, depending on the nature of assistance involved. It is not, like making friends, a reflection of self-selection, however. Our data this time suggest that the destination environment itself is the most probable basis for the behavior observed, although the data supporting such an assignment of 'determinacy' are not conclusive. This assertion, however, is supported by those about economic and educational similarities among homeowners, as well as by the nature of personal similarities felt shared by suburbanites.

We can further assess the influence, or lack of it, of the new residential settings by arraying time-budget information from Phase I to Phase III with respect to the change represented in the experience of individuals. We classified the change in people's participation in specific activities on weekdays and on Sundays in terms of whether these comparisons showed a decrease in the time devoted to the activity, the same amount of time devoted, or an increase. We counted, for example, someone who did not perform the activity in Phase I but did do it in Phase III in the 'increase' category, just like someone who did it both times but increased the amount of time devoted to it. The rules underlying assignment to the other categories are logically similar.

We found that formal visits at home increase for those in all categories, not just those who had moved to houses. Rates of increase differed slightly, in favor of those moving to houses, averaging about 10 percent for houses and about 4 percent for apartments.

On the other hand, we found that those in downtown apartments meet their friends in public establishments of various kinds slightly more than do others. In this case, an aggregate gain of 14 percent contrasts favorably with gains of 11 percent in downtown houses, 7 percent in suburban apartments and 10 percent in suburban houses. The *amount* of increase in *time* spent with friends in public buildings, which is substantial on the part of those in downtown apartments, is hidden by this form of classification.

We must remember also that women moving to suburban houses had expected to entertain more at home after the move. Time-budget trend data show that they did, but only slightly more than the others—and only more so on weekdays. Looking at these data in terms of change from Phase I to Phase II and then again from Phase II to Phase III shows that there was very little increase in entertaining at home in Phase II (if anything, it decreases), while the period during which increased entertaining began was only after some months following the move.

In addition, we saw in Chapter 6 that husbands living in houses eat out with friends most frequently. This activity differs from seeing friends in public places in that it is much more specific. The trend data indicate that the amount of increase of this activity among them is approximately twice the increase found among those in apartment houses. This increase, when linked with an absence of pre-move differences in this regard, suggests that post-move factors provide an explanation. Nonetheless, it is difficult to claim that this is a function of the housing type, but it is more likely, as implied in the last chapter that this has to do with the relative affluence and seniority of this category of men.

In general, then, we need to account for relatively few differences in interpersonal relations. The most significant of them, where people make their friendships, is something characteristic of these people before they come to their new housing, generally reflecting the presence or absence of children. In contrast, some of the extremely marginal differences in inter-personal relationships, such as mutual aid and weekday visiting by wives, reflect a slight influence from the home environment. Finally, while a main difference in the daily life of men, eating out with friends, increases in association with a move to a single-family house, this 'dynamic' relation is likely spurious. By and large, then, our analysis of interpersonal relations among the families sampled does not provide strong support for either self-selection or environmental determinism.

Organizational Activity

In the previous chapter, we looked at the organizations which husbands and wives joined after their moves, noting that about the same percent-age of persons in the various categories of residential environment was likely to join an organization. At this point, we must ask whether those moving to houses continued the greater participation we had noted *before* the move.

About 45 percent of the wives, regardless of housing type or location, participate as much in organizations to which they previously belonged following their move, while a strong minority of about 38 percent say that they participate less. Since about only 20 percent say they participate more, the aggregate change is one of somewhat less continuing participa-tion, a change effective across the board.

The reasons women advance for lowered continuing participation vary by location. The suburban wives, especially those who moved to houses, feel that the organizations in which they no longer participate as actively are too far away. Those living downtown state that they are doing other things instead—consistent with the presence of alternative spatial opportunities.

While the men in downtown apartments and in suburban houses follow the same pattern, those in downtown houses and suburban apartments are more likely to continue participation the same as before and less likely to decrease participation; for these latter two groups, there is little aggregate change in participation. However, when they decrease their level of organizational activity, the suburban and downtown apartment husbands give the same reasons as their wives. In addition to this, the men in downtown houses who decrease their involvement claim time pressures because of the need to work on their new homes, while those in suburban houses cite job pressures.

That people bring over to their respective new homes approximately equal percentages of their former participation means that those in houses have more because they *started with more.*

Church attendance was shown in Chapter 6 as most characteristic of families living in houses and least characteristic of those in downtown apartments. Already in Phase I, church attendance differentiated those choosing homes from those choosing apartments. When comparing the stated frequency of attendance given in Phase I with that in Phase III, we see that the post-move differences reflect the original dispositions of the mover, not the characteristics of the environment to which they moved. Every category of environment is associated with a decline in attendance. The decline is sharp (54% lost and 8% gained, a 46% net loss) in downtown apartments, but it is usually mild (for example, a 6% net loss in suburban houses). There is no characteristic change according to the type of move made.

The time-budget data on the same phenomenon, but with reference to the preceding Sunday, show a very slight gain of about 5 percent in aggregate among those in suburbia, compared to a 4 percent loss in downtown houses and no difference (but 94% 'no participation') in downtown apartments.

As might be expected, the farther that people moved geographically, the more likely they were to change the church to which they go (assuming that they do belong to a church). Hence, those remaining within the downtown zone are most likely to retain membership in a church within the same square mile area as before; 42 percent of them do so. Among all the other churchgoers who moved, only 18 percent go to the same place in Phase III that they did in Phase I. None of those moving downtown from the suburbs did so, and only 15 percent of those moving from the intermediate area went back out on Sundays. Smaller differences separated those remaining within the suburbs (18%), those moving there from intermediate areas, (15%), and those moving to the suburbs from downtown (11%). Nonetheless, that about one in eight newly decentralized churchgoing suburbanites did return to the same church to which they previously belonged, in what by definition is a reasonable distance away, helps explain the length of journey shown in Figure 6.1.

The data on children suggest somewhat more of an association between housing type and religious practice than do the changes recorded for the adults. Among the children in suburban houses, 26 percent of them increased their attendance at church on the Sunday recorded in the time budget, compared to 7 percent who decreased, a 19 percent net increase. This contrasts sharply with those in suburban apartments, of whom only 6 percent increased, while 9 percent decreased, a net decrease of 3 percent. Although the increase in suburban houses is strongly present regardless of what type of residence a child moved from, it is most pronounced among those who moved from low-rise apartments to houses (39%).

Hence, while patterns of churchgoing owe very much to preexisting behavior and loyalty, there is some evidence among the *children* of different emphasis according to their current housing type.

Commuting

I indicated the integral place of commuting with moves downtown in the previous two chapters. At this point, we must pursue not absolute distances or travel times but rather what the changes meant to the families involved.

For example, the preceding two chapters showed women moving downtown as disproportionately far from their work before the move and comfortably close afterward. It is not surprising, then, to find that about 60 percent of them decreased the length of their journey, compared to about 40 percent who increased their journey, although by somewhat shorter distances. In contrast, more than three-quarters of the women in all the other categories increased their distance to work as a consequence of the moves. Women moving to suburban houses were affected most negatively.

The above picture describes those wives who did *not* change their jobs while in the process of moving. The few who did change their jobs simultaneously present no clearcut pattern of advantage or disadvantage.

Husbands moving to downtown had not been disadvantaged in terms of distance—only travel time. Our trend analysis shows that no category of men had a net decrease in distance to their jobs, although the men who moved to downtown apartments most nearly broke even. Those moving to suburban houses had the greatest increases in distance. Table 7.8 shows these changes in distance to work for those not changing jobs.

It was, however, those *moving toward* the center who had the greatest deficit for which to compensate in distance to work. Hence, it is not surprising to see that, among those moving downtown from more remote areas, three times as many women decreased their distance to work as increased it, compared to the ratio of more than 3 to 1 in favor of an *increase* among those remaining within the downtown area. Although all categories of suburban movers incur net gains in distance, those moving from more central locations incur the worst increases, particularly since the data mapped in Chapter 6 indicate that a good many suburbanites continue to work in the center. The husbands' data are very similar to the wives' in this respect.

An analysis of the effect of change in *housing* to husbands' distances to work shows that the move to the house clearly involves more of a trade-off with distance to work than is the move to an apartment. This is, of course, a classic trade-off often cited. In the case of the present sample, the move from an apartment to a home involves an increased commute for the husband 83 percent of the time, while a move from a home to an apartment involves an increase only 28 percent of the time.

Furthermore, those choosing to live in houses demonstrate consistently greater increases in distance to work than those choosing apartments, regardless of the kind of housing from which they are moving: *from houses,* 55.8 percent increase when moving to other houses and 28.2 percent to

Table 7.8
Change in Length of Work Trip after Moving, by Destination
Housing Type and Location

Change in Distance in Miles
Percentage of Wives/Husbands for Each Environment

Destination Environment	1 + less		Up to 1 less		No change		Up to 1 more		1 to 5 more		5 + more		(N)	
	Wife	Husband	Wife	Husband	Wife	Husband	Wife	Husband	Wife	Husband	Wife	Husband	Wife	Husband
Apartment downtown	19.2	22.3	13.5	7.4	44.2	38.9	9.6	14.8	13.5	11.1	0.0	5.6	(52)	(54)
House downtown	11.8	15.3	5.9	16.9	29.4	23.7	17.6	18.6	23.5	22.0	11.8	3.4	(17)	(59)
Apartment suburbs	11.1	24.9	7.9	8.1	7.9	20.8	6.3	9.4	30.2	17.4	36.5	19.5	(63)	(149)
House suburbs	7.3	10.9	2.4	7.5	4.9	9.5	2.4	10.2	34.1	28.6	48.8	33.3	(41)	(147)
Total													(173)	(411)
Missing Information													(—)	(136)

apartments; *from low-rise apartments,* 60.4 percent to houses and 46.2 percent to high-rises; and *from high-rises,* 82.9 percent to houses and 45.6 percent to other high-rise apartments.

Nonetheless, as indicated in Chapter 5, distance is translated into travel time via the mechanism of mode of travel. We saw in the last chapter the downtown emphasis on mass transit compared to the suburban emphasis on driving. Given these differences, the only context in which we found abnormally long *durations* of commute to work was among men living in suburban houses. This does not mean, however, that the moves did not have different effects, given the disproportionately high travel times we previously found among both men and women destined for downtown apartments.

The trend data indicate that the greatest decreases are enjoyed by both husbands and wives moving to downtown apartments, even if this does not result in a situation of overall travel efficiency compared to all other categories. Women moving to downtown houses achieve somewhat less pronounced decreases in time than do men in suburban apartments. Women in both suburban housing types, though only men moving to suburban houses, encounter significant increases in commuting time. Table 7.9 indicates these changes.

As would be expected, the centralizers get the largest decreases in time (over 60% of both husbands and wives in this category doing so). Those remaining downtown show a slight decrease among the wives and a slight increase among the husbands. Those remaining within the suburbs show a slight increase (by 20% in aggregate for the wives, with the husbands remaining unchanged: about 35% increasing and 35% decreasing). On the other hand more than 60 percent of the wives and 50 percent of the husbands increased their commuting time if decentralizing out to the suburbs. Table 7.10 indicates this finding.

The time budgets reflect time usage during a particular day, rather than respondents' images of travel time in the abstract. The same comparative relationships remain, when gauged by time-budget data, contrasting the downtown high-rise residents with the others. Wives within this one category of residence show a decrease in travel time more frequently than an increase, while those in all the others report net gains in travel time. Among the husbands, those living in suburban houses do not show the considerable increase in travel time their own words had suggested, indi-

Table 7.9
Change in Duration of Work Trip after Moving, by Destination
Housing Type and Location

Change in Duration in Minutes
Percentage of Wives/Husbands for Each Environment

Destination Environment	10 + less		Up to 10 less		No change		Up to 10 more		10 + more		(N)	
	Wife	Husband	Wife	Husband	Wife	Husband	Wife	Husband	Wife	Husband	Wife	Husband
Apartment downtown	22.6	18.9	41.9	34.0	12.9	22.6	22.6	18.9	0.0	5.7	(31)	(53)
House downtown	0.0	13.4	45.5	25.0	18.2	19.2	18.2	25.0	18.2	17.3	(11)	(52)
Apartment suburbs	7.9	20.5	18.4	24.4	13.2	18.9	34.2	19.7	26.3	16.5	(38)	(127)
House suburbs	6.7	8.5	23.3	14.0	13.3	24.0	26.7	24.8	30.0	28.7	(30)	(129)
Total											(100)	(361)
Missing Information											(—)	(186)

Table 7.10
Change in Duration of Work Trip, by Location Change

	Change in Duration of Work Trip in Minutes Percentage of Wives/Husbands for Each Location Change											
	10 + less		Up to 10 less		No change		Up to 10 more		10 + more		(N)	
Location Change	Wife	Husband	Wife	Husband	Wife	Husband	Wife	Husband	Wife	Husband	Wife	Husband
Downtown to downtown	10.2	7.5	30.8	29.9	33.3	22.4	5.1	23.9	20.5	16.4	(39)	(67)
Outside Toronto to downtown and centralizers	25.0	31.6	37.5	28.9	20.8	18.4	12.5	18.4	4.2	2.6	(24)	(38)
Suburbs to suburbs	10.0	14.2	20.0	20.8	20.0	27.4	16.7	21.7	33.3	16.0	(30)	(106)
Outside Toronto to suburbs and decentralizers	13.6	14.7	9.1	18.0	16.7	17.3	24.2	22.7	36.4	27.3	(66)	(150)
Total											(159)	(361)
Missing Information											(—)	(186)

cating about an equal number of gains and losses. This is, nevertheless, in sharp contrast to the twice as many men in downtown apartments who decreased their time as increased it. The time budgets show that men in downtown houses, as well as those in suburban apartments, on balance have made slight increases in their travel time.

In sum, the one category of mover whose mobility appeared predicated upon the reduction of deficits in commuting time is the one whose changes in that regard appear to bring about the most post-move benefits. People whose moves were not as closely related to commuting, but rather to other aspects of their home environment, incurred in most cases an increase in travel time to work. Nonetheless, it must be kept in mind that no matter how sharp the increases or decreases, the final pattern is one in which only those living in suburban houses may, by some criteria, be shown to be at a strong disadvantage (presumably sustained in recognition of other benefits they are incurring).

Commercial Activity

We may legitimately pursue several aspects of change in commercial activity in this section: frequency of activity, travel mode, and location. In Chapter 6, we saw that suburbanites shop for clothing more frequently than those moving downtown, that downtown residents utilize public entertainment more fully, and that women in downtown apartments eat out most frequently. Let us look at these findings one by one.

Since there was no category of mover shopping for clothing more frequently than any other before the move, the existence of observable differences between suburbanites and downtown residents following the move suggests change. The nature of change, in this case, turns out to be twosided. Women moving downtown *decreased* the frequency of their shopping for clothes rather sharply (47% in both downtown apartments and homes shopped less, while only 31% in the apartments and 20% in the houses shopped more, an aggregate decrease of about 20%). In contrast, 48 percent of those in suburban apartments increased, compared to 25 percent who decreased, while the comparable figures among those who moved to suburban houses are 33.3 percent and 31.8 percent, a modest aggregate increase.

Changes in location are not responsible for these trends. It is difficult to specify exactly what did cause the simultaneous contraction and expansion of shopping activity in the respective locations; none of the social characteristics we measured is related.

People patronize places of commercial entertainment less from Phases I through III. Despite a hectic period of recreational activity immediately following the move by those who moved downtown, the overall trend in this area is one of decrease. For example, although those in downtown houses are the greatest users of entertainment facilities, they also demonstrate the greatest decrease in use. That they and the residents of downtown apartments still lead in such usage has to be considered a function of self-selection based on prior activity, not situated behavior.

In answer to our direct question about restaurant meals, wives gave no evidence of differences in increase or decrease according to home environment. Again, differences among the categories of residence are those that existed before the move.

In contrast, the mode of travel involved in commercial activity is highly related to the nature of the destination environment. In Chapter 6, we saw that mode of travel varies for shopping, but not for entertainment. With respect to grocery shopping, for example, there was a home-apartment split regarding the use of the automobile. Table 7.11 shows the change in percentage use of the automobile in the different phases according to the type of housing change undertaken. Those who moved to houses retain the same level of automobile usage for grocery shopping *if moving from*

Table 7.11
Use of Car in Grocery Shopping, by Change in Housing Type
(*Percentage*)

	Change in Housing Type						
Phase of Study	House to house	Other to house	Apartment to house	Apartment to apartment	Other to apartment	House to apartment	
Phase I	90.5	76.8	75.0	65.7	62.0	72.3	
Phase II	91.6	88.5	81.7	60.2	55.9	52.2	
Phase III	89.3	86.2	91.1	55.7	59.1	59.2	
(N)	(164)	(74)	(58)	(158)	(66)	(44)	(564)
Missing Information or Not Applicable							27

another house; if, on the other hand, they move to a house from an apartment, they move from a lower level of automobile usage to a higher one.
In contrast, those moving from one high-rise to another lower their auto
usage for grocery shopping from an already low level, while those moving
there from a house lower their usage from a somewhat higher level. Although the changes in usage show a persistently strong effect by the new
housing type, one must note as well some degree of self-selection; all categories of apartment movers started with a lower level of auto usage for
grocery shopping than did any category of house mover.

The data indicate the same pattern with shopping for sundries, except
that the self-selective pattern is not as strong as with groceries. Those
moving from apartments to houses show marked increases in auto use,
while those moving to apartments show equally marked decreases; those
remaining within these two housing types demonstrate unchanging high
and low rates of utilization, respectively. Table 7.12 presents these data.

Those downtown use public transit to shop for clothing, while those in
the suburbs do not. Analyzing those who live downtown according to locational changes shows that people who stayed downtown make little
change in their 33 percent utilization rate of public transit, while those
who moved downtown from the suburbs increase from o to 29.4 percent.
Surprisingly, perhaps, those who moved downtown from intermediate locations show only a token increase of 22 to 25 percent usage, although it
is likely that their move to an even more central location is predicated on
more efficient use of the mass transportation they had already become ac-
customed to using.

Table 7.12
Use of Car in Sundry Shopping, by Change in Housing Type
(*Percentage*)

Phase of Study	House to house	Other to house	Apartment to house	Apartment to apartment	Other to apartment	House to apartment	
Phase I	78.4	51.9	39.7	31.0	37.7	57.8	
Phase II	75.5	71.0	64.3	31.1	23.8	22.5	
Phase III	81.5	66.7	77.5	28.8	15.5	33.3	
(N)	(164)	(74)	(58)	(158)	(66)	(44)	(564)
Missing Information or Not Applicable							27

An examination of the extent that people change their shopping habits upon moving helps clarify the location of commercial facilities they visit.

Most people patronize different stores for groceries and sundries after moving. This is particularly so among those making moves of a centralizing or decentralizing character; among these, fewer than 10 percent retain the same shopping habits for groceries, and under 5 percent go to the same places for sundries. Nonetheless, these figures are only 29 percent and 25 percent respectively for those remaining within the downtown zone and 16 percent and 12 percent among those remaining within suburbia.

In contrast, much higher percentages continue to go to the same locations for clothing, restaurants, and entertainment. Regardless of whether people move to or remain within downtown, about 50 percent of the downtown residents continue to shop in the same places for clothing—predominantly the downtown shopping area. Slightly over 30 percent of both those remaining in or moving to suburbia continue to patronize the same locations for clothing as before; many suburbanites still go downtown for clothing.

Since places of entertainment are not equally distributed about the city and are not generally considered chosen on the basis of efficient access, it is not surprising that we find a comparably high-retention rate of locations utilized, without distinction according to the kind of locational change undertaken.

Our analysis of the changes in location of places patronized within the year *following* the move, from Phase II to Phase III, helps support what respondents said about the differential rates of adaptation to the different residential settings. Those living in downtown apartments had already settled on over 70 percent of the places where they shop for groceries and sundries, the two most changeable types of commerce, by Phase II. Those who moved to suburban houses still utilized in Phase III only about 35 percent of the places selected as of Phase II. Consistent with the direct relationship of length of time needed for adaptation to single-family housing and suburban location, the two intermediate categories (downtown houses and suburban apartments) have intermediate rates of just about 50 percent change from Phase II to Phase III. In any case, the suburban house population, with greater distances to cover, greater flexibility given their use of the car, less presence of facilities at hand to 'fall into,' and a high level of selectivity in their shopping behavior, certainly indicate that their behavior immediately following the move cannot be construed as final.

As a result of these differing commutes and commercial travel habits, it is not surprising to see considerable differences in the number of miles families drive per month. More than half the families in suburban houses, the greatest consumers of automobile miles, run up a total of over 1,200 miles per month. Only 38 percent of the families sharing suburban locations but located instead in high-rise apartments exceed this minimum mileage. These suburban percentages, on the other hand, compare to 29.9 percent of those in downtown apartments and 25.1 percent of those in downtown houses who drive that much. The latter are also more likely to demonstrate considerably lower average monthly mileages. About a quarter of all the downtown families drive fewer than 600 miles a month, compared to one in seven families in suburban apartments and one in eight in suburban houses.

Pastimes

We can examine the basis for the findings reported in Chapter 6 on recreational activity by looking at respondent reports of pastimes they initiated or increased in activity after moving and at trend analyses of selected activities as gathered by the time budget.

We saw gardening in Chapter 6 as a widespread preoccupation of homeowners. In Chapter 5, we saw it also as a preexisting interest of those moving to houses. At this point, let us look at the families who in Phase III were shown to participate in gardening. Did a disproportionate number of these start or increase their participation in this activity only after the move to houses; or, on the other hand, did the lion's share of gardening simply come with these respondents from their previous homes?

Among the homeowners, 45 percent of the wives and 52 percent of the husbands living downtown, as well as 30 percent and 27 percent respectively of the suburbanites took up gardening only after the move to the new house, surely reflective of the normative demands for 'proper' maintenance of a house. These percentages are particularly high for those moving from apartments, as 54 percent of the wives and 40 percent of the husbands moving from low-rise apartments to houses and about 60 percent of both spouses moving from high-rise to houses started gardening only after the move.

Even those who already gardened in their homes before moving were likely to increase the amount of time devoted to it after the move. This increase is particularly marked among the husbands. In downtown houses, 64 percent of them devote more time after the move, compared to an increase among 52 percent of those in suburban houses.

Sports participation was central at the time people chose to move to apartments, although we did not observe long-run, differential behavior to any appreciable extent in the last chapter. Since most families have some prior acquaintance with sports, *increases* are most meaningful to observe here. A considerably higher percentage of women who moved to high-rise apartments than those who moved to houses claim to have increased their participation in sports. About 45 percent of participants in high rise report increases since the move, compared to only about 30 percent among those in single houses. These increases, furthermore, appear to reflect the opportunities gained by changes in housing type; about 50 percent of those moving to apartments from single houses and low-rise apartments increase their participation, compared to only 36 percent of those moving from one apartment to another.

The time budgets, however, indicate no great changes in participation in sports from Phase I to Phase III. They record an across-the-board, modest increase on weekdays and an equally modest decline for all categories on Sundays. Nonetheless, this tends to hide a significantly greater increase from Phase I to Phase II for both husbands and wives moving to high-rise apartments, accompanied by a general decline among these respondents from Phase II to Phase III.

Hence, respondent reports of increased participation after moving are not inaccurate; these reports are merely incomplete with respect to longer-range behavior. While the home environment did provide for the fulfillment of the desired behavior after the move, there is no necessity that this behavior continue indefinitely, particularly if not a high-priority item in people's lives. Nonetheless, this is more evidence that those moving to high-rise make immediate use of the new residence, in contrast to the longer period of adaptation taken by people moving to houses.

Listening to stereo is a male pastime emphasized in high-rise apartments, according to data in Chapter 6. Almost 10 percent of the husbands in the downtown high-rise and 4 percent in the suburban high-rise, moreover, say that such participation originated after their moves, compared to none living in houses. Although these are not significantly large percentages, they reflect *only* men who had moved to high-rise *from other forms of housing,* as if stereo were a form of *adaptation* to high-rise.

Among those who already listened to stereo before the move, men in apartments are twice as likely to have increased this activity following the move than those who moved to houses (about 17% to 8½%). This is particularly true of those moving from lower-rise alternatives to apartments, although those moving from any housing type to an apartment are more likely to increase stereo listening than their counterparts who move instead to houses.

Suburbanites appear to bring card playing with them, as the modest increase in time devoted to this pastime by those moving to and within suburbia is less than the increase found among those moving to and within downtown. The characteristic situation is the continuation of previous amounts of time devoted to this activity, which presumably ensures a higher level of participation among those now living in the suburbs.

Going to the theater, a favorite pastime of those living downtown, is another which does not increase as a function of changes in housing type or location. Nonetheless, among all those who chose suburbia, the families making decentralizing moves showed greater declines than did those remaining outside the central city. Among those moving to the suburbs from downtown, 40 percent say they devote less time to theater following the move, compared to just under 30 percent among those remaining outside. Theater going, then, primarily reflects *preexisting* interests and rates of participation, which help to account for the choice of downtown housing.

We found photography a hobby most frequently engaged in among those in downtown apartments. The husbands in this case show striking gains in pursuit of this pastime. Although few are taking it up for the first time, 46 percent of the men in downtown high-rise increase their participation in photography, compared to an average of 19 percent within all the other categories. While those in suburban apartments do not nearly approach those in downtown apartments in this regard, they still show more activity of this sort than do those in the single-family homes. Photography may thus be one answer to the question of what form of creative activity is potentially compatible with relatively small, high-rise quarters.

We saw in the last chapter that men and women in downtown houses are uniquely less likely to have an interest in watching television, just as had been the case before their move. The time budget indicates that, subsequent to the move, these people are the only ones not sustaining a substantial increase in their amount of television watching. Both husbands and wives in all the other categories of housing and location increase their television viewing by 15 to 20 percent. The wives in downtown houses show a net increase of only 3.7 percent, and their husbands show a net decrease of 7.9 percent.

On Sundays, the husbands in downtown houses do show a net increase of about 14 percent, but this is overshadowed by considerably larger increases among all the others. Women in downtown houses, in contrast, show the largest net increase on Sundays, 14 percent, but this still does not bring them to the point of equality with the others.

On balance, the residents of downtown houses appear to *bring with them* a predisposition against great concentration on television watching, which the context of their new homes and location does not distort; the other housing types do not, perhaps, present as time-consuming challenges in the realm of home repair which limits the amount of time available for watching television.

Children moving to houses show a greater decline in television viewing. This decline is particularly marked among those moving to houses from apartments.

Sports participation increases the most among children moving to apartments (62% in suburban apartments versus 48.6% in suburban houses). Although the numbers involved are smaller, the percentage increase is very much higher among those moving from houses to apartments than among those moving either from one apartment to another or from an apartment to a house (about 85% versus about 50%).

In neither of the above two cases are house-apartment differences a function of the ages of the children involved. They occur regardless of whether the children are in their young or older teens.

Although we found that people in homes read more than do those in apartments, this does not reflect a unique post-move increase in reading. Modest increases were found among all categories of movers, with the subsequent emphasis among homeowners reflecting their preexisting habits.

In sum, this material on pastimes presents much the same picture as do the other subject areas. In some cases, pastimes which reflect the demands or opportunities of particular housing types or locations are developed more fully following the move. In other cases, in contrast, the emphasis discovered following the move reflects instead preexisting differences within the population (which were not necessarily irrelevant to the choice of housing type and location).

Housekeeping Activity

In the preceding chapter, we saw that different forms of housework vary according to various combinations of housing type and location. With respect to food preparation, for example, those in downtown apartments are less active than the others, the position they occupied with respect to *all* forms of housework on weekdays before their move.

Our trend analysis shows that this lower level of activity cannot be seen as a function of the move, since 25 percent more women in downtown apartments increased their attention to food preparation than decreased it following the move, while there is a net decrease in time devoted to food preparation in all the other categories. Inasmuch as we found the number of children in the family responsible for some differences in housekeeping time before the move, subsequent changes among the downtown-apartment group may reflect to some extent the postmove increases in their families.

Suburbanites spend more time washing dishes. What this reflects, however, is not a major increase among all those moving to suburbia, although the suburban apartment wives do show a 17 percent net increase, the largest of the groups. Rather, there is an 8 percent decrease in downtown houses following the move, which joins with the already low figure in downtown apartments, where participation increases by only a little (6%), forming a generally lower level than that seen in suburban areas.

We saw that those who moved to downtown apartments continue to do less indoor cleaning than others. This is hardly an effect of the environment, inasmuch as those in downtown apartments are the only group not showing a net decline in activity. Although housework generally went up from Phase I to Phase II throughout all categories, surely as a function of the move, time devoted to housework then tended to go down even further by the end of the first year of residence. In downtown apartments, almost exactly a third increase, decrease, and remain the same in their devotion to housework, while the typical pattern in each of the other categories shows 45 percent decreasing and 36 percent increasing, a net decrease of 9 percent. Nonetheless, since participation in the downtown apartments started at a lower level, these women still contribute the least of this form of housework, surely a function of self-selection.

The situation behind time devoted to laundering is similar to that behind dishwashing. In this case it is the apartment dwellers who do the least on weekdays. The group performing the least activity in this regard before the move, the downtown high-rise group again, remains relatively stable, while those in suburban apartments show a net decrease of 13 percent. Since we recorded very slight increases of 7.5 and 1.4 percent for the downtown and suburban house groups, a resulting home-apartment dichotomy occurs which partly reflects self-selection and partly reflects a decrease whose origins are unknown.

Husbands devote time to home repairs both on weekdays and on Sundays. In this case, the trend data indicate the influence of the housing type chosen, inasmuch as the premove behavior patterns were not in this direction. Table 7.13 shows that those moving to houses increase performance of this activity both on weekdays and Sundays, while those moving to apartments decrease sharply in this respect. That this happens is surely no surprise.

Table 7.13
Change in Time for Husband's Home-Maintenance Activity from
Phases I to III, by Destination Housing Type and Location
(*Percentage*)

		Destination Housing Type and Location			
Change in Time		Downtown apartment	Downtown house	Suburban apartment	Suburban house
Weekdays	(N) =	(51)	(38)	(123)	(142)
Less		11.8	5.3	13.8	7.7
Same		84.3	81.6	79.7	78.2
More		3.9	13.2	6.5	14.1
Sunday	(N) =	(48)	(36)	(120)	(138)
Less		29.2	8.3	21.7	18.1
Same		66.7	69.4	74.2	62.3
More		4.2	22.2	4.2	19.6

RECAPITULATION

Both parts of this chapter, the first concerned with fulfillment of specific expectations and the degree that elements of housing were anticipated, and the second dealing with the specific areas of social differentiation and behavior, come down supporting the presence of a considerable degree of *both* self-selection and post-move 'situated behavior' as applicable to a number of specific aspects and implications of housing type and location. While the first section includes summaries of the implications of these data in tabular format, the discussion throughout the second part of the chapter to this point has not been amenable to such a summary display. Therefore, as a form of recapitulation, a listing is presented in Table 7.14 of the effects cited in Chapter 6 and pursued through one or another form of datum and analysis in this chapter. This table attempts to assess the relative degrees of influence from self-selection, on the one hand, and the postmove environment, on the other.

This table indicates that a roughly equal number of phenomena are explained with reference to each perspective, according to the nature of people's motivations in some cases and the opportunities and requirements of the environment in other cases.

In many of the cases involving a continuation of previously existing social behavior, the environment is causally spurious, although not necessarily irrelevant. Such factors as family size, and, in some cases, working status of the wife and socioeconomic status, explain not only the behavior involved but, to some degree, the environmental choice as well; in the real world, however, they all occur together in a package, helping to explain the particular kinds of behavior found within a given residential setting.

Our answer, then, to the 'nature versus nurture' question is, simply, 'both,' but not necessarily at the same time with respect to the same issue. Each has its place in a total system of explanation. There is no need to be dogmatic about the one form of explanation or the other.

Table 7.14
Situated Behavior, by Type of Relation to Residential Environment

	Downtown apartment	Downtown house	Suburban apartment	Suburban house	House	Apartment	Downtown	Suburbs
1. Personal trait similarity among neighbors					*			*
2. Knowledge of neighbors		†			†			
3. Where friends first met				†	*			*
4. Mutual aid patterns					†			
5. Differential participation in organizations						*		
6. Differential types of organizations joined					*			*
7. Church attendance—adults					†			
8. Church attendance—children					†*			
9. Commuting decrease	†							
10. Commuting increase				*				
11. Frequency of clothes shopping					*			*
12. Frequency of commercial entertainment	†							
13. Frequency of restaurant meals (wives)							†	
14. Mode of transportation for groceries—car					†*			
15. Change of location—shopping goods					*			
16. Gardening					†*			
17. Sports participation						*		*

18. Stereo				
19. Photography	*			*
20. Theatergoing	†			
21. Television	†	†		†
22. Reading		†		
23. Food preparation—women	†	†	†	
24. Washing dishes—women	†	†		
25. Laundry—women	†	†	†	
26. Indoor cleaning—women	†	†	*	
27. Home maintenance—men		†		

Key: * = Behavior appearing in response to new residential context.

† = Behavior or expectation carried over from previous home.

NOTES

[1] See Charles Tilly, *An Urban World* (1974), for an analogous, triangular schema, designed to put into perspective the various factors considered throughout urban sociology more generally. An even more recent work, drawn in (small) part on the present project results, elaborates three competing theories of urban sociology which represent these same considerations (Fischer, 1976).

[2] A recent study using personality tests suggests that suburban neighboring patterns do not really reflect self-selection, since the underlying personality traits conducive to neighboring are more closely related to factors which covary with suburban location than to suburban location itself (Baldassare and Fischer, 1975). Nonetheless, if the covariates, the housing type, and the resultant behaviors all occur together as a package, the relation of neighboring to suburban residence (in our case, residence in suburban *houses*) is not coincidental, even though we should not attribute causal effects to the residential environment.

Chapter Eight

Evaluation

WHAT THEY THINK,
WHAT THEY PLAN

To this point, I have described and analyzed how people found their new housing, why they moved and to where, what phenomena appeared in the new environment, and the extent that such phenomena were either brought into or developed within the destination environment. While this may constitute a variety of concerns, it does not touch upon how the respondents reacted to their new homes and locations. We do not know what people think of their homes and locations. We do not know the consequences of such problems as arose. We do not know what the new residential settings mean in the lives and plans of these respondents.

In Chapter 8, levels of satisfaction and dissatisfaction, together with the physical elements contributing to them are assessed. We must place such an assessment, however, into a larger perspective, for which the respondents' own plans for their family mobility appear to provide a basis.

EVALUATION AND ITS COMPONENTS

One measure of satisfaction consists of direct answers to questions about how respondents "feel" about their new home, location, and neighborhood, respectively. Answers consisted of a closed-ended choice among items on a five-point scale: very satisfied, mostly satisfied, neither satisfied nor dissatisfied, mostly dissatisfied, and very dissatisfied.

We also asked a great number of other evaluative questions in the interviews. These included, for example, the orientations represented in answer to master-coded, open-ended questions, counts of the number of environmental elements with which respondents claim to be satisfied or dissatisfied, statements of intentions to move, and a self-anchoring scale measuring where current housing fits with the best and worst housing that people envisaged available for themselves.

The simple, direct question appears to tap environmental satisfaction most directly, without the more specific associations and derivations connected with the other evaluative questions. In any case, there are no contradictions among these measures, which are highly related, though not statistically identical, due to the connotations of the more specific questions. For example, only 29 percent of the wives who expressed satisfaction with under fifteen of the items on the checklist of elements of the new home said that they were definitely satisfied with their home, while 48 percent of those citing over fifteen elements claimed to be definitely satisfied.

Although I give the respondents' 'feelings' primacy in terms of general evaluation, I shall cite the other measures as appropriate.

Tables 8.1 through 8.3 indicate the feelings of husbands and wives about their new home environments. In general, these tables relate a high degree of satisfaction. Whether the response is about the new home, the new location, or the new neighborhood, and whether given by husband or wife, around 90 percent of the feelings are in the definitely satisfied or

Table 8.1

Feelings about the New Home, by Housing Type and Location
(Percentage)

Housing Type and Location	Feelings about New Home (Phase III)											
	Definitely satisfied		Mostly satisfied		Not satisfied Not dissatisfied		Mostly dissatisfied		Definitely dissatisfied		(N)	
	Wife	Husband	Wife	Husband	Wife	Husband	Wife	Husband	Wife	Husband	Wife	Husband
Apartment downtown	23.9	20.4	64.2	64.8	6.0	11.1	6.0	1.9	0.0	1.9	(67)	(54)
House downtown	52.6	54.8	44.9	42.9	2.6	0.0	0.0	2.4	0.0	0.0	(78)	(42)
Apartment suburbs	24.2	26.8	53.0	56.9	14.6	12.4	6.6	2.6	1.5	1.3	(198)	(153)
House suburbs	53.2	50.6	45.0	45.7	1.4	3.1	0.5	0.0	0.0	0.6	(218)	(162)
(N)											(561)	(411)
Missing Information											(32)	(38)

Table 8.2
Feelings about the New Location, by Housing Type and Location
(*Percentage*)

Housing Type and Location	Feelings about New Location (Phase III)											
	Definitely satisfied		Mostly satisfied		Not satisfied Not dissatisfied		Mostly dissatisfied		Definitely dissatisfied		(N)	
	Wife	Husband	Wife	Husband	Wife	Husband	Wife	Husband	Wife	Husband	Wife	Husband
Apartment downtown	44.8	41.1	50.7	53.6	4.5	3.6	0.0	1.8	0.0	0.0	(67)	(56)
House downtown	72.5	69.8	22.5	30.2	3.8	0.0	1.3	0.0	0.0	0.0	(80)	(43)
Apartment suburbs	46.5	36.5	44.9	54.7	4.5	6.9	2.0	0.6	2.0	1.3	(198)	(159)
House suburbs	43.3	48.2	46.0	45.7	7.9	4.3	2.8	1.8	0.0	0.0	(215)	(164)
(N)											(560)	(422)
Missing Information											(33)	(27)

Table 8.3

Feelings about the New Neighborhood, by Housing Type and Location
(*Percentage*)

| Housing Type and Location | Feelings about New Neighborhood (Phase III) | | | | | | | | | | | |
| | Definitely satisfied | | Mostly satisfied | | Not satisfied Not dissatisfied | | Mostly dissatisfied | | Definitely dissatisfied | | (N) | |
	Wife	Husband	Wife	Husband	Wife	Husband	Wife	Husband	Wife	Husband	Wife	Husband
Apartment downtown	31.3	33.9	55.2	51.8	11.9	12.5	1.5	1.8	0.0	0.0	(67)	(56)
House downtown	65.8	44.4	26.6	42.2	6.3	8.9	0.0	4.4	1.3	0.0	(79)	(45)
Apartment suburbs	34.3	33.3	46.5	54.1	18.2	7.5	0.5	3.1	0.5	1.9	(198)	(159)
House suburbs	43.7	46.4	45.6	47.0	7.9	4.8	1.9	1.2	0.9	0.6	(215)	(166)
(N)											(559)	(426)
Missing Information											(34)	(23)

mostly satisfied categories. More of the remaining answers are in the neutral than on the dissatisfied side of the scale.

Specific differences deserve attention according to the home environment to which people moved. Those who moved to single-family homes are more than twice as likely to be definitely satisfied *with their homes* as those who moved to high-rise apartments. These figures are not quite reversed in the mostly satisfied category, with the remainder of the answers among the apartment dwellers more likely to fall into the neutral and dissatisfied categories. Although Table 8.1 shows satisfaction among most families regardless of housing type, it shows also a higher level among those who move to houses than to apartments.

The families clearly demonstrating the most definite satisfaction on *location* are those living in downtown houses. About 70 percent of these families indicate definite satisfaction, compared to around 45 percent of those in the other categories. These results, indicated in Table 8.2, suggest an independence of the dimensions of housing type and location (cf. Onibokun, 1974). It is perhaps surprising that those moving to downtown houses stand alone, so far above their companions in downtown apartments, on locational satisfaction, since the latter used locational criteria so heavily in their choice of new housing. I shall return to this question later in this chapter.

Table 8.3 deals specifically with feelings about the new neighborhood. There is much less difference by housing type and location with this dimension of satisfaction. Nonetheless, the wives (only) downtown evince the greater percentage of definite satisfaction, while men and women living in houses are somewhat more likely (by about 10%) than those in apartments to indicate definite satisfaction with their neighborhoods. If the study were to have sampled polar neighborhood types, similar to our consideration of housing type and location, more dramatic findings might have appeared in this regard.

Overall, the downtown-house families give evidence of the greatest multidimensional satisfaction, while those in apartments of all types demonstrate the least (although no particular evidence of dissatisfaction).

Such findings are entirely consistent with those from other recent studies of high-rise housing in Canada. One study by the Social Planning Council of Metropolitan Toronto (1973), which utilized a more representative sample of apartment dwellers throughout the Toronto area and included many of the same measurement instruments, came up with identical findings. Another study, on condominium buyers in Vancouver, found 50 percent of their respondents expressing extremely satisfied responses and another 43 percent reporting moderate satisfaction (Hamilton and Roberts, 1973, p. 46).

Another form of confirmation of a high level of satisfaction with all forms of housing and location reported comes in answer to the question in Phase III about whether respondents "feel at ease" in their new homes. Upwards of 89 percent among the husbands and 90 percent among the wives do feel at ease by Phase III. Although the differences are extremely narrow and surely not significant in any way, husbands who move to houses and wives who move to apartments are marginally more at ease. Those most at ease are the women in downtown high-rise apartments, 96 percent of whom feel this way.

Thus, although some clear differences in degree of satisfaction are defined, there is hardly evidence of hostility to any form of housing or location studied, let alone simmering discontent. This is quite contrary to what we are led to believe by those who dismiss apartment or downtown living as unsuitable for families.

This is analogous to the situation concerning social contact among residents of high-rise apartments, which had been posited by others as virtually nonexistent but which emerged as alive and well in Chapters 5 and 6. The different nature, but not amount, of social contact among those living in a high-rise is explained in unemotional terms with respect to the paths which families follow in the course of making social acquaintances. In the present case, we must find an unemotional solution to the confrontation between popular claims of family discontent in high-rise settings and the high degree of satisfaction reported to us by families living there. I shall turn to this later in the chapter.

First, however, it may be instructive to look more closely at the various elements of the home environment found most satisfactory and unsatisfactory in the various settings.

Tables 8.4 and 8.5 show by housing type and location the considerable differentiation of elements found satisfactory by those exposed to them.

Those who have moved to downtown high-rise apartments cite locational elements most frequently. Such aspects as good public transportation, proximity to shopping, closeness to downtown, and access to both work and play are by far the most satisfactory elements of their home environment. They rate aspects of their homes and neighborhoods far less favorably.

In contrast, those living in downtown houses show much the same level of satisfaction with these locational aspects, sharing as they do the same part of town. In addition, however, they indicate a considerably higher appreciation for such critical elements of the dwelling unit as its size, layout, appearance, quality, and storage capacity. They appreciate several aspects of the neighborhood, including its appearance and the characteristics of neighbors. Those in downtown houses give evidence of satisfaction with all the major dimensions constituting the residential context.

Those in suburban apartments, however, are not consistently satisfied with any dimension, nor is there a level of satisfaction on any single element as high as the highest level accorded by either of the two downtown groups. They do, however, demonstrate a much higher than average satisfaction with their proximity to recreation facilities and to shopping. They appreciate their proximity to open space. Many aspects of their own apartments, such as the number of bedrooms and bathrooms, storage space, and parking are appreciated.

Finally, those who moved to suburban single-family homes are extremely satisfied with most aspects of their homes, but indicate relatively little satisfaction with any aspect of their location except their access to schools and to open space.

These findings are not surprising, since they reflect, in part, that which people expected before they moved. As we saw in the previous chapter, most of what people expected to find as benefits are represented among these satisfactions after the move. Nonetheless, the extent of differentiation in what satisfies which families goes far beyond what they expected.

We must note that although the percentage of persons responding favorably to items judged most satisfactory within each category of housing type and location does vary somewhat, with those living in suburban apartments showing the least consensus about satisfactory elements of the environment, those in every residential category nonetheless demonstrate satisfaction of a reasonably high level with one or another group of elements. Although the nature of the checklist used in the interviewing was intended for purposes of a complete inventory of relevant elements; the *profile* of elements to which residents turn in the search for satisfaction in

TABLE 8.4

Mention of Specific Satisfactions within Categories of Housing Type and Location (Wives, Phase III) (*Percentage*)

(All bars, regardless of shading, originate at zero.)

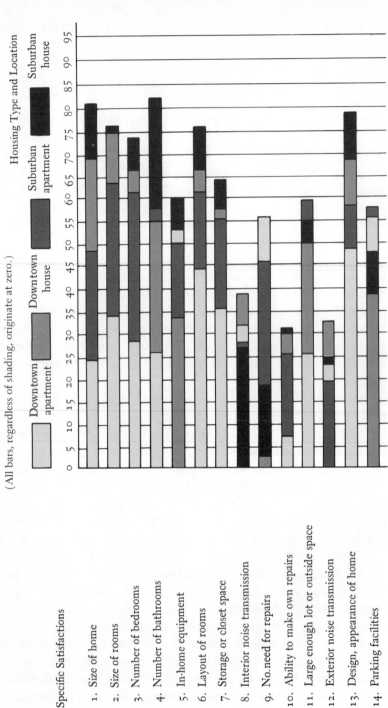

Housing Type and Location

Downtown apartment | Downtown house | Suburban apartment | Suburban house

Specific Satisfactions

1. Size of home
2. Size of rooms
3. Number of bedrooms
4. Number of bathrooms
5. In-home equipment
6. Layout of rooms
7. Storage or closet space
8. Interior noise transmission
9. No need for repairs
10. Ability to make own repairs
11. Large enough lot or outside space
12. Exterior noise transmission
13. Design, appearance of home
14. Parking facilities

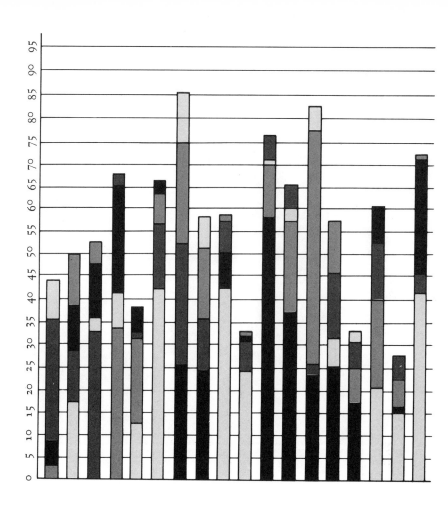

15. Management or developer
16. Social character of neighborhood
17. Type of neighbors/co-tenants
18. Distance to country/green spaces
19. Schools—quality
20. Design, appearance of neighborhood
21. Public transportation facilities
22. Short distance to work
23. Short distance to friends
24. Short distance to relatives
25. Short distance to shopping
26. Short distance to recreation facilities
27. Short distance to downtown area
28. Neighborhood facilities—adequate
29. Neighborhood facilities—convenient
30. Schools—location
31. Housing costs
32. Quality of home

TABLE 8.5

Mention of Specific Satisfactions within Categories of Housing Type and Location (Husbands, Phase III) (*Percentage*)

(All bars, regardless of shading, originate at zero.)

Housing Type and Location

Downtown apartment
Downtown house
Suburban apartment
Suburban house

Specific Satisfactions

1. Size of home
2. Size of rooms
3. Number of bedrooms
4. Number of bathrooms
5. In-home equipment
6. Layout of rooms
7. Storage or closet space
8. Interior noise transmission
9. No need for repairs
10. Ability to make own repairs
11. Large enough lot or outside space
12. Exterior noise transmission
13. Design, appearance of home
14. Parking facilities

0 5 10 15 20 25 30 35 40 45 50 55 60 65 70 75 80 85 90 95

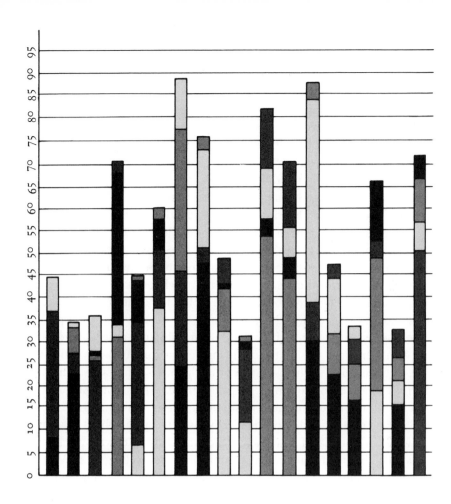

15. Management or developer
16. Social character of neighborhood
17. Type of neighbors/co-tenants
18. Distance to country/green spaces
19. Schools—quality
20. Design, appearance of neighborhood
21. Public transportation facilities
22. Short distance to work
23. Short distance to friends
24. Short distance to relatives
25. Short distance to shopping
26. Short distance to recreation facilities
27. Short distance to downtown area
28. Neighborhood facilities—adequate
29. Neighborhood facilities—convenient
30. Schools—location
31. Housing costs
32. Quality of home

their home environments is a different one for each of the environmental categories.

This is not surprising, since people had chosen these environments for different reasons. While this finding of different profiles of evaluative criteria does not rule out the ultimate presence of common goals or needs in housing, what this says is that different elements are contributing to the satisfaction expressed in the different categories. It may be possible at any given time for people to be happy with their home environment without a list of *universal* user needs being satisfied across the board.

Answers to another type of question further illustrate the differentiation of criteria employed to evaluate housing. We asked each respondent, when evaluating a good place to live, to indicate the relative importance of the dwelling unit, the location, and the neighborhood. We presented each combination of two of these three to the respondent for a dichotomous choice. We mentioned the pairs and the items within each pair in random order, so as not to bias the outcome through order of presentation. What emerged was that those living downtown, husbands and wives alike, rated location as the most salient of the three dimensions. Those in suburbia, regardless of housing type, placed the dwelling unit first.

Next in importance for those in suburbia were neighbor and neighborhood characteristics, with location clearly last. In contrast, both husbands and wives in downtown apartments and husbands in downtown houses placed neighborhood characteristics last, behind the dwelling unit. Women in downtown houses put neighborhood second and the dwelling unit last, although, as the data just presented indicate, these women are also well satisfied with their houses.

The suburban emphasis on homes and lack of emphasis on location is consistent with the thrust of previous research. The stress on location among those living downtown is also consistent with previous work. However, in the latter case, the emphasis on location even among those living in detached houses helps to explain the persistence of downtown homeowners in attempting to maintain the residential character of the areas in which they live; it is not a matter of indifference to them where they live. They do not consider a home of similar quality in another part of town an adequate substitution for that which they have already, which is difficult to replace if lost. Traditionally, the developer or politician anxious to see 'higher' levels of development in central areas of the city has not compre-

hended the relevance of both housing type *and* location among the downtown homeowners.

Children's views of their new homes are parallel to those of their parents. Their general level of satisfaction is high. The degree of satisfaction
in houses is much higher than that in apartments. Most children say that
they are at ease by Phase III, although, like their parents, those moving to
houses feel they took longer to adjust.

We compared the children's views about their new settings to reports
of what the parents thought about their children's reactions. The adult
views of their children's evaluations accurately mirrored what the children
thought in most cases, although the impressions of fathers were slightly
more accurate than those of mothers.

Like the parents, the children in different settings found different
grounds for satisfaction in the different types of residence. Given the numbers of children involved in the study, the main comparison, as before, is
between those living in suburban apartments and in suburban houses.
Children living in suburban apartments find the bulk of their satisfactions
with their new homes in site characteristics, particularly recreation facilities (38%), and social aspects of the neighborhood (20%). Aspects of the
dwelling unit (16%) are only secondary. In contrast, those living in suburban houses find 58 percent of their satisfactions in characteristics of the
dwelling unit, 17 percent in site characteristics, and only 4 percent with
the neighborhood more generally.

Those living in suburban apartments show the least satisfaction with
the elements in the dimensions of environment they chose as most important. This is consistent, however, with the data of the previous three chapters showing the generally residual character of the suburban high-rise regarding both its choice and the nature of the opportunities families find
within it. While the suburban high-rise is not without its benefits, they
are not of high priority in the lives of its residents.

This is indicated further by the number of dissatisfactions which people
report regarding specific elements of their new home environments.

Residents of suburban apartments are likely to cite the greatest number
of elements on our checklist as sources of dissatisfaction.[1] About 55 percent of wives and husbands cite five or more of them as sources of dissatisfaction. Although the residents of downtown apartments are the next
most likely to cite five or more sources of dissatisfaction, 49 percent and

40 percent respectively, the latter percentage represents a considerable drop from the 55 percent found among the husbands in suburban apartments. Those living in houses, whether suburban or downtown, are even less likely to single out five or more sources of dissatisfaction, only about 35 percent doing so.

As shown in Tables 8.6 and 8.7, the families living in downtown apartments are most dissatisfied first with the size and the capacities of their dwelling units and, second, with some of the typical aspects of the conventional high-rise building. The former considerations include the size of the dwelling and its rooms, the number of bedrooms, the amount of storage space, and room layout. The latter include an inability to make repairs personally, noise transmission, and management practices. These families share with their neighbors in downtown houses the regret that they are so far away from the country or other open, green space.

In contrast, those in single-family homes downtown do not have as many characteristic complaints about house and location. They, as well as suburban homeowners, would prefer more outside space. The wives in particular mention problems with the number of bathrooms and with the adequacy of parking space. The only problem of any significance is housing cost, but this is not a problem unique to those in downtown houses, as it is mentioned relatively equally by families in all types of housing and location.

In the eyes of its residents, the suburban high-rise apartment has the disadvantages of both suburban location and high-rise living. I have already enumerated the latter. The former include difficulties with public transportation and distance from downtown. Women in suburban apartments also have greater problems with access to workplace than do women in the other categories.

This problem is a more general one for men; the only category with an unusually *low* percentage of husbands mentioning distance to work is that of men in downtown houses.

In addition to these locational difficulties, the wives in suburban houses characteristically find access to recreational facilities insufficient. Both husbands and wives also find dissatisfaction in the aesthetics of their predominantly new neighborhoods, and they share with those in downtown houses some dissatisfaction with the size of their lots, which they feel are too small.

As with items promoting satisfaction, different elements contribute to different profiles of dissatisfaction in the different combinations of housing and location. The dimensions of housing and location are important for dissatisfaction, with the high-rise apartment and the suburban location incurring the most criticism. Hence, people criticize the suburban apartment on two counts, while they deem the downtown house negative on neither. The downtown apartment and the suburban house each becomes the focus of criticism on one dimension, but not the other.

We may view dissatisfaction with particular elements of the environment in terms of whether those in given housing types and locations place high priority on them. Those living in downtown apartments gave highest priority to the locational dimension, which they did not mention frequently with dissatisfaction. The housing dimension, however, was second—and the subject of considerable dissatisfaction. I shall skip the downtown house, which received little expression of dissatisfaction from its occupants. Those in suburban apartments singled out their environment as deficient with respect to housing type and location; since they had established the dwelling unit as the highest priority dimension of home environment, this combination of deficiency and priority indicates the possibility of stress. Much less stress, however, would be expected among those in suburban houses, whose dimension of greatest expressed dissatisfaction is location, which we saw as of lowest priority to them.

Reference, then, to specific sources of dissatisfaction, within the perspective of the priorities assigned the different dimensions of environment by specific categories of families, helps to explain the differences in level of satisfaction separating homeowners from apartment renters. It is particularly noteworthy that those in downtown houses are so satisfied with their locations, since location is of such high priority to them, while suburban homeowners are satisfied with their dwelling units.

Nonetheless, we can ask about the importance of the *individual items* which families cited as unsatisfactory. When a respondent singled out any item on the checklist as unsatisfactory, we asked whether this item was important or unimportant.

Those living in apartments note that they view a greater percentage of unsatisfactory elements as important than do those in houses. Women living in apartments deemed important about 62 percent of the elements chosen, compared to about 50 percent by those living in houses. Among

TABLE 8.6

Mention of Specific Dissatisfactions within Categories of Housing Type and Location (Wives, Phase II) (*Percentage*)

(All bars, regardless of shading, originate at zero.)

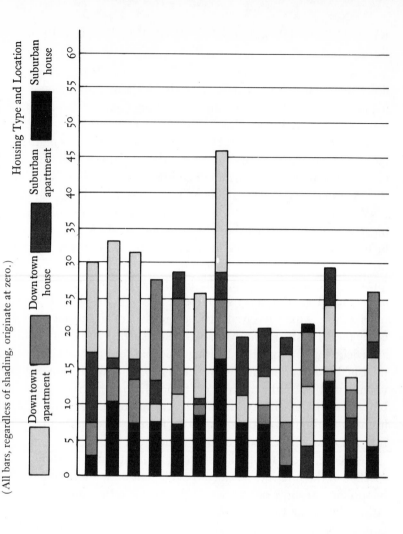

Housing Type and Location

Down town apartment   Down town house   Suburban apartment   Suburban house

Specific Dissatisfactions

1. Size of home
2. Size of rooms
3. Number of bedrooms
4. Number of bathrooms
5. In-home equipment
6. Layout of rooms
7. Storage or closet space
8. Interior noise transmission
9. Need for repairs
10. Inability to make own repairs
11. Lot or outside space too small
12. Exterior noise transmission
13. Design, appearance of home
14. Parking facilities

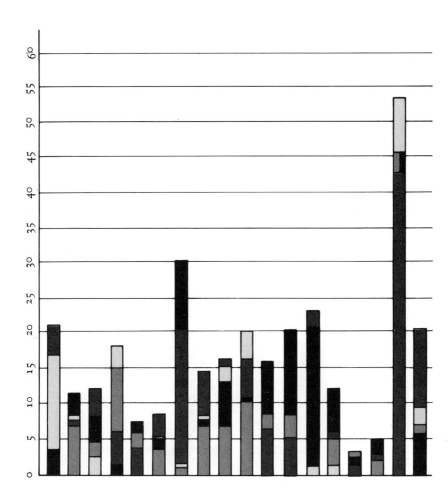

15. Management or developer
16. Social character of neighborhood
17. Type of neighbors/co-tenants
18. Distance to country/green spaces
19. Schools—quality
20. Design, appearance of neighborhood
21. Public transportation facilities
22. Long distance to work
23. Long distance to friends
24. Long distance to relatives
25. Long distance to shopping
26. Long distance to recreation facilities
27. Long distance to downtown area
28. Neighborhood facilities—inadequate
29. Neighborhood facilities—inconvenient
30. Schools—location
31. Housing costs
32. Quality of home

TABLE 8.7

Mention of Specific Dissatisfactions within Categories of Housing Type and Location (Husbands, Phase III) (*Percentage*)

(All bars, regardless of shading, originate at zero.)

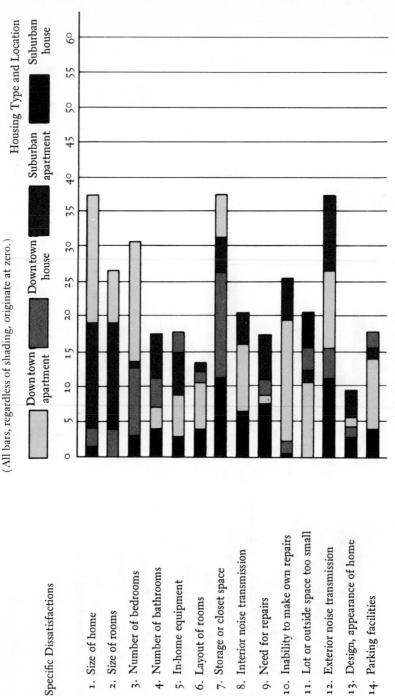

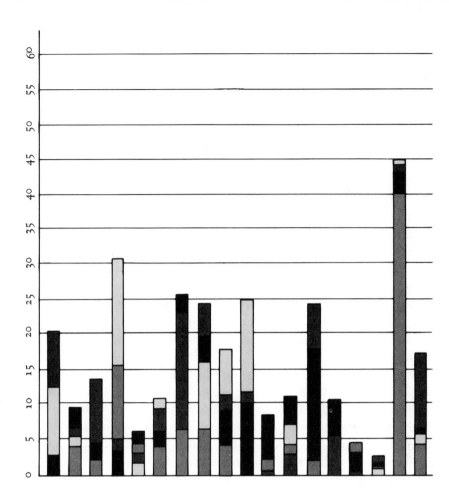

15. Management or developer
16. Social character of neighborhood
17. Type of neighbors/co-tenants
18. Distance to country/green spaces
19. Schools—quality
20. Design, appearance of neighborhood
21. Public transportation facilities
22. Long distance to work
23. Long distance to friends
24. Long distance to relatives
25. Long distance to shopping
26. Long distance to recreation facilities
27. Long distance to downtown area
28. Neighborhood facilities—inadequate
29. Neighborhood facilities—inconvenient
30. Schools—location
31. Housing costs
32. Quality of home

the husbands, these same figures were approximately 65 percent and 48 percent, respectively.

Those in apartments do not concentrate on just a few items when they judge unsatisfactory items as important. *Most* elements mentioned by any number of apartment dwellers as unsatisfactory are also seen by at least 50 percent as important.

People moving to houses, in contrast, agree upon relatively fewer items as important. Both downtown and suburban homeowners, though, view cost and repairs as serious. Suburban homeowners treat such additional elements as schools and neighbor characteristics as important.

Some understanding of why apartment dwellers see their problems as more important than do homeowners may lie in the realm of what the respondents can do about them. We asked respondents whether they could remedy each element deemed unsatisfactory without moving. Homeowners feel they can remedy about 50 percent of the items they mentioned without moving, compared to only about 20 percent among residents of high-rise apartments.

Although homeowners feel they can do little about problems of location, lot size, and interior layout, they feel able to work on such difficulties as repairs, parking, and the number of bedrooms and baths. Renters feel relatively powerless about most aspects of their dwellings, in addition to sharing the feeling of homeowners about lacking control over more macroscopic elements of their neighborhood and city.

About those elements they feel they *can* remedy, the apartment dwellers believe they have to follow a different path than the homeowners, turning more to tactics of political organization to achieve results, in comparison to direct and personal action. People may view deficiencies less seriously if they feel some sense of potential control over the remedy, a situation largely lacking among apartment renters.

I must raise the special position of the apartment condominium owner again in this connection. The importance of personal control in the condominium is indicated by a comparison of answers by suburban apartment owners and renters to the checklists on items of satisfaction. Close to 60 percent of the former list their ability to make repairs as a satisfaction, compared to only 15 percent of the latter.[2]

Where a respondent deemed an element of the environment incapable of remedy from its unsatisfactory state without moving, we asked whether he or she would consider moving in that regard. Although homeowners are considerably more resistant to moving on these grounds than apartment dwellers, it is noteworthy that among neither the wives nor the husbands living in apartments is there any great tendency to consider moving because of these unfixable problems. The wife does not consider moving in about two-thirds of the cases, compared to 60 percent among the husbands.

The greatest potential precipitators of moving among those in a high rise, regardless of sex or location, are the size of the dwelling unit and the number of bedrooms. Nonetheless, regardless of the importance of these elements of home environment and an inability of occupants to alter their problematic characteristics, they do not to any great extent predispose apartment residents to move.

At this point, there are several paradoxes. Those moving to apartments have greater numbers of dissatisfactions, show a greater coincidence of these dissatisfactions with high priority dimensions of environment, treat these dissatisfactions as more important, and cannot fix them without moving. Although the degree with which they are satisfied with their housing and location is clearly less than that of the homeowners, nonetheless the overwhelming pattern is one of satisfaction. Apart from a tendency of interviewees to put a good face on things, which always lurks as a danger in surveys, what could account for the high level of satisfaction found among those in apartments? In addition, if so much of importance cannot be remedied in the apartment, why do people consider moving to it?

The answer to these questions appears to lie in the general plan of events which constitutes each family's mobility cycle, as they see it.

WHAT THEY PLAN:
THE FAMILY MOBILITY CYCLE

We must return to the paradigm in Chapter 1, which allows for the possibility that families will change housing according to the life plan of a given family, without the necessity of strain and hence the necessity for dissatisfaction with the residential environment occupied prior to any move. When addressing the question of why, when faced with a number of important, unchangeable, and unsatisfactory aspects of their housing, families in high-rise apartments report satisfaction and little predisposition to move in that regard, we discover that most of them never intended this particular home as anything but interim accommodation. It is as interim accommodation that it is found satisfactory. They do not choose to move because of the deficiencies of the high-rise, because they expect to be moving anyway. Many aspects of this phenomenon require exploration.

When we first interviewed our respondent families, before they moved to their new houses and apartments, we asked about their likelihood of moving again within the next five years. Sixty-six percent of the husbands and 57 percent of the wives moving to downtown apartments expressed this likelihood as very great, while another 29 percent of the husbands and 33 percent of the wives suggested that it was possible. Only about 5 and 9 percent, respectively, said that a repeat move was not likely. These data are indicated in. Table 8.8. Among those about to move to suburban apartments, a somewhat smaller percentage of both husbands and wives considered a repeat move as very likely, but nonetheless fewer than 20 percent of both husbands and wives felt one *not* likely within the next five years.

The apartment movers were clearly going to interim accommodation.

In contrast, about 70 percent of the wives and about 60 percent of the husbands felt that a move from the single-family home was not likely in the next five years. Only very small percentages of movers to houses saw

Table 8.8
Pre-move Likelihood of Moving Again in Next Five Years, by De
Housing Type and Location
(*Percentage*)

Destination Environment	Likelihood of Moving Again							
	Very great		Possible		Not likely			
	Wife	Husband	Wife	Husband	Wife	Husband	Wife	Husband
Downtown apartment	57.4	65.9	33.3	29.4	9.3	4.7	(108)	(85)
Downtown house	4.3	13.3	25.8	28.3	69.9	58.3	(93)	(60)
Apartment suburbs	35.4	43.1	45.6	40.6	18.9	16.2	(285)	(197)
House suburbs	4.8	5.0	20.8	31.2	74.4	63.8	(207)	(141)
Resale house suburbs	3.2	9.3	22.2	32.6	74.6	58.1	(63)	(43)
Total							(756)	(526)
No answer							(5)	(1)

the likelihood of another move as very great. In addition, movers to houses considered almost all additional moves foreseen as a function of a future job transfer. This contrasts strongly with the high percentage of apartment movers who saw future moves as a function of a desired change in housing type or tenure (accounting for approximately half the reasons for an anticipated move on the part of apartment movers).

Thus, even at the time that apartment movers were physically carrying out the first stages of one cycle of mobility, based on specific motives relevant to the setting to which they were moving, they were also planning for their removal from that site to still another residential setting with highly different characteristics, which would satisfy a different set of goals.

The case of the condominium high rise is interesting in this regard, since it incorporates a desired form of tenure with a less preferred type of housing. It is not surprising, then, to find 45 percent of the families moving to condominium apartments state that the likelihood of repeat mobility is very great or possible, with the remainder considering it not likely. This distribution is virtually midway between the extremes presented by those buying houses and by those renting apartments.

This surely does not suggest that condominium apartments satisfy the housing requirements of families occupying them just because ownership is provided. But, on the other hand, it does indicate the potential for more stability and greater long-term commitment than among apartment renters.

The likelihood of moving again certainly had not diminished after about the first year and a quarter in the new apartments. During the Phase III interviews, 75 percent of the wives in downtown apartments and 52 percent of those in suburban apartments thought the possibility of a move within the next five years as very great, while only 6 percent and 11 percent, respectively, felt it not likely. Among the husbands, the percentages anticipating future moves are even higher.

Furthermore, a reasonably high percentage of those expecting a future move thought it likely to take place within one year. About 50 percent of husbands and wives in downtown apartments and 37 percent of those in suburban apartments who expected a future move thought that it would take place within the year.

Although those in houses were by Phase III more likely to consider the possibility of moving again (only about 60% of the wives and about 50% of the husbands considering it unlikely), only about 5 percent of the wives and about 8 percent of the husbands expected that it would take place within a year.

Since we were particularly eager to understand the extent that future mobility shed light on preferences regarding housing types, we also asked respondents whether they realistically anticipated moving in the future to a *more satisfactory home*. Among those living in apartments, 81 percent of the wives and about 87 percent of the husbands answer in the affirmative. In contrast, among those now living in houses, only 39 percent of the wives and 45 percent of the husbands do so.

When asked the characteristics of the more satisfactory home, well over two-thirds within every category specify the single-family, detached house. Among the wives, 67 percent of those living in downtown apartments who expect more satisfactory housing specify the single house, while over three-quarters who are living in suburban apartments do so. Close to 80 percent of those already in houses who foresee an improvement take this path as well. Among the husbands, close to 80 percent of those now in apartments, without significant differences according to location, specify the house, as compared to almost 90 percent of those now in houses.

Furthermore, among those in high-rise, only about 10 percent of husbands and wives see high-rise housing as their ultimate goal.

There are considerable differences with respect to the location to which respondents feel they realistically aspire, according to their current combination of housing type and location. Those in downtown apartments not only want houses, but they want houses in the suburbs or in rural areas. *Only 10 percent of this group of wives and 13 percent of their husbands plan to remain in or near the downtown area.* While their current motives strongly emphasize the downtown, while utilizing the high-rise apartment because it is there, the criteria behind their current housing choice are clearly temporary. At present, their motives are rational, and they are largely fulfilled. Yet, these respondents have aspirations with an almost totally different content.

Among those in downtown houses, however, not only do fewer anticipate moving, but far fewer foresee decentralization. Among the potential movers, 43 percent want to remain downtown, compared to 20 percent desiring to move either to the suburbs or to rural areas. Another 14 percent would like to move to a small town, outside the Toronto sphere of influence. When combining this distribution with that of the majority of downtown residents not wishing to move again, a strong commitment to a future in the downtown area is shown by those in the downtown houses.

Surely the homeowners and apartment dwellers present contrasting pictures of commitment to downtown neighborhoods and housing. It is no wonder that they stand on opposite sides of the fence on issues of neighborhood preservation. Clearly their motives and interests are different. Clearly also, future policy formulation must consider these interests as different. There are different markets providing occupants for the apartments than for the homes. The substitution of one kind of dwelling unit for another after redevelopment, private or public, may be an appropriate statistical equivalence, but its social basis is unsound.

Those already in the suburbs, whether in houses or apartments, show a strong commitment to suburbs or even more rustic settings. Roughly 40 percent of both husbands and wives who anticipate an improvement in housing would remain within the suburbs, and about another 25 percent would move out even further to rural areas. About another 10 percent would prefer moving to a small town. Only about 5 percent would consider moving downtown. Just as suburbanites were largely not interested in downtown areas when planning the move studied, their quasi-rural orientation extends also into the future.

These data suggest, then, that the majority of people moving to houses and to apartments are at different stages of a family mobility cycle. Most of the former have attained their aspirations in housing, with marginal improvements in design or location possible in the future. On the other hand, those moving to apartments have done so for good and logical reasons, connected in large part to the opportunities available in the destination environment; but they are in Stage 2 in the family mobility cycle, where they move to make incremental changes in their residential settings, moves which do not necessarily bear on what they really want to achieve.

We analyzed combinations of answers to some of the above-mentioned questions to approximate operationalizing the family-mobility cycle. We classified families as belonging to Stage 3 (approximation of the ideal) if they did not give financial obstacles as a reason for not moving to more satisfactory housing. Families moving *only* for job changes were also placed in Stage 3. Families were placed in Stage 2 (incremental change—unblocked mobility) if they foresaw a move to a more satisfactory home and gave reasons for mobility having to do with housing, not job change. If they did not foresee a move because of financial limitations, families were placed in another Stage-2 category of blocked movers; only nine wives and ten husbands fit that category.

Table 8.9 indicates the resultant distribution of families in stages in the moving cycle by housing type and location. Just over 80 percent of the families in downtown apartments and 75 percent in suburban apartments fall in Stage 2, incremental change. In contrast, the vast majority of families in detached houses are in Stage 3, the approximation of the ideal.

There is a variety of additional evidence supporting different orientations toward mobility and housing separating the families in apartments from those in houses.

We assessed where families thought they stood in a sequence of progress toward housing goals, by showing them a ladder whose rungs were to indicate the steps toward the best and the worst housing they could envisage for themselves. We asked them where on the ladder they would

Table 8.9
Stage in Mobility Cycle, by Housing Type and Location

Housing Type and Location	Stage in Mobility Cycle			
	III. Approximation of the ideal (%)	II. Incremental change (%)	II. Blocked mobility (%)	(N)
Apartment downtown				
Wife	16.7	83.3	0.0	(60)
Husband	18.5	81.5	0.0	(54)
House downtown				
Wife	80.5	15.6	3.9	(77)
Husband	62.2	33.3	4.4	(45)
Apartment suburbs				
Wife	22.0	76.8	1.1	(190)
Husband	22.8	75.3	1.9	(158)
House suburbs				
Wife	77.7	20.5	1.9	(215)
Husband	72.8	24.1	3.2	(158)
Total				
Wife				(542)
Husband				(415)
Missing Information				
Wife				(51)
Husband				(34)

place their Phase III home. Although a great number of families rated their homes very highly on the scale, more than 60 percent of those in houses placed themselves on one of the top two steps on the ladder, while a majority of those in apartments placed themselves somewhere below the first two steps.

Evidence on the different orientation of families in the different categories of residence is offered in answers to several questions of an attitudinal nature. We asked people to rate responses to the following statements about housing and location on a five-point scale ranging from strongly agree to strongly disagree:

1. Ultimately, with economic conditions favorable, a detached home is the most desirable goal for families like mine.
2. With transportation as it is today, even someone on the fringe of metropolitan areas has easy access to everything in town he needs.

3. Suburban lot sizes and street patterns are more suitable for raising children than are those in in-city residential areas.

4. Children can be brought up just as well in high-rise apartments as in any other type of housing.

The first and fourth of these questions obviously deal with attitudinal aspects of the polar housing types, while the middle two questions deal with certain spatial aspects of suburbs and downtown areas.

A clear majority of husbands and wives in all the combinations of housing type and location supported the first question, on the detached home as a goal. As Table 8.10 indicates, over 60 percent of husbands and wives in apartments agreed with the statement while about 80 percent of those in houses do so. Although not shown in the table there are no appreciable differences on *strength* of agreement among those who agree; about an equal number of them 'strongly agree' and 'agree' with the statement.

Only those living in downtown houses fail to support the second question on the accessibility of the downtown to those living on the fringe of the metropolitan area. The husbands living in downtown apartments agree with this statement to a degree which is virtually indistinguishable from that of the men already living in the suburbs; a majority of their wives support this statement, but this falls about 15 percent short of the level

Table 8.10

Agreement with Each of Four Attitudinal Statements on Home Environment within Categories of Housing Type and Location

(*Percentage*)

Housing Type and Location	Attitudinal Statements							
	1. Single housing as a goal		2. Fringe areas accessible		3. Children need suburban space		4. High rise not for child raising	
	Wife	Husband	Wife	Husband	Wife	Husband	Wife	Husband
Apartment downtown	61.2	61.4	56.7	63.1	65.7	73.7	16.1	14.0
House downtown	81.3	79.6	40.1	38.7	25.1	20.5	8.8	4.5
Apartment suburbs	68.1	62.3	74.1	62.3	75.8	78.0	40.9	32.3
House suburbs	83.0	91.7	71.4	66.7	83.4	83.9	8.3	9.5

of agreement given by those already in the suburbs. In any case, families in downtown high-rise offer attitudes oriented toward the suburbs much more than do those in downtown houses.

Question 3 goes even further in tying the downtown-suburban polarity to child raising, something particularly relevant to husbands and wives in the stage in the life cycle found in the present sample. In this case, the difference between those in downtown houses and all the others is even more extreme. Only 21 percent of the husbands and 25 percent of the wives in downtown houses agree with the statement, compared to the vast majority of persons in the other categories. Nearly 74 percent of the husbands and 66 percent of the wives living in downtown apartments agree, and another 12 and 13 percent, respectively, are undecided. Although these figures are not entirely coincident with those of the families already in suburbia, they are so close to them and so far from the responses given by those in downtown houses as to be virtually indistinguishable from the established suburban response.

The final statement, on bringing up children in high-rise apartments just as well as anywhere else, is disapproved of by a majority of persons in every housing category. Strongest support for the statement comes from families in suburban apartments, where 32 percent of the husbands and 41 percent of the wives agree. Responses of families in downtown high-rise apartments are in this instance almost at the level of families already owning houses.

In light of the high level of disagreement with what many families were in fact doing, we assessed responses to this last statement according to whether families in high-rise had children. We divided families in terms of whether (1) they had children both before and after their move, (2) they had children only after moving, or (3) they had no children at either point studied.

Although the presence of children both before and after the move to the apartment signaled greater acceptance of the idea of raising children in apartments, at no time did a majority of husbands and wives in such families agree with this statement. Three times as many families who moved to the high-rise without children but who then had babies disagreed with the statement as agreed, showing no expectation of raising their children within high-rise. Furthermore, those who are childless are even more opposed to raising children in high-rise; particularly among the husbands, their experience in high-rise has certainly not predisposed them to consider raising children there.

It is not surprising that families who have not as yet had children are so conventional in their attitudes toward housing and location. An earlier study (Loewy and Snaith, 1968) indicated that the foremost criterion utilized among newly engaged and newly married couples in choosing their housing is its suitability for children.

In short, both the housing aspirations and attitudes of most of the apartment dwellers studied show the basis for the movement to detached houses and, increasingly, suburban or small town locations which is so firmly rooted in cultural traditions. The Social Planning Council Study (1973) of families in high-rise apartments showed that 67 percent of the heads of households had grown up in family-owned houses, and the popular support given this ideal in the face of contemporary trends to the contrary is apparently of considerable strength. The presence of a contrary housing market at one point in time may dictate where people live after any single move, but does not necessarily affect what they think or what they plan.

RECAPITULATION AND DISCUSSION

At least three questions developed during the course of the analysis of evaluation in this chapter: (1) Why are apartment dwellers unlikely to move in response to difficulties experienced? (2) Why are there differences in degree of satisfaction between those in apartments and those in houses? (3) Despite the difficulties in question one and the factors brought forward in answer to question two, why do apartment dwellers still overwhelmingly express satisfaction, at least mild satisfaction, with their home?

Answers to these three questions are intertwined, but can now be answered relatively succinctly.

Apartment dwellers do not consider moving because of their difficulties, because most of them had never intended to stay in the first place. Their plans call for subsequent movement, toward lower rise housing and suburban locations, and are supported by a strong belief in conventional attitudes about family housing and location.

That families expect to move vitiates the buildup of strain in the residential environment, making blanket disenchantment with the high-rise home unnecessary, regardless of the presence of elements in the home environment which are not considered satisfactory. The data of Chapter 7 do show that most expectations are in fact fulfilled, regardless of the type of housing and location to which families move. The benefits which people expect are largely rational readings of the opportunities available in the destination environment, so that although a given home environment may not maximize all possible criteria for judgment, it succeeds reasonably well in providing what was expected. Furthermore, respondents who have not in fact approximated their ideal in the current home give clear evidence that most of them feel that they can and will move on to a better home. That they feel *able* to progress toward satisfaction of other criteria in housing removes the necessity to judge the current environment on anything other than the grounds on which it was originally chosen. On this basis, we can understand why such a very high percentage of families evaluated their homes as satisfactory.

Extremely few of the families indicate that they feel their future mobility is blocked. We expect that families in high-rise apartments who aspire eventually to reach other forms of housing but who feel incapable of achieving their aspirations should feel far less satisfied with their current housing. Moreover, they cannot feel as flexible in judging current housing on short-term criteria while knowing that their period of residence will in fact be long term. There are hints of this in the current data, but the number of persons feeling blocked is far too small to support inferences. A recent extension of this reasoning to subsamples of residents in public housing by Kennedy (1975) does, however, support this hypothesis.

Yet, beyond the initial level of general satisfaction characteristic of most families, regardless of housing type, there are clear-cut differences in the degree of satisfaction separating most homeowners from most apartment dwellers studied. Although both groups filled their own expectations reasonably well, these expectations are related to types of housing with clearly differing lengths of residence, known to be such in advance of the move. Since the evidence is overwhelming that most apartment dwellers intend to move again to homes and, in some cases, locations which are considerably different in form and in opportunities provided, the benefits which the apartment families expect during their stay in the apartment are largely not the same as those to which they ultimately aspire. Hence, it is understandable that, while some expectations are surely fulfilled, the fulfillment of expectations relating to only temporary and not ultimate aspirations produces a lesser level of satisfaction than that associated with approximation of the ideal, regardless of what the actual character of these expectations and aspirations might be.

We can see vastly differing levels of satisfaction by separating out those within *each* housing type who see it as their ideal versus those who see it as a place for incremental change. Table 8.11, for example, shows that among the relatively few families in downtown apartments classified as in Stage 3 of the family-mobility cycle, 50 percent of the wives are definitely satisfied with their apartments, compared to only 20 percent of those in Stage 2, with figures of 33.3 percent and 18.6 percent for the respective stages among the husbands. Among those in suburban apartments, the corresponding percentages are 35.7 percent and 21.2 percent for the wives and

Table 8.11
Respondents Definitely Satisfied with Home, by Stage in the Mobility Cycle
and Category of Housing Type and Location
(Percentage)

Housing Type and Location

Stage in the Mobility Cycle	Downtown apartment				Downtown house				Apartment suburbs				House suburbs				Total			
	Wife		Husband		Wife		Husband		Wife		Husband		Wife		Husband		Wife		Husband	
	(%)	(N)	(%)	(N)	(%)	(N)	(%)	(N)	(%)	(N)	(%)	(N)	(%)	(N)	(%)	(N)	(%)	(N)	(%)	(N)
III. Approximation of the ideal	50	(10)	33.3	(9)	53.3	(60)	74.1	(27)	35.7	(42)	47.1	(34)	59.3	(167)	58.0	(112)	54.1	(279)	57.1	(182)
II. Incremental change	20	(50)	18.6	(43)	50.0	(12)	28.1	(13)	21.2	(146)	20.2	(114)	36.4	(44)	32.4	(37)	23.3	(270)	22.2	(207)
II. Blocked mobility	—		—		33.3	(3)	0.0	(2)	0.0	(2)	33.3	(3)	0.0	(4)	80.0	(5)	11.1	(9)	50.0	(10)
N																		(558)		(399)
Missing Information																		(35)		(50)

47.1 percent and 20.2 percent for the husbands. The figures are consistently in this direction as well for those living in houses, as would surely be expected. Some percentages for the handful of people classified in the blocked category are in the right direction, but others are not; the base numbers are so small, however, that these percentages are clearly subject to wild fluctuation.

In any case, since so many apartment dwellers are clearly following terms of reference of limited duration and receiving limited, though positive, feedback, it is fortunate that adaptation to the attractions of the apartment environment occurs much more quickly than in the detached houses. Quick adaptation for the fulfillment of interim goals among families expecting recurrent mobility in the near future is a phenomenon of the high-rise apartment.

Although the apartment movers discover a great many more aspects with which they are dissatisfied than those moving to houses, this in itself does not mean that the respondents consider them as relevant or important. Nonetheless, that most apartment dwellers feel they can do nothing about most of these elements of housing and that these dissatisfactions reflect dimensions of the home environment which apartment dwellers consider of relatively high priority in their present stage in the moving cycle, helps contribute to the lower level of satisfaction characteristic of the apartment dwellers.

High-rise apartments are hardly medieval instruments of torture. The ways in which they satisfy and in which they fall short are largely based on criteria which flow from the plans and aspirations of apartment dwellers rather than from absolutely good or bad aspects of the home environment.

The critical dynamic, then, behind the realism of the evaluations given by respondents and what they mean for the assessment of the implications of types of housing is whether apartment dwellers do in fact move on to other housing, as they expect. This is the subject of Chapter 9.

However, before turning to this critical assessment, it may be useful to express succinctly the fabric of behaviors, social differentiation, aspirations for differential mobility, and resultant satisfaction represented by the various housing types and locations. In Chapter 6, passing reference was made to a factor analysis confirming the postmove clusters of variables, but this discussion was omitted at that time because the emerging packages of phenomena would have been incomplete without inclusion of the data on evaluation and plans for future mobility brought forward in the present chapter. Therefore, let us examine briefly the types of factors which merge various discrete findings of Chapters 6 through 8.

We performed a factor analysis similar in procedure and intent to that described in Chapter 5 on the many variables shown relevant for the post-move implications of the housing types and locations studied. To do this we put 170 variables into the rotated factor analysis. This number exaggerates the diversity of the input, since the quantification of some otherwise qualitative variables once again required the creation of several items out of one.

We have seen so far that the emergent postmove pattern includes aspects both of self-selection and 'situated behavior.' Hence, it is not surprising to find the post-move results more differentiated than in the Chapter 5 factor analysis. Twice as many factors (20) met standard criteria of sufficient size than was the case before the move. Although the absolute amount of variance explained is, in my opinion, meaningless in this exercise, for reasons explained in Chapter 5, the total amount explained is 46.4 percent, with the first ten factors accounting for 30.9 percent.

Since the reason for performing this factor analysis is to observe whether the previous interpretative linking of variables from the discrete findings is consistent with patterns emerging from this more succinct though unthinking method of analysis, let us turn directly to the nature of the factors which appeared.

Eighteen of the twenty factors include housing type and/or location as essential elements in the clusters they represent—the various housing types and locations appearing individually and in combination. According to the particular factor involved, aspects of social distribution, behavior, aspirations for mobility, and evaluation are joined together, as was the case without the benefit of factor analysis. Let us look at the factors one by one.

Factor 1—Stage 3 in Family-Mobility Cycle
(Variance explained 6.4%)
Factor 1 brings together homeowners both in the suburbs and downtown, who are definitely satisfied with their new homes and who do not anticipate moves to more satisfactory homes. They have above average interests in gardening, go to church on Sundays, and spend time with their neigh-

bors, who are similar to themselves. The opposite side of this coin has families in high-rise apartments who expect to move shortly to suburban housing. Although the current housing of the latter allows easy access to groceries and sundries, it occupies a low place on the ladder in terms of where these families think they will eventually wind up.

Factor 2—Neighboring in Suburban Homes
(Variance explained 6.0%)

Factor 2 refers to husbands, who exchange several kinds of mutual aid with their neighbors, and expect the same in return. The husband knows a number of people in his neighborhood well. He participates actively in organizations. This factor is devoted almost entirely to a description of the man and his relations with neighbors in suburban houses, with only meager evidence in the factor that the opposite is found in people who live in downtown houses; the factor does not include relevant details about how their life is different.

Factor 3—Working Wife in Apartment (Variance explained 3.4%)

Factor 3 describes the working wife without children, who has a high level of education, high personal and family income, and who lives in a downtown or suburban apartment. Her opposite is a woman who spends the greatest part of her day in cleaning, shopping, and caring for children.

Factor 4—Suburban Women (Variance explained 2.8%)

Factor 4 mainly identifies women living in the suburbs, showing that they support the statements that suburbia is suitably accessible to necessary land uses and that suburbs are the best place to bring up children. What these women have most in common in this factor is their attitudinal support for the suburbs. This contrasts strongly with women in downtown houses but not, to any significant degree, downtown apartments.

Factor 5—Automobile Emphasis in Suburban Houses
(Variance explained 3.1%)

Factor 5 shows that families owning houses in the suburbs own more cars *and* use them for grocery and sundry shopping. It is not irrelevant that these people who drive so much claim to be definitely satisfied with their new *homes*, most of all finding satisfaction in the amount of space discovered in the home, for which the distance to be overcome by automobile is a trade-off. The above families contrast with apartment renters, regardless of location, who are less likely to drive everywhere.

Factor 6—Intensive Neighboring (Variance explained 2.0%)
Factor 6 does not refer to housing type or location. Rather, it assembles those people who know a lot about their neighbors and feel similar to them. These people offer the various types of mutual aid, including child care. The neighborhood has a high degree of priority to them, and they meet their neighbors informally inside the neighborhood. While the single-family dwelling loads only on the positive side of this factor, it is a very weak aspect of the factor (.116). The opposite side of the factor includes, without any spatial reference, people who do not perform or expect mutual aid and who are not particularly happy with or involved in the neighborhood.

Factor 7—Suburban versus Downtown Apartments
(Variance explained 2.7%)
Factor 7 contrasts families in suburban apartments, who have children, who spend a greater amount of time in the care of children, and who go to church, with those in downtown apartments, where the wife is more likely to work, have higher income, and be childless.

Factor 8—The Woman About Town (Variance explained 1.8%)
Factor 8 focuses on the use of time by wives living in suburban houses, whose husbands are in managerial positions with high incomes. These women spend the greater portion of their time in public places, with friends and neighbors, shopping, in restaurants, in church, and in transit. When at home on Sundays, they spend a greater than average amount of time gardening. This contrasts with the activities of working wives in this factor.

Factor 9—Apartment Downtown (Variance explained 1.3%)
Factor 9 looks at the interpersonal relations, attitudes, and mobility aspirations of families in downtown apartments, who plan to move to suburban houses in the foreseeable future. While they like their current location, they are not very well acquainted with their neighbors, and they

anticipate moving to a more satisfactory home. This contrasts with families living at present in suburban houses, who have already achieved what the former group wishes to accomplish.

Factor 10—Friendship in Downtown Houses (Variance explained 1.4%)
Factor 10 is relatively simple and indicates that women in downtown houses are more closely associated with their friends and neighbors than they are with their relatives.

Factor 11—Characteristics of Families in Downtown Houses
(Variance explained 2.0%)
Factor 11 shows that the families in downtown houses have a high degree of education, with husbands in professional or technical occupations. Family income is high, as is the husband's income. The husband prefers to take public transit to work. Husband and wife have an above-average interest in the theater. They both participate in organizations frequently. They contrast with those living in suburban apartments.

Factor 12—Mobility Differences among Apartment Renters
(Variance explained 1.3%)
Factor 12 contrasts the mobility potential of families in downtown apartments with those in suburban apartments, showing greater expected mobility on the part of the former. Although they expect to move to a more satisfactory home, both husbands and wives in downtown apartments stress satisfaction with their current location.

Factor 13—Satisfaction and Mobility Differences between Downtown
Apartments and Houses (Variance explained 2.0%)
Factor 13 contrasts the definite satisfaction with house, location and neighborhood of those living in downtown houses with the lesser degree of satisfaction associated with home and neighborhood of those in downtown apartments. It contrasts as well the great expectations of future mobility among the apartment dwellers with opposite expectations among those in the downtown houses.

Factor 14—Life Style in the Suburban House (Variance explained 1.5%)
Factor 14 brings together certain recreational interests, aspects of neighboring, and aspects of performance of mutual aid among both husbands

and wives in the suburban house. It presents a contrast with families living downtown. A major component of this factor is whether these families feel they can expect to "shoot the breeze" with their neighbors, with the suburban-house families on the positive side.

Factor 15—Mutual Aid (Variance explained 1.4%)
In Factor 15 there is a polarization on whether women, primarily, exchange the various forms of mutual aid, with the exception of borrowing or lending money. No reference is made to housing type or location.

Factor 16—Downtown Apartment Transients
(Variance explained 1.3%)
Factor 16 simply puts together some of the major characteristics of families living in downtown apartments. The wife takes public transit to work, and both spouses see a more satisfactory home as one in the suburbs. This is put into contrast with women spending a greater degree of time on weekdays in cleaning and shopping.

Factor 17—Permanent Residents of Downtown Apartments versus
Temporary Residents of Suburban Apartments (Variance explained 1.3%)
In Factor 17 a contrast is made between those residents of downtown apartments who expect to stay there and those who feel they are living in suburban apartments only temporarily. The former place a higher priority on location than do the latter, who emphasize neighborhood characteristics instead.

Factor 18—Orientations of Downtown Homeowners
(Variance explained 1.3%)
The behavioral and attitudinal support for the downtown location held by those living in downtown houses is indicated in Factor 18. These people do not think that accessibility to the advantages of the city is equally available to those living in the suburbs. The wife in such families spends a considerable amount of time on weekdays in restaurants and other public places.

Factor 19—Apartments versus Houses (Variance explained 1.6%)
In Factor 19, families living in apartments who disagree with the conventional goal of single-family housing are contrasted with families living

in houses who support this goal. The latter are more likely to be interested in gardening and to have met their neighbors within their current neighborhoods.

Factor 20—Where Met Friends (Variance explained 1.6%)
This final factor loads most heavily on whether wives and husbands met their friends through nonlocal communities of interest or in their current neighborhoods. The former path to friendship is seen as typical of residents of suburban apartments, while families making local contact with neighbors live in a variety of residential settings. Meeting families in the neighborhood is closely associated with an above average interest in gardening.

The factor analysis surely supports the descriptions given in these chapters of a differentiation process whereby persons with diverse backgrounds come to diverse residential settings, where they end up doing diverse things. It illustrates once again how the process of differentiation is not an absolute and final sorting of persons, but rather is compounded by clear-cut plans which residents have for future mobility, which are supported by differential attitudes toward housing and location in the city. While at any one time within a given housing market, we can see people appearing to make different choices and performing different daily routines, the life plans they have before them show a very much greater similarity of residential aspirations (but by no means monolithic).

The key point to emerge in this particular chapter about evaluation, both in the discrete analysis and in the factor analysis, is the centrality of the assumption among the persons in this particular study that their future mobility, in pursuit of conventional housing goals, will be relatively unhindered. On this assumption lies the logic joining the various responses they give. Let us therefore turn to a detailed examination of the validity of this assumption.

NOTES

[1] Operationally, enumeration of satisfactions and dissatisfactions was independent. A particular environmental element may be cited in both respects, and the two types of rating were not conducted simultaneously.

[2] Other differences between the two groups are as expected. Owners express more satisfaction with financial aspects than renters. Having probably shopped more carefully, owners are much more satisfied with such clearly observable aspects of their homes as size, number of bedrooms and bathrooms, and interior equipment. Owners, on the other hand, are no more happy and sometimes less happy with what they find, especially the "quality" of their housing, when it comes to many of the functional aspects of their apartment homes which only become apparent over time.

Chapter Nine

Temporal Validation

Time enables the evaluation of many things—hunches, investments, assumptions, and predictions. It simply takes time to see if a purported effect or intention reaches fulfillment as anticipated.

In this analysis, we have observed various short- and long-range expectations and experiences in housing, which vary among the families studied with the choice of high-rise and single-family housing. Furthermore, residents' evaluations of high-rise apartments as mildly satisfactory appear based on a conception of them as transitory, short-range habitats for these families; most residents of high rises intended to move in the near future to more self-contained, often more decentralized residential settings, to realize higher priority benefits than those they acknowledge receiving in the high rise. We can understand the positive evaluations of high rise only within the context of assumptions of future mobility.

Hence, carrying the longitudinal study beyond initial adaptation enables some assessment of what these families do in the longer run. It provides some measure of validation of the assumptions basic to people's evaluative framework.

In this chapter, we shall look at who moved again, where, and why. We shall focus on the realism of the assumptions held by the residents, as well as on what would have been predicted on the basis of information gathered in the first three phases of the study.

THE HOUSING MARKET AS CONTEXT

Before we turn to what happened, however, we must take a short look at the state of the housing market which served as context for the aspirations and mobility of our respondents. Although one of the crucial features of the present sample is its representation of families likely to have more economic freedom in the housing market than the average, what these families do is still affected by objective conditions in the housing market. The families studied are not so affluent that they can choose *anything* they wish, and we indicated in Chapter 5 some of the economic limitations on what they chose as a basis for entering this study.

During the period studied, supplies of the kind of housing to which most people aspired became much shorter than before. Toronto used to be a city predominantly of single-family, detached houses. As recently as 1961, 55.7 percent of the housing stock in Metropolitan Toronto consisted of such homes, although by 1967 this had sunk to 50.4 percent. During this same time, the percentage of apartments and flats, not counting attached, low-rise housing, increased from 26.7 percent to 33.3 percent (Simmons, 1974, p. 11).

Although there was some balance in the overall distribution of housing units in the total market in Metropolitan Toronto, the ratio of completions was dramatically in favor of high-rise apartments. In 1969, the year the study commenced, only 18.6 percent of the dwelling units completed in the entire Toronto census metropolitan area, roughly equivalent to Toronto and the suburbs covered in the present study, were in the form of single-family, detached houses, while 69.1 percent were in apartments and flats. With some minor fluctuations, this ratio of completions continued throughout the period of the study. The percentage of completions in single-family housing varied from a low of 14.3 percent in 1970 to a high of 26 percent in 1973, while the percentage of apartments completed varied from a high of 71.4 percent in 1970 to a low of 51.4 percent in 1973.[1]

This trend brought the percentage of detached houses by 1971 to the point of relative equality with apartments, 41 percent of the housing stock in Metropolitan Toronto in the former, and 40 percent in the latter. This represented dramatic change in only ten years! (Metroplan, 1974, p. 8.)

Hence, although houses were always available for sale during this period and while additions were made to the supply of single-family housing, the balance of available housing was shifting rapidly from single and detached to the high-rise.[2]

It is no great surprise that the price of what houses were available on the market rose sharply. The average selling price of homes sold through the Multiple Listing Service of the Real Estate Board of Metropolitan Toronto is the most cited barometer of housing cost in Toronto. During the period from 1969 through 1974, the average selling price almost doubled. In 1969, it was $28,945. By 1972, it had worked its way up to $32,513. But in 1973, it jumped to $40,605, and in 1974, to $52,806.[3]

At the same time, the city continued to expand rapidly in population, as an active centre of employment opportunities within Canada. What this means is that the sector of families in the present study who anticipated moving from multiple dwellings to low-rise, hopefully detached housing in the near future had the concrete obstacles of availability and cost facing them.

This is the context which immediately affects families in Toronto. While severe, it is not unique. Between 1970 and 1974, for example, the cost of a house being resold in the United States rose an average of almost 20 percent, while the cost of new houses went up by about one-sixth (*The New York Times*, 1975).

ONWARD, DOWNWARD, AND OUTWARD

As mentioned in Chapter 3, we sent mail questionnaires to the families studied approximately four years and two months after the move of record. Supplemented by follow-up telephone calls as necessary, responses were received from 81 percent of the original Phase I sample. This ranged from 71 percent of the families moving to downtown high rises up to 93 percent among those moving to downtown houses. Although this level of response is less than that in Phase II, although more than the response in Phase III, the individual respondents are not exactly equivalent to any other single group, since some families who responded in Phase I but not in II or III were retrieved for Phase IV, while a very few who responded in all the previous phases could not be reached in Phase IV. Hence, in tables in which Phase IV data are compared with data from earlier phases, the number of families represented does not always total 617, due to the possibility of noncoincidence between the appearance of a respondent in Phase IV and in one or more earlier phases.

One of our critical tasks in Phase IV was to ascertain to the fullest possible extent the subsequent mobility of the respondents with whom we had started nearly five years earlier. Hence, although we acknowledged the right of any respondent family not to participate actively in the study any further if it did not wish to, we attempted to establish the incidence and nature of repeat mobility among nonrespondents whenever possible through *indirect* methods.

Our information on respondents' repeat mobility is on three different levels of confidence, according to the source. The definitive returns, which we use exclusively when analyzing mobility in conjunction with other responses given by families in Phase IV, represent those families who did answer the questionnaire. The second level of mobility data refers also to respondents whose current addresses were retrieved either through the respondents themselves when refusing a telephone interview, through the person named by the respondent in Phase III who would always know where to find them, or through the telephone company's directory assistance operator. The most inclusive, but least reliable, set of data on subsequent mobility contains all of the preceding cases, plus those where information was supplied either from driver license files or by the post office when the latter returned a questionnaire.[4]

Whatever the data set consulted, the picture is the same. Great numbers of persons moved. About 45 percent of the Phase I families moved at least one *additional* time beyond the move recorded as the basis for this study. In fact, about 18 percent of the sample moved at least two more times. Among the movers, 4 percent did not remain as much as a year in the new homes which we studied, and another 23.6 percent stayed only a year. Moving after up to 2, 3, and 4 years are 37.2 percent, 20.4 percent, and 14.8 percent respectively. This shows that over 60 percent of the repeat moves made their second move no more than about two years after their first move.

Although it is impossible to say exactly what happened to those who could not be traced, they almost undoubtedly represented an even higher percentage of subsequent mobility.

We were able to trace the subsequent mobility of 69 families who did not answer the questionnaire—about half the difference between the number of Phase I and IV respondents; 87 percent of these traceable nonrespondents had moved.[5]

Therefore, by whatever criteria employed, repeat mobility in the present sample was common, frequent, and relatively immediate.

Who moved? Just as the anticipation of repeat mobility was not equally distributed throughout the sample, neither was actual repeat mobility. In broad terms, almost all families living in apartments moved at least once again, while virtually none of those who had moved to houses did so. Among those living in downtown high-rise apartments, 86.4 percent moved, while 75 percent of their suburban counterparts did so. However, the repeat mobility would have been even higher within the suburban apartment group had it not included the small subsample of families who had bought condominium apartments. Using the most detailed figures available, since the condominium sample is so small, 53 percent remained in their condominium apartments through at least the first four years, while 47 percent moved. Subtracting the condominium subsample from

the other suburban apartment dwellers leaves the latter with a repeat mobility rate of 83 percent. Reducing the condominium group to include
only those who responded to the questionnaire still indicates 42 percent
moving and 58 percent remaining. It is astonishing how well these figures,
whether 53 or 58 percent, agree with what the respondents themselves
had predicted before moving to these apartments (about 55% predicted
they would remain). We may say the same, of course, for most other respondents as well.

Among those who had moved to houses, only about 15 percent moved
again, representing 13.6 percent of the families in downtown houses and
16.4 percent of the families in suburban houses.

Certainly, the aggregate expectation among families in the contrasting
housing types were upheld.

A major component, moreover, of anticipated mobility was the type
of environment *to which* people would move. For example, those in downtown apartments showed strong indications of future mobility to more
self-contained units and to the suburbs, while those in downtown houses
were more oriented to remaining in comparable neighborhoods downtown. Those in suburban apartments wished for more self-contained units
and possibly more peripheral locations, the latter shared with those in
suburban houses, assuming they wished to move.

Table 9.1 shows the high degree of realization of these aspirations, as
of Phase IV. Starting with the entire Phase I sample, we see that among
those who moved to downtown apartments, only 16.5 percent were known
to still reside in one, four years and a few months later. More had moved
to suburbs than to any single location, more than 3 times as many decentralizing as moving elsewhere downtown.

Table 9.2 indicates locational information relevant to those who moved.
Only 22.5 percent of those who moved from downtown high-rise apartments remained downtown, with 25.4 percent moving out but not as far
as the suburbs, 33.8 percent to the suburbs, and 18.3 percent out of town.

Those who had moved to downtown high-rise apartments also fulfilled their anticipations regarding a further change in housing type. Table
9.3 indicates specific trends regarding housing type for those moving again.

Figure 9.1 indicates graphically the extent and nature of movement
among those in the downtown apartments, linking the housing type and
location to which they moved as part of the study to their last known ad-

Table 9.1
Phase IV Housing Type and Location of All Respondents, by Phase II
Housing Type and Location

Phase IV Housing Type and Location		Phase II Housing Type and Location				
		Apartment downtown (%)	House downtown (%)	Apartment suburbs (%)	House suburbs (%)	(N)
Did not move—Same place		10.1	80.9	19.9	68.8	
	Apartment downtown	6.4	1.1	1.4	0.0	
	House downtown	4.6	1.1	1.0	0.0	
	Apartment suburbs	6.4	0.0	7.7	1.1	
	House suburbs	11.0	0.0	15.0	6.3	
Moved to	Beyond Toronto area	11.9	5.3	9.4	8.8	
	In between downtown and suburban zones	16.5	3.2	10.3	1.8	
	Low-rise multiple dwelling in either downtown or suburbs	7.4	2.1	15.0	0.7	
Don't Know		25.7	6.4	20.3	12.5	
Total Families		109	94	286	272	(761)

Table 9.2
Last-known Location of Repeat Movers, by Phase II Housing Type and Location

Housing Type and Location	Phase IV—Last-known Location				
	Downtown (%)	Suburbs (%)	In-between (%)	Out-of-Toronto Area (%)	(N)
Phase II					
Apartment downtown	22.5	33.8	25.4	18.3	(71)
House downtown	33.3	0.0	25.0	41.7	(12)
Apartment suburbs	4.7	62.6	17.0	15.8	(171)
House suburbs	2.0	41.1	9.8	47.1	(51)
(N)					(305)

Table 9.3
Last-known Housing Type of Repeat Movers, by Phase II Housing Type and Location

Housing Type and Location	Phase IV: Last-known Housing Type			
	Single-family detached house (%)	Low-rise multiple dwelling (%)	High-rise apartment (%)	(N)
Phase II				
Apartment downtown	40.0	22.9	37.1	(70)
House downtown	66.7	25.0	8.3	(12)
Apartment suburbs	45.3	32.6	22.1	(172)
House suburbs	81.6	12.2	6.1	(49)
(N)				(303)

dress. Although the map is slightly oversimplified, lumping as one the families who did the same thing, it provides the basis for noting marked contrasts to the actions of the families in the other categories of housing type and location.

Table 9.1 shows a highly different pattern among those who had moved to downtown houses. We know with confidence that most of them have remained in the same residence. Among the handful who moved, three-quarters either remained in the downtown or moved out of Toronto completely, while none at all moved into the suburbs. Two-thirds of those who moved from downtown single-family homes went to single-family homes once again, and another 25 percent remained in the realm of a low rise. Only 8.3 percent of the movers (representing exactly one family) changed to a high-rise.

Among those who had moved to suburban high-rise apartments, hardly any made repeat moves downtown, while the vast majority remained sub-urbanites. Specifically, only 4.7 percent of the movers went downtown, while 62.6 percent remained in the suburbs. Another 17 percent moved somewhat closer to but not within the downtown area, while 15.8 percent moved out of town. Only 22 percent of those moving from suburban high-rise chose high-rise apartments again, while in contrast 45.3 percent moved to single-family homes and 32.6 percent found another kind of low-rise accommodation.

Very few of those who had moved to suburban houses made qualitative

FIGURE 9.1.
RELATION OF NEW HOME AND LAST-KNOWN SUBSEQUENT HOME, of all respondents whose new home was a downtown apartment.

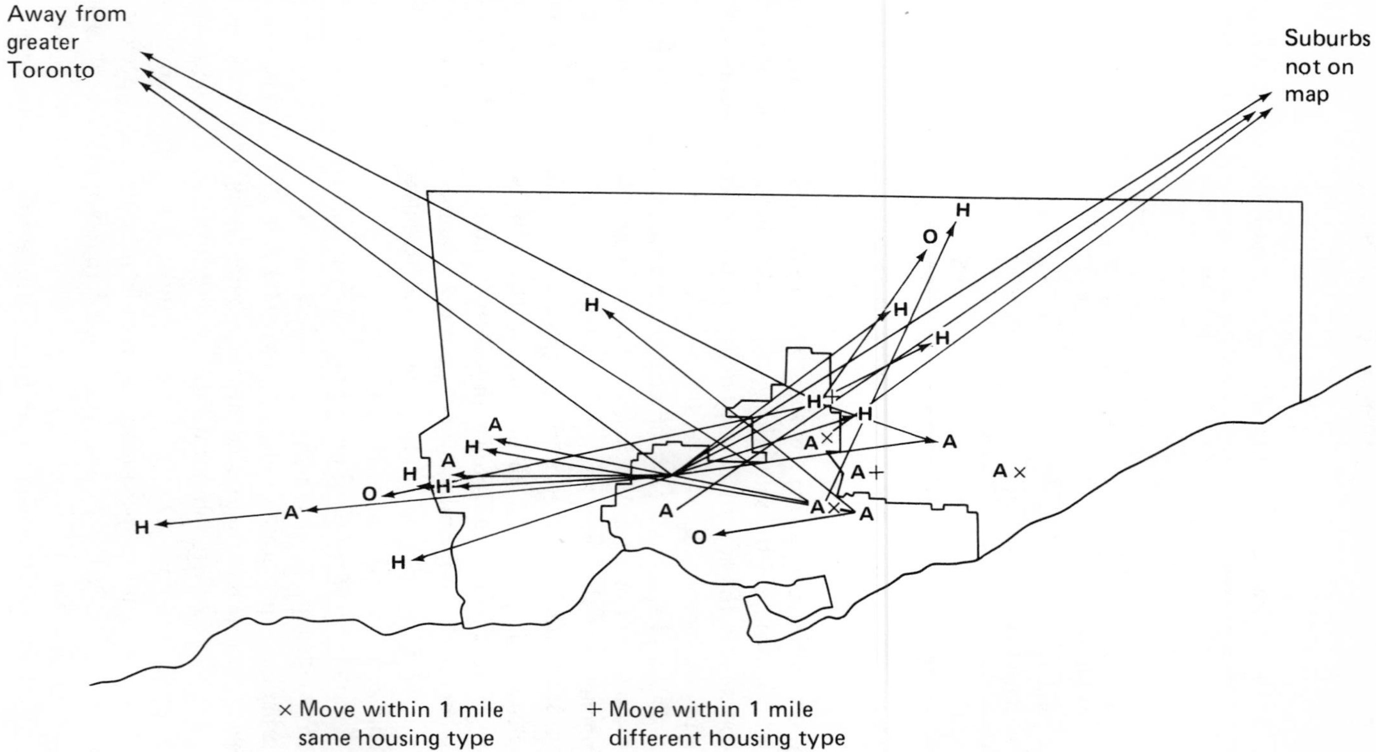

Away from
greater
Toronto

Suburbs
not on
map

× Move within 1 mile
same housing type

+ Move within 1 mile
different housing type

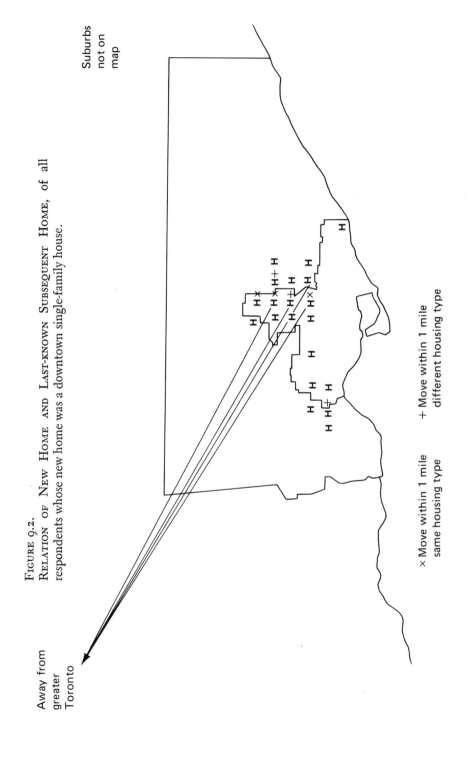

FIGURE 9.2.
RELATION OF NEW HOME AND LAST-KNOWN SUBSEQUENT HOME, of all respondents whose new home was a downtown single-family house.

Away from greater Toronto

Suburbs not on map

× Move within 1 mile same housing type

+ Move within 1 mile different housing type

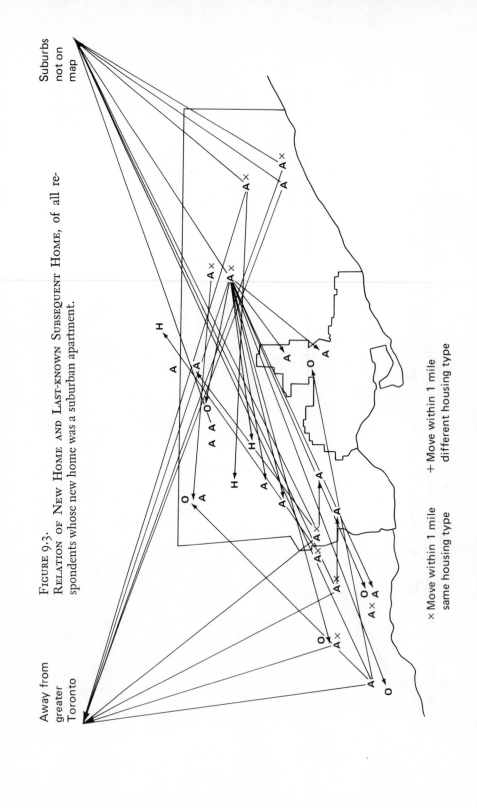

FIGURE 9.3.
RELATION OF NEW HOME AND LAST-KNOWN SUBSEQUENT HOME, of all respondents whose new home was a suburban apartment.

Away from
greater
Toronto

Suburbs
not on
map

× Move within 1 mile
same housing type

+ Move within 1 mile
different housing type

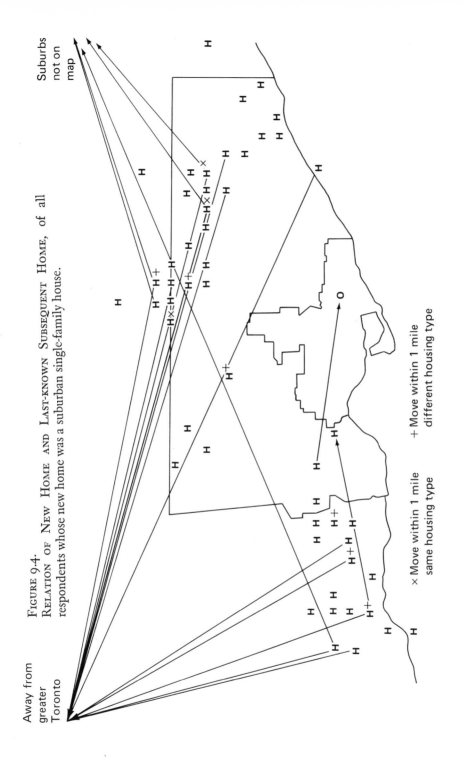

FIGURE 9.4.
RELATION OF NEW HOME AND LAST-KNOWN SUBSEQUENT HOME, of all
respondents whose new home was a suburban single-family house.

Away from
greater
Toronto

Suburbs
not on
map

× Move within 1 mile
same housing type

+ Move within 1 mile
different housing type

changes in housing type. Most of those who subsequently moved chose another single-family house in the suburbs of Toronto or migrated to another city. The only family to move downtown chose a townhouse. When making inter-city moves, most respondents nonetheless remained in single-family homes. Almost 8.2 percent of suburban homeowners who moved remained in detached houses; only 6.1 percent chose a high-rise apartment, while 12.2 percent occupied a low-rise multiple dwelling.

Figures 9.2, 9.3 and 9.4 all contrast with Figure 9.1 and with each other in terms of the *extent* of repeat mobility, *direction* of these moves, and the *housing type* at the origin and destination of each move. The maps, together with the foregoing data, indicate that where there is a financial way, there is surely a will among the respondents to move in the direction of self-contained housing and, among the apartment renters, to suburban locations. On the other hand, those families already in single-family housing are shown as steadfastly loyal to this form of housing, as well as to the location which they 'originally' chose.

Most moves from what people classify as approximating their ideal in housing reflect job changes as we expected, not the desire for more appropriate housing.

The net result for the whole sample is a distribution of families, some four years and two months after their initial moves of record, which is more heavily skewed toward residence in single-family homes and toward suburbia than at the outset. That this has happened, in spite of a housing market with opposite trends with respect to housing type, is a tribute to the strength of the intentions of these families, as well as to their financial ability to manage such moves.

THE STRENGTH OF EXPECTATIONS

In 1955, Rossi wrote that the best way of predicting whether a family would actually move is to ask them their intentions beforehand. Rossi's observation appears well founded, according to the foregoing findings.

It is possible, however, that the apparent strengths of intentions and assumptions about future mobility are spurious—that those who had intended to move are actually no more likely to have done so than those who had not. It is possible that characteristics of the high-rise apartment or other factors in the lives of high-rise residents spur them on to repeat mobility regardless of the nature of their original intentions. Retention of a single-family house may also be related to something other than original intentions. Whether individuals as well as aggregates follow expected patterns is crucial for our understanding of the basis and validity of the evaluations which individuals offer. If their assumptions of future mobility are valid, the nature and basis of their evaluations become more plausible.

Our first measure of intended repeat mobility is the direct question on this subject from Phase I, before the respondents had yet moved to their new homes of record. This is perhaps the most important of the measures, because it was taken before people could base opinions or intentions on the experience of living in their new homes. Table 9.4 shows that, with two minor exceptions due almost certainly to chance variation within the smallest cells, those husbands and wives moving to all the combinations of housing type and location who had thought the likelihood very great or possible that they would move again were in fact more likely to do so than those thinking repeat mobility not likely. Regardless of housing type, the expectation of future mobility was followed by appropriate actions.

Nonetheless, the same table indicates as well that the repeat mobility *from particular housing types* is only modified, not greatly influenced, by the type of expectations people have. For example, 77.8 percent of the few wives and 100 percent of the even fewer husbands who moved to

Table 9.4
Percentage Moved before Phase IV among Those Expressing Pre-move Degrees of Intention to Move Again, by Phase II Housing Type and Location

Phase II Housing Type and Location	Pre-move Intention to Move Again											
	Very great				Possible				Not likely			
	Wife		Husband		Wife		Husband		Wife		Husband	
	(%)	(N)	(%)	(N)	(%)	(N)	(%)	(N)	(%)	(N)	(%)	(N)
Apartment downtown	87.8	(62)	82.2	(45)	88.0	(25)	94.4	(18)	77.8	(9)	100.0	(3)
House downtown	0.0	(3)	14.3	(7)	20.8	(24)	11.8	(17)	11.7	(60)	9.4	(32)
Apartment suburbs	91.4	(81)	90.4	(73)	72.1	(104)	68.9	(61)	56.3	(48)	40.7	(27)
House suburbs	50.0	(12)	50.0	(8)	22.9	(48)	29.6	(54)	18.1	(177)	16.0	(106)

downtown high-rise apartments and who thought it not likely that they would move again within five years did so anyway; 56.3 percent and 40.7 percent of the wives and husbands entering suburban apartments with the same disposition in fact moved subsequently. While the percentages of repeat mobility among 'apartment movers' without the intention of repeat mobility are, but for the cells based on tiny (N)'s, lower than among those who had thought it likely or possible that they would move, they are still very much higher than the percentages of repeat mobility among those who moved to houses.

Thus, while the intentions held by most people appear well confirmed and while these intentions do appear to have some independence from the environments in which they are found, the high-rise building is nonetheless associated with far more repeat mobility than one can expect only on the basis of intentions.

Such relative independence between the two sources of influence does not, however, diminish the validity of respondents' assumptions underlying their evaluation of housing.

The expectation of moving is partially fulfilled as soon as Phase III. Among the families where husband or wife in Phase I had thought it possible or likely that they would move once again, 13.2 percent had already done so before Phase III, compared to less than one-half of 1 percent among those originally considering themselves unlikely to move again.

Furthermore, the goals underlying the intentions of future mobility among apartment dwellers are confirmed by our examination of *where* those who had expected to move again in Phase I found themselves in Phase IV. Table 9.5 indicates that those who had the greatest expectations of repeat mobility (regardless of sex or location) were also those most likely to occupy the generally accepted housing goal—the suburban single-family house, after one or more repeat moves. Hence, people's assumptions of future mobility are important not only in understanding repeat mobility but also in understanding both the rationale behind the move and the evaluation of the housing from which this move takes place.

As we saw in Chapter 8, intentions of subsequent mobility enable feelings of satisfaction with an environment which does not fulfill people's ultimate housing aspirations. This means that the presence of satisfaction in a high-rise apartment is not something which serves to deter repeat mo-

Table 9.5

Percentage of Repeat Movers from Apartments Occupying Suburban Houses in Phase IV, by Pre-move Intention to Move Again

Phase II Residence	Pre-move Intention to Move Again											
	Very great				Possible				Not likely			
	Wife		Husband		Wife		Husband		Wife		Husband	
	(%)	(N)	(%)	(N)	(%)	(N)	(%)	(N)	(%)	(N)	(%)	(N)
Apartment downtown	21.4	(42)	22.2	(36)	15.0	(20)	17.6	(17)	0	(7)	0	(3)
Apartment suburbs	34.7	(72)	32.8	(64)	19.2	(14)	19.5	(41)	15.4	(26)	18.2	(11)

bility, since it is partly made possible by the intention to move again. Hence, we find that those families who in Phase III expressed definite satisfaction with living in high-rise apartments were not any less likely to move thereafter to suburban houses than those with lesser degrees of satisfaction. In fact, among the wives there is a slight tendency to the contrary. Roughly 20 percent of the apartment families moved to suburban houses regardless of their degree of satisfaction with these apartments.

The relative influences of prior expectations and of satisfaction in housing on repeat mobility are indicated in Table 9.6. This table shows that *regardless* of the level of satisfaction among families after the first year (high or low), those who had thought the likelihood in Phase I of moving again within five years was "very great" or "possible" were much more likely to have proceeded to do so than those deeming it "not likely." Indeed, in almost all categories, there is a correspondingly great difference in repeat mobility between those saying "very great" and "possible."

Furthermore, among those who had predicted their repeat mobility as "very great," there is very little variation in the high percentages of those who moved again, regardless of their degree of satisfaction with their 'interim' housing. Definite satisfaction, then, did not deter respondents with high expectations of moving, nor did lower levels of satisfaction provide extraordinary incentive to others.

Table 9.6
Percentage Repeat Mobility, by Pre-move Expectations of Future Mobility and Feelings about the Phase II Home in Phase III

Pre-move Expectations of Future Mobility	Feelings about Phase II Home after More than a Year									
	Definitely Satisfied		Mostly satisfied		Neither satisfied nor dissatisfied		Mostly dissatisfied		Definitely dissatisfied	
	(%)	(N)	(%)	(N)	(%)	(N)	(%)	(N)	(%)	(N)
Wives										
Very great	85.7	(42)	83.9	(62)	88.9	(9)	85.7	(7)	100.0	(2)
Possible	36.5	(63)	57.3	(89)	91.7	(12)	50.0	(6)	100.0	(1)
Not likely	17.3	(110)	28.3	(113)	53.8	(13)	100.0	(5)	00.0	(1)
Husbands										
Very great	80.0	(30)	77.8	(54)	83.3	(12)	100.0	(2)	100.0	(2)
Possible	34.0	(47)	54.7	(53)	57.1	(7)	66.7	(3)	100.0	(1)
Not likely	11.9	(59)	29.3	(58)	40.0	(5)		(0)		(0)

It is only in those cases where expectations of future mobility were not as great that repeat mobility is directly related to lower levels of satisfaction with new housing.

Levels of locational satisfaction, on the other hand, are *totally* unrelated to repeat mobility, while levels of neighborhood satisfaction show only very weak relationships of the same pattern taken by satisfaction with the home.

Other information provided in Phase IV helps confirm the existence of valid though short-range reasons for some of the original moves and hence the grounds for the evaluations given. The overwhelming majority in every category of home environment said that, had they been able to make the 'original' move over again, knowing what they learned in the process, they would still have moved to the same homes. Those who had moved to suburban apartments were least likely to say they would have done it again, but yet a full 74 percent of them said that they would have. Those in single-family houses downtown are the most likely to repeat, at 90.6 percent. Downtown apartments and suburban houses are about equal, half way between these two extremes.

The kinds of motive reflected in such answers are expressed by representative respondents as follows:

"It was a very pleasant place to live and suited our life style at the time."

"At the time, we didn't have kids. It was a nice apartment as apartments go, and it was in a very convenient location for the subway. . . ."

A very strong theme among those who wished that they had chosen an alternative was the feeling that by not buying a house at the earlier time, they had bypassed their chance to enter the market for single-family houses, given the subsequent increase in the price of houses.

What we observed happening through Phase IV is not the end of the moving cycle for the families involved. Their lives, of course, continue even after the study. We find that even in Phase IV families still living in apartments say that they are far more likely to move in the future than those living in houses. Among families in downtown apartments, 96 percent say the possibility of their moving is very great or possible (divided exactly in half). Moreover, 44.4 percent of them expect to move to a detached house, while another 38.9 percent expect to move to a low-rise multiple dwelling, with only 16.7 percent expecting to remain in high-rise housing. Among those in suburban high-rise apartments, 71 percent expect a future move (with somewhat more than half stating this as a very great likelihood). Among the suburban apartment dwellers, 40.4 percent expect to move to single-family housing, 29.8 percent to low-rise attached housing, with the remaining 29.8 percent expecting to remain in high-rise housing.

Hence, the same intentions which, shortly after their original move of record, speeded the move of many families from high-rise to lower-rise forms of housing appear strongly among those still in high-rise. If the result is the same among them as it was among their former colleagues, one may expect that only a handful of the hundreds of families with which we started will remain in high-rise over the long run.

There is one change, however, observable in the goals of those who have stayed in or drifted to new downtown high-rise apartments over the years. At this point, a very much higher percentage of the few that are still there desire to remain within the downtown zone. While, previously, most expressed preferences for suburban moves, now 42.1 percent express a desire to remain downtown, compared to 37 percent who would decentralize, with the remainder showing an interest in other situations.

These data surely confirm the place of the family-mobility cycle in understanding residential mobility and hence in assessing the implications of contrasting housing types and locations. I suggested in Chapters 1 and 2 that the context of explanation in this case is a wide one, including many factors at many times. The fact of cyclical mobility oriented to but not necessary always advancing toward a goal does not exclude the fact that in many moves, particularly within Stage 2 of the moving cycle, extremely pragmatic concerns help form the decision to move and the choice of where to relocate. Many of these single factors have formed the central part of more restrictive theories of mobility. We saw in Chapter 5 that such factors as household size, the working status of the wife, and family income play a part in some kinds of moves, with no one such factor explaining all Stage 2 moves.

With aid of data from Phase IV, we can examine the influence that factors such as these had on the extent and nature of repeat mobility, viewing their effect over a much longer period, in contrast to a single move at a single point in time.

THE RELEVANCE OF SELECTED
FACTORS OVER TIME

Size of Household

In the move upon which this study focuses, we did not find size of household related to change in housing types as expected. The largest families were more likely to occupy suburban houses already.

When we turn to movement between Phases II and IV, we see, as Table 9.7 shows, that the relation between repeat mobility and size of family is completely inverse.

That this occurs in aggregate, however, does not mean that large families remain in high-rise as steadfastly as they appear to remain in single-family houses. There were few large families in the downtown high-rise apartments, and virtually everybody moved out of them in any case. However, a breakdown of repeat mobility by family size within the suburban apartment subsample shows that, contrary to the aggregate trend, the largest families were most likely to move out during the period of study. Between 83 and 85 percent of families with four or more members made a repeat move; only 56 percent of childless couples moved again, while 65 percent of families with just one child repeated their move.

No such pattern emerges among those in houses, who report that about 40 percent of their subsequent moves were based on the simple criterion of job change. In any case, those in houses already have relatively large quarters, more able to handle a large family than the conventional apartment.

The aggregate is pieced together from the pattern of families, who, within each category of housing type and location, have differing family sizes and rates of mobility, whose agglomeration makes a beautiful but spurious relation, one which is not found applicable to any of the disaggregated categories of home environment.

Table 9.7
Repeat Mobility, by Size of Family in Phase IV

| Size of Family | Repeat Mobility | | (N) |
	Did not move again (%)	Moved again (%)	
1	27.3	72.7	(11)
2	39.5	60.5	(81)
3	46.6	53.4	(118)
4	47.5	52.5	(219)
5	69.8	30.2	(116)
6	74.5	25.5	(47)
7	83.3	16.7	(12)
8	100.0	0.0	(1)
10	100.0	0.0	(2)
12	100.0	0.0	(1)
Total			(608)
Missing Information			(9)

A sorting process has in any case occurred over time, as less than 5 percent of the families with more than four members live in high-rise apartments by Phase IV. Of the 23 families who are living in downtown high-rise apartments at this time, 13 of them have two or fewer members, while seven have only one child. Among the 84 families in suburban apartments, somewhat more are likely to have children; however, only 11 percent of these families have more than two children (all but two of those families having three). In contrast, over 40 percent of the families in houses, whether downtown or suburban, have three or more children.

Despite this sorting out process, seen to its fullest effect among the larger families who four years before had moved to suburban apartments, there is no indication through this time period that families are more likely to move merely because they are big. This is indicated in still another way by an analysis of the answers to the Phase IV question on the likelihood of still another move within the five year period following Phase IV. Again, there is an indirect relationship between family size and mobility (this time reflecting intention). What these data suggest is that the pressures of total family size can be understood only within the context of where people live already. Large families in high-rise apartments do expect to move away, while families in houses have selected these dwellings partly for the very purpose of accommodating their numbers.

Change in Household Size

Although the absolute size of families is unlikely to precipitate change except in unfavorable settings, a change in family size is more likely to create pressures requiring action, even though this action, as we saw in Chapter 5, may be the move from one apartment to another for the purpose of gaining space. In that chapter we saw also that growing families were more likely to move to the suburbs.

Unfortunately, our measures were not sufficient to document whether babies were causes or effects of the moves around which we had designed the study. However, our assessment of change in family size since the first move from the perspective of Phase IV enables us to determine whether moves to houses were followed by greater numbers of offspring, as hypothesized.

In actuality, the opposite was true. Family increases were more likely to occur among those who had moved to high-rise apartments. Among those who had moved to downtown high-rise apartments, 44 percent had one or more children in the four years and two months after their move, as did 36 percent of those who had moved to suburban apartments. Additional children were born to only 30 and 24 percent of those in downtown and suburban houses, respectively.

These figures surely do not support popular claims, often based on experiences in countries with extreme housing shortages, that high-rise living is a form of birth control. Nonetheless, one must interpret the present findings only in light of expectations of continued mobility on the part of these families to more self-sufficient quarters, which most of them in fact realized during this period of just over four years. Table 9.8 shows that an increase in family size is more highly related to repeat mobility in all but the suburban houses. The exception represented by the last category is hardly surprising, as this is the housing type generally thought most appropriate for child raising, from which people would not move when having more children.

The kind of sentiment involved was clearly expressed by one respondent:

"I felt the need for a home and backyard for the children—and privacy. A house became important once the child was born—that is with respect to the logistics of getting in and out of the home. . . . We needed a place for the children to play. *I didn't want my child to be an elevator baby."*

Overall, 57 percent of those with additions to the family moved again between Phases II and IV, compared to only 41 percent among those without additions.

The pressures of increased family size remain, as only 35 percent of the families who had two or more children in the more than four years after their 'first' move think it not likely they will move again in the next five years, compared to 41 percent of those with one addition, and 50 percent of those undergoing no change.

In addition, almost one family in seven *decreased* by one or more persons, some of them through children growing up and leaving the premises and others through separation and divorce. Families with decreases are also less likely to think that they will remain in place, resembling the families whose numbers have increased in propensity to move—helping to form a set of relations in which those undergoing the least change are most likely to remain and those undergoing the most change are most likely to move.

Although the maps and discussion in the first section of this chapter make the point obvious, I should note in this connection that the expected finding confirmed in Chapter 5, that families having more chil-

Table 9.8
Percentage Repeat Mobility, by Increase in Family Size and
Phase II Housing Type and Location

Housing Type and Location (Phase II)	Increase in Family Size					
	2 or more		1		No change	
	% Repeat mobility	(N)	% Repeat mobility	(N)	% Repeat mobility	(N)
Apartment downtown	92.3	(13)	90.5	(21)	81.6	(38)
House downtown	18.2	(11)	20.0	(15)	6.5	(46)
Apartment suburbs	94.4	(18)	83.1	(59)	68.2	(110)
House suburbs	20	(10)	11.1	(45)	21.6	(139)
Inapplicable or Missing Information						(92)

dren move out to the suburbs, is certainly confirmed once again in the longer range behavior of the present sample. The downtown high-rise respondents fulfill clearly expressed intentions in so doing. Although the respondents whose life styles and intentions reflect suburban orientations do largely fulfill such desires, this does not mean that the families in downtown houses do not also provide what they regard as satisfactory homes for their children. The latter simply represent a different submarket, with different orientations and criteria, but satisfied and loyal. Neither of these two subgroups is anxious for the product of the other.

Wife's Work Status

We have seen that the work status of the wife is congruent with downtown location. Nonetheless, we have seen also that families in apartments trade-off central location to maximize other goals. Hence, it is not surprising that whether or not a woman works is completely unrelated to repeat mobility. Forty-eight percent of the working wives moved again, compared to 46 percent of nonworking wives.

On the other hand, if families move again, the relation of working status to choice of housing type and location is similar to what we observed in the original moves (although a greater percentage of all wives in the study were working in Phase IV than was the case in Phase I). In any case, among those whose repeat moves took them to downtown high-rise apartments, 82 percent worked, as was true of 72 percent of those moving to suburban apartments. In contrast, in Phase IV, 38 percent of those moving to downtown houses and 49 percent of those moving to suburban houses had paid employment. Among those who remained in their Phase II settings, much the same proclivities to work are exhibited. Table 9.9 shows these breakdowns.

That the wife's work status is a partial determinant of *where* to move though *not an incentive to do so* is reflected by the relatively minor difference of 10 percent in the percentages of those who anticipate future mobility between working and nonworking wives (the former more likely to move again). This difference is small in comparison with the difference accounted for by other factors inducing future mobility.

Table 9.9
Percentage of Working Wives, by Repeat Mobility and
Selected Phase IV Housing Type and Location*

Housing Type and Location (Phase IV)	No repeat move: Remain in residences cited		Repeat move to residences cited	
	(%)	(N)	(%)	(N)
Apartment downtown	70.0	(10)	81.8	(11)
House downtown	43.2	(74)	37.5	(8)
Apartment suburbs	71.7	(53)	72.0	(25)
House suburbs	48.0	(173)	49.3	(67)
Inapplicable or Missing Information				(196)

* Those beyond basic cross-classification omitted.

Change in Family Income

We saw in Chapter 5 that family income was lowest among those who moved to suburban apartments. These people had the fewest strong rationales for the choice of their new homes; in many respects, they were there because they did not see better alternatives available within the limitations of their incomes, despite what benefits they foresaw. The alternatives to which they aspired required increases in income. Hence, we can ask whether increases in family income are associated with repeat mobility, particularly among those who had moved to suburban apartments.

In the whole sample, increase in income is only weakly related to repeat mobility. In line with economic trends, we divided the sample into those whose family income increased by 50 percent or more, whose increase was 25 to 49 percent, and whose family income did not increase as much as 25 percent. This produced categories containing 27 percent, 42 percent, and 31 percent, respectively. Among those with the largest increase, 55 percent moved again, compared to about 45 percent in each of the other two categories.

Nonetheless, families who had moved to suburban apartments with greater increases in income were more likely to move again than those with lesser increases, even though there was a general propensity to move again in any case. Among those whose incomes increased by over 50 percent, 85 percent of the families undertook repeat moves, compared to 75 percent among those with 25 to 49 percent increases and 67 percent among those with lesser increases. Among all the other families in the study, such a relationship disappears entirely. Among those living in houses, the families with the larger increases in income were slightly more likely to remain, perhaps paying for the high cost of these houses with expected increases in income.[6] It is noteworthy that those who between Phases II and IV *moved to* each combination of housing type and location were more likely to have received large increases in family income than those who *remained within* them in this period. Table 9.10 indicates this phenomenon.

Moreover, when families in suburban high-rise apartments sustain healthy increases in pay, they not only move, but they move away from this setting. Forty-seven percent of those with the biggest increases moved to one or another form of low-rise housing, compared to 38.6 percent and 30.6 percent among the other two categories, respectively.

We found the same proclivity toward repeat mobility among those still in suburban apartments in Phase IV. Almost 65 percent of those who enjoyed the largest amount of increase in family income expect to move

Table 9.10

Percentage with Increases in Family Income over 50 Percent, by Repeat Mobility and Selected Phase IV Housing Type and Location*

Housing Type and Location (Phase IV)	Mobility Status			
	No repeat move: Remain in residences cited		Repeat move to residences cited	
	(%)	(N)	(%)	(N)
Apartment downtown	9.1	(11)	25.0	(12)
House downtown	31.0	(71)	75.0	(8)
Apartment suburbs	17.0	(9)	18.5	(27)
House suburbs	22.4	(170)	27.7	(65)
Inapplicable or Missing Information				(253)

* Those beyond basic cross-classification omitted.

again within five years, compared to 31 and 35 percent among the other two categories.

Once again, however, increases in income are not associated with intended repeat mobility in any of the other categories. Hence, while income is critical as a limiting factor when people desire a change already, it is not something which has an independent effect on movement. As with other factors, it is crucial to understand the current stage which families occupy in their mobility cycle. The homeowners have already approximated their ideal, with subsequent moves usually based on something other than the financial ability to move. However, increases in income help those in suburban apartments realize a strong intention to move somewhere else.

In short, the data from Phase IV of the study confirm not only the strength of respondents' intentions and the validity of their assumptions, but also our interpretation of the place of certain factors in explaining mobility.

We may pursue still another form of validation with data from Phase IV by assessing whether we find over the longer run some of the typical behaviors and evaluations which had emerged after the first year and several months of residence.

LONG-RUN PATTERNS

We can discover whether some of the findings about home environment in Phase III accurately reflect long range patterns, by focusing on questionnaire data given by those who did not undertake repeat mobility.

We were, for example, surprised that those who had moved to houses did not show consistently greater amounts of social contact with neighbors than those in apartments in Phase III. The former did have more of some kinds of contact with neighbors, but not all.

Among those, however, who remained in their new settings to Phase IV, minor differences started to appear in favor of those living in houses, particularly suburban houses. Among those in suburban houses, 31 percent named neighbors as the people they see most frequently, as do 27 percent of those in downtown houses, compared to 20 percent in downtown apartments and 14.3 percent in suburban apartments. The emergence of this pattern surely does not signal an enormous difference among these categories, but it is in the direction expected.

What this reflects, however, is somewhat of a decline in this form of neighbor contact among those in the apartments, with only very modest increases among those in houses; the difference most likely reflects the dissimilar mobility of the neighbors with whom our respondent families had come in contact. The original group with whom the apartment families had moved in has largely dispersed to other quarters.

On the other hand, neighbors have yet to become prominent in the realm of *personal* contact, as no more than 9 percent of the families in any category named neighbors as the most intimate contact they have outside their own immediate families.

We saw in Chapter 6 that families living in houses were more likely to expect *material* aid from their neighbors, while those living in suburbs were most likely to expect *personal* companionship and assistance. By Phase IV, however, families living in houses were more likely to expect *all* the types of mutual aid about which we asked from their neighbors than were those still living in apartments.

As Table 9.11 indicates, the differences at times are narrow, and in one case, that of borrowing among families in downtown high-rise, there is an exception (although based on the very smallest number of cases of families remaining in their Phase II homes). Nonetheless, the pattern is relatively consistent and, at times, strong.

These data suggest the deeper development of interpersonal relationships among those who remained in homes but not apartments. Data from the earlier phases were less suggestive of problems concerning contact because most of the apartment residents studied were living there *only* during the *initial* period, when no marked problems of social contact were observed. Nonetheless, those whom we studied do not reflect the greater population, which is increasingly troubled by the inability of large numbers of families to proceed through their anticipated moving cycle, remaining longer than expected in high-rise accommodation. I advise extrapolating present findings to this unstudied group, as the many, scattered, 'residual' residents of high-rise may in fact face problems in contact *proportionate* to the length of their own residence and the mobility of their neighbors.

Duration of travel time to work was one factor behind the choice of downtown locations, even though no single category of home environ-

Table 9.11

Expectation of Selected Types of Mutual Aid from Neighbors, by Housing Type and Location among Non-Repeat Movers

Housing Type and Location (Nonrepeat Movers Only)	Types of Mutual Aid (Percentage expected from neighbors)							
	Borrowing cash		Borrowing food staple or tool		"Shooting the breeze"		Babysitting in emergency*	
	(%)	(N)	(%)	(N)	(%)	(N)	(%)	(N)
Apartment downtown	54.5	(11)	90.9	(11)	45.5	(11)	33.3	(6)
House downtown	68.0	(75)	85.7	(77)	79.7	(74)	90.7	(54)
Apartment suburbs	52.6	(57)	77.2	(57)	68.5	(54)	57.1	(42)
House suburbs	65.5	(194)	94.7	(189)	88.0	(183)	83.1	(172)

* Families with children only.

ment wound up with an unqualified net advantage in commuting after the move.

The longitudinal data from Phase IV indicate that those men who remain in the downtown houses have far and away the shortest average commute, 76 percent of them under half an hour. Those with the longest commutes are the men who remained in downtown high-rise apartments, 50 percent of whom travel more than 45 minutes each way to work; clearly, the men who erased the greatest discrepancy in travel time to work by moving to downtown high-rise apartments lost this advantage, something which did not occur among residents of downtown houses. Although men in suburban houses have a somewhat longer commute than those in suburban apartments, the difference is no longer great, with a majority in both categories claiming commutes of less than half an hour.

Among the wives, a very different pattern emerges. Those in downtown apartments match their husbands as the most *dis*advantaged in Phase IV; only 42.9 percent of them are within half an hour of work. Those living in suburban houses are closest to work. Since Phase III, many wives in suburban houses have started to work, and it is common for jobs taken by suburban housewives to be within relatively easy access of home by car; 84.3 percent of the working wives in suburban houses travel less than half an hour to their jobs.

In sum, these data indicate the strength and meaning of the choice of downtown residence among the men in downtown houses. Furthermore, husbands and wives moving to downtown apartments do not necessarily retain travel time as a benefit. These data also show flexibility on the part of many working wives, who find work relatively near home.[7]

We saw that residents of houses were more definitely satisfied with their homes in Phase III than were those moving to apartments, even though both reported satisfaction. We did not put the same measure of satisfaction on the mail questionnaires; we relied instead on a count of the number of specific elements of housing, location, and neighborhood on the questionnaire which the respondents found satisfactory and unsatisfactory. We had found this type of count highly related in other phases to the direct question on satisfaction.

One might expect that those remaining in the same apartment for as long as four years and some months would be considerably more satisfied than the general average might have shown for all the families in that category in Phase III. Nonetheless, comparison of those families who remained in their dwelling units through Phase IV shows that the apartment occupants deem *far* fewer elements satisfactory than do house dwellers. Of a possible 29 items, more than 50 percent of those living in houses found over 24 to be at least partially satisfactory, while about 90 percent found over 20 as satisfactory. In contrast, only 27 percent of those in downtown high rise and 39 percent of those in suburban high rise judged over 24 items as satisfactory, while a total of only 55 percent and 63 percent, respectively, did so for over 20 items, a considerable difference.

The converse is true about items found at least partially unsatisfactory. Close to 30 percent of the apartment dwellers found over 10 items unsatisfactory, compared to just under half that many among the homeowners. Over all, however, the differences by housing type and location regarding dissatisfaction are less compelling than those regarding satisfaction, as between about 50 and 60 percent of the families in all the categories have six or more elements with which they are dissatisfied. It is largely the extreme numbers of dissatisfactions cited by some families that put the apartments in a somewhat poorer light in this regard.

This picture is not inconsistent with that presented in Phase III; while there were differences in the level of satisfaction, there was no great sign of a general feeling of dissatisfaction with any of the dwelling units.

Nonetheless, this does not mean that certain problems are not characteristically present in the various environmental contexts. A number of these were discussed in detail in Chapter 8. Table 9.12 may be compared with Tables 8.4 and 8.5, as they all represent satisfaction with approximately the same elements of environment but at two different points in time, Phases IV and III, respectively. The general level of satisfaction reported is higher in Phase IV. While we may attribute some of this increase to a real increase in satisfaction with these elements, particularly by those who have chosen to remain in the same residence, we must give some weight to the response format of the mail questionnaire. The questionnaire predisposes positive answers to a visible series of questions, in contrast to the selection process used during the interviews in Phases I through III.

In any case, when we look at the specific elements which refer to location, the differences between categories of home environment follow the

Table 9.12
Aspects of Residential Environment Found Satisfactory (Phase IV), by
Housing Type and Location among Non-Repeat movers

| Aspects Found Satisfactory | Housing Type and Location (Non-repeat movers only) | | | |
	Apartment downtown (N=11) (%)	House downtown (N=76) (%)	Apartment suburbs (N=57) (%)	House suburbs (N=187) (%)
Space in home	45.5	92.1	80.7	94.1
Size of rooms	90.9	93.4	80.7	95.7
Number of bedrooms	45.5	88.2	82.5	88.2
Number of bathrooms	63.6	80.3	82.5	93.6
In-home equipment	81.8	90.8	78.9	95.2
Storage or closet space	54.5	69.7	61.4	82.9
Noise	63.6	78.9	61.4	81.1
Repairs/alterations	90.9	76.3	64.9	80.2
Size of lot or outside space	72.7	85.5	71.9	81.8
Design, appearance of home	90.9	92.1	84.2	96.3
Parking facilities	81.8	81.6	71.9	93.0
Management or developer	90.9	22.4	70.2	39.0
Social character of neighborhood	100.0	96.1	84.2	91.4
Type of neighbors/co-tenants	100.0	88.2	82.5	82.4
Distance to country/ green spaces	72.7	75.0	93.0	91.4
Schools	54.5	76.3	70.2	84.5
Design, appearance of neighborhood	90.9	93.4	87.7	97.3
Transportation facilities	100.0	97.4	86.0	74.9
Distance to job/work	90.9	93.4	82.5	79.7
Location of friends	81.8	93.4	89.5	90.4
Location of relatives	81.8	67.1	64.9	82.4
Distance to shopping	100.0	98.7	98.2	90.4
Distance to recreation facilities	81.8	88.2	93.0	87.2
Distance to downtown area	90.9	98.7	80.7	79.1
Housing costs	45.5	73.7	56.1	76.5
Quality of home	81.8	94.7	73.7	93.0
Neighborhood facilities	90.9	92.1	89.5	89.8
Scenery	100.0	90.8	87.7	89.8

same pattern that they did in Phase III. Families living downtown are more likely to cite public transportation, access to their job, and access to downtown as satisfactory than are those living in the suburbs. The latter, on the other hand, are more likely to find satisfaction in their access to green spaces and the country. Families living in suburban houses are most likely to be uniquely disadvantaged with their access to work and to shopping. Those living in suburban apartments are the most satisfied with their access to recreational facilities, as before.

With respect to aspects of the dwelling unit, the disadvantages seen more than three years earlier in the downtown apartments are still reflected in lower levels of satisfaction by those still living there: the amount of space in the home, the number of bedrooms, the number of baths, and storage. Those in downtown apartments share with their suburban counterparts a low degree of satisfaction with the cost of housing; this is less of a concern now among the homeowners, who are more likely to benefit from inflation. Apartment dwellers are more satisfied with questions of management, but only because this is inapplicable to homeowners once beyond developers' warrantee periods.

Homeowners are more likely to be satisfied with the mechanical equipment in their homes than are apartment dwellers, a considerable change in response on the part of those living in downtown houses. It is highly likely, however, that the intense amount of work which the families in downtown houses undertook after moving helped make this aspect of their housing more satisfactory—something which they *can* do through their own efforts which the apartment occupants can not (except perhaps in condominiums or co-ops).

In Phase III, homeowners had been somewhat more favorable about the social characteristics of their neighborhoods and of their immediate neighbors. Among those who chose to remain there is a reasonable degree of satisfaction within all categories, topped by the 100 percent citation of these elements on the part of the eleven families left in downtown high-rise apartments.

On dissatisfactions, the locational disadvantages of the suburban house are clearly represented in Table 9.13 for those who did not move through Phase IV. These families are the most troubled with public transportation, access to shopping, access to downtown, and access to recreation. While those living in suburban apartments do not share problems in reaching

Table 9.13
Aspects of Residential Environment Found Unsatisfactory (Phase IV), by
Housing Type and Location among Non-Repeat Movers

Aspects Found Unsatisfactory	Housing Type and Location (Non-repeat movers only)			
	Apartment downtown (N=11) (%)	House downtown (N=76) (%)	Apartment suburbs (N=57) (%)	House suburbs (N=187) (%)
Size of rooms	18.2	28.9	29.8	27.3
Space in home	63.6	25.0	40.4	18.2
Number of bedrooms	54.5	21.1	26.3	18.7
Number of bathrooms	36.4	21.1	24.6	11.2
In-home equipment	36.4	23.7	31.6	9.1
Storage or closet space	63.6	48.7	47.4	32.1
Noise	45.5	35.5	52.6	29.9
Repairs/alterations	36.4	47.4	35.1	19.3
Size of lot or outside space	18.2	30.3	19.3	35.3
Design, appearance of home	18.2	31.6	28.1	12.3
Parking facilities	36.4	25.0	31.6	9.1
Management or developer	63.6	1.3	47.4	4.3
Social character of neighborhood	18.2	15.8	28.1	28.9
Type of neighbors/co-tenants	18.2	15.8	33.3	17.6
Distance to country/ green spaces	27.3	36.8	12.3	11.8
Schools	0.0	21.1	10.5	21.9
Design, appearance of neighborhood	0.0	17.1	19.3	15.5
Transportation facilities	0.0	10.5	26.3	34.2
Distance to job/work	18.2	10.5	33.3	27.8
Location of friends	36.4	17.1	17.5	21.9
Location of relatives	36.4	22.4	29.8	20.3
Distance to shopping	0.0	6.6	3.5	16.6
Distance to recreation facilities	9.1	15.8	8.8	23.5
Distance to downtown area	9.1	2.6	35.1	32.6
Housing costs	54.5	40.8	54.5	37.4
Quality of home	18.2	17.1	38.6	20.9
Neighborhood facilities	0.0	13.2	15.8	21.9
Scenery	9.1	18.4	19.3	27.3

stores or places of recreation, they do share with those in suburban houses concerns about public transportation and access to downtown; they are even more likely to complain about access to their jobs than are those in suburban houses, although both are high in this respect. Families living downtown, on the other hand, are more dissatisfied with their access to the country or green spaces.

Turning to the scale of the dwelling unit, dissatisfaction in downtown apartments continues with number of bedrooms, baths, storage space, total living space, home equipment, and noise. The last three concerns are shared by suburban apartment residents. Those in downtown houses, despite whatever improvements they have made, still have more dissatis-factions with equipment and repairs than those living in generally newer suburban houses.

Those living in apartments are more dissatisfied with housing costs. More than half the apartment dwellers are also at least partially dissatis-fied with the management of their buildings, and suburban apartment dwellers are particularly concerned about the quality of their buildings.

Homeowners are more dissatisfied with the size of their grounds (per-haps because they have some with which they can be dissatisfied). Fami-lies living in suburban houses have the least problems with parking.

Suburbanites are more likely to find difficulty with the social character-istics of their neighborhood and neighbors, although it is the families in suburban *apartments* who stress this most fully (nearly 3 out of 10). Only the families in downtown high-rise show no dissatisfaction whatever with the design of their neighborhoods, although this is not an element about which strong dissatisfaction is shown in any case.

Some altered evaluations of specific elements of the home environment appear in Phase IV, reflecting actual changes made by the respondents (e.g., modernizing or enlarging a home) or beyond their control (e.g., changes in characteristics of neighbors). Nonetheless, most evaluations are not significantly different than those made about three years earlier.

In short, the longer range actions and opinions of the families studied confirm strongly the potency of the expectations and intentions origi-nally held by these families. These data show also a degree of stability in the evaluation of specific aspects of the environment, as well as in general satisfaction. They show some changes in interpersonal contact with time, as well as additional confirmation of the locational orientation and loyalty of the downtown house group, in contrast to those families who had moved to downtown apartments.

We have now looked, throughout various chapters, at a number of aspects of environmental choice, human behavior, and residential satisfaction. What remains is the more interpretative question of what the various findings suggest, both for the scientific perspectives and the urban housing policy concerns with which I began. I turn to these in Chapter 10.

NOTES

[1] Central Mortgage and Housing Corporation, Ontario Regional Office, Toronto.

[2] Although official figures do not differentiate within the apartment and flat category between walk-up and elevator apartments, the overwhelming majority of completions were of the latter type.

[3] Real Estate Board of Metropolitan Toronto.

[4] The former is inaccurate when a family moves out of the Province of Ontario, and the latter is of inconsistent validity, to put it most positively.

[5] Unlisted telephone numbers are an obstacle to telephone interviews but not to the determination of repeat mobility, as operators are careful to establish that it is really 'such and such' a family that has an unlisted number.

[6] A common, recent phenomenon in the Toronto area is for young couples to purchase houses to the limits permitted by more lenient lending regulations, under the assumption of continued inflation in wages and property values, while their loan commitments remain stable.

[7] Undoubtedly, much more can be made out of the different orientation to careers popularly assumed to characterize men and women and reflected in the present data. Unfortunately, the nature and orientation of the present set of data do not encourage further elaboration.

Chapter Ten

Some Applications and Implications

In the preceding nine chapters, I have dealt theoretically and empirically with environmental choice, human behavior, and housing satisfaction. In this, the final chapter, I shall not attempt a résumé. Given the diversity of the material covered, a résumé would be both lengthy and redundant.

I shall instead, attempt to identify the major messages. To some extent, this involves a greater degree of personal interpretation of the facts than in previous chapters,[1] but I see this as a major obligation, given that I have been so close to the subject during the conception, execution, and analysis of the project described.

There are many levels at which this work can be taken. The most obvious form of inquiry concerns what the present data might say as a basis for the creation of better apartments, houses, and residential areas. How can one make better high-rise apartments? What about the suburban house?

Considerable material, assembled and presented in Chapters 5 through 9, bears on this type of question. One can isolate a number of prominent themes from this material. Here are four.

1. Despite our observation of a general level of satisfaction in high-rise apartments, a number of characteristic problems are open to remedy. A number of the buildings, as conventionally built today, are deficient in terms of soundproofing, storage space, square footage, and in the number of rooms available to any given family. Beyond these initial deficiencies in conception and construction, the apartment dweller feels unable either to remedy such problems or to adapt his home environment to the changing needs of his family without the necessity to move. While still residing in the high-rise apartment, he is highly dependent on the performance of management personnel. In addition, apartment dwellers, realizing the economic differences between ownership and tenancy and largely desirous of

the former, are increasingly more upset at the escalation of monthly housing costs.

Such types of complaints are hardly original, nor kept secret. Nonetheless, they are not as yet compensated for in the design and management
of high-rise buildings. The condominium, of course, solves some problems
of tenure and management, but the condominium owner is still locked
into the decisions made by the governing boards of individual building
projects and by decisions made regarding the physical plan long before
his arrival.

Others may argue that market forces, which we showed in Chapter 2
to have helped decide the number of bedrooms and the amount of soundproofing in a given building, actively militate against remedies, lest the
price for doing so force out the very people who report these dissatisfactions but who survive the experience at present. The various pieces of
data, whether with respect to compromises which tenants knew they were
making at the time of choice, short-range observations based on experience, or longer-run evaluations made by those who stayed, add up to a consistent set of criticisms about certain aspects of the high-rise apartment
building, remedies for which would clearly result in better buildings.

2. On the other hand, certain aspects of high-rise projects were shown
to be of critical importance in the minds and short-run activities of high-
rise dwellers. Recreation facilities, both for adults and for children, were a
major attraction in the rental of apartments, and apartment dwellers utilized them heavily during the period immediately after moving. We saw
that they do not continue the same level of utilization thereafter, however.
That the greatest number of residents do not appear to use the facilities
at any time does not appear to negate the importance of these facilities for
the people involved. Other goals of a more critical nature dictate a subsequent move elsewhere. Although the recreation facilities are therefore related neither to continuing behavior nor to ultimate aspirations, they are
a central positive focus to many moving to the high rise, almost alone as
an attraction in that setting.

Families also appreciate the mixture of land uses often found within
apartment complexes (or, at a somewhat more macro level, immediately
adjacent to apartment complexes).

The higher level of servicing becoming more common in North American high-density projects is not necessarily high on the list of priorities which most people have about housing. They appreciate servicing when they postpone achievement of higher-level priorities in housing. Although planners and intellectuals approve of high standards of local servicing, it appears clear that a great number of families will trade such standards off in return for more self-sufficient types of housing. Such a trade-off was surely characteristic of the movers to suburban houses in the present study. The friction between optimizing servicing and residential self-containment is a dilemma found in many nations (cf. Michelson, 1976).

3. Despite the trade-offs they have rationally made and the great deal of satisfaction which they express, the families in suburban houses express great amounts of dissatisfaction with the kind of access they have to places of recreation, shopping, and work. They are seldom within walking distance to any of these places, and they feel that public transportation is not sufficiently well developed.[2] Such a feeling of remoteness is particularly characteristic of the housewife, who may not have a second car for use, and who, in any case, does not have the excuse to get away from home during the average day, as do those in paid employment. Those with jobs away from home must take the trouble to travel to them, but once outside the 'gravitational pull' of their homes, they have greater opportunities to utilize nonlocal facilities 'on the way.' It is interesting to note the great increase in the percentage of the suburban wives who in the long run undertake outside employment.

Although such employment tends to bring a person more into contact with other parts of the world beyond the home, it does not mean that attention should not be given to a greater mixture of land uses in low-density areas. Although a certain number of the suburban homeowners feel that strict segregation of land uses helps maintain the value of their properties this does not mean that well-planned services with strong functional boundaries, yet more accessible to residents of surrounding areas on foot, would be undesirable. Distance is not necessarily the only way to protect the integrity of residential areas; when areas are totally planned, so that the resident knows what can or cannot be subsequently placed where, he feels 'safe' regarding his investment (Werthman, et al., 1965).

Although suburban homeowners do not require an increase in services as a prerequisite for satisfaction, which they already feel, we should expect such improvements in land-use planning to remove some of the less satisfactory aspects of life in suburban areas.

4. Still another major practical theme has to do with the right of self-contained houses in and near the downtown area to exist in the future. Given the economics involved in purchasing homes in which only one or a few families live and replacing them by buildings to be inhabited by many, there is typically a one-way process wherein apartment houses (or offices) replace detached homes. At best, cities point with pride to areas where detached houses or other forms of low-rise accommodation are rehabilitated and conserved. But it is rare to encounter the replacement of high density by low density housing. There is, then, a consistent reduction in the number of self-contained units, with the constant threat of nearly total elimination.

The data indicate without ambiguity that families living in houses in the downtown area find them highly attractive because of the location. They value access to the downtown and the opportunities within it. They do not find it a matter of indifference in comparison to living in the suburbs. They are close to work. They utilize culture and entertainment centered on the downtown; they participate in civic groups. Unlike their companions in high-rise downtown apartments, they do not aspire to live elsewhere, and they do remain in the downtown area. On the other hand, it is not *just* location which underlies their satisfaction and loyalty, but that they live in the housing type to which they aspire.

Hence, the downtown house is a product with solid, though surely not universal, support. If houses disappear from the downtown area, relocation to houses in other, more peripheral areas would not substitute, given the values and priorities of the residents of the downtown houses; nor would relocation to a downtown apartment.

Furthermore, since these families live near and are good patrons of what the downtown has to offer, it is highly desirable for the future vitality of the downtown area to have them continue to live nearby. This is something which many American cities currently do not have as an advantage. Cities like Toronto which still have a stable population in decent housing close to the center should be taking steps to retain such a population, whose family structures, incomes, and experiences demand that they continue to live in something approximating the self-contained dwelling.[3]

This suggests that steps should be taken to preserve the supply of downtown single-family homes, despite the wishes of both developers and of some property owners desirous of reaping the benefits of one-way change. What happens in a project-by-project, house-by-house process which goes in only one direction is the removal of the downtown house as a viable part of the housing market.

Since apartment dwellers are not typically rooted in the local neighborhoods in which their buildings are found, nor do they retain long-term loyalties to the downtown area, there is no necessity to confine apartment developments to *established* central residential areas. Since most cities have areas containing such land uses as underutilized railway yards, outdated factory buildings and warehouses, and the like, there is generally a considerable amount of land within easy access of the opportunities and attractions of the center city for many additional units of high-density housing, without the need to make irreplaceable inroads in the stock of self-contained housing.

Merely preserving or improving the current housing stock is not enough. Provision must also be made for the channeling of needed additions to the housing stock. They must not remain a continual threat to existing neighborhoods, even if the latter are aided or protected at any one time by government programs or by-laws, which are generally highly impermanent, providing scant protection.

Extraordinary feats of land assembly may be required, not to speak of cooperation between the private sector and the public sector. However, making various persons in these sectors act rationally and responsibly seems preferable to the inevitable removal of housing which families currently appreciate and which provides them with benefits far exceeding the dwelling units themselves.

Although the persons we studied in the present research were relatively affluent, the same phenomenon applies in spades to those poorer people who also live in existing housing near the city center. Although the quality of the housing in which many of these people live may leave considerable room for improvement, their proximity to downtown sources of employment, to low-cost public transportation and to a variety of commercial and institutional services provides for a living environment which is normally far more efficient and supportive than that found in connection with 'better' housing in peripheral areas. A major problem in the Toronto area is that more affluent people are buying out the poor and the landlords of the poor and rehabilitating the units. While this has its benefits for some segments of the population and for many forms of commerce, it has rather more negative implications regarding the housing market, viewed in its widest environmental capacity, for poorer people.

These four themes represent aspects of housing policy and design which could be acted upon overnight, albeit with some need for strong resolve in doing so, to improve the situation of those living in various settings studied. Nonetheless, when observing closely the various outcomes of the study, one cannot help but be struck by the fact that despite whatever negative features are indicated about various forms of housing, most families are nevertheless at least minimally satisfied with it. Despite the fact that many of them move, they are not moving simply because these elements of their environments are causing them undue strain.

While it is imperative that housing be designed and built as appropriately as possible, the study suggests that this is surely not all that is relevant in the provision of housing. People's evaluation of their housing is not based just on the physical characteristics of the units and the neighborhoods in which they live but on a more complex set of criteria with reference to both the lives of the families and the housing market more generally.

I shall return to the development of the implications of this situation, but first I must consider another area of application of the present study results. Our data bear strongly on *theoretical* arguments about self-selection in housing, on the one hand, and on environmental determinism, on the other.

Although disciplined thinking by theorists should have avoided the creation of an 'either-or' situation, the theoretical problem had been posed on whether 'the' explanation for people's behavior in given residential areas comes from either human rationality in choice (self-selection) or the influence of spatial components of the environment (environmental determinism). Having removed an absolute faith in either type of explanation alone in Chapter 1, I still had to ask: 'To what extent does man make the environment or environment make the man? And in what ways?'

We conducted an analysis of many bases on which people might sort themselves out residentially, and we assessed many forms of behavior considered relevant regarding self-selection and determinism before and after families moved, with special attention to determining times and places of origin. I presented these phenomena in Chapters 5, 6, 7, and 9. The discussion focused on financial aspects, neighbor characteristics, life-cycle stage, interpersonal relations, organizational activity, commuting, commercial activity, recreational activity, and housekeeping activity.

All the various phenomena assessed did not follow just a single pattern. There was clear evidence of self-selection, although in some instances this was based on additional social attributes that the families moving to a given housing type and/or location had in common. These attributes were directly related to choice of environment and to certain aspects of behavior, contributing to a spurious illusion that people picked home environments in order to do things that were actually concomitants of their social makeup. Nonetheless, given the nature of interrelations among social attributes, behavior, and environment, these three are most fruitfully seen as part of a common 'package.' Understanding of the life and problems in a given environmental context requires an understanding of the social and physical components of this whole package, no less so than if there were only direct relationships between environment and behavior. The working and family statuses of the wife are two important attributes in this regard.

On the other hand, no smaller number of phenomena reflect the spatial opportunities experienced in the destination environment. Differentiation of types of person and of behavior according to destination environment is found to be very much more complex after the move than could have been predicted on the basis of self-selective factors utilized by the respondents before the move.

What people will do, for example, when in a situation which provides well-defined opportunities, in contrast to one which does not, is well illustrated by patterns of shopping, use of recreational facilties, and good public transportation. Families with shopping facilities well integrated into their complexes were very much more likely to go shopping on foot, foregoing to some extent selectivity in the nature of everyday shopping goods. When the land use was conveniently near, people used it. In contrast, those without commercial facilities immediately present not only traveled by car but went to even more distant destinations, becoming somewhat more choosy in their shopping patterns.

The presence of on-site recreational facilities among persons who clearly saw them as an attraction led in the short run to a very much higher degree of utilization of this kind of facility.

Among families moving downtown, there were the cultural and entertainment facilities of the downtown area, to which they had much greater access than suburbanites. Intensive utilization, which actually preexisted and influenced the move downtown, continued within the setting, in comparison to a decline among those moving to less favorable locations.

Where public transportation is excellent and available, as among the downtown respondents, all of whom were very close to the subway, it is clearly utilized, leading to a focus on the downtown area rather than an equal degree of movement in all directions. Downtown families are highly satisfied with their location and the degree of access to various places they enjoy; they do not appear to suffer from any loss in flexibility by not driving automobiles everywhere. In fact, the moves of many families to downtown high-rise apartments had appeared predicated on the use of mass transit.

Such short-run pursuit of desired activities in favorable settings, which is not always continued in the long run, particularly among apartment dwellers who may trade them off for something else, indicates as well the perspective with which environmental opportunity must be taken—it allows intensive usage to occur where desired but by no means forces people to do what they never wanted or no longer wish.

One of our critical findings lay in our *failure* to support previous assertions of a deficit in social interaction among families in high-rise apartments, particularly in the short run. The major difference found was not in amount or in place of contact, but rather in the way people originally met those who became their friends. This, in turn, was related to people's family structures, which, for their part, have a bearing on the kind of building to which they will move. The buildings themselves also maintain both spatial and normative obstacles to alternate forms of contact among families who do not have children to help speed their mutual acquaintance. Without local channels to friendship, families typically rely on channels associated with communities of interest rather than communities of physical proximity.

Nonetheless, despite the high degree of self-selection, as well as the behavioral patterns emerging as functions of environmental situations after the move, the pattern of answers to various questions at several phases of the study suggests strongly that what people do at any given time is not necessarily what they would be doing were they to have achieved their aspirations. In short, what they quite willingly and happily do in a given setting is not necessarily consistent with their attitudes on what is best for them to do.

That this occurs without any signs of undue stress or strain is contrary to my assumptions when first undertaking the study. I was forced to change my interpretation on the prevalence and consequences of some alternative paths through the paradigm of residential mobility presented in Chapter 1.

I assumed at the outset that a particular type of person, 'Person A,' would, whenever possible, choose a type of housing and/or location which would maximize his opportunities to fulfill his most important behavioral requirements. Hence, Person A would match himself with 'Environment A,' Person B, with Environment B, and so on. If, on the other hand, Person A, through objective exigencies or lack of foresight, wound up in Environment B, he would evaluate the opportunities available for his type (which would have been found in Environment A), resulting in dissatisfaction and the possibility of stress or strain.

In fact, what the various results suggest is that Person A may well rationally choose Environment B, to enjoy the behavior associated with the opportunities in Environment B for an interim period, while waiting for the most appropriate and feasible time to go to Environment A and to satisfy more central behavioral goals.

What all this suggests is that while much behavior found associated with the different housing types and locations is in large part *a function of the situation* in which people find themselves, partly through the application of motivated choice and partly through the spatial characteristics of the environment, this behavior is not necessarily consistent with their ultimate aspirations, either in housing or in behavior.

The inconsistency between current behavior and deep-seated attitudes or aspirations is not harmful in and of itself. The match between environment and behavior is clearly made with some degree of forethought on the part of the people involved, and most of the people in our sample eventually achieve that to which they aspire.

The discrepancy between current behavior and long-range aspirations simply requires the adoption of a dynamic perspective with which to view these phenomena. It is not as though the choice of Environment B at Time 1, leading to a performance typifing the behavior pattern expected of a Person B, precludes someone who wants to become Person A reaching Environment A at Time 2, 3, 4, or 5, in the future. Families are simply staging their moves in a sequence, taking on environments and behavior quite different from those ultimately intended for periods which they explicitly regard as temporary.

During residence in an environment regarded as temporary, people evaluate it with respect to only a partial subset of all the criteria upon which housing can be potentially judged. It is important to realize the extent that families who had moved to homes which they regarded as highly temporary (high-rise apartment homes) achieved many of the benefits that they intended very soon after having arrived there, consistent with the temporary length of tenure intended. In sharp contrast, those moving to houses took longer to achieve many of their expectations. Were the former moves not most frequently conceived as interim moves, way-stations to somewhere else, it would have been more difficult to base evaluation only on the particular subset of criteria employed, as many of the criteria being put aside temporarily were actually of much higher priority in the minds of the apartment dwellers (i.e., the amount of private, inside space and its control).

Thus, the results suggest strongly that the choice of high-rise apartments and their evaluation thereafter were made on one set of grounds, while the attitudes and intentions of the very people who choose these dwelling units support a different form of choice in housing, focusing on very different criteria of evaluation. Understanding this discrepancy requires a model incorporating the notion of sequential movement, leading to a goal which may remain consistent for at least one period in the lifetime of a family. Satisfaction with an environment which would at face value be thought incongruent with ultimate goals or aspirations, is, within this perspective, not inconceivable.[4]

This type of apparent disparity between attitude and behavior, when viewed only in a static perspective, is a new variation on an old theme in social science. This type of discrepancy has been observed most notably in ethnic relations,[5] although it has been applied to a number of other situations, such as political behavior (Brannon et al., 1973). The upshot of most of this literature is that behavior is strongly influenced by interpersonal pressures present in the actual situation under which it occurs but which are not present when people tell others what they think (their attitudes).

This literature says that while both behavior and attitudes may remain stable within their own frame of reference (the latter important for people's identity), it is critical for the understanding of what is possible in the real world (i.e., opportunities for minority groups, etc.) to rely more on what people do than on what they say they do.

In the present case, what people say they want and prefer is very highly related to what they try to and succeed in getting for themselves at a later point in time, when, as in the case of most families in the present sample, their objective circumstances may make this more feasible. The 'success' rate, for example, of the Phase II apartment dwellers moving to other forms of housing, and, in the case of the downtown apartments dwellers, to more suburban locations, is impressive. In this respect, the behavior involved (long-range moving behavior) is highly consistent with their attitudes.

What is inconsistent is their behavior *at any point in time* with the behavior which would follow from the attitudes they express about housing. The discrepancy in this case is based not on peer pressures of any kind but rather on the possibility and even desirability of carrying out one form of behavioral emphasis consistent with the spatial opportunities in which it is situated at one point in time, while actively planning and awaiting a different form of behavior in a setting which is congruent with attitudes and aspirations.

Hence, this kind of discrepancy between behavior and attitude is something about which people are aware and with which they are actively coping, wherever possible.

The most critical aspect of this dynamic set of relationships is that the assumption of future mobility be valid, so that families can postpone desired behaviors and high-priority criteria in the security that there *will be* a long run for them. Thus, among the families in high-rise apartments, what most of them do is not necessarily what they want to do in the long run; but what they *think* of what they now do is based on whether they can do what they want in the long run.

Satisfaction in the high-rise is based partly on assumptions of future mobility. Even the faults so clearly identified are taken in stride if families think that they are shortly moving elsewhere. If they cannot make this assumption, then they must face these faults as long-term problems, a situation confronting increasing numbers of urban Canadians.

Given the importance, then, of the possibility of long run mobility toward a goal (normally the self-contained housing unit), it might be relevant to ask on what the long run depends for the satisfaction of these widely held aspirations. Although this proceeds beyond the practical and theoretical origins of the present study, such a consideration has been made a necessary requirement for an understanding of the problem—and hence its solution.

The answer to this question emerges from the preceding discussion: *what satisfies families in high-rise apartments in the short run is not what would satisfy them in the long run, nor in the short run either if they could not move elsewhere in the long run.* Therefore, for the components of the high-rise apartments which do satisfy them in the short run, such as the recreation facilities, to have their effects as intended, some assurance of the validity of apartment families' long-run assumptions is essential. What this involves is:

1. an adequate supply of low-rise, self-contained housing, and
2. a sufficiently low *cost* of the available supply, so that it may be considered feasible.

Obviously, supply and cost are related to one another. Nonetheless, each without the other is insufficient, particularly with the pressures of demand. The recent decade in Toronto specifically and other cities more generally has seen the formation of new families among an unusually large group of young people, together with additional housing needs created by large amounts of in-migration and immigration. This has created a demand for great numbers of new housing units, which was largely channeled into the construction of high-rise apartments. While this may have filled the bill in the short run, most of these same families may be expected to be in the pursuit of their own family mobility cycles, where a high rise is for many but a stepping stone to housing which comes closer to fulfilling personal aspirations and cultural goals.[6] Certainly, the analysis of age differentials in housing preferences among the present sample does not indicate a growing acceptance of high-rise living.

Nonetheless, at the very time that such unprecedented demand was being filled by building high and dense, this choice of response to demand created severe pressures against the fulfillment of that to which many of the families ultimately aspired. These pressures were related not only to the *availability* of self-contained units, but also to *cost*. As the figures in Chapter 9 indicate, the purchase cost of the average house in Toronto has doubled in just five years. Since mortgage rates have climbed as well during this time, the financial burden of home ownership has reached unprecedented heights, narrowing the field of prospective homeowners objectively.

Some politicians and developers suggest that people will just have to adapt to the high rise, eventually accepting it just as they did modern conveyances, like the car and airplane. This point of view stresses that the main problem with the high rise is its novelty; people are not used to it and hence resist it. They argue also that municipal by-laws unwittingly hinder the design and construction of more optimal high-rise buildings. According to this view, the current 'problem' will disappear once people gain greater exposure to high-rise apartments and as design and construction improve with experience and legal reform.

The data of the present study do not validate the preceding points of view. They show that people with experience in high-rise apartments are, if anything, less likely to desire them in the future. Furthermore, they show that even after experience in a high-rise apartment (at a time when the housing market supports apartment construction and resists house construction), people's aspirations for houses are tough, potent, and unyielding. These attitudes remain largely unchanged over the time covered by this study, and they are related to a considerable amount of supportive consumer activity. It is difficult to erase childhood experiences and a generally shared cultural conception of the good life just because the housing market is allowed to run in a particular direction at a given point in history.

Although I have outlined some steps which might be taken to improve potential satisfaction among those living in high-rise apartments, as well as in some of the other settings mentioned, it is not clear that this approach is the most *meaningful* way either to improve satisfaction in high-rise apartments or to satisfy the housing needs and desires of families, the single largest submarket in housing. If the satisfaction which people have in the high-rise is based on the premise of a subsequent move to a house or the equivalent, then the surest path to satisfaction lies not in tinkering with the art of building a better high-rise; it lies in creating sufficient numbers of houses, so that both the quantitative *and* qualitative dimensions of the supply side of the market are sufficient for the promise of future mobility to be valid for more than just the very affluent segment of society.

The challenge lies not in creating great numbers of units of a particular kind, in response to perceived economic realities or to some imagined universal set of user needs. It lies in taking the necessary steps to bring back balance in the housing market, so that the various submarkets, for families and for various types of younger and older persons, find something corresponding to their requirements.

For years Canada has put annual goals forward regarding the number of housing starts and completions, to ensure an adequate supply of housing. This has not traditionally included the specification of who (very likely someone already housed in objectively acceptable housing) is actively in the market for additional housing nor what this segment of the population actually requires. What this study shows is that satisfaction with certain types of existing housing is at least partly a function of the availability of more desirable forms of housing.

As the market now stands, the surest way to improve satisfaction with high-rise housing, particularly for the less-affluent sectors of the population, would be to build more detached houses at affordable prices.

Although single-family houses have been allowed to become bigger, more ornate, and more expensive, in correlation with rises in the price of land on which they are built, claims by home builders that the public will not settle for less than a deluxe version of the single-family house are not supported by recent experiences (nor by the data in this study). It is not the ornate features of the house that serve as the major attraction to the respondents surveyed, but rather some of its most basic characteristics—control of the premises, relative economic security, self-containment, and private, open space. These are found in basic houses as well as in deluxe houses.

In Ontario, recent government programs made available very basic, small houses without frills, built by the private sector acting under cost restrictions. These homes elicited such consumer response that sales had to occur via a lottery to ensure fairness. While families living in mansions may not create undue clamor for so-called 'no-frills' houses, the picture looks considerably different to the family who can move out of a high-rise apartment to what approximates their ideal only if basic houses are built. That home builders heard demands in favor of frills from people who were affluent enough to dare look for new houses in recent times avoids the plight of many others who saw no purpose in looking. We must also take into consideration the requirements of less affluent families, whose mobility is now blocked by the relative unavailability of houses they can realistically consider. It is this group which suffers the greatest difficulties with the high-rise apartment at present.

The discussion to this point raises, therefore, a question of different nature. I have stressed that while user needs are identifiable for remedy and that while some of the characteristic behaviors found in residential settings are understandable according to both expected and experienced opportunities made possible within the spatial parameters of the home environment, satisfaction is most critically related to the general shape of the housing market. If, then, the housing market is so closely related to user satisfaction, why does the market not respond by providing a more balanced selection of newly completed housing units? If consumer preference is as clearly articulated as it appears to be, why has the recent trend been in exactly the opposite direction of consumer preference? In short, why were great numbers of families left in what, at best, they considered a way station, without at the same time providing for the construction of their final stop? Why should there have been a need for a study like ours?

Questions of this sort point out a sensitive situation in the social and physical sciences. Scientists and policy makers alike have become aware of the importance of evaluative studies, tracing the implications of certain environments or environmental practices. The recent upsurge in interest concerning ecology generally and pollution more specifically has been accompanied by the requirement that environmental impact assessments be made more regularly. There is a growing acceptance for policy to appear to reflect what happens to the people principally affected by any given environment or environmental practice.

Such assessments generally focus on what happens *in reaction to* and generally subsequent to the environment or practice under focus. This follows generally accepted scientific principles of cause and effect. There is nothing wrong with this. It is essential. Assessments of the real and diverse consequences of environmental actions are long overdue.

Yet, the discovery of a set of consequences publicly deemed unsatisfactory does not necessarily mean that a revised set of environmental practices or interventions into the environment itself can then be instituted, even if one *knows* how to change the stimulus to produce responses viewed more favorably. For, to change the existing situation may also require some change in the status quo for those persons or forces who are responsible for it—or for those who are charged with the responsibility for making such changes (who are often not the users).

Basically, history does not start at the time that the stimulus starts to have its response. The stimulus is itself the product of a number of assumptions, actions, and actors. The creation of a given environment or environmental practice may reflect actions taken in self-interest by relatively few people, actions taken by persons attempting to speak for the public good although not necessarily affected by the situation themselves, by perceptions (sometimes indirect) of how things are thought to work, by existing practices in government, economics, and social structure, and by the existing state and supply of natural and man-made resources, at a minimum.

Merely because we may discover an unfavorable set of consequences about a practice does not mean that more favorable alternatives can be implemented easily within the same set of 'antecedent conditions' as produced the status quo. Hence, in terms of studying the implications of a given environment or environmental practice for the purpose of contributing to an actual improvement in the situation studied, the traditional mode of studying cause and effect, only with respect to conditions subsequent to the stimulus, is insufficient.

A 'two-way' model, which takes into consideration both antecedent and subsequent conditions, is required. This approach must say not only what are the implications and why did they happen, but for a solution to be put into force, what would have to be done to the conditions which brought about the problem studied in the first place.

On the current problem of high-rise housing, suggestions of how to ameliorate the specific physical elements which appear negative would be a treatment of the symptoms rather than of the disease. We might create better buildings; but we are not attacking the general question, satisfaction as related to aspiration, which is based on the distribution of completions in the housing market more generally, the maldistribution of which helped define the study of families in high-rise apartments as a problem. If consumer demand justifies only a fraction of the units of high-rise housing as were built, why were so many built?

As our study was formulated along traditional, scientific lines, we concentrated on implications of these selected settings for their users. This means that the focus of our efforts was not, unfortunately, on a detailed analysis of the antecedent conditions influencing this particular housing market. This would have been another study,[7] certainly as demanding as the present one. It is fortunate, though, that the pattern of responses suggested as much as it did about 'external' bases for evaluation; we could all too easily have compartmentalized satisfaction with specific aspects of home environment and taken it in isolation from other phenomena in the real world.

Nonetheless, certain facts about the antecedent conditions relevant to the present case appear obvious to the interested layman, which help underscore the ultimate nature of the problem emerging in this analysis. The large growth in the percentage of high-rise housing starts reflects specific economic assumptions and practices which are largely taken for granted and which are allowed to have their effects. Because these practices are taken for granted and not thought subject to control or direction, trends, such as that of the high-rise, have the appearance of being inevitable. Yet, a close look at the situation would indicate that what is inevitable is only thought to be so because those in a position to take appropriate steps to the contrary feel it inadvisable or difficult to do so. What are some of these assumptions?

A major assumption which underlies decisions on the qualitative nature of housing is that land is a commodity, to be bought and sold for profit. This puts land in the same position as gold, stamp collections, and hog bellies. It is possible to make a decent living by buying and selling land without, in the meanwhile, doing anything to improve the land or to construct housing. Real estate is often considered a safe investment in the cities of urban Canada, although gambles are more frequently involved in some parts of American cities. Since land typically appreciates over time and in response to the efforts of persons in surrounding areas, the land speculator finds it possible to make profits almost purely on the skills of judicious buying and selling, not necessarily on the basis of planning, design, or construction.

As Smith put it (1970), the price of real estate has a ratchet-like effect. It may go up in response to one or another stimulus, but it rarely if ever comes very far down. Hence, one person's speculation assists the next one's.

Since land value has become an increasingly large percentage of the cost of housing, whether paid in the form of rent or purchase price, the value of land used for housing helps determine the cost of the final product (cf. Dennis and Fish, 1973, p. 79). A house, for example, built on a costly lot is going to cost more than the same house built on a cheap lot. Furthermore, it is standard practice for housing to be made more ornate and expensive when built on an expensive lot, inasmuch as the development industry feels that it is not suitable to put a cheap house on an expensive lot, even if the total cost might turn out to be less.

Moreover, the cost of land affects not only the cost of the completed unit, but, perhaps even more important, also the qualitative nature of the building to be built. When land gets too expensive for the construction and sale of detached houses, with respect to their potential market, then it is customary to seek the construction of multiple dwellings of one or another kind. A typical reaction to this problem has been the erection of high-rise apartments, as the greatest density can be put on a given site this way, dividing the cost of the land among a greater number of potential residents.

Building high-rise on one piece of expensive land creates a greater likelihood that the same will happen on other tracts of land for sale, by serving as an example in setting the prices on these latter tracts. The general process then narrows the range of consumer options.

Thus, in the absence of checks against land speculation, not only does the cost of housing rise substantially, but the kind of housing which gets built gets limited to the high-rise, the medium to high density low-rise, or the very expensive single-family housing, depending on the situation.

The discussion to this point has centered on speculation in the sale of land and its effect on the type and cost of housing. However, a great number of speculators are ordinary men and women who buy and sell houses in which they live or houses which they may own for purposes of income. The lively trade in such units, without limitations on profit, tends also to drive up the general price of housing, since vendors, not surprisingly, are reluctant to take any less than the maximum they can get for the homes that they sell.

Many persons in the development industry also blame the shortage of serviced land in the greater Toronto area for the high cost of land—and its subsequent implications for building. The requirement that land be fully serviced before development, when coupled with the lack of widespread provision of such services, has led to intensive bidding among developers for whatever land is available for development in the foreseeable future. This, of course, drives up the price.

Nonetheless, this last factor alone cannot be seen as the sole explanation of the current situation. One large developer in the Toronto area, for example, explained to an assembled group of visiting experts on housing how his firm had bought the land for a large new project many years before. The firm started selling homes at $42,000 apiece, but within two years raised them to $74,000. The developer was asked why such an increase was necessary, since it was far above and beyond even inflationary increases in materials and wages and since the land had been purchased so many years before. He answered that if the developer down the road could command $74,000 for new houses, he would be a fool not to ask this as well. The basic price of a new house in that area then becomes $74,000, regardless of the cost ingredients which went into the recipe.

The same developer then went on to state that he was reluctantly building a greater percentage of multiple dwellings in his project than planned because too few people could afford $74,000 houses. When speculation occurs at all stages and among all actors in development, housing prices go ever upward, and trends take shape in the nature of development.

Other factors as well help add to this trend. Building codes are frequently outdated, requiring that developers utilize proven and sound, but unduly costly techniques and materials. These codes often prohibit the use of mass production in housing, which, although hardly a total solution to cost, nonetheless can help save some money.

Municipalities help drive up the cost of housing when they take long periods of time to decide whether they like proposed projects, in the absence of universalistic criteria on which to make that judgment sooner. They take time also in sheer bureaucratic inertia.

In combination, these factors and doubtless others have an effect which individual political leaders and developers alike feel they cannot alter, as each person plays only a partial role in the total game whose current rules bring about the skewed distribution of the kinds of housing being built.

There is, however, nothing sacred about any of these assumptions or practices, apart from the fact that some people currently make money through their perpetuation. It is not inevitable that land be used in speculative fashion nor that people use their residences as a form of old-age security which *outruns* the general rate of inflation. If everyone in fact requires housing as a necessity of life, it is questionable whether it should be subject to speculation in the commodity market, analogous to other substances. In Sweden, for example, a capital gains tax of 100 percent has been placed on property for the first two years of ownership, with a slowly declining capital gains tax thereafter (above the rate of inflation plus improvements made to property). This helps take some of the incentive out of speculative turnovers of real estate. In that country, there are other measures as well which attempt the same thing. Farmers, for example, are not normally allowed to sell land for nonagricultural uses without permission. Any piece of land may be purchased by a municipality when it is up for sale if the municipality feels that the proposed cost or use is unwise.

Similarly, the other practices which join with speculation in boosting the price and hence the type of housing, can, if desired, be streamlined to eliminate the increases in cost they cause.

What is required for amelioration is to ask first what the actual problem is whose symptoms are observed. Then answers should be given which deal with the genesis of the problem, not just the symptoms. Pragmatic answers to pragmatic questions have a potential for solving problems. Signs of great legislative or administrative action which only deal with putting a new cover on an old book are not likely to have any basic positive effect.

I do not favor government ownership or control of housing per se. This simply involves the substitution of one bureaucracy for another, and the existing private bureaucracies are at least forced to be streamlined by pressures of survival. If part of the problems already come from the lack of efficient activity on the part of some levels of government, then one could hardly expect great solutions to come from government takeovers.

What I do favor is the application of policies under which there will be rewards for the production of needed types of housing, at relevant prices, but which at the same time eliminate practices which serve no positive purposes for the common good and which tend to have draconian consequences on the nature of the housing market. Taxation policies and other forms of legislation can do this without the need for government entrepreneurship or the elimination of the profit motive on the part of the development industry.[8]

A recent emphasis on high density, *low-rise* housing, which places more people on a given piece of land than with completely detached houses but less than with high-rise apartments, has emerged in official circles. Although this may answer some of the problems of the high-rise, it does not provide for all the amenities which people typically seek in detached housing, nor, without other kinds of subsidies, does it compensate builders for what they would otherwise earn on a high-rise apartment. It will be interesting to see the extent that low rise, high density housing proves or does not prove to be a happy compromise.

In any case, there would be no need to compromise but for the high cost which land has been allowed to assume. Were the problem to be faced directly, other types of answers might result.

Accommodating additions to the population with the use of a reasonable percentage of relatively self-contained houses, is, admittedly, not an unmitigated blessing. Houses use up more land, some of which may be agriculturally valuable. Spreading services around larger areas is more costly than concentrating them. It is generally more difficult to arrange for public transportation in low density areas. While thorough developmental planning and the provision of appropriate transit facilities oriented toward the most common nodal points would surely ameliorate some of the problems of sprawl, the public costs of doing so would admittedly be higher than providing services in only limited areas and letting people pile up there. Nonetheless, relatively low densities must be contrasted in all relevant respects with the present system, which links lower total public costs to additional costs which individual residents must pay directly to speculators in return for no product at all. One must wonder whether the cost of controlled, planned suburban development would be really less of a value were land removed from the realm of speculation than the costs incurred under the present system, including large profits simply for the transfer of land.

In any case, even if differences in cost were to remain, one must ask whether the average family would or would not consider it worth the price, provided it were not extreme, to have the chance to achieve its housing aspirations. In the meanwhile, before achieving their aspirations, they would also have the leeway to be satisfied with other forms of housing (such as high-rise), judging them only on selected interim criteria. At present, the data of the present study indicate that families can and do brave considerable adversity to achieve what they value in housing.

My answer, then, is that the current wave of high-rise housing is not an inevitability. It is only inevitable as long as policy makers choose to continue support of the assumptions and the practices which make it desirable for developers to provide the highest density accommodation they can manage.

There is no use pretending that a change of these assumptions and practices would not involve some people's oxen being gored. While property ownership would not be threatened, making excess profits from property turnover would be.

At present, however, a very great number of ordinary families are bloodied every day. One wonders at the trepidation over goring a few in order to provide a healthier situation for the great majority of people, insofar as the goal is a universalistic system in which nobody would stand to lose—simply not to *gain* at the expense of their fellow citizens, while doing nothing of value for them.

Moreover, we have often thought trends inevitable until such time as they inevitably changed, due to one or another good reason. This happened to tenements. This happened to postwar suburban growth. Indeed, it has happened in Scandinavia with this very trend of building high-rise apartments.

While the social structure and legislation of different countries contain profound differences, the varieties of experience in housing and the change in clear-cut trends occurring in so many places indicate the inadvisability in treating current trends too literally without thinking first about how they got to be the way they are and whether one should intervene. Should one evaluate current trends as unfavorable, the careful analysis of the conditions antecedent to them should almost certainly provide a basis for constructive change toward the direction of more favorable alternatives.

I have, by this time, strayed considerably from the implications of the several combinations of housing type and location on which this book focuses. This is, however, a function of the various findings of the present study. It is and was possible to isolate many behavioral implications associated with these selected environments. It is and was possible to isolate a number of both promising and problematic aspects of the physical environment. Nonetheless, the emergent theme arising from these data is that these positive and problematic factors in the home environment only gain salience with knowledge of the state of the housing market, together with what this market implies about provision for the normally expected moving cycle of individual families.

In essence, this suggests that while user needs are real and should be optimized, they are relatively trivial in comparison to qualitative aspects of supply in explaining family satisfaction. This suggests that the path to large-scale amelioration, although incorporating what many designers and builders surely already know, to achieve better houses, apartments, and neighborhoods, lies in the direction of understanding more fully under what conditions people can get what they wish, eliminating the process whereby excess profits by speculators and anachronistic practices within government chambers help determine what gets built.

Surely this is preferable to the current situation, in which citizens are told to adjust their aspirations and to try to like that which they do not.

In whose employ, then, are the policy makers whose actions or lack thereof underlie that which becomes defined as inevitable? To optimize the social implications of housing, actions speak louder than words. Sooner or later, it becomes clear whether actions are addressed to the basic problems whose symptoms are bemoaned or whether actions are but words.

NOTES

[1] I welcome the expression of other interpretations, although clearly standing by those presented at this time.

[2] Toronto has an unusually well-developed system of mass transportation, with extensive routes of bus service feeding into two 'trunk' subway lines which focus on the downtown area. One can travel from almost anywhere to almost anywhere else on a single fare during most of the waking hours of the day. Relatively safe service contin-

ues in many areas almost around the clock. Nonetheless, the act of getting to a bus stop and waiting up to 20 or 30 minutes in winter cold and wind, with or without small children or packages, tends to reduce the feeling that a family in a low density, peripheral location actually does have a high degree of access to facilities outside of home. Although recent experiments with dial-a-bus and the possible inception of new forms of fast, light rail transit suggest that transit planners are trying to better their existing achievements, the current problem documented is simply one of suburbanites feeling unwilling or unable to get where they want or need to go via public transit.

[3] In Toronto there is at present much debate about requiring new downtown office buildings to include a minimum amount of apartments in them. Although the orientations of downtown apartment dwellers in the current study are surely at odds with those of families living in downtown houses regarding the ultimate desirability of downtown as a place to live, leading to higher repeat mobility out of the center, such people nonetheless were shown to value proximity to the center and to use the facilities of the area during their relatively short stays in the downtown area. Hence, if the rents of the proposed apartments in office buildings were low enough to be feasible to these young families, such a proposal would probably bring about the provision of housing which would be appreciated by those living there, even if for relatively short periods of tenure.

[4] In fact, it is extremely consistent with literature on the effects of extreme amounts of overcrowding cited in Chapter 2, which shows that those most likely to survive unscathed are persons with a degree of optimism as to what is going to happen to them during the period of time which follows the overcrowding (Biderman et al., 1963).

[5] A fascinating review of much of this literature, from LaPierre to the present, is found in a recent work by Deutscher (1973).

[6] It is worth noting that just because immigrants may come from countries without great amounts of detached housing this does not stop them from quickly demonstrating aspirations for what Canadians have as goals. Using original cultural background as a rationale for building multiple dwellings, without considering objective circumstances and aspirations, is simply a form of stereotyping.

[7] But, see Dennis and Fish (1973) for much that is relevant to this approach and for the discussion which follows.

[8] In 1974 a series of government policies came forward in Ontario, intended to ameliorate the cost of land and the effects of speculation, as well as to speed up the production of new housing units. Its effect to date is not entirely clear, not least because it does not cover all contingencies nor provide disincentives large enough to drastically change the nature of what gets built.

REFERENCES

Abu-Lughod, J. 1960. A survey of center-city residents. In *Housing choices and constraints*, eds. N. Foote; J. Abu-Lughod; M. M. Foley; and L. Winnick, pp. 387–447. New York: McGraw-Hill.

Adams, J. S. 1969. Directional bias in intra-urban migration. *Economic Geography* 45:302–323.

Alexander, C. 1964. *Notes on the synthesis of form*. Cambridge, Mass.: Harvard University Press.

————. 1973. A city is not a tree. In *Surviving the city*, ed. J. Gabree, pp. 106–136. New York: Ballantine Books.

Alexander, C.; S. Ishikawa; and M. Silverstein. 1968. *A pattern language which generates multi-service centers*. Berkeley, Calif.: Center for Environmental Structure.

————, et al. 1969. *Houses generated by patterns*. Berkeley, Calif.: Center for Environmental Structure.

Altman, I. 1973. Some perspectives on the study of man-environment phenomena. In *Environmental design research, vol. 2: Symposia and workshops*, ed. W. F. Preiser, pp. 99–113. Stroudsburg, Pa.: Dowden, Hutchinson & Ross.

American Behavioral Scientist. 1966. Issue devoted to *The multi-national comparative time budget research project*, ed. A. Szalai, 10 (4):1–31.

American Public Health Association. 1946. *An appraisal method for measuring the quality of housing*. New York: The Association.

Anderson, J. n.d. *Space-time-budgets: potentialities and limitations*. Discussion paper no. 33. London: Graduate School of Geography, London School of Economics.

————. 1970. *Time budgets and human geography: notes and references*. Discussion paper no. 36. London: Graduate School of Geography, London School of Economics.

Anderson, J. R. 1973. *Evaluating housing for families of low and moderate income: a bibliography*. Housing, Research and Development. Urbana, Ill.: University of Illinois.

Anderson, J. R., et al. 1974. *Resident satisfaction: criteria for the evaluation of housing for low and moderate families*. Paper presented at Conference In 74.

Angrist, S. S. 1974. Dimensions of well-being in public housing families. *Environment and Behavior* 6:495–516.

Ansbacher, H. L. 1967. Life style: a historical and systematic review. *Journal of Individual Psychology* 23:191–212.

Appleyard, D.; K. Lynch; and J. R. Myer. 1964. *The view from the road.* Cambridge, Mass.: M.I.T.

Ardrey, R. 1966. *The territorial imperative.* New York: Atheneum.

Baldassare, M., and Claude S. Fischer. 1975. Suburban life powerlessness and need for affiliation. *Urban Affairs Quarterly* 10:314–326.

Ball, D. W. 1973. *Microecology: social situations and intimate space.* Indianapolis: Bobbs-Merrill.

Barbey, G., and C. Gelber. 1973. *The relationship between the built environment and human behavior: a survey and analysis of the existing literature.* Lousanne: Institute for Research on the Built Environment, Federal Institute of Technology.

Barker, R. C. 1968. *Ecological psychology.* Stanford, Calif.: Stanford University Press.

Barrett, F. A. 1973. *Residential search behaviour.* Geographical Monograph no. 1. Toronto: York University.

Bechtel, R. B. 1970. Human movement and architecture. In *Environmental psychology,* ed. H. M. Proshansky, et al., pp. 642–645. New York: Holt, Rinehart & Winston.

———. 1975. The semantic differential and other paper-and-pencil tests. In *Behavioral research methods in environmental design,* ed. W. Michelson, pp. 41–78. Stroudsburg, Pa.: Dowden, Hutchinson & Ross.

Beck, R. 1970. Spatial meaning and the properties of the environment. In *Environmental psychology,* ed. H. M. Proshansky, et al., pp. 134–141. New York: Holt, Rinehart & Winston.

Becker, F. D. 1974. *Design for living: the resident's view of multi family housing.* Ithaca, N.Y.: Center for Urban Development Research, Cornell University.

Becker, G. S. 1965. A theory of the allocation of time. *Economic Journal* 75: 493–517.

Beldo & Willmarth, Incorporated. 1968. *An exploration of human needs as a guide to planning urban transportation.* Paper prepared for Barton-Aschman Associates, Inc., Chicago.

Bell, G.; E. Randall; and J. E. R. Roeder. 1973. *Urban environments and human behavior: an annotated bibliography.* Stroudsburg, Pa.: Dowden, Hutchinson & Ross.

Bell, W. 1958. Social choice, life styles and suburban residence. In *The suburban community,* ed. W. M. Dobriner, pp. 225–247. New York: Putman.

———. 1968. The city, suburb, and a theory of social choice. In *The new urbanization,* ed. S. Greer, et al., pp. 132–168. New York: St. Martin's.

Bendix, R. 1962. *Max Weber: An intellectual portrait*. Garden City, N.Y.: Doubleday (Anchor).

Berger, B. M. 1960. *The working-class suburb: a study of auto workers in suburbia*. Berkeley, Calif.: University of California Press.

———. 1963. The sociology of leisure: some suggestions. In *Work and leisure: a contemporary social problem*, ed. E. O. Smigel. New Haven, Conn.: College and University Press, pp. 21–40.

Beshers, J. 1962. *Urban social structure*. New York: Free Press.

Biderman, A., et al. 1963. *Historical incidents of extreme overcrowding*. Washington, D.C.: Bureau of Social Science Research.

Booth, A., and S. Welch. 1973. *The effects of crowding: a cross-national study*. Ottawa, Ont.: Ministry of State for Urban Affairs, mimeographed.

Bott, E. 1957. *Family and social network*. London: Tavistock.

Brannon, R., et al. 1973. Attitude and action: a field experiment joined to a general population survey. *American Sociological Review* 38:625–636.

Broady, M. 1968. *Planning for people*. London: National Council of Social Service.

Brolin, B., and J. Zeisel. 1968. Mass housing: social research and design. *Architectural Forum* 129:66–71.

Brown, L. A., and E. G. Moore. 1970. The intra-urban migration process: a perspective. *General Systems* 15:109–122.

Burby, R. J., III. 1974. Environmental amenities and new community governance: results of a nationwide study. In *Man-environment interactions: evaluations and applications, part 1*, ed. D. H. Carson, pp. 101–123. Stroudsburg, Pa.: Dowden, Hutchinson & Ross.

Burch, W. R., Jr.; N. H. Cheek, Jr.; and L. Taylor, eds. 1972. *Social behavior, natural resources, and the environment*. New York: Harper & Row.

Burgess, E. W. 1925. The growth of the city. Chapter 2 in *The city*, ed. R. E. Park; E. W. Burgess; and R. McKenzie. Chicago: University of Chicago Press.

Burns, T. 1968. Urban styles of life. In *The future of the city region: vol. 2*, pp. 43–61. Working Paper. London: Centre for Urban and Community Studies.

Butler, E. W., et al. 1968. *Moving behavior and residential choice: a national survey*. Chapel Hill, N.C.: Center for Urban and Regional Studies, Institute for Research in Social Science, University of North Carolina.

Buttimer, A. 1972. Social space and the planning of residential areas. *Environment and Behavior* 4:279–318.

———. 1973. Social space in interdisciplinary perspective. In *Surviving the city*, ed. J. Gabree, pp. 15–29. New York: Ballantine Books.

Calhoun, J. B. 1963. Population density and social pathology. In *The urban condition*, ed. L. J. Duhl, pp. 33–43. New York: Basic Books.

Canadian Council on Social Development. 1973. *Beyond shelter*. Ottawa, Ont.: Canadian Council on Social Development.

Canter, D., and R. Thorne. 1972. Attitudes to housing: a cross cultural comparison. *Environment and Behavior* 4:3–32.

Capilano College Conference Centre, in conjunction with Seneca College of Applied Arts and Technology. 1975. *Condominiums: concepts and challenges*, Transcript of seminar, January 27–28, 1975.

Caplow, T. 1949. The social ecology of Guatemala City. *Social Forces* 28: 113–133.

Caplow, T., and R. Forman. 1950. Neighborhood interaction in a homogeneous community. *American Sociological Review* 15:357–366.

Cappon, D. 1972. Mental health in the high rise. In *Canadian housing: a reader*, ed. K. S. Sayegh, pp. 149–151. Waterloo, Ont.: University of Waterloo.

Carlstein, T., et al. 1968. *Individars dygnsbanor i några hushallstyper*. Lund: Institute for Cultural Geography, University of Lund.

Chapin, F. S. 1966a. *Time budget studies and city planning*. Paper presented at the time-budget round-table at the Sixth World Congress of Sociology, Evian, France.

———. 1966b. The use of time budgets in the study of urban living patterns. *Research Previews*, vol. 13. Chapel Hill: University of North Carolina, Institute for Research in Social Science.

———. 1968. Activity systems and urban structure: a working schema. *The American Institute of Planners, Journal*, 34:11–18.

———. 1970a. New planning techniques: activity analysis or the human use of urban space. *Town and Country Planning* 38:345–348.

———. 1970b. *Some exploratory directions in time-budget research*. Paper presented at the Seventh World Congress of Sociology, Varna, Bulgaria.

———. 1971. Free time activities and the quality of urban life. *The American Institute of Planners, Journal* 37:411–417.

———. 1974. *Human activity patterns in the city: things people do in time and in space*. New York: Wiley Interscience.

Chapin, F. S., and R. K. Brail. 1969. Human activity systems in the metropolitan United States. *Environment and Behavior* 1:107–130.

Chapin, F. S., and H. C. Hightower. 1965. Household activity patterns and land use. *The American Institute of Planners, Journal* 31:222–231.

———. 1966. *Household activity systems—a pilot investigation*. Chapel Hill, N.C.: Institute for Research in Social Science, University of North Carolina.

Chapin, F. S., and T. H. Logan. 1968. Patterns of time and space use. In *The quality of the urban environment*, ed. H. S. Perloff, pp. 305–332. Baltimore: The Johns Hopkins Press, for Resources for the Future, Inc.

Clark, S. D. 1966. *The suburban society*. Toronto: University of Toronto Press.

Clarke, W. A. V., and M. Cadwallader. 1973. Locational stress and residential mobility. *Environment and Behavior* 5:29–41.

Coit, E. 1965. *Report on family living in high apartment buildings.* Washington, D.C.: Public Housing Administration.

Condominium Research Associates. 1970. *National survey of condominium owners.* Ottawa, Ont.: Central Mortgage and Housing Corporation.

Converse, P. E. 1968. Time budgets. In *International encyclopedia of social sciences,* ed. D. L. Sills, 16:42–47. New York: Macmillan and Free Press.

Craik, K. H. 1970a. The environmental dispositions of environmental decision-makers. *The American Academy of Political and Social Science, The Annals* 389:87–94.

————. 1970b. Environmental psychology. In *New directions in psychology,* ed. K. Craik, et al., 4:1–121. New York: Holt, Rinehart & Winston.

Crawford, P., and A. Virgin. 1971. *The effects of high rise living on school behavior.* Toronto: Board of Education of the Borough of North York.

Cullen, I. G. 1973. Space, time and the disruption of behavior in cities. *Society and Leisure* 5(1):71–91.

Cullen, I.; V. Godson; and S. Major. 1971. *The structure of activity patterns.* Paper presented at the meeting of the Regional Science Association, London.

Cullen, I., and V. Godson. 1972. *Networks of urban activities: the structure of activity patterns.* London: Joint Unit for Planning Research, University College London and The London School of Economics.

Cullen, I., and V. Nichols. n.d. *Networks project: report on the tabulations of the pilot time-budget survey of the Bartlett School of Architecture.* Seminar Paper 14, 2d ser. London: Joint Unit for Planning Research, University College London and The London School of Economics.

Cullingworth, V. B. 1965. *English housing trends: a report on the Rountree Trust Housing Study.* Occasional papers on social administration, no. 13 London: G. Bell.

Dahlgren, R.; J. Hellberg; and G. Lindberg. 1971. *Boendeaktiviteter och omgivning.* Lund: Institutionen för byggnadsfunktionslära, Tekniska Hogskolan.

Dalén, I., and L. Holm. 1965. *Bättre bostäder,* Stockholm; Prisma.

Daniel, R. E. 1969. *Local residential mobility: a selected and annotated bibliography.* Exchange Bibliography 104. Monticello, Ill.: Council of Planning Librarians.

Darke, J., and R. Darke. 1969a. *Suburban housing estates: social composition and social characteristics.* Working Paper, CES WP 40. London: Centre for Environmental Studies.

————. 1969b. *Physical and social factors in neighbor relations.* Working Paper, CES WP 41. London: Centre for Environmental Studies.

Daun, Åke. 1974. *Förortsliv.* Stockholm: Prisma.

De Grazia, S. 1964. *Of time, work, and leisure.* New York: Doubleday.

Dennis, M., and S. Fish. 1973. *Programs in search of a policy: low income housing in Canada.* Toronto: A. M. Hakkert.

Denton, T. 1973. *Social relations and physical environment: a critical bibliographic review.* St. Catharines, Ont.: Urban Studies Institute, Brock University.

Department of the Environment. 1972. *The estate outside the dwelling.* London: Her Majesty's Stationary Office.

Deutscher, I. 1973. *What we say/what we do.* Glenview, Ill.: Scott, Foresman.

Dobriner, W. M., ed. 1958. *The suburban community.* New York: Putman.

Downs, R. M. 1970. The cognitive structure of an urban shopping center. *Environment and Behavior* 2:13–39.

Downs, R., and D. Stea eds. 1973. *Image and environment.* Chicago: Aldine.

Duncan, O. D., and Beverly Duncan. 1957. Residential distribution and occupational stratification. In *Cities and society,* ed. P. K. Hatt and A. J. Reiss, pp. 283–296. New York: Free Press.

Durlak, J. G.; J. Layman; and J. McClain. 1973. *The school environment: a study of user patterns.* Toronto: Division of Social Sciences, York University.

Eberts, E. H. 1972. Social and personality correlates of personal space. In *Environmental design: research and practice; Proceedings of the EDRA 3/AR 8 Conference,* January 1972, University of California at Los Angeles, ed. W. J. Mitchell, pp. 211–219.

Efran, M. G., and J. A. Cheyne. 1974. Affective concomitants of the invasion of shared space. *Journal of Personality and Social Psychology* 29:219–226.

Egerö, B. 1967. *Ny bostad i ytterstad.* Göteborg: Sociologiska Institutionen, Göteborgs Universitet.

Ekland, B. 1966. *Retrieving mobile cases in longitudinal surveys.* Paper presented at the Annual Meeting of the American Sociological Association, Miami Beach, Florida.

Elliott, D. H.; A. S. Harvey; and D. Procos. 1973. *An overview of the Halifax Time-Budget Study.* Paper presented for the Second Annual Colloquium of the Working Group on Time-Budgets and Social Activities. Berlin, D.D.R.

Ermuth, F. 1974. *Residential satisfaction and urban environmental preferences.* Geographical Monograph no. 3. Toronto: York University.

Esser, A. H. 1973. Structures of man-environment relations. In *Environmental design research, vol. 2: Symposia and workshops,* ed. W. F. Preiser, pp. 114–123. Stroudsburg, Pa.: Dowden, Hutchinson & Ross.

Esser, A. H.; A. S. Chamberlain; E. D. Chapple; and N. S. Kline. 1970. Territoriality of patients on a research ward. In *Environmental psychology,* ed. H. Proshansky, et al., pp. 208–214. New York: Holt, Rinehart & Winston.

Evans, G. W., and R. B. Howard. 1972. A methodological investigation of personal space. In *Environmental design: research and practice: Proceedings of the EDRA 3/AR 8 Conference,* January 1972, University of California at Los Angeles, ed. W. J. Mitchell, pp. 221–228.

Fanning, D. M. 1967. Families in flats. *British Medical Journal* 18:382–386.

Farr, L. E. 1967. Medical consequences of environmental noises. *Journal of the American Medical Association* 202:171–174.

Fava, S. F. 1956. Suburbanism as a way of life. *American Sociological Review* 21:34–37.

Feldheim, P., and G. Manz. 1973. Time-budgets and social activities. *Society and Leisure* 5(1):7–9.

Feldman, A. S., and C. Tilly. 1960. The interaction of social and physical space. *American Sociological Review* 25:877–884.

Felson, M. 1974. The pitfalls of fancy analysis. *Sociology and Social Research* 58:399–402.

Festinger, L. 1957. *A theory of cognitive dissonance.* New York: Row, Peterson.

Festinger, L.; S. Schachter; and K. Back. 1950. *Social pressures in informal groups.* New York: Harper.

Firey, W. 1947. *Land use in central Boston.* Cambridge, Mass.: Harvard University Press.

Fischer, C. S. 1976. *The urban experience.* New York: Harcourt Brace Jovanovich, Inc.

Fischer, C. S., et al. 1974. *Crowding studies and urban life: a critical review.* Working Paper no. 242. Berkeley, Calif.: Institute of Urban and Regional Development, University of California.

Foley, D. L. 1964. An approach to metropolitan spatial structure. In *Explorations into urban structure,* M. M. Webber, et al., pp. 21–78. Philadelphia: University of Pennsylvania Press.

Foote, N. N. 1961. Methods for study of meaning in use of time. In *Aging and leisure,* ed., R. W. Kleemeier, pp. 155–176. New York: Oxford University Press.

Fraser, G. 1972. *Fighting back: urban renewal in Trefann Court.* Toronto: A. M. Hakkert.

Freedman, J., et al. 1971. The effect of crowding on human task performance. *Journal of Applied Social Psychology* 1:7–25.

Fried, M. 1973. *The world of the urban working class.* Cambridge, Mass.: Harvard University Press.

Fried, M., and P. Gleicher. 1961. Some sources of residential satisfaction in an urban slum. *The American Institute of Planners, Journal.* 27:305–315.

Gad, G.; R. Peddie; and J. Punter. 1973. Ethnic differences in the residential search process. In *The form of cities in central Canada: selected papers,* ed. L. S. Bourne; R. MacKinnon; and J. Simmons, pp. 168–180. Toronto: University of Toronto Press.

Galle, O.; W. R. Gove; and J. M. McPherson. 1974. Population density and pathology: what are the relationships for man? In *Comparative urban structure,* ed. K. Schwirian, pp. 198–213. Toronto and Lexington, Mass.: Heath.

Gans, H. J. 1962a. *The urban villagers.* New York: Free Press.

————. 1962b. Urbanism and suburbanism as ways of life: a re-evaluation of some definitions. In *Human behavior and social processes*, ed. A. M. Rose, pp. 625–648. Boston: Houghton Mifflin.

————. 1963. Effects of the move from city to suburb. In *The urban condition*, ed. L. J. Duhl, pp. 184–198. New York: Basic Books.

————. 1967. *The Levittowners*. New York: Pantheon Books.

————. 1968. *People and plans*. New York: Basic Books.

Ginzberg, E.; I. E. Berg; et al. 1966. *Life styles of educated women*. New York: Free Press.

Glazer, N. 1965. Slum dwellings do not make a slum. *New York Times Magazine*, November 21, pp. 55ff.

Goffman, E. 1959. *The presentation of self in everyday life*. New York: Free Press.

————. 1963. *Behavior in public places*, Garden City, N.Y.: Doubleday (Anchor).

————. 1971. *Relations in public*. New York: Harper & Row.

Goldstein, S., and K. Mayer. 1964. Migration and the journey to work. *Social Forces* 42:472–481.

Goodey, B. 1972. Displays for mating. *Design and Environment* 3:46–53.

Gordon, H., and P. Molin, 1972. *Man bara anpassar sig helt enkelt*, Stockholm: Pan.

Gordon, R. E.; K. K. Gordon; and M. Gunther. 1961. *The split level trap*. New York: Random House.

Gould, P. R. 1966. *On mental maps*. Inter-University community of mathematical geographers, Discussion Paper no. 9. Ann Arbor, Mich.: University of Michigan.

Govaerts, F. 1969. *Loisirs des femmes et temps libre*. Brussels: Université Libre de Bruxelles.

Greer, S. 1956. Urbanism reconsidered: a comparative analysis of local areas in a metropolis. *American Sociological Review* 21:19–25.

————. 1972. *The urbane view*. New York: Oxford University Press.

Gutenschwager, G. A. 1973. The time budget-activity systems perspective in urban research and planning. *The American Institute of Planners, Journal* 39:378–387.

Gutman, R. 1963. Population mobility in the American middle class. In *The urban condition*, ed. L. J. Duhl, pp. 172–183. New York: Basic Books.

————. 1972. The questions architects ask. In *People and buildings*, ed. R. Gutman, pp. 337–369. New York: Basic Books.

Hall, E. T. 1966. *The hidden dimension*. Garden City, N.Y.: Doubleday.

Hamilton, S. W., and R. Roberts. 1973. *Condominium development ownership*. Vancouver: Real Estate Board of Greater Vancouver.

Hammer, P. G., and F. S. Chapin. 1972. *Human time allocation: a case study of Washington, D.C.* Chapel Hill, N.C.: Center for Urban and Regional Studies, Institute for Research in Social Science, University of North Carolina.

Hartman, C. 1963a. Social values and housing orientation. *Journal of Social Issues* 19(2):113–131.

———. 1963b. The limitations of public housing: relocation choices in a working-class community. *The American Institute of Planners, Journal* 24:283–296.

Harvey, A. S., and D. Procos. 1974. *Suburb and satellite contrasted: an exploration of activity patterns and urban form.* Paper presented at 3rd Advanced Studies Institute in Regional Science, Karlsruhe, Germany.

Hemmens, G. C. 1966. *The structure of urban activity linkages.* Chapel Hill, N.C.: Center of Urban and Regional Studies, Institute for Research in Social Science, University of North Carolina.

———. 1970. Analysis and simulation of urban activity patterns. *Socioeconomic Planning Sciences* 4:53–66.

Hightower, H. C. 1965. *Recreational activity analysis: toward a spatial and aspatial methodology for urban planning.* Ph.D. dissertation. Chapel Hill, N.C.: University of North Carolina.

Hinshaw, M. L., and K. J. Allott. 1973. Environmental preferences of future housing consumers. In *Housing urban America*, eds. J. Pynoos; R. Schafer; and C. W. Hartman, pp. 191–200. Chicago: Aldine.

Hitchcock, J. R. 1968. *Urbanness and daily activity patterns.* Ph.D. dissertation. Chapel Hill, N.C.: University of North Carolina.

Homenuck, H. P. M. 1973. *A study of high rise: effects, preferences, and perceptions.* Toronto: Institute of Environmental Research, Inc.

Howard, E. 1898. *Tomorrow: a peaceful path to real reform.* London: S. Sonnenschein. Republished as *Garden cities of tomorrow*, ed. F. J. Osborn, 1965, Cambridge, Mass.: M.I.T. Press.

Hägerstrand, T. 1970. What about people in regional science? *Papers and Proceedings of the Regional Science Association* 24:7–21.

———. 1972. The impact of social organization and environment upon the time-use of individuals in households. In *Plan International*, Swedish Society for Town and Country Planning, pp. 24–30.

Ittelson, W. H.; H. M. Proshansky; L. G. Rivlin; and G. W. Winkel. 1974. *An introduction to environmental psychology.* New York: Holt, Rinehart & Winston.

Jacobs, J. 1961. *The death and life of great American cities.* New York: Random House.

Jephcott, P. 1971. *Homes in high flats: some of the human problems involved in multi-story housing.* Edinburgh: Oliver and Boyd.

Johannis, T. B., Jr., and C. N. Bull. 1971. Non-work time and leisure: three areas of future growth and development. *Society and Leisure* 3(2):109–115.

Johnston, R. J. n.d. Towards a general model of intra-urban residential patterns. *Progress in Geography*, 4:85–124.

Jonassen, C. T. 1949. Cultural variables in the ecology of an ethnic group. *American Sociological Review*, 14:32–41.

Kataoka, S. M. 1972. Using proxemic indicators and instruments to analyze classroom interaction, curriculum planning, and curriculum implementation. In *Environmental design: research and practice: Proceedings of the EDRA 3/AR 8 Conference*, January 1972, University of California at Los Angeles, ed. W. J. Mitchell, pp. 241–248.

Katz, R. D. 1963. *Intensity of development and livability of multi-family housing projects*. Washington, D.C.: U.S. Government Printing Office.

Keats, J. 1962. *The crack in the picture window*. New York: Ballantine Books.

Keller, S. 1968. *The urban neighborhood*. New York: Random House.

Kennedy, L. W. 1975. *Residential mobility as a cyclical process: the evaluation of the home environment both before and after the move*. Doctoral dissertation, Toronto: University of Toronto (abridged version published as Major Report no. 3, Toronto: Centre for Urban and Community Studies, University of Toronto).

Klopfer, P. H. 1969. *Habitats and territories*. New York: Basic Books.

Kolaja, J. 1969. *Social system and time and space: an introduction to the theory of recurrent behavior*. Pittsburgh: Duquesne University Press.

Kramer, J. ed. 1972. *North American suburbs*. Berkeley, Calif.: Glendessary Press.

Krantz, B. 1968. *Lägenheter och markutrymman i Baronbackarna, Örebro*, Stockholm: Statens Institut för Byggnadsforskning.

Krantz, P. 1970. What do people do all day? *Behavioral Science* 15:286–291).

Kumove, L. 1966. *A preliminary study of the social implications of high density living conditions*. Toronto: Social Planning Council of Metropolitan Toronto, mimeographed.

Kuper, L. 1953. *Living in towns*. London: Cresset.

Ladd, F. C. 1970. Black youths share their environment: neighborhood maps. *Environment and Behavior* 2:74–99.

Langner, T. S., and S. T. Michael. 1963. *Life stress and mental health*. New York: Free Press.

Lansing, J. B. 1966. *Residential location and urban mobility: the second wave of interviews*. Ann Arbor, Mich.: Survey Research Center, Institute for Social Research, University of Michigan.

Lansing, J. B.; R. W. Marans; and R. B. Zehner. 1970. *Planned residential environments*. Ann Arbor, Mich.: Report prepared for the U.S. Department of Transportation, Bureau of Public Roads.

Lasswell, T. E. 1974. The measurement of social science inputs to architectural programming. In *Putting sociology to work*, ed. A. B. Shoskak, pp. 155–162. New York: David McKay.

Lawton, M. P. 1972. Some beginnings of an ecological psychology of old age. In *Environment and the social sciences: perspectives and applications*, eds. J. F. Wohlwill and D. H. Carson, pp. 114–125. Washington, D.C.: American Psychological Association.

Le Corbusier. 1929. *The city of tomorrow and its planning*. New York: Payson and Clarke.

Lee, R. G. 1972. The social definition of outdoor recreational places. In *Social behavior, natural resources, and the environment*, ed. W. R. Burch, Jr.; N. H. Cheek, Jr.; and L. Taylor, pp. 68–84. New York: Harper & Row.

Lee, T. R. 1968. Urban neighborhood as a socio-spatial schema. *Human Relations* 21:241–67.

———. 1970. Perceived distance as a function of direction in the city. *Environment and Behavior* 2:40–51.

———. 1972. The effect of the built environment on human behavior. *Ekistics* 34:20–24.

Lindberg, G., and J. Hellberg. 1975. Strategic decisions in research design. In *Behavioral research methods in environmental design*, ed. W. Michelson, pp. 9–40. Stroudsburg, Pa.: Dowden, Hutchinson & Ross.

Lipman, M. 1969. Social effects of the housing environment. In *The right to housing*, ed. M. Wheeler, pp. 171–189. Montreal: Harvest House.

Loewy, R., and W. Snaith, Inc. 1968. *The motivations toward homes and housing*. Monograph prepared for the Project Home Committee. New York: Project Home.

Long, N. E. 1958. The local community as an ecology of games. *American Journal of Sociology* 64:251–261.

Loo, C. M. 1974. *Crowding and behavior*. New York: MSS Information Corporation.

Loring, W. C. 1956. Housing characteristics and social disorganization. *Social Problems* 3:160–168.

Lowenthal, D. 1972. Research in environmental perception and behavior. *Environment and Behavior* 4:333–342.

Lowenthal, D., and M. Riel. 1972. The nature of perceived and imagined environments. *Environment and Behavior* 4:189–208.

Lundberg, G. A.; M. Komarovsky; and M. A. McInerny. 1934. *Leisure a suburban study*. New York: Columbia University Press.

Lynch, K. 1960. *The image of the city*. Cambridge, Mass.: M.I.T. Press and Harvard University Press.

Lynch, K., and L. Rodwin. 1958. A theory of urban form. *The American Institute of Planners, Journal* 24:201–214.

MacMurray, T. 1971. Aspects of time and the study of activity patterns. *Town Planning Review* 42:195–209.

Mann, M. 1973. *Workers on the move: the sociology of relocation*. Cambridge: Cambridge University Press.

Manning, P. 1970. Office design: a study of environment. In *Environmental psychology*, ed. H. M. Proshansky, et al. pp. 463–483. New York: Holt, Rinehart & Winston.

Manz, G. 1973. People's requirement and use of time. *Society and Leisure* 5(1):11–15.

Marans, R. W. 1975. Survey research. In *Behavioral research methods in environmental design*, ed. W. Michelson, pp. 119–179. Stroudsburg, Pa.: Dowden, Hutchinson & Ross.

Marris, P. 1961. *Family and social change in an African city*. Evanston, Ill.: Northwestern University Press.

Martin, W. T. 1956. The structuring of social relationships engendered by suburban residence. *American Sociological Review* 21:446–453.

Martini, S. 1974. *Nyere forstadsmiljøer*. Copenhagen: Tekniska forlag.

Maslow, A. H. 1943. A theory of human motivation. *Psychological Review* 50:370–396.

Meier, R. L. 1959. Human time allocation: a basis for social accounts. *The American Institute of Planners, Journal* 25:27–33.

————. 1962. *A communications theory of urban growth*. Cambridge, Mass.: M.I.T. Press.

Merton, R. K. 1948. The social psychology of housing. In *Current trends in social psychology*, ed. W. Dennis et al., pp. 163–217. Pittsburgh: University of Pittsburgh Press.

————. 1949. Patterns of influence: a study of interpersonal influence and communications behavior in a local community. In *Communications research 1948–49*, eds. P. Lazarsfeld and F. N. Stanton, pp. 180–219. New York: Harper.

Metroplan. 1974. *What kind of city?: a profile of Metropolitan Toronto*. Toronto: Municipality of Metropolitan Toronto.

Michelson, W. 1961. *Adult voluntary associations in Levittown, New Jersey*. Senior thesis, Princeton: Princeton University.

————. 1965. *Value orientations and urban form*. Ph.D. dissertation, Cambridge, Mass.: Harvard University.

————. 1966. An empirical analysis of urban environmental preference. *The American Institute of Planners, Journal* 32:355–360.

————. 1967. Potential candidates for the designers' paradise: a social analysis from a nationwide survey. *Social Forces* 46:190–196.

————. 1968a. *Ecological thought and its application to school functioning*. Paper presented at the Fourteenth Annual Eastern Research Institute of the Association for Supervision and Curriculum Development, National Education Assoc. (Available on microfilm from NEA.)

————. 1968b. Urban sociology as an aid to urban physical development: some research strategies. *The American Institute of Planners, Journal* 34:105–108.

————. 1970a. Analytic sampling for design information: a survey of housing experience. In *EDRA 1: Proceedings of the First Annual Environment Design Research Association Conference*, June 1968, North Carolina State University, Raleigh, ed. H. Sanoff and S. Cohen, pp. 183–197.

————. 1970b rev. ed., 1976. *Man and his urban environment: a sociological approach*. Reading, Mass.: Addison-Wesley.

————. 1971a. The case of the equine fountain. *Design and Environment* 2:28–31, 59.

————. 1971b. Some like it hot: social participation and environmental use as functions of the season. *American Journal of Sociology* 76:1072–1083.

————. 1973a. *Environmental change.* Research Paper no. 60. Toronto: Dept. of Sociology and Centre for Urban and Community Studies, University of Toronto.

————. 1973b. *The place of time in the longitudinal evaluation of spatial structures by women.* Research Paper no. 61. Toronto: Centre for Urban and Community Studies, University of Toronto.

————. 1973c. *Residential mobility as a deficit compensating process.* Paper presented to the Canadian Sociology and Anthropology Association, Kingston, Ontario.

————. 1973d. Some inductive comments on sociology of leisure. *Society and Leisure* 5(1):177–88.

————. 1973e. Discretionary and nondiscretionary aspects of activity and social contact in residential selection. In *The form of cities in central Canada: selected papers.* eds. L. S. Bourne; R. MacKinnon; and J. Simmons, pp. 180–198. Toronto: University of Toronto Press.

————. 1974. The reconciliation of "subjective" and "objective" data on physical environment in the community: the case of social contact in high-rise apartments. In *The community: approaches and applications,* ed. M. P. Effrat, pp. 147–173. New York: Free Press.

————. ed. 1975a. *Behavioral research methods in environmental design.* Stroudsburg, Pa.: Dowden, Hutchinson & Ross.

————. 1975b. A conceptual introduction to the use of the time-budget for purposes of physical planning. In *Proceedings of the working group on time budgets and social activities,* 1. Toronto: Centre for Urban and Community Studies, University of Toronto.

————. 1975c. Urbanism as ways of living: the changing views of planning researchers. *Ekistics* 40:20–26.

————. 1976. *Reversing the inevitable trend: new housing in Sweden and Denmark.* Research Paper no. 79. Toronto: Centre for Urban and Community Studies, University of Toronto.

Michelson, W.; D. Belgue; and J. Stewart. 1973. Intentions and expectations in differential residential selection. *Journal of Marriage and the Family* 35:189–196.

Michelson, W., and K. Garland. 1974. *The differential role of crowded homes and dense residential areas in the incidence of selected symptoms of human pathology.* Research Paper no. 67. Toronto: Centre for Urban and Community Studies, University of Toronto.

Michelson, W., and P. Reed. 1970. *The theoretical status and operational usage of life style in environmental research.* Research Paper no. 36.

Toronto: Centre for Urban and Community Studies, University of Toronto.

――――. 1975. The time-budget. In *Behavioral research methods in environmental design*, ed. W. Michelson, pp. 180–234. Stroudsburg, Pa.: Dowden, Hutchinson & Ross.

Mitchell, R. E. 1971. Some social implications of high density housing. *American Sociological Review* 36:18–29.

Moore, E. G. 1972. *Residential mobility in the city*. Washington, D.C.: Association of American Geographers, Resource Paper no. 13.

Moore, W. E. 1963. *Man, time, and society*. New York: Wiley.

Moore, W. 1969. *The vertical ghetto*. New York: Random House.

Moriarty, B. M. 1974. Socio economic status and residential locational choice. *Environment and Behavior* 6:448–469.

Morris, R. N., and J. Mogey. 1965. *The sociology of housing: studies of Berinsfield*. London: Routledge & Kegan Paul.

Murdie, R. A. 1969. *Factorial ecology of Metropolitan Toronto, 1951–1961: an essay on the social geography of the city*. Chicago: Department of Geography, Research Paper no. 116, University of Chicago.

New York Times. 1975. The ivy-covered cottage, nearly an impossible dream. New York: New York Times, p. E9, May 11, 1975.

Newman, O. 1972. *Defensible space*. New York: Macmillan.

Newman, S. 1974. *The residential environment and the desire to move*. Ann Arbor, Mich.: University of Michigan, Institute for Social Research.

Norcross, C. 1973. *Townhouses and condominiums: residents' likes and dislikes*. Washington, D.C.: Urban Land Institute.

Ogburn, W. F. 1946. Inventions of local transportation and the patterns of cities. *Social Forces* 24:373–379.

Onibokun, A. G. 1974. Evaluating consumers' satisfaction with housing: an application of a systems approach. *The American Institute of Planners, Journal* 40:189–200.

Orleans, P. 1967. Urban experimentation and urban sociology. In *Science engineering, and the city*, ed. P. Orleans. Washington, D.C.: National Academy of Science.

Ottensmann, J. 1972. *Systems of urban activities: an interpretative review of the literature*. Paper presented for the Center for Urban and Regional Studies, University of North Carolina, Chapel Hill.

Palmer, J. D. 1970. The many clocks of man. *Natural History* 79(4):52–59.

Park, R. E. 1952. *Human communities*. Glencoe: Free Press.

Park, R. E.; E. W. Burgess; and R. D. McKenzie. 1925. *The city*. Chicago: University of Chicago Press.

Perin, C. 1970. *With man in mind*. Cambridge, Mass.: M.I.T. Press.

Perry, C. 1966. The neighborhood unit formula. In *Urban housing*, eds. W. L. C. Wheaton; G. Milgram; and M. E. Meyerson, pp. 94–109. New York: Free Press.

Peterson, G. L. 1967. A model of preference: qualitative analysis of the perception of the visual appearance of residential neighborhoods. *Journal of Regional Science* 7:19–32.

Plant, J. S. 1957. The personality and an urban area. In *Cities and society*, eds. P. K. Hatt and A. Reiss, pp. 647–665. New York: Free Press.

Proshansky, H. M.; W. H. Ittelson; and L. G. Rivlin. 1970. The influence of the physical environment on behavior: some basic assumptions. In *Environmental psychology*, eds. H. M. Proshansky, et al., pp. 27–37. New York: Holt, Rinehart & Winston.

Proshansky, H. M.; W. H. Ittelson; and L. G. Rivlin, eds. 1970. *Environmental psychology*. New York: Holt, Rinehart & Winston.

Pyron, B. 1972. Form and diversity in human habitats: judgmental and attitude responses. *Environment and Behavior* 4:87–120.

Quinn, J. A. 1950. *Human ecology*. New York: Prentice-Hall.

Rainwater, L. 1966. Fear and the house-as-haven in the lower class. *The American Institute of Planners, Journal* 32:23–31.

Rapoport, A. 1969. *House form and culture*. Englewood Cliffs, N.J.: Prentice-Hall.

———. 1973. An approach to the construction of man-environment theory. In *Environmental design research, vol. 2: Symposia and workshops*, pp. 124–135, ed. W. F. Preiser. Stroudsburg, Pa.: Dowden, Hutchinson & Ross.

Raven, J. 1967. Sociological evidence on housing: 2, the home environment. *The Architectural Review* 142:236–240.

Reed, P. 1972. *Situated interaction: normative and non-normative bases of patterned social behavior*. Research Paper no. 55. Toronto: Centre for Urban and Community Studies, University of Toronto.

Reiner, T. A. 1963. *The place of the ideal community in urban planning*. Philadelphia: University of Pennsylvania Press.

Reissman, L. 1954. Class, leisure, and social participation. *American Sociological Review* 19:76–84.

Riesman, D. 1950. *The lonely crowd* (abridged). New Haven, Conn.: Yale University Press.

———. 1958. The suburban sadness. In *The suburban community*, ed. W. Dobriner, pp. 375–408. New York: Putnam.

Riis, J. A. 1890. *How the other half lives*. New York: Scribner.

Robinson, I. M.; W. C. Baer; T. K. Banerjee; and P. G. Flachsbart. 1975. Trade-off games. In *Behavioral research methods in environmental design*, ed. W. Michelson, pp. 79–118. Stroudsburg, Pa.: Dowden, Hutchinson & Ross.

Robinson, J. P. 1969. Social change as measured by time-budgets. *Journal of Leisure Research* 1:75–77.

Robinson, W. S. 1950. Ecological correlations and the behavior of individuals. *American Sociological Review* 15:351–57.

Roos, P. D. 1970. Jurisdiction: an ecological concept. In *Environmental psychology*, eds. H. M. Proshansky, et al. pp. 239–246. New York: Holt, Rinehart & Winston.

Rosenberg, G. 1968. High population densities in relation to social behavior. *Ekistics* 25:425–427.

Rosengren, W. R., and S. DeVault. 1970. The sociology of time and space in an obstetrical hospital. In *Environmental psychology*, ed. H. M. Proshansky, et al., pp. 439–453. New York: Holt, Rinehart & Winston.

Rosow, I. 1961. The social effects of the physical environment. *The American Institute of Planners, Journal* 27:127–133.

———. 1967. *Social integration of the aged.* New York: Free Press.

Ross, L. H. 1961. Reasons for moves to and from a central city area. *Social Forces* 40:261–263.

———. 1965. Uptown and downtown: a study of middle-class residential areas. *American Sociological Review.* 30:255–259.

Rossi, P. 1955. *Why families move.* Glencoe, Ill.: Free Press.

Rushton, G. 1968. The scaling of locational preferences. In *Behavioral problems in geography: a symposium*, eds. K. R. Cox and R. G. Golledge, pp. 197–227. Studies in Geography no. 17. Evanston, Ill.: Northwestern University.

Sabagh, G.; M. D. Van Arsdol, Jr.; and E. W. Butler. 1969. Some determinants of intra-metropolitan residential mobility: conceptual considerations. *Social Forces* 48:88–98.

Sandahl, D. A. 1972. Conceptions of self as individual orientations to the spatial environment. In *Environmental design: research and practice: Proceedings of the EDRA 3/AR 8 Conference*, January 1972, University of California at Los Angeles, ed. W. J. Mitchell, pp. 231–238.

Sanoff, H. and M. Sawhney. 1971. *Residential livability: a socio-physical perspective.* Raleigh, N.C.: Urban Affairs & Community Service Center, North Carolina State University.

Sayegh, K. S. ed. 1972. *Canadian housing: a reader.* Waterloo, Ont.: Faculty of Environmental Studies, University of Waterloo.

Schmitt, R. C. 1963. Implications of density in Hong Kong. *The American Institute of Planners, Journal* 24:210–217.

———. 1966. Density, health, and social organization. *The American Institute of Planners, Journal* 32:38–40.

Schorr, A. L. 1963. *Slums and social insecurity.* Washington, D.C.: Department of Health Education and Welfare, Research Report no. 1, Social Security Administration and Division of Research and Statistics.

Sewell, W. D. 1971. Environmental perceptions and attitudes of engineers and public health officials. *Environment and Behavior* 3:23–59.

Shulman, N. 1972. *Urban social networks: an investigation of personal networks in an urban setting.* Toronto: Ph.D. dissertation, University of Toronto.

Simmel, G. 1957. The metropolis and mental life. In *Cities and society*, eds. P. K. Hatt and A. Reiss, Jr., pp. 635–646. New York: Free Press.

Simmons, J. W. 1968. Changing residence in the city, a review of intra-urban mobility. *The Geographical Review* 58:622–651.

———. 1974. *Patterns of residential movement in metropolitan Toronto*. Research Publications no. 13. Toronto: Dept. of Geography, University of Toronto.

Smith, J. F. 1973. *Elrond, an architectural study*. Kingston, Ont.: Elrond College.

Smith, W. F. 1970. *Housing: the social and economic elements*. Berkeley, Calif.: University of California Press.

Social Planning Council of Metropolitan Toronto. 1973. *Families in high rise apartments*. Toronto: The Council.

Sommer, R. 1969. *Personal space*. Englewood Cliffs, N.J.: Prentice-Hall.

———. 1972. *Design awareness*. San Francisco: Rinehart.

Sonnenfeld, J. 1966. Variable values in space and landscape: an inquiry into the nature of environmental necessity. *Journal of Social Issues* 22(4): 71–82.

———. 1972. Social interaction and environmental relationship. *Environment and Behavior* 4:267–277.

Sorokin, P. A., and C. Q. Berger. 1939. *Time budgets of human behavior*. Cambridge, Mass.: Harvard University Press.

Spectorsky, A. C. 1955. *The exurbanites*. Philadelphia: Lippincott.

Staikov, Z. 1970. *Time budget as a methodological basis for planning and forecasting of social phenomena and processes*. Paper presented to the 7th World Congress of Sociology, Varna, Bulgaria.

———. 1973. Modelling and programming of time-budget (methodological issues). *Society and Leisure* 5(1):31–47.

Statistics Canada. 1974. *Perspective Canada*. Ottawa, Ont.: Information Canada.

Stea, D. 1970. Space, territory and human movements. In *Environmental psychology*, eds. H. M. Proshansky, et al., 37–42. New York: Holt, Rinehart & Winston.

Steffens, J. L. 1931. *Autobiography*. New York: Harcourt, Brace & World.

———. 1957. *The shame of the cities*. New York: Hill and Wang.

Stewart, W. F. R. 1970. *Children in flats: a family study*. London: National Society for the Prevention of Cruelty to Children.

Stokols, D. 1972. A social-psychological model of human crowding phenomena. *The American Institute of Planners, Journal* 38:72–83.

Stokols, D.; M. Rall; B. Pinner; and J. Schopler. 1973. Physical, social and personal determinants of the perception of crowding. *Environment and Behavior* 5:87–115.

Stone, P. J. 1970. *Technical issues and solutions suggested by the international time budget project*. Paper presented to the 7th World Congress of sociology, Varna, Bulgaria.

Strauss, A. L. 1961. *Images of the American city*. New York: Free Press.

Studer, R. G. 1970. The dynamics of behavior-contingent physical systems. In *Environmental psychology*, eds. H. M. Proshansky, et al., pp. 56–76. New York: Holt, Rinehart & Winston.

———. 1973. Man-environment relations: discovery or design. In *Environmental design research: vol. 2, Symposia and workshops*, ed. W. F. Preiser, pp. 136–151. Stroudsburg, Pa.: Dowden, Hutchinson & Ross.

Suttles, G. D. 1972. *The social construction of communities*. Chicago: University of Chicago Press.

Swan, J. A. 1972. Public responses to air pollution. In *Environment and the social sciences: perspectives and applications*, eds. J. F. Wohlwill and D. H. Carson, pp. 66–74. Washington, D.C.: American Psychological Association.

Swedner, H.; I. Becker; and U. Krahg-Schou. 1967. *Forslag till miljöforskningsprogram*. Stockholm: Stockholms Stads Generalplanberedning.

Swedner, H., and D. Yague. 1970. Proposals for a nomenclature for human activities with particular reference to cultural activities. *Society and Leisure*. 2(4):119–47.

Szalai, A., et al. 1972. *The use of time*. The Hague: Mouton.

Tilly, C. 1961. Occupational rank and grade of residence in a metropolis. *American Journal of Sociology* 67:323–330.

———. 1974. *An urban world*. Boston: Little, Brown.

Tilly, C., and H. C. Brown. 1967. On uprooting, kinship and the auspices of migration. *International Journal of Comparative Sociology* 8:139–164.

Tognacci, L. N.; R. H. Weigel; M. F. Wideen; and D. T. A. Vernon. 1972. Environmental quality: how universal is public concern? *Environment and Behavior* 4:73–86.

Tomeh, A. K. 1964. Informal group participation and residential patterns. *American Journal of Sociology* 70:28–35.

———. 1969. Empirical considerations on the problem of social integration. *Sociological Inquiry* 39:65–76.

Toran, M. 1973. Environmental stress and flexibility in the housing process. In *Environmental design research: vol. 1, Selected papers*, ed. W. F. Preiser, pp. 47–58. Stroudsburg, Pa.: Dowden, Hutchinson & Ross.

Tunnard, C., and H. H. Reed. 1955. *American skyline*. Boston: Houghton Mifflin.

U.S. House of Representatives Committee on Banking and Currency, Ad Hoc Sub-Committee on Urban Growth. 1970. *The quality of urban life*. Washington: U.S. Government Printing Office.

Vernon, R. 1962. *The myth and reality of our urban problems*. Cambridge: Joint Center for Urban Studies of M.I.T. and Harvard University.

Wallace, A. F. C. 1952. *Housing and social structure: a preliminary survey, with particular reference to multi-storey, low rent, public housing projects*. Philadelphia: Philadelphia Housing Authority.

Warner, W. L., et al. 1963. *Yankee city*. New Haven, Conn.: Yale University Press.

Warner, W. L., and P. S. Lunt. 1941. *The social life of a modern community*. New Haven, Conn.: Yale University Press.

Warner, W. L.; M. Meeker; and K. Eells. 1957. *Social class in America*. Gloucester, Mass.: Peter Smith.

Webber, M. 1963. Order in diversity: community without propinquity. In *Cities and space*, ed. L. Wingo, pp. 23–54. Baltimore: The Johns Hopkins Press.

Weiss, S. F.; R. J. Burby, III; and R. B. Zehner. 1974. *Evaluation of new communities, selected preliminary findings*. Washington, D.C.: Proceedings of a seminar held at the National Science Foundation, Center for Urban & Regional Studies, University of North Carolina.

Wekerle, G. R. 1974. *Vertical village: the social world of a high rise complex*. Ph.D. dissertation. Evanston, Ill.: Northwestern University.

Wekerle, G., and E. Hall, 1972. High rise living: can the same design serve young and old? *Ekistics* 33:186–191.

Wellman, B. 1971. Who needs neighborhoods? In *Citizen participation*, ed. J. A. Draper, pp. 282–287. Toronto: New Press.

Wellman, B., et al. 1971. *The uses of community: community ties and support systems*. Research Paper no. 47. Toronto: Centre for Urban and Community Studies, University of Toronto.

Werthman, C. et al. 1965. *Planning and the purchase decision: why people buy in planned communities*. Reprint no. 10. Berkeley, Calif.: Institute of Regional Development, Center for Planning and Development Research, University of California.

Wheeler, J. O. 1968. Residential location by occupational status. *Urban Studies* 5:24–32.

Whitelaw, J. S., and J. S. Gregson. 1972. *Search procedure in the intra-urban migration process*. Monash Publications in Geography no. 2. Melbourne: Monash University.

Whyte, W. H., Jr. 1956. *The organization man*. Garden City, N.Y.: Doubleday (Anchor).

———. 1957. Are cities un-American?. In *The exploding metropolis*. ed. W. H. Whyte, Jr., pp. 1–31, Garden City, N.Y.: Doubleday (Anchor).

Willems, E. P. 1973. Behavioral ecology as a perspective for man-environment research. In *Environmental design, research: vol. 2, Symposia and workshops*, ed. W. F. Preiser, pp. 152–165. Stroudsburg, Pa.: Dowden, Hutchinson & Ross.

Willis, M. 1954. *Environment and the home*. London: London County Council, Architect's Department.

Willmott, P. 1963. *The evolution of a community*. London: Routledge & Kegan Paul.

———. 1973. Social research and new communities. In *Surviving the city*, ed. J. Gabree, pp. 252–272. New York: Ballantine Books.

Willmott, P., and M. Young, 1960. *Family and class in a London suburb.* London: Routledge & Kegan Paul.

Wilner, D. M., et al. 1962. *The housing environment and family life: a longitudinal study of the effects of housing on morbidity and mental health.* Baltimore: The Johns Hopkins Press.

Wilson, R. L. 1962. Livability of the city: attitudes and urban development In *Urban growth dynamics*, eds. F. S. Chapin, Jr., and S. Weiss, pp. 359–399. New York: John Wiley & Sons.

Winsborough, H. M. 1974. The social consequences of high population density. In *Comparative urban structure*, ed. K. Schwirian, pp. 193–198. Toronto and Lexington, Mass.: D. C. Heath.

Wirth, L. 1938. Urbanism as a way of life. *American Journal of Sociology* 44:1–24.

Wohlwill, J. F. 1966. The physical environment: a problem for a psychology of stimulation. *Journal of Social Issues* 22(4):29–38.

————. 1973. The environment is not in the head! In *Environmental design research: vol. 2, Symposia and workshops*, ed. W. F. Preiser, pp. 166–181. Stroudsburg, Pa.: Dowden, Hutchinson & Ross.

Wohlwill, J. F., and D. H. Carson, eds. 1972. *Environment and the social sciences: perspectives and applications.* Washington, D.C.: American Psychological Association.

Wolpert, J. 1966. Migration as an adjustment to environmental stress. *Journal of Social Issues* 22(4):92–102.

Young, M. and P. Willmott. 1957. *Family and kinship in east London.* London: Routledge & Kegan Paul.

Zehner, R. B., and F. S. Chapin, Jr. 1974. *Across the city line: a white community in transition.* Lexington, Mass.: Lexington Books.

Zeisel, J. 1975. *Sociology and architectural design.* New York: Russell Sage Foundation.

Zelan, J. 1968. Does suburbia make a difference: an exercise in secondary analysis. In *Urbanism in world perspective*, ed. S. F. Fava, pp. 401–408. New York: Thomas Y. Crowell.

Zlutnick, S., and I. Altman. 1972. Crowding and human behavior. In *Environment and the social sciences*, eds. J. F. Wohlwill and D. H. Carson, pp. 44–58. Washington, D.C.: American Psychological Association.

INDEX